The Metamorphosis of U.S.-Korea Relations

Lexington Studies on Korea's Place in International Relations

Series Editor: Jongwoo Han, The Korean War Legacy Foundation & World History Digital Education Foundation

This series publishes trailblazing research by pioneering scholars on contemporary Korean issues. Transformative events in the early twenty-first century have marked a watershed for South and North Korea in many areas, including political economy, democracy, international power politics and security, ongoing disputes over the past with China and Japan, and North Korea's nuclear and missile programs, to name a few. Furthermore, post-modern cultural influences and the global advent of digital technology have led to the diversification of Korea's culture, religion, sports, diasporic community, and inter-Korean linguistic differences, as well as the Korean Wave. This series aims to explore and dissect these issues to further understanding of contemporary Korean life and politics.

Recent Titles in This Series

The Metamorphosis of U.S.–Korea Relations: The Korean Question Revisited, By Jongwoo Han

Diplomacy, Trade, and South Korea's Rise to International Influence, Edited by Dennis Patterson and Jangsup Choi

The Construction of Korean Culture in Korean Language Textbooks: Ideologies and Textbooks, By Dong Bae Lee

Korea and the World: New Frontier in Korean Studies, Edited by Gregg Brazinsky

The Metamorphosis of U.S.-Korea Relations

The Korean Question Revisited

Jongwoo Han

LEXINGTON BOOKS
Lanham • Boulder • New York • London

Published by Lexington Books
An imprint of The Rowman & Littlefield Publishing Group, Inc.
4501 Forbes Boulevard, Suite 200, Lanham, Maryland 20706
www.rowman.com

86-90 Paul Street, London EC2A 4NE

Copyright © 2022 by The Rowman & Littlefield Publishing Group, Inc.

All rights reserved. No part of this book may be reproduced in any form or by any electronic or mechanical means, including information storage and retrieval systems, without written permission from the publisher, except by a reviewer who may quote passages in a review.

British Library Cataloguing in Publication Information Available

Library of Congress Cataloging-in-Publication Data

Names: Han, Jongwoo, 1962- author.
Title: The metamorphosis of U.S.-Korea relations : the Korean question revisited / Jongwoo Han.
Description: Lanham : Lexington Books, [2022] | Series: Lexington studies on Korea's place in international relations | Includes bibliographical references and index.
Identifiers: LCCN 2022001882 (print) | LCCN 2022001883 (ebook) | ISBN 9781498582810 (cloth) | ISBN 9781498582834 (paperback) | ISBN 9781498582827 (epub)
Subjects: LCSH: United States—Foreign relations—Korea. | Korea—Foreign relations—United States. | United States—Foreign relations—1989- | United States—Foreign relations—20th century. | Korea—Foreign relations—1945-
Classification: LCC E183.8.K6 H36 2022 (print) | LCC E183.8.K6 (ebook) | DDC 327.730519—dc23/eng/20220119
LC record available at https://lccn.loc.gov/2022001882
LC ebook record available at https://lccn.loc.gov/2022001883

Contents

List of Figures, Tables, and Map — vii

Acknowledgments — ix

Introduction — 1

1 Origins of the Korean Question and the Consequences of the Korean War — 19

2 Encounter of Isolationist Joseon and Expansionist America — 67

3 The Two Korean Wars — 111

4 North Korean Quagmire: The Last Phase of U.S. Encounter? — 161

5 Upshots of Encounters — 197

6 The Corean Question Revisited — 231

Bibliography — 253

Index — 267

About the Author — 279

List of Figures, Tables, and Map

FIGURES

Figure 0.1	U.S.-Korea Encounters: Major Milestones	7
Figure 4.1	Conceptualization of U.S. Korea Policy: Regime Change, Regime Denial, and Regime Recognition	170
Figure 5.1	How Asia-Pacific Nations See Each Other	225
Figure 5.2	Changes in Chinese Views of Japanese	225
Figure 5.3	Chinese Views on Japanese Contrition	226
Figure 5.4	Japanese Views of Chinese Turn More Negative over the Past Decade	227

TABLES

Table 1.1	Total Casualties of the Pacific War by Nation and Type	59
Table 1.2	Divergent Paths: South Korea and North Korea, 1960–2010	62
Table 2.1	Major Milestones in the History of U.S.-Korea Relations	90
Table 3.1	Timeline of U.S. Policy toward Korea Leading up to the Korean War	140
Table 4.1	Major Events surrounding DPRK	167
Table 4.2	North Korea's Exports and Imports, 2007–2012	172
Table 5.1	Top 10 Korean Exports, Progress from 1967 to 2009	198
Table 5.2	Major Indicators, the United States and the ROK	199
Table 5.3	Top Export Partners for U.S. Goods, 2012	200
Table 5.4	Korea's Goods Export Partners, 2012	200

Table 5.5	Korean War Veterans Dispatched by State (over 40,000)	201
Table 5.6	Top 10 States (Goods Exporters to Korea, 2012)	202
Table 5.7	Top 10 States (Jobs from U.S. Exports to Korea, per 100,000 Residents, 2012)	203
Table 5.8	Congressional District Exports to Korea	205
Table 5.9	Top 10 Districts of Korean American Community	205
Table 5.10	East Asian Countries' Potential	221

MAP

Map 1.1	The Seward-Shufeldt Line vs. the Theodore-Franklin Line	22

Acknowledgments

Has my generation ever experienced anything like COVID-19? At the present moment, the world is in a state of shock. From the midst of quarantine, I have been venting my anger over this situation as well as an even stronger virus that has infected us along the lines of truth and falsehood. I was only able to breathe thanks to the comforting presence of the gravel track beside the Old Erie Canal and the peaceful trails that meander through Green Lakes Park near my home, where I hike and bike until those feelings transform into ideas, patterns, and something more constructive.

When I first arrived in the United States about 30 years ago, I had a burning question: "Why had the U.S. excluded Korea from its defensive perimeter in January 1950, just a few months prior to the outbreak of the Korean War?" As I traced back along the roots of the relationship that developed between these two nations, I kept finding myself becoming enraged over the whole affair—how these two strangers first met, broke apart, then reconnected, with two very opposite outcomes: South Korea and North Korea.

By adopting a holistic perspective, I now hope to bring some closure to my question about the proper place of Korea in U.S. history and vice versa. This relationship has produced a long history of warfare as well as a postcolonial model of sustainable development but also serious threats to global security.

When I received my doctorate in 1997, my dissertation was not on this topic. I wanted to return to Korea but have remained rooted, for some mysterious reasons, in Syracuse for the past 30 years. Why have I stayed so long? I still don't know why, but it turns out that my stay has something to do with tracing the roots of U.S.-Korea relations, preserving the voices of Korean War veterans, and collaborating with American teachers of history and social sciences on the vital task of preserving our bilateral history for future generations. Each of these experiences has led me to grow and advance toward grasping the key to questions I have tried to answer.

I am fortunate for the opportunity to consider such essential questions on the historical place of this international relationship, not just from my own personal perspective but in broader scholarly contexts. Through my involvement in Syracuse University's academic exchange with North Korea's Kim Chaek University of Technology from 2002 to 2010, I was able to sense more acutely the pains of the road ahead for a divided Korea. Also, since 2011, it has been my great honor to interview Korean War veterans from all 22 countries that came to Korea's aid. These interviews and curricular resources based on these oral histories are now available to the public through the Korean War Legacy Foundation (www.koreanwarlegacy.org). Having also recently researched and written on South Korea's unprecedented simultaneous achievement of democratization and economic development, I am finding myself uniquely positioned to lay out a comprehensive account of U.S.-Korea relations.

Now, as editor of the Lexington Books series on Korea's place in international relations, I can say my own book is to be added to the series as the fifth volume. To Lexington Books and its acquisition editor, Joseph Parry, of course, I am deeply grateful for the continued recognition of my questions and research. Also, Sara Noakes, acquisitions assistant of Lexington Books, has been extremely helpful in the last phase of this book publication. Professor Moon Chung-in, chairman of the Sejong Institute of Republic of Korea, has provided me with his encouraging and insightful comments and suggestions so that I can sharpen the main perspectives and arguments of this book, which is recounting the one-and-a-half-century-old history of bilateral encounters. I am deeply indebted to his scholarly advice and unflagging support for my book publications.

In this quest, Eric Berlin has served as my editor, helping me to articulate my questions and answers into writing. I feel fortunate to have him as my copy editor and friend. At the final editing stage, my former teacher and friend Blanca Gallardo gave her enthusiastic support to go over this book and give it a final read before publication. I also want to give special thanks to my wife Kyunghee Lee, who was also a classmate of my alma mater, the department of political science of Yonsei University, and has been a source of encouragement and inspiration for works and life in Syracuse. Diagrams and charts that depict complex ideas and events-loaded histories in the encounters between the United States and both North and South Korea were made by my daughter Hyemin Han, who spent many hours preparing impeccable graphics for her father's book.

Finally, I want to dedicate this book to my friends, the social science and history teachers who will help fill any gaps in the histories of how these nations first encountered each other, what they experienced, and where they may be heading for generations to come. —Jongwoo Han

P.S. Now I have more concrete answers as to why I have been anchored in Syracuse: Ambassador Pyo Wook Han—who established Korea's embassy in Washington, DC, witnessed the UN resolution to aid Korea, and met President Truman to request aid for the war and post-war reconstruction—was a graduate of SU's Philosophy Department (class of 1942). Also, I found that Robert T. Oliver, who worked as foreign affairs advisor to Korea's first president, Syngman Rhee, also taught at SU. Also, as mentioned, vivid memories of my North Korean brothers and sisters in Syracuse still reverberate. Finally, I was able to complete the all-22 country Korean War veterans' digital archive having started to interview Korean War Veterans Association's Syracuse Chapter 105 in 2011. For all of these reasons and more, I am deeply thankful for how my journey has unfolded. Now, to me, Syracuse no longer remains just a city in the United States that has nothing to do with Korea. Rather Syracuse has been a destined trail for my rediscovery of the place of Korea in U.S. history.

Introduction

UNWITTING CREATOR OF THE KOREAN QUESTION

One of the most conspicuous outcomes of the 47th G7 summit, held on June 11–13, 2021, in Cornwall, the United Kingdom, is that Washington successfully rallied Western allies against China and Russia. Shortly after the summit and with support from its allies, U.S. president Joseph Biden met with Russia's Vladimir Putin on June 16, 2021, at Geneva Lake, Switzerland, and temporarily stitched up America's severely strained relationship with Russia, through which I think Washington consolidated its war fronts into one, China.

With China's rise as the world's largest economy and its apparent desire to challenge America's unilateral hegemony, the Corea[1] question has resurfaced: South Korea's heavy reliance on the Chinese market and China's leverage against North Korea have intensified South Korea's instances of sidings with China significantly enough to call into question the expected loyalty that the United States has acquired through its decisive commitment starting with the Korean War. The Moon administration's Korean Peninsula Peace Process, aggressively embracing the North Korean regime and leveraging Beijing toward its own goal of maintaining its China market and normalization with Pyeongyang, has provoked some cacophony between Washington and Seoul. China has, in turn, attempted to regain its conventional leverages against South Korea while maintaining control over North Korea.

This book contends that the long history of America's intercourse[2] with Corea opened the Pandora's box of the Corean Question by signing a treaty with Corea in 1882 and establishing the Seward-Shufeldt (SS) Line. In turn, the decline of China's suzerainty over the Korean Peninsula and the fall of Russian power with the consequential rise of Japanese power in the region—resulting in changes from the SS Line to the Theodore-Franklin Line

(President Theodore Roosevelt-President Franklin Roosevelt), the colonization of Corea, Korean division, and the Korean War—have nearly brought the American position full circle to that first encounter in Pyeongyang, where the American schooner, *the General Sherman*, ignited the first unfortunate encounter between the United States and Corea in 1866. As details show, the United States is the party most responsible first, for opening the Pandora's box of the Corean Question and then, for the contemporary disparity between North and South Korea. Ultimately, this book argues, the United States must uphold its 1882 commitment by normalizing relations with North Korea, which will in turn bring closure to the "Corean Question."

Here again, the "Corean Question" has now been raised by all parties involved. For the United States, options of dropping Korea again from its line of defense or strengthening its leverage against Seoul through carrots and sticks include President Trump's threats to increase by fivefold South Korea's burden of the cost sharing for U.S. Forces in Korea. China, on the other hand, has tried placing pressure on South Korea by demonstrating Beijing's control of the flow of Chinese tourists to Korea in 2017, for example, when Seoul decided to accept the American Terminal High Altitude Area Defense (THAAD) missile system and by raising nontariff barriers against South Korean products. As President-Elect Biden signaled the normalization of the U.S.-South Korea military alliance, Beijing has been signaling President Xi's visit to Seoul in order for Seoul not to move out of its control. The most striking aspect of the new Korean question is that South Korea is now trying to strike a balance between Washington and Beijing in order to maintain access to the world's largest market and, at the same time, keep its traditional ally.

Is this the final outcome of American efforts to open Corea about two hundred years ago? If not, what will the eventual geopolitical landscape of the Korean Peninsula be in the near future? Would Washington finally decide to agree to end the Korean War and normalize its relationship with North Korea? Would Beijing allow Washington to move ahead with U.S.-North Korea normalization? Would Koreans be able to reunite themselves in the vortex of Sino-U.S. confrontation and power competitions over their Peninsula?

The "Korean Question" points to Korea's fall from its 1910 colonization by Japan, which was supported by the United States even after its official 1882 treaty, to the perpetuation of its 1945 division and the Korean War, and to the contemporary showdown between Pyeongyang and Washington over North Korea's program of weapons of mass destruction. It serves as a typical story of scapegoating by powerful countries in the history of international power politics. Precedents are not rare, but only Poland's experience regarding its powerful neighbors, Germany and the Soviet Union, appears to match the Korean case in scale and scope in twentieth-century international political history.

Among many factors, this book urges that the policy of the United States regarding Korea in particular and Asia in general be answerable for the Korean Question, and for what the contemporary Korean nations have faced as explained above. Specifically, Washington aggressively engaged in opening the Joseon dynasty in 1882 and then yielded it in 1905. After a long silence, Washington occupied and halved the Korean Peninsula and then, deserted it again until the outbreak of the Korean War in 1950. With regard to its Asian policy in general, Washington left it to Japan, its only ally in the region, until the latter threw its dagger into America. China has long been a central concern to the United States as the world's biggest market. However, the United States has also always struggled with Japan in its competition for the Chinese market, which was a decisive reason for the Pacific War.

Washington's policy toward Korea can be characterized as erratic, zigzagging, or even strategically muddled. Washington has acted like a poker player who can't choose whether to call, raise, or fold and has vacillated between attempts at regime opening and recognition and regime change, especially with Pyeongyang (Han, 2009:109). From this perspective, the principal aim of this book is to account for the historical origins of the "Korean Question" by delving into the history of the encounters between the United States and Korea. This book concludes that the current nuclear showdown between North Korea and the United States is nothing new but an instance of déjà vu of the disastrous 1866 encounter in which America's General Sherman was burned down in the Daedong River near Pyeongyang, the current capital of North Korea. Starting with 1866, the arc of the Korea-U.S. encounter seems to have reached the final critical point of whether Washington commits to fulfilling its original intent of establishing a relationship with Korea by resolving the nuclear showdown with North Korea and, once and for all, normalizing its relationship with Pyeongyang, thus closing the circle of America's encounter with the Korean Peninsula.

In fact, Pyeongyang's equally erratic, irrational, and perilous nuclear brinkmanship and general disregard for the well-being and human rights of its own citizens make it blameworthy for Washington's reluctance to normalize the relationship with Pyeongyang. However, there is an alternative view that Pyeongyang's all-in strategy of using its nuclear wager primarily has been intended to demand Washington's attention in order to initiate bilateral talks, to extricate itself from dysfunctional alliances with Beijing and Moscow, and then to partner with a new big brother, the United States (Han, 2009:105, 108). South Korea's Nobel Peace Prize winner and former South Korean president Kim Dae-jung once said that "Every one of Pyeongyang's moves has always been politically motivated and strategically calculated." Former

North Korea leader Kim Jong-il made clear to President Kim Dae-jung that "only America is capable of providing the military security and large-scale economic aid his country needs" (Han, 2009:108). Based on this premise, this book makes a bold claim that United States' inconsistent and contradictory Korea policy in the broad context of its Asia strategy in the late nineteenth and twentieth centuries is the prime source of the Korean Question.

A SHORT SURVEY OF THE ENCOUNTER

The encounter of the United States with the Korean Peninsula has taken place over less than two centuries. In fact, the United States had not even celebrated its first centennial of independence when it first encountered what it called "Corea" in 1866. For Korea, the sudden appearance of the United States on its shores interrupted a long history of isolation. For about 5,000 years, it had shared its history with nobody but its larger neighbor and suzerain, China. American demands for Corea to open launched the story of their unhappy marriage, which soon came to involve spats, betrayals, apathy, and a reluctant reunion in a 20th century war, leading to the creation of two different Koreas. The first 84 years after the American blackship, the General Sherman, intruded into Korea and unilaterally made armed demands for a relationship can only be justified if we accept the perspective of the dominant culture in the history of humanity. This arbitrary usurping of Korea's sovereignty took a dramatic turn, however, when the United States became willing to sacrifice its own citizens in order to deter communist invasion of North Korea. Nevertheless, America's primary motivation was not to save Korean lives; its national interest lay in maintaining Korea as a buffer against communism and protecting Japan. Meaningful transformation in America's view toward Korea came about only after two contrasting Koreas emerged: the communist but failed state in the north and the prosperous America-backed free-capitalist democracy in the south.

My fascination with the history of U.S.-Korea relations cannot be attributed solely to the fact that I am a patriotic Korean American with a background in international relations. Rather, I have been mesmerized for years by the way that the international tensions encircling the Korean Peninsula have not substantially changed or abated since the Joseon dynasty first fell prey to fierce competition among the superpowers that surrounded it in the late nineteenth century.

To many readers, this claim may sound unrealistic since the Republic of Korea has risen to become one of the world's most vibrant democracies and industrial powerhouses, yet its heavy dependence on exports to China, the United States, and Japan leaves it highly vulnerable to the whims of these superpowers, who also happen to be some of the strongest military powers in the world. Moreover, South Korea has always been exposed to high levels of threat from its neighbors, including North Korea's weapons of mass destruction, Japan's recent attempts to rearm and reform its constitutional limits, with its record of mass killings in the Pacific War, China's retort to American hegemony with its "One Belt One Road" initiative, and Russia's desperate attempts to regain global influence in the post–Cold War era. With regard to global security, the Korean Peninsula has been an object of competition among the world's strongest military and economic powers: the United States, China, Russia, Great Britain, and Japan.

The puzzle at the core of this book is how best to explain Korea's rude awakening from centuries of self-isolation, its helpless exposure to the ruthless maneuvers of nineteenth-century Western imperial competition, and its eventual fall to colonialism. Why was Korea split against its will as the first victim of bipolar Cold War politics and then kept divided as reckless provocations from North Korea's failed state continued, raising the chances of clashes among North Korea, the United States, China, and Japan? The most obvious answer to this admittedly loaded question is that Korea had not transformed thoroughly enough to resist the power politics in the region. Among many other elements and variables that could elucidate these issues, this book argues that the United States played a transformative role in Korean history through acts such as forcing the Joseon dynasty open, dividing the nation, and witnessing South Korea's unprecedented rise from the ashes alongside North Korea's economic failure. An overview of this relationship's development will provide some necessary context. As historical evidence will bear out, the United States, in the process of forming a relationship with Korea, inadvertently forsook its own liberal and Christian values by first committing to the Korean nation and then voluntarily and recklessly forsaking it, though such claims may sound naïve in light of the cold-blooded reality of international power politics.

A useful metaphor for such a relationship is a marriage between two strangers from backgrounds that diverge not just culturally but socioeconomically and personally as well. Familial metaphors have been used in the major historical discourse to shed light on Korea's reasons for expecting the United States to support Korean independence in the late nineteenth century. For instance, when Syngman Rhee as leader of the independence movement beseeched President Theodore Roosevelt for protection against Japanese occupation, as Wilz (1985) aptly notes, "he likely viewed the United States through a Confucian lens as a big brother" (244).

What's more, this sense of betrayal has diminished little in Korea's contemporary discourse. Quoting George M. McCune, Kraus (2015:159) indicates that "the United States had unwittingly made Korea the tragic victim of far-reaching international rivalries" by stating that Korea would be liberated from colonial rule "in due course." Both McCune and Kraus criticize the paternalistic nature of U.S. policy toward Korea, stating that the nation "is still looked upon as a stepchild in high government circles in Washington." Similarly, Wilz (1985:244) argues that "[Korea] had come to view the United States as Korea's elder brother, and according to the Confucianist ethical system that animated their thoughts, an elder brother was obliged to protect his younger brother." Even King Gojong, who endured the tumult and humiliation of having to surrender the Joseon's sovereignty to Japan, confessed in an 1897 interview with Horace Allen, then U.S. minister to the Joseon, "We feel that America is to us as an Elder Brother" (Wilz, 1985:249). Though the causal links between these details will receive more attention in later chapters, these examples should suffice to show that the use of such interpersonal metaphors for the bond between the United States and Korea bears fruit. Figure 0.1 demonstrates how America's expansionist and open-door policy coincided with Korea's isolationist policy and how such an encounter eventually resulted in Korea's fall to Japan, the division of the Peninsula, America's reluctant involvement in the Korean War, and disparate policy for the two Koreas.

1. America's opening of the Joseon dynasty and recognition of the regime in the era of "The Continued Expansion of the United States' Interests" (1866–1898), which entailed the General Sherman Incident (1866) and the Shinmiyangyo (1871)
2. America's vacillation between regime recognition and regime denial toward Korea in the era of "Defending U.S. International Interests" (1899–1913), which included President Theodore Roosevelt's consent to Japanese control of Korea
3. America's complete disregard for Korea in the eras of "WWI and Wilsonian Diplomacy" (1914–1920), "Interwar Diplomacy" (1921–1936) and "Diplomacy and the Road to Another War" (1937–1945), with Korea under Japanese colonial control
4. America's reluctant regime recognition of South Korea in "The Early Cold War" (1945–1952) and the Korean War (1950–1953) and
5. America's assertive regime recognition of South Korea and vacillation from aggressive regime change to tacit regime denial and then intermittent regime engagement of North Korea in the era of "Entrenchment of a Bipolar Foreign Policy" (1953–1990).

As shown in figure 0.1, the Joseon dynasty was by far America's most important target corresponding to U.S. expansionism from 1866 to 1898 as written in the State Department's "Milestones in the History of U.S. Foreign Relations." The State Department secretary showed great interest in opening the Joseon dynasty and investigating the General Sherman incident. Due to

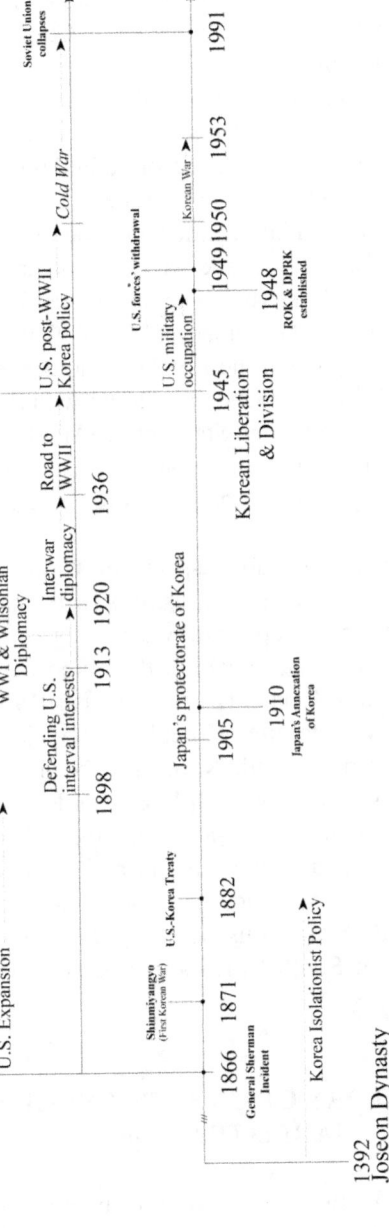

Figure 0.1 U.S.-Korea Encounters: Major Milestones. *Source*: Created by the author.

this American expansionist stance, Korea was forced to accept the General Sherman's arbitrary demand to open and experienced defeat in 1871, when American expeditionary forces invaded Ganghwa Island. Literally speaking, this was the first Korean War, but it is more commonly known as the Shinmiyangyo. The 1882 Treaty of Peace, Amity, Commerce, and Navigation between the United States and Korea was the final achievement of U.S. expansionist policy. However, this eagerness on the American side for intercourse with Korea evaporated when the United States, under President Theodore Roosevelt's leadership, got into the mode of defending international interests within the period from 1899 until the outbreak of World War I. President Roosevelt, as will be described later, anticipated the rise of Japan as a regional power with the consequential decline of the Russian Empire, one of the most powerful nations in Western power dynamics. During the periods of World War I and Wilsonian Diplomacy (1914–1920), Interwar Diplomacy (1921–1936), and Diplomacy and the Road to Another War of World War II (1937–1945), when the United States was tied up with diplomacy, Korea was completely ignored. Until the United States ended World War II against Japan, Korea was not even on its radar. Alas, Korea was cut in half when the United States broke silence to reluctantly engage with Korea again, as will be spelled out in subsequent chapters.

Unfortunately, many problematic aspects of U.S.-Korea relations since 1945 remain unresolved, with the Peninsula still technically at war as the ceasefire in 1953 has not been replaced by a peace treaty. In recent decades, however, the United States has developed unprecedented closeness with South Korea through developments such as the 1953 Mutual Defense Alliance Treaty, and by becoming Korea's second largest destination for exports. Along similar lines, South Korea has become America's seventh largest trading partner, which may seem like a sudden and drastic shift from the United States' century-and-a-half-long practice of betting to folding.

Today, the United States is facing military and economic challenges from China—Korea's former suzerain and, at the same time, its main enemy in the Korean War. The United States, this book argues, bears responsibility both directly and indirectly for South Korea's democratization and rise to world economic power.

THE HISTORY OF UNEVEN ENCOUNTER: JARED DIAMOND

Korea's place in East Asian ancient cultural history is well recognized for passing on major cultural and religious arts, craftsmanship, ideas, and philosophy to Japan. As Oliver (1944:18–19) observes,

The custom, traditions, and civilization of the Korean people are their own; they have influenced their neighbors at least as much as they have been influenced themselves. The development of Japan in pre-Commodore Perry times began with its importation of Korean culture.

Nathan (1954:17) echoes Oliver's point, saying, "many of Korea's contributions reached the world by way of their influence on the Japanese. Centuries ago, the Japanese adopted many Korean artistic techniques and religious ideas. In turn, they often added a distinctive Japanese touch." Oliver (1944:19) also indicates that "Korea's history as an independent country is far older than that of Greece or Italy—about as old as that of Egypt, Abyssinia, and the Hebrew tribes. In comparison with Korea," he says, "England, France, Germany, and Russia—to say nothing of the United States and the Latin American countries—are all newcomers to the world family of nations." Nathan (1954:17), in his epoch-making post–Korean War report for the UN Korean Reconstruction Agency in 1954, mentions how Korea's heritage developed over millennia:

> They are proud, for example, that Koreans printed books with moveable metal type before the Gutenberg bible, that they compiled an encyclopedia before Diderot, that they built an astronomical observatory a century and a half before the Holy Roman Empire. . . . Compared to such a long history of civilization of Korea, the first wave of European immigration that arrived in Massachusetts Bay was in 1620. For most of the 17th and 18th centuries, America's expansion witnessed the massacre of Native Americans as well as the introduction of the slave trade. Although the US, in the midst of an industrial revolution and territorial expansion, officially opened relations with China in 1844 (Treaty of Wangxia) and Japan in 1854 (Treaty of Kanagawa), relations with Korea remained closed. Secretary of State William Seward, under Presidents Lincoln and Johnson, was one of the political leaders most focused on U.S. strategic interests in the Pacific and Asia, including Korea.

Jared Diamond's (1997:16) claim that "the modern world has been shaped by the history of interactions among disparate peoples, the reverberations of which still resound" is one of the few that make sense of the stark contrasts that have crystalized between North Korea and South Korea, two nations that shared the same history for thousands of years until military occupation by the Soviet Union and the United States: "History followed different courses for different peoples because of differences among peoples' environments," Diamond says, "not because of biological differences among peoples themselves." America's determination to put Asia within its sphere of influence was expected to result in a series of encounters with Asian countries, China,

Japan, and Corea, which were embedded with quite different or opposite cultures and economic and political systems.

In this early encounter with Asian countries, Washington found Japan to be the most compatible Asian partner as non-white and non-Christian but the Yankee of the East, or Great Britain in Asia and went hand in hand with Tokyo in America's most important moments of foreign-policy decisions during the late nineteenth and early twentieth centuries. The merit of that relationship lay in Japan's rapid rise as a powerful competitor to Western powers within a half-century from the Meiji Reformation in 1868 to the Washington Conference in 1920–1921.

However, they were intrinsically distinct from each other, with such contrasts having continuously surfaced throughout their strained partnership as disastrous as any modern history can identify. LaFeber characterizes such radical differences as follows:

> It is a singular fact that in Japan, where the individual is sacrificed to the community, he would seem perfectly happy and contented; while in America, where exactly the opposite takes place, and the community is sacrificed to the individual, the latter is in a perpetual state of uproarious clamor for his rights. (LaFeber, 1997:30)

They fought against each other as the principal enemy during the World War II while their veiled alliance pushed Corea into the status of a colony and a divided nation after all. Diamond's argument that history followed different courses for different peoples because of differences among peoples' environments has found its validity in East Asian modern history as well.

In fact, according to LaFeber (1997:50), Washington was aware of the consequences of its move with Tokyo on the destinies of two East Asian countries, China and Corea, that America's strong alignment with Japan might endanger the status of Korea and China. In fact, the early twentieth-century history witnessed that with full support, Washington allowed Japan to colonize Corea in 1905 and to destroy China in the pre–Pacific War from 1931, when Japan invaded Manchuria.

In this encounter of America with Asia, both religious and racist values and attitudes shaped the natures of the intercourses. After successful expansions to the West, the United States was ready to move on to the Pacific Ocean with the victorious spirit of Manifest Destiny ideology, which

> came to mean that Americans ("with the calm confidence of a Christian holding 4 aces," as frontier writer Mark Twain later phrased it) believed they had God-given rights to spread both their new political institutions and successful

commerce across the continent, then into Latin America, and to uplift, among others the benighted Europeans and Asians. (LaFeber, 1997:10)

Therefore, from the beginning of the encounters, Asia's long history and Confucian and other philosophical backgrounds were objects to be corrected, punished, and infused with American and Western cultures, religion, and political and economic systems.

Put simply, Korea's modern history mirrors that of the United States. Thus, by reflecting on its relationship with Korea, the United States can gain insights into many questions about itself: who it is, what it stands for, and where it is heading. Conversely, by reflecting on its encounter with the United States, Korea can learn analogous lessons about itself. Such bilateral histories have much to offer, greatly expanding our comprehension of the interwoven factors involved as well as the interrelated contexts within which they exist. In fact, much of what the Korean nation has experienced from the end of the Joseon until now mirrors quite substantially certain aspects of U.S. international and East Asian policy, whereas the actions of the United States are the only possible explanation for the realities that South Korea and North Korea have come to represent in contemporary international affairs.

Was the American decision to intervene in the Korean War purely in that country's interest? No, it was mainly to deter the expansion of the new ideology of communism being led by the Soviet Union, which had shaped post–World War II international politics as one pole of the Cold War rivalry. Nevertheless, in its new commitment to Korea, Washington made the first major sacrifice of losing 36,547 American lives with 1.8 million soldiers deployed in the Korean theater. In this war, Washington faced a new China that had converted to communism on October 1, 1949. The Republic of China was no longer an old, emasculated suzerain of the old Confucian Korea. Due to China's intervention in October 1950 in the Korean War, the United States did not have an immediate victory. Rather, in the Korean War against North Korea (a Soviet satellite) and China, Washington, the principal victor of World War II, had to swallow the insult of signing the Armistice on July 27, 1953.

This new international Cold War rivalry created an environment that forced Washington to make an almost permanent commitment to stationing troops in the southern half of the Peninsula. In the overarching history of U.S.-Korea relations from 1866 to 1953, Washington finally decided to formally recognize the Republic of Korea, which, this book reasons, was the first occasion of abiding by the good offices provision of the Treaty of Peace, Amity, Commerce, and Navigation of 1882. In the Cold War rivalry system, Washington had no choice but to recognize the regime in the south as its own satellite country that served to demonstrate the superiority of America's democracy and capitalism as well as being the last stronghold for deterring Soviet imperialism. As enumerated in many official and declassified documents produced by the American government, the Korean Peninsula also was viewed as a buffer zone to protect Japan from being communized. Despite being of secondary importance in Washington's choice to station troops in the Korean Peninsula, South Korea was the perfect case where Washington could speak into the microphone on the global stage and show that America's free democracy and capitalism were better than the Soviet Union's centralized socialist economy and totalitarian communist dictatorship.

In this way, South Korea was fully supported by the U.S. government in terms of economy, the military, and America's nuclear umbrella. Ironically, though, South Korea's rapid economic development and substantial democratization—accomplished by the Five-Year Economic Development Plan in 1962 while anti-military and antiauthoritarian demonstrations were being led by university students and civic forces—happened to exemplify the Washington versus Moscow rivalry. To the United States, South Korea's rise to an economic power and a model of democracy in Asia served as a perfect example to promote the superiority of the American ideology of free capitalistic democracy against its own World War II ally but soon-to-be prime antagonist in the last half of the twentieth century. South Korea's story of being the "Miracle on the Han River" has become much more appealing to Washington in its efforts to win the ideological competition against communism as Soviet-backed North Korea's economy attracted world attention for mass hunger in the late 1990s.

Therefore, Washington decided to recognize the South Korean regime as one of its most important allies for posing a stark contrast against the failures of the communist ideology as well as to contain communist expansion in Asia. In contrast, Washington's policy toward North Korea during the Cold War was to ignore and deny its existence mainly due to no longer needing to deal with Pyongyang since Washington just dealt with Moscow, which had a tight grip on Pyongyang.

The single most contributing factor to such transformative changes in Washington's policy toward South Korea, from complete abandonment to full commitment, was the October 1, 1953, Mutual Defense Treaty between the United States and the Republic of Korea, which was the direct outcome of the Korean War. This defense treaty in the twentieth century between the United States and South Korea was the second document to substantially change the nature of encounters between the two countries. In fact, I am not sure whether Washington is aware of the differences and similarities between the two treaties it established with Korea—the 1882 and 1953 treaties—in terms of U.S. policy toward Korea. As discussed, the 1882 Treaty of Peace, Amity, Commerce and Navigation also had a provision of good offices—meaning mutual responsibility to come to each other's aid if one partner is endangered by foreign forces—and was unilaterally discarded by President Theodore Roosevelt in 1905. The 1953 mutual defense treaty had a similar but much stronger and more specific commitment on the part of the United States toward South Korea. Throughout the chapters in this book, Diamond's thesis on the disparities caused by encounters between different cultures and societies will be addressed as a way of explaining the consequences of America's encounters with North and South Korea.

ANALYTICAL FRAMEWORKS: AMERICA'S REGIME DENIAL OF NORTH KOREA AND HEGEMONIC BEHAVIOR

The most serious consequence of the Korean War is that the United States, with a bitter memory of not winning the war against communism, has intensified its perception of North Korea as one of the most deplorable rogue countries in the world, as clearly expressed by the Bush administration's designation of North Korea as an Axis of Evil in 2002. Except for the Trump administration, Washington has never committed to having any direct talks with North Korea's top leader since the Korean War. Rather, the United States has waited for North Korea to collapse somehow. Despite no shortage of scholarly attempts, there appears to be no coherent framework or theory to comprehend such American hatred against North Korea and no intention to normalize the relationship.

This book conceptualizes such American attitudes and policy on North Korea as a mixture of "regime change" and "regime denial" since the breakout of the Korean War. Gasiorowski (1996), Waltz (2000), and Owen (2010) indicate America's reliance on both overt and covert attempts to deal with political regimes that pose potential threats to its own national interests by replacing those regimes with more Washington-friendly governments. They define regime change as alterations of fundamental political institutions in countries by armed forces and various operations. Washington has deployed such tactics and strategies for many years dealing with anti-American regimes all over the world, especially in Latin America.

Conceptually, regime change comes with regime promotion that would replace those regimes targeted for Washington to remove. However, the concept of regime change does not capture the whole picture of America's North Korea policy since the breakout of the Korean War. Rather, most of America's attitudes and actual policy implementations against North Korea can be better explained with the notion of denial of a North Korean regime. Chapter 6 will detail notions of regime change, regime promotion, and regime denial in historical contexts of America's overall Korea policy. In sum, the concept of regime denial resulted from three phenomena: Washington's disinterest in and hostility toward the communist regime in North, its unwillingness to break the status quo on the Korean Peninsula, and finally strategic reasons to promote the figure most closely representing the image of America's model ally, the South Korean regime.

To Washington, these combinations of regime change and promotion in a divided nation are the most realistic options for legitimizing what the United States argues South Korea exemplifies: capitalism and free democracy. Among Washington's many reasons for denying Pyeongyang is that considering military actions against North Korea is unrealistic, given that such a course may also devastate South Korea, whose capital lies only 40 minutes away from the North's long-range cannons which are concentrated in the demilitarized zone (DMZ). In contrast, the realistic option perfectly suits Washington's desire to avoid harming its international prestige and to maintain hegemonic position by upholding its own economic and political ideals realized in the South. In this realistic option, the denial of North Korean regime occupies a central position.

America's encounter with Korea will complete its full circle if and when Washington is ready to give up its traditional policies of either regime change or regime denial and move toward establishing an official state relationship with North Korea. However, such radical transformation from regime change to regime recognition in America's North Korea policy could only be feasible if Washington is willing to recognize North Korea as a nuclear power. It is almost an impossible proposition that Pyeongyang would renounce its nuclear weapons because it is well aware of its vulnerability without its own asymmetric nuclear weapon system in the face of South Korea's far better economic and military capacities as well as the world's most dreaded military power, the United States.

SUMMARY OF CHAPTERS

This book aims to recount the trajectory of U.S.-Korean relations centering on the Korean Question of how the destiny of the Korean nation has been shaped through the historical evolution of its encounters with the United States. This chapter briefly discussed the essence and realities of the Korean Question, unwittingly created by a series of ever-shifting American policies toward Korea, first opening, deserting, and dividing the Korean nation, in 1882, in 1905, and in 1945, respectively, and then finally committing reluctantly during the Korean War, and espousing the two opposite policies of regime change in the North and regime recognition in the South. After a brief survey of the encounters between the United States and Korea, the chapter, in order to explain such an incoherent policy toward Korea and uneven developments of the divided Korean nation, makes reference to the findings of Jared Diamond's historical research into the causes of uneven development and unequal relationships between societies, cultures, and countries as they encounter each other. A theoretical conceptualization of America's two opposite approaches to North and South Korea is attempted through the notions of "regime denial" and "regime recognition."

Chapter 1 will delve into the historical background of how the Korean Question originated and the consequences of that Korean Question to the Korean nation. Rare historical documents written by two principal architects in opening the self-confining Joseon dynasty, then-state secretary William Seward and Commodore Robert Shufeldt, will be examined. Further, this chapter will analyze both how this original SS Line had taken a dramatically opposite turn due to President Theodore Roosevelt's abandoning America's treaty with Corea and how such a change resulted in warfare on the Korean Peninsula and subsequent radical disparities between North and South Korea. In order to shed light on the original aspects of the SS Line and its policy foci, this chapter looks into Secretary of State William Seward's vision for achieving American hegemony in the Asian market by opening Corea and making the Pacific an American lake. Next, Commodore Robert Shufeldt's efforts are retraced to see how he succeeded in executing Secretary Seward's vision. In particular, Shufeldt's letters to Navy Secretary Thompson and family will be intensively referenced, along with other documents, to reveal the rationales underlying American leadership. Lastly, this chapter evaluates the impact of President Franklin Roosevelt's Korea policy, how the rationale behind Theodore Roosevelt's abandonment of Corea to Japan resurfaced in his cousin's plan of placing Korea under the tutelage of superpowers, thus dividing the Peninsula in the end, as implemented by President Truman. The decisions of these four American leaders are the factors most responsible, as this book will show, for the history of Korea's encounters with the United States.

Chapter 2 will delve into the bilateral history of U.S.-Korea encounters with U.S. blackship diplomacy literally running up against Corea's tradition of isolationism, detailing the first encounter of the General Sherman incident in 1866, the Treaty of Peace, Amity, Commerce, and Navigation between the United States and Corea in 1882, America's abandonment of that treaty in 1905, and Washington's long silence on Corea from 1910 to 1945. As a conclusion to this chapter, this book discusses how Corea's requests that Washington invoke the good offices provision of the 1882 treaty when Japan suddenly posed a lethal threat to Corea in the early twentieth century was flatly ignored. Subsequently, this chapter examines the Korea policy of President Theodore Roosevelt, who was most responsible for America's vacillation from the original intent of the SS Line, dropping Corea from the U.S.-initiated treaty of 1882 and initiating the tragedy of Korea's suffering under colonial control by the Japanese.

Chapter 3 introduces two Korean Wars, the first in 1871 and the second in 1950. Usually, when we talk about the Korean War, we talk about the second one from 1950 to 1953 in which 36,574 American soldiers were killed in action and which served as a dramatic turning point in Washington's policy toward the Korean Peninsula, mainly due to the advent of a new ideological warfare with its former World War II ally, the Soviet Union. The first Korean War took place in 1882 with roughly 400 Corean and two American casualties. Fourteen U.S. Navy and Marine Corps service members were awarded America's highest military decoration, the Medal of Honor, which, this book argues, serves as one of the reasons to call it a war. Recommendations by two major political leaders of President Truman's administration, General Albert Wedemeyer and then-acting secretary of states James Webb, which could have dramatically changed America's post–World War II Korea policy, will also be discussed. Finally, the transformative role of the Korean War in America's Korea approach and its lingering effects upon the power dynamics between the United States and China will be examined.

In chapter 4, this book looks upon today's showdown between Pyeongyang and Washington on North Korea's nuclear status and potential threats to the United States and the region as a ship's steering wheel returning to the original point of its efforts to open Joseon in 1866. The chapter will conceptualize Washington's approaches to Korea, with regime opening in 1882, regime abandonment in 1905, the bifurcative approaches of regime change against North Korea and strong regime recognition of South Korea during and after the Korean War, and finally regime denial of North Korea in the Cold War era.

Chapter 5 will investigate the consequences of America's encounters with Korea in general and its disparate policies toward North and South Korea. Specifically, major economic indicators will be studied to evaluate positive outcomes of the encounter between the United States and South Korea as a case study exemplifying one side of Jared Diamond's hypothesis that encounters between different societies and people result in uneven developments. The Korean War will be reconsidered first from the perspective of the resurrection of Kilroy, the hand-drawn figure emblematic of veterans first from World War II and next from that of the Korean War, with the sacrifice and experience of the latter critically contributing to the transformation of Washington's view of the Korean Peninsula. South Korea's splendid economic success in the wake of the war will be reviewed as one of the legacies of the Korean War and of America's decisive intervention. Lastly, America's

Asian policy and the North Korean question will be briefly revisited in the context of the century-old antagonism among the three East Asian countries.

Chapter 6, the conclusion of this book, will revisit the Korean Question with a short summary and an epilogue. More specifically, this final chapter assesses the transformational impacts of the Korean War in 1950 on Washington's fundamental perspectives on the Korean Peninsula. In one sense, that transformation can be explained by the transition from the SS Line to the Theodore-Franklin Line, which may offer one path toward resolving the "Corean Question" in the conclusion.

NOTES

1. Before the modern era, "Corea" was used among Westerners to mean the Joseon dynasty (1392–1910) in particular and Korea more broadly. "Corea" is the romanized spelling and pronunciation of the Goguryeo Kingdom (BC 37–668) during the Three Kingdoms periods: the Silla Kingdom (BC 57–935) and the Baekje Kingdom (BC 18–660). Two eras come later: the Goryeo Kingdom (918–1392) and the Joseon dynasty (1392–1910, including the Great Han Empire (1897–1910). Regarding the origin of this spelling, Savage-Landor (1895: 22) used it in his seminal book, *Corea or Cho-sen* [Joseon] – *The Land of the Morning Calm* (1895): "The real native name now used is Cho-sen [Joseon], though occasionally in the vernacular the kingdom goes by the name Gori, or antiquated Korai. Here 'Gori' or 'Korai' means Goguryeo Kingdom." He continues: "There is no doubt that the origin of the word Corea is Korai, which is an abbreviation of Ko-Korai, a small kingdom in the mountains of Fuyu, a little further north, whence the brave and warlike people probably descended, who conquered old Cho-sen." In general, this book uses "Corea" when conveying foreigners' perspectives, and "Joseon" or "Korea" when referring to the nation before its division by the United States and the USSR in 1945. In this book, "Corea" generally indicates the Korean nation from its first identification by Westerners till it was colonized by Japan while Korea denotes the nation after World War II and now even though both "Corea" and "Korea" can interchangeably mean the same in such phrases as "Corean Question" and "Korean Question."

2. Despite its very sensitive and gender-biased implications in the use of "intercourse," this book occasionally uses it in order to reveal the historical contexts and backgrounds in the conventional usages in American foreign policies and the nature of America's encounters with other societies. It was widely used by many foreign-policy leaders including William Seward and Robert Shufeldt, who were two most important American leaders in the encounters, opening, and official treaty with Corea. Shufeldt used it in his May of 1880 letters to Navy Secretary R. H. Thompson as is also the case for Seward's many letters to American diplomats in China in the late 1990s and other politicians.

Chapter 1

Origins of the Korean Question and the Consequences of the Korean War

COMPLETION OF THE GREAT CIRCLE ROUTE: THE SEWARD-SHUFELDT LINE

In tracing the history of the encounters that have taken place between Korea and the United States, this book begins its historical investigation by making it clear that it was the United States and not Korea that first sought to establish official relations. Considering how heavily South Korea currently depends on the U.S. market, technology transfer, and military assistance and security umbrellas, many assume it was Korea that asked for a relationship with America in the late nineteenth century. At that time, China maintained tight suzerainty over Korea, which matched well with Korea's voluntary attachment to Beijing. Korea's strong stance of belonging to the center of China's Confucian world order at that time had been anchored in the Korean ideology of *sadae*, meaning service to the great. However, after the first unofficial encounter between the United State and Korea in 1866, Secretary of State William Seward, having already established official relations with China and Japan in 1844 and 1854 respectively, made clear that U.S. control of Korea would be the logical next step.

Seward had shown his obsessive interests in Asia in the 1850s. From 1846 to 1848, America had won a major war against Mexico and was able to expand immensely toward the West, absorbing California and much of the Southwest into the Union. Such domestic territorial expansion ran parallel to industrial expansion. Seward urged Americans to take their eyes off the European markets and passionately promoted his idea of conquering a new but bigger market in Asia. He believed that "the American continent was soon to become the center of the world's production and communications," he urged "Americans to take their eyes off the western hemisphere where, he was sure, the United States was inevitably going to be supreme, and focus on the incredible potential of Asia, 'the prize,' the chief theatre of events in the world's great hereafter," as he termed it. The key to Asia was commerce, "which [,] surviving dynasties and empires . . . continues, as in former ages, to be a chief fertilizer" for both Europe and Asia (LaFeber, 1997:27).

Such bold and epoch-making ideas and visions in America's working its way into the Asian market were followed with rigorous and expeditious preparations by the best marine experts surveying the navigational routes toward Asia, which resulted in the completion of the navigational route of the Great Circle or the Seward-Shufeldt (SS) Line, this book claims. An American naval officer, John Rodgers, led a survey expedition through the waters surrounding Japan and along China's coasts between 1853 and 1856. Investigating this Great Circle Route thoroughly, Commodore Rodgers also echoed the vision of William Seward and Secretary of Treasury Walker that "the commercial possibilities [of Asia] are so vast as to dazzle sober calculation" (LaFeber, 1997:25).

The most decisive and critical beginning to the creation of this Great Circle was, however, initiated by Secretary Seward's purchasing Alaska from Russia in 1867 and, then, in correspondence to his nephew George Seward, the U.S. minister to China, finally calling for the opening of Corea.

The extension and eventual completion of the Great Circle were accomplished with a series of American policy acts: first, allying with Japan, which paved the way for Americans by settling a delicate territorial dispute with Russia in 1875 by annexing the Kuril Islands in line with the Aleutian Islands in exchange for Sakhalin, off Siberia's coast; second ratifying the treaty with Corea (the Joseon dynasty) in 1882; and finally acquiring the Philippines. In late autumn 1898, at the end of the Spanish-American War, President William McKinley pressured Spain to renounce all the Philippines, which was critical in America's strategic control of trading route leading to the millions of China and Korea as well as those of Southeast Asian countries.

Robert Shufeldt's Final Stroke in the Great Circle Route

Secretary Seward's dream of opening Corea was finally achieved by the American expeditionist Commodore Robert Wilson Shufeldt, who successfully followed up on Secretary Seward's call for intercourse with Korea by convincing the Joseon dynasty (Corea, 1392–1910) to sign the Treaty of Peace, Amity, Commerce, and Navigation with the United States in 1882. This American mission was completed after a series of unfortunate violent incidents. In 1871, the year of Shinmi, of the Sheep according to the Chinese zodiac, an American invasion of Joseon by means of an amphibious landing in Incheon ended up killing about 400 Joseon soldiers to avenge the

American crew members who died in the burning-down of the *General Sherman*, an American schooner, in 1866. This *Shinmiyangyo* set an unfortunate precedent, which this book sees as the first Korean War between the United States and Korea (the Joseon dynasty).[1]

The next question that naturally arises is, what compelled the United States to so ardently pursue official relations with the Joseon at that time? Even though there is abundant evidence in nineteenth-century literature and documentation that Corea was needed as a safe haven for shipwrecked American merchants, the Corean market was otherwise too small to attract interest from American capitalism. Perhaps Corea's market was not big enough to meet the expansionist appetites of imperialism. Then, what was it the United States wanted from Corea, other than waystations for safe haven between Japan and China?

American leaders such as Secretary William Seward and Commodore Robert Shufeldt, this book argues, saw the Pacific Ocean, and the whole Asian market for that matter, as America's biggest national interest, especially since the Atlantic Ocean, had already been dominated by European competitors in the late nineteenth century. Moreover, Corea was the only Asian country that had refused intercourse[2] (trade) with the West. Making the Pacific Ocean into a kind of American Lake, and establishing American dominance in the Asian market, a handful of leaders in Washington believed that Corea was the last remaining target for conquest after America's successful opening of Japan in 1854. With Commodore Perry's 1854 Treaty of Kanagawa, Japan became a trophy for America as the first Asian country to ever be opened. By contrast, America's treaty with China in 1844 was an easy follow-up on European imperialist penetrations into China through the Opium War from 1839 to 1842. Furthermore, by means of intercourse with Corea, the United States could compete more effectively against European powers and rise to become the next world hegemon by dominating the Asian market through tight control over the Pacific Ocean, which was viewed as potentially the largest market of the twentieth century.

William Seward and Robert Shufeldt shared the same thinking and vision for achieving their American goal by acquiring Corea and completing the SS Line as illustrated in map 1.1,[3] this book argues. This started with Seward's acquisition of Alaska, naturally linking it with the Aleutian and Kuril Islands through treaties with Japan, the Philippines, and the Samoan Islands to make a perfect perimeter for the American era of the Pacific and hegemony in the Asian market. Linking these islands and countries through the SS Line would lead the Pacific and Asian market to become at no distant day the commercial domain of America. Initiating intercourse with Corea was Commodore Shufeldt's finishing touch on the plan for achieving American hegemony in the coming twentieth century. In addition to serving as another link in the

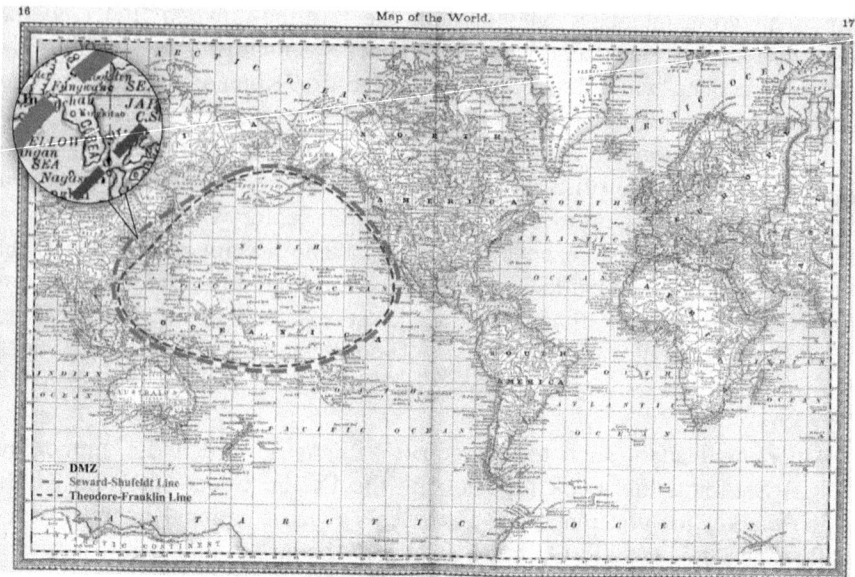

Map 1.1 The Seward-Shufeldt Line vs. The Theodore-Franklin Line. *Source:* Library of Congress Geography and Map Division. Call Number G1200.H37 1882, modified by Maranda Wilkinson.

chain binding East to West, it would give the U.S. moral precedence in Corea by establishing the relationship without violent force, unlike what occurred with European penetration into China.

THE COREAN QUESTION: CONCEPTUALIZATION

This American vision incorporating Corea as part of American hegemony in Asia, this book argues, was the origin of the so-called "Corean Question." At the same time, by pushing to establish relations with Corea in 1882, a Pandora's box of woes was opened, giving rise to questions that have not been resolved to this day. Moreover, this book argues that the original American dominance in the Pacific Ocean and Asian market was established by the Seward-Shufeldt, or "SS," Line.

Regarding the "Corean Question," two important historical observations deserve attention. In America's process of opening Corea, first, China's thousand years of accepted authority over Corea was severely damaged and even severed by Japanese victory in the Sino-Japanese War of 1894–1895. In fact, China's demands that the United States recognize Chinese suzerainty over Corea in its 1882 treaty with Corea were officially refused by Commodore

Shufeldt even though the treaty negotiations had been aided and facilitated by China. Second, when Japan surprised President Theodore Roosevelt by crushing the Russian fleet in the Russo-Japanese War in 1904–1905, Korea's place in the original SS Line changed dramatically. President Roosevelt breached the treaty and traded control of Corea to Japan for its suzerainty over the Philippines because his decision to do so did not affect the American interest reflected in the original SS Line as long as Tokyo remained friendly to Washington. Thus, the first and most important factor in the "Corean Question" was America's attempt to extricate Corea from Chinese control.

In President Theodore Roosevelt's decision to trade Corea for the Philippines, while it remained within the SS Line, the only change was Korea's loss of independence and 35 years of Japanese colonial control till the end of World War II. Such a dramatic shift of American policy from a consistent desire to establish a relationship to complete abandonment of Corea was a short-term outcome of the encounter that Americans desperately wanted to achieve from the encounter. In turn, Korea's place on the map of America's zeal for hegemony over the Pacific was completely lost. In 1941, Japan attacked Pearl Harbor, which opened World War II, during which President Franklin Roosevelt laid the foundations for militarily occupying Korea. At the end of the war, Korea would be liberated from 35 years of brutal colonial control under Japan, an occupation which was the legacy of President Theodore Roosevelt's policy on Corea in the late nineteenth century. Contemplated by President Franklin Roosevelt and executed by President Truman to defeat Japan, the Soviet Union was invited into the northern Korean Peninsula as a result of American military occupation of the south.

The Seward-Shufeldt idea of keeping Corea as an equal treaty partner in its Pacific-Asia dominance was dropped in favor of the Theodore-Franklin Line, which allowed Japan to have Corea while occupying the Philippines. In map 1.1 the Theodore-Franklin Line visibly denotes Washington's willful renouncement of the Korean Peninsula as its direct sphere of influence. When such decisions as the Theodore-Franklin and its identical Acheson Line were made in 1950 by Washington, the Korean nation had tragically suffered: In 1905 with President Theodore Roosevelt's decision to renounce Corea, that country eventually fell to Japan as its colony, and in 1950, the Korean War broke out. In other words, the essence of the Korean Question in this book is about this shift by Washington from the original SS Line to the Theodore-Franklin Line, which means either inclusion or exclusion of the Korean Peninsula in America's grand vision of making the Pacific Ocean and Asia as an American sphere of influence. In such American decisions, it did not matter to the United States whether Corea maintained independence or not, provided that Corea became part of the SS Line. Therefore, as long as the United States aligned with Japan, which had annexed Corea in 1910, Washington would not bat an eye when Japan moved to seize colonial control of that country. Corea was not an end but a means in the 1882 treaty, and America's continuing goal was to establish and maintain American dominance in the Pacific and Asian market, at least up until the outbreak of the Korean War in 1950.

Another dramatic swing in Korea's value to U.S. national interests took place on January 12, 1950, when Secretary of State Acheson announced the American defensive perimeter, which excluded the Korean Peninsula from America's original SS Line. We must remember here that Corea remained within the Theodore-Franklin Line even after it fell under Japanese control; however, the Korean Peninsula was completely dropped by the Acheson Line. Strangely, on the original SS Line, Korea was the only country or territory attached to the Eurasian continent bordering with China and Russia, whereas all of the others were islands, including Japan and the Philippines.

America's treaty with Corea in 1882 extricated Corea from China and Russia, and the Acheson Line of January 12, 1950, was to return Corea to what it used to be. Upon Acheson's clarification, which served as an inadvertent invitation for a communist attack on South Korea, Russia and China did not hesitate to recover control over the Korean Peninsula. The Korean War from 1950 to 1953 was waged by the North's communist regime of Kim Il-sung, backed by China, an old suzerain, and Russia, who wanted harbors that would not freeze in the winter. In this war, the United States, for the first time, had to face China as a main enemy, which started the new international bipolar system of the Cold War and lasted officially until the collapse of the Soviet Union in 1991.

That dramatic exclusion of Korea from the American defensive perimeter rekindled hegemonic competition over the Peninsula when such competitions were thought to have come to an end with America's victory in World War II. Metamorphosed into communist countries, the Soviet Union and the People's Republic of China were vigilantly awaiting an opportunity to challenge U.S. supremacy in the Korean Peninsula, which eventually raised again the question of the place of the Peninsula in the power competitions among Washington, Moscow, and Beijing in the East Asian region. It was high time for China to regain suzerainty there and for Russia to redeem itself for its defeat in the Russo-Japanese War and in the competition for the Pacific Ocean in the early twentieth century.

Can it be realistically said that the Cold War has ended? This book argues that the Cold War in the Korean Peninsula has never ended as the Korean War technically has not been replaced by a peace treaty. In fact, the Korean War produced two troubling outcomes: a provocative North Korea with nuclear and ICBM technologies, and a challenge from a rising China. The United

States is still colliding with China on the same defensive perimeter of the Seward-Shufeldt and Acheson Lines.

The prediction of Secretary Seward and Commodore Shufeldt was accurate—that the Asian market would become the world's largest if the three East Asian countries' GDP together could account for more than one-third of the world's total GDP. However, America's choice of Japan over China in the late nineteenth century and its decision not to include liberated Korea within its defensive perimeter seem to have brought about scenarios such as contemporary showdowns with China and North Korea. Through the Korean War (1950–1953), the United States finally achieved control over the half of the Korean Peninsula by occupying South Korea as its inevitable defensive line, sacrificing 36,594 men and women, deploying roughly 1.8 million soldiers in the Korean theater during the 3-year war, investing enormous amounts of dollars and technology, and currently deploying about 25,000 American soldiers in South Korea. The Corean Question of whether America can continue its original commitment to Korea and vision of having Corea play an essential role in U.S. hegemony in the Pacific and Asian region temporarily appeared to have been answered.

Power Struggles between the United States and China over Korea

In its conclusion, this book claims that the origin of the "Corean Question" was the power struggle for control of the Korean Peninsula between the United States and China. Competition over the Peninsula, due to the strategic importance of its geopolitical location, was the origin of the Corean question. The reason for this book's main argument that the United States is the party most responsible for such a question as Korea's place in the region, as well as in American national interest, is simply that the United States raised the issue of relations in the first place and then committed itself to official intercourse with Korea through the 1882 treaty. One of the main questions implicit in this "Corean Question" is whether the United States will uphold its commitment and start viewing Korea as an end and not a means. This book reasons that the United States has reached the final stage of completing its original commitment to the Korean Peninsula, as the Korean chip—which is still split and in conflict between north and south, and always surrounded by the same superpowers—has become too valuable for the United States to lose. South Korea's rise as an economic powerhouse in the global economy and its strategic value to the reality of China's challenge to America's unilateral hegemonic status in the global power pyramid has become so valuable to the national interest of the United States that U.S. dominance in global politics would be seriously damaged without Korea.

The Corean question is about the power struggle over the strategic location of the Korean Peninsula between the United States and other powers that have fallen and risen in the region since the late nineteenth century. In this struggle, Japan also served as a means for Washington when the latter did not want to maintain its original commitment to Korea. It was President Theodore Roosevelt's policy to contain Russian power by aligning with Japan and maintaining American power in the region, which included U.S. control over the Korean Peninsula. America's intention to initiate intercourse with Corea through the 1882 treaty was deserted and in fact had run its full course and taken advantage of the geopolitical value of the Korean Peninsula in early twentieth-century U.S. Asian policy. The human and economic commitment that Washington had to make during the Korean War in the advent of the Cold War rivalry began to cause a substantive transformation in America's commitment to Korea and has come almost full circle for a completion.

At the core of the history of these competitions for global power that have driven the destiny of the Korean nation lies an antagonism between the United States and China that remains unresolved. When Commodore Shufeldt officially loosened the ties of Corean isolationism and voluntary loyalty to the Sinocentric worldview and, further, when Japan defeated China and Russia within an interval of a decade, Washington thought it had achieved the goal of making the Pacific Ocean an American lake, especially with America's rise as a new hegemon in world politics after leading the victory in World War II. However, once these two regional powers of Russia and China had been resurrected, equipped with the ideology of communism, they began to test Washington's commitment to Korea in 1950. President Truman's decision to call, in response to the bet placed by the communists, unfolded a new set of international rivalries toward the Korean Peninsula. Known as the Cold War, this bipolar rivalry between Washington and Moscow/Beijing entailed strong commitment and support for the regime in the south and aggressive regime change (northern advance during the Korean War) or strategic regime denial (no need for Washington to directly engage Pyeongyang in the presence of the Soviet Union).

The current North Korean crisis stems from the end of such bipolar Cold War politics that crystalized in the wake of the Soviet Union's collapse in 1991. Now, Washington has to deal, in a much more direct way, with North Korea's isolationism and unwavering desire to deal with Washington by possessing weapons that can pose serious threat to American leadership in the international non-proliferation regime. In returning full circle, Washington must now tackle the game that Pyeongyang is playing with the bargaining chips of nuclear weapons for U.S. recognition of its own regime and economic aid. This book asks what rationale Washington has for its 70-year animosity against Pyeongyang. Is it merely because of North Korea's stubborn will to possess nuclear and ICBM capabilities?

In fact, the U.S. government has provided both financial and military aid to the three most infamous nuclear proliferating countries of Israel, India, and Pakistan. Comparing North Korea with these countries, which have acquired hundreds of nuclear weapons and ICBM technologies, there seems to be insufficient justification for the United States to be bluntly antagonistic toward Pyeongyang, except for two reasons. First, North Korea was America's main enemy in the Korean War. Second, the United States did not win in the war against such a small satellite state of the Soviet Union. How can we justify Washington's ignoring the first three countries' proliferation activities and providing assistance while at the same time refusing to countenance a compromise with North Korea. From this perspective, the Corean Question is about bilateral competitions between China and the United States over the strategic geopolitical value of the Korean Peninsula in relation to their ultimate national interests.

Such an observation leads to the following point—that Washington seems to view North Korea as a part of its China problem, calling to mind the issue of the "Thucydides Trap," which points to China's challenge to American hegemony in contemporary international power politics. In fact, Pyeongyang is maintaining a very close alliance with Beijing while even South Korea has to increase its economic and security interdependence as China rises to become a global power, making itself a direct counterpart to the United States in a G2 world. Thus, as shown in map 1.1, North Korea remains a big part of the Corean Question, leaving the question of whether the United States will carry through with its original intention and commitment to having relations with Korea to Washington.

Can Korea Trust the United States?

Another critical aspect of the "Corean Question" is whether Korea can trust the United States, considering the holistic view of American decisions made throughout the one-and-a-half-century history of unilateral actions from 1866 to the contemporary Korean questions raised so far. Those American actions served to play the game of extricating Corea from China's influence, enhancing U.S. status in the region, and maximizing its influence in the largest market, which Secretary of State Seward had envisioned. Thus, if the United States abruptly folded in this game—and finally abandoned Korea, cut it in half, then committed to supporting the South while antagonizing the North—shouldn't Washington be considered as the single most important factor leading up to the current situation of the Korean nation? The question is, in light of a rising China, whether South Korea can trust the United States and its stance on the resolution of North Korean issues. This book argues that the transition from the SS Line to the Theodore-Franklin Line in America's Asian and Korea policy is the reason why the "Corean Question" remains unresolved, and posits that this is a legitimate question for South Korea on the bases that the United States betrayed its own treaty and commitment, traded Korea to Japan, and has ultimately been the most critical factor leading to the Korean War and the 75-year-old division and confrontation. This legitimate question forms the core of the so-called "Corean Question," this book argues, which Washington ought to consider more fully.

To some, it may sound absurd to bring morality and ethics into real politics and international affairs, but the treaty with Corea that the United States so eagerly sought and signed in 1882 clearly laid out that Corea was an independent country, which was a strategic excuse for extricating Korea from Chinese suzerainty. In addition, a provision of "good offices" was knowingly broken by President Theodore Roosevelt in 1905 by trading Corea to Japan for the control of Philippines. As a historical fact, Korea was abandoned by its treaty counterpart to Japan for 35 years of colonial rule (1910–1945) and then halved against its will by the United States upon being liberated in 1945. Even though the United States came to fight at the same time, Secretary Acheson's declaration excluding the Korean Peninsula from the U.S. defensive perimeter on January 12, 1950, about six months before North Korean communists attacked the South, served as an inadvertent signal for Stalin and Mao's approval of Kim Il-sung's plan to launch the Korean War.

The American Question of Korea

Finally, whose question is the "Corean Question"? Surely, the Corean Question raised in the late nineteenth century is about Korea or the Korean Peninsula. However, this question could never have been raised if the United States had not attempted to open Corea against its will. Alternatively, perhaps a better way to answer this question is to point out that the United States prompted the Corean Question, which in turn has become one of the main issues in U.S. foreign policy. Thus, this book argues that intrinsically the Corean Question is the question of America's policy on the Korean Peninsula. This, in turn, has become the determining factor in the life or death of the Korean nation.

By answering Commodore Shufeldt's call to establish the treaty in 1882, Joseon leaders thought that Corea would have a distant but benign neighbor to help rebuff bullying from old neighbors nearby. However, their wish opened the Pandora's Box of the Corean Question and became a death knell for the Korean nation in 1905, when Theodore Roosevelt signaled to Japan to do what Japan had wanted since its victory in the 1894 Sino-Japanese War. Since then, the destiny of the Korean nation was to become a global gladiatorial contest and a powder keg, which was ignited in the Korean War in 1950.

By inviting the Soviet Union, its soon-to-be most threatening enemy, into the Korean Peninsula and overestimating Japan's military capacity at the end of World War II when Japan was about to collapse under nuclear bombs, Washington committed another grave blunder in chopping the Korean nation in half and sowing antagonism between the North and the South. President Franklin Roosevelt's idea of installing a trusteeship for Korea that was comprised of superpowers revealed the contemporary epitome of the Corean Question, which was realized by the Truman administration in 1945. To make a long story short, Corea's place in the original SS Line in the late nineteenth century was dropped from the Theodore-Franklin Line, even though its location remained within the American defensive perimeter.

In the mid-twentieth century, Washington made the most critical blunder in its Korea policy, by treating Korea as a poker chip in its Asian policy—to the extent of even dropping the location of the Korean Peninsula, not to mention the Korean nation, from the Theodore-Franklin Line. In other words, the Acheson Line eliminated the Korean Peninsula from the original SS Line. It was due to this inadvertent signal to Stalin and Kim Il-sung that the Korean War broke out. What if Secretary of State Dean Acheson had not changed the Theodore-Franklin Line in his National Press Club speech on January 12, 1950, and had not excluded Korea from the American defensive line, would Stalin have approved Kim Il-sung's plan to attack South Korea? This book reasons that Stalin would not have permitted Kim's attack while he could or might have persuaded Kim to look for another gaffe on the part of Washington, which did not grasp the full understanding of its former World War II ally but soon-to-be principal enemy, despite warning signs such as George Kennan's Telegram X, Moscow's Berlin blockade, and civil disturbances stirred up by communist forces in Greece and Turkey.

Thus, the Corean Question has become an American question about America's commitment to its own Korean policy. As examined, Korea's modern destiny was remarkably affected by a series of American initiatives, renunciations of original policies, and misjudgments that resulted in the Theodore-Franklin Line and further retreat from it. The Korean War, however, served as a watershed for another sudden turn from the Theodore-Franklin Line. President Truman, after dividing, occupying, and withdrawing from the Korean Peninsula and allowing Secretary Acheson to exclude Korea from the American defensive line, reclaimed American ownership of the Corean Question by deciding within a week to intervene in the communist invasion of South Korea on June 25, 1950.

Chapter 1

THE COREAN QUESTION: SEWARD AND SHUFELDT

Based on the conceptualization of the Corean Question in the previous sections, the next two sections will examine historical documents written by both William Seward and Robert Shufeldt that will reveal America's nascent ideas and visions on the Asian market as well as questions on the status of Corea in an ambitious U.S. Asia policy. Secretary Seward considered the burning down of the *General Sherman* and the killing of some crew members as an opportunity to initiate an official intercourse with Corea and exchanged many correspondences and reports with his nephew George Seward, who was the minister to China. The letter this book analyzes is from the "Seward Family Digital Archives" from the University of Rochester. Following the Seward's heraldic voices, Commodore Shufeldt delivered the treaty with Corea in 1882 and completed the Great Circle Route for the United States. His original ideas, visions, thoughts, and policy recommendations on the assessments on power dynamics around the Corean Peninsula in the late nineteenth century and the essential nature of the Corean Question are well reflected in his two reports to Secretary of the Navy R. H. Thompson.

William Seward Opening the Pandora's Box of the Corean Question

It is vital, here, to distinguish between Seward's policies for North America and for the world. Like the proponents of Manifest Destiny 20 years prior, Seward believed that all of North America would ultimately fall under the control of the U.S. government and system. Secretary Seward said in 1867 that "Nature meant this whole continent to be sooner or later, part of the American Union. Canada and Mexico would not be colonies but rather states, just as Texas, California, and Oregon had become." Seen in this light, the Alaskan purchase was the first step in bringing about this new union. However, his attitude toward overseas territory was quite different. Seward felt that American influence and domination would come about, not by the acquisition of colonies or military conquest but by the growth of "world-wide foreign commerce" (Swartout, Jr., 1974:97). William Seward was one of the strongest mercantilists and promotors of international trade. Even though it was the late but successful catch-up of the industrial revolution, the nineteenth century, he declared, was the American century of Westward expansion, the manufacturing revolution and becoming the world's top trading country.

One big difference between Secretary of State William Seward and President Theodore Roosevelt regarding U.S. policy in opening Korea was Japan's relative place on the world's power map. During Seward's heyday, which overlapped with Japan's Meiji Reform in 1868, modernization of

Japan was just getting underway. However, Japan's rise, to the point of walking shoulder to shoulder with early risers from the West, such as Great Britain and the United States, was swift. The interval between the eras of Seward and Roosevelt was clearly reflected in Seward's view of Japan. To Seward, Japan was only half-civilized. He told U.S. minister to Japan Robert H. Pruyn that "Japan was semi-barbarous, the government being relatively enlightened, but the people and the ruling classes not yet reconciled to the opening of the country" while the Korean government was not even ready to think about opening itself up to foreigners (Swartout, Jr., 1974:100).

Secretary Seward took the same approach when news arrived of the death in Korea of the French missionaries and the crew of the American merchant ship, the *General Sherman*, both in 1866. Seward's desire for the growth of the American share in the Asian market, coupled with his reaction to this news, led him to propose a joint expedition with the French designed to avenge the dead and force a commercial treaty (Swartout, Jr., 1974:102). This proposal was soon dropped, but Korea was not forgotten. In January 1868, Seward wrote that the Americans' illegal excavation of royal tombs in Korea was "unendurable," but that "the United States was eager to proceed with such moderation there so as not to bring into question American dignity and liberality in relation to rude and unorganized Eastern communities" (Swartout, Jr., 1974:102). It was his cultural and religious attitude and sense of superiority,[4] as Swartout Jr. explains that actually allowed such conclusions to be drawn in the first place.

The following document,[5] written by Secretary Seward on October 14, 1868 to nephew and deputy George Seward, then U.S. minister to China in Shanghai, clearly reveals details of how Secretary Seward approached the opening of Corea:

French authorities, are withheld

At the same time, I am to inform you, though not now for the first time, that the Government of the United States is profoundly affected by the reports which have reached this country of the destruction of the merchant vessel "General Sherman" and the murder of her numerous crew in the waters of Corea.

During a period of several months we have been receiving, from our consuls and from Admiral Bell, statements which, although vague, uncertain and unsupported by authentic evidence, have nevertheless concurred in (forcing)[6] bringing to (the) a [9] conviction that a barbarous and inhuman massacre has been committed upon (American) citizens of the U.S., but whether with the sanction of the Corean Government is at present entirely unascertained. The subject is at the same time embarrassed by the reported fact that the vessel was employed in violation of the laws of the U.S. and of international law, in supplying the Coreans with contraband articles of commerce to (sustain them) be used [10] in their defense against the naval expedition undertaken by France as a (~~Christian for~~) just visitation provoked by the murder of twelve, unoffending French (writing unclear) in the peninsula.

This government has . . . thus far confined itself . . . to the duty of obtaining full, complete and reliable information concerning the facts. Not only Admiral [11] Bell but yourself and many consular correspondents have been instructed to procure and communicate such information. The scene of these injuries is, however, so remote that answer (~~to our inquiries~~) are not yet due. They may perhaps be expected within the next three months.

In the meantime, I have to [12] submit for your consideration what at the present moment seems to the President to be a proper form for future proceedings in the event that the information conflicted shall verify the case as it is now supposed to stand. That plan is, that you shall apply to the Chinese government for its good offices (several phrases crossed out) [13] and (~~guaranty of~~) for a safe conduct to an agent of this Government who shall proceed to the seat of government at Corea. Such agent will be authorized to ask, –

1st—That such indemnities shall be paid for the use of the families and relations of the persons murdered as will be sufficient in some degree to compensate for their great loss and will at the same time afford satisfactory reason to expect that [14] the atrocious crime will not hereafter be repeated.

2nd—That a treaty substantially similar to our treaties with Japan or China, shall be at once acceded to us by the government of Corea, subject to ratification by the President, with the advice and consent of the Senate of the United States.

3rd—That all the commercial and social advantages which are to be stipulated by such a treaty [15] in favor of the United States, shall be open to all the Western Powers that shall choose, concurrently or thereafter, to negotiate with the Corean Government.

4th—That a categorical answer by the Corean Government be given to the demands thus made, which answer shall be conveyed to us through the good offices of the Chinese Imperial Government, which good offices are to be preliminarily secured for that purpose. [16]

5th—In the event of a refusal of the Corean Government, to accede to these terms, the U.S. will (~~resort to such~~) then consider what measure of reprisal for the aforementioned are warranted by the laws of nations and the injuries of the case.

You are authorized to sound the Chinese government upon this subject in some confidential manner, preserving confidence on your part if the Chinese government shall desire you do so. If, on the other hand, [17] their answer to your request for their good offices shall be favorable and no objections to its publicity shall be made by theirs, there will then be no reason why you should not make the affair the subject of (unclear writing) and friendly communication with the representatives of the other Western Powers at Peking.

Your opinion upon the plan which I have submitted is requested, and I shall be thankful [18] for any suggestions you may make by way of improvement upon it. Your opinion is especially desired as to the amount which should be asked by way of indemnity, so that on the one side the exaction of it may not be unnecessarily vindictive, while, on the other side, it shall carry with it a proper moral weight.

After the supposition that the Chinese government will think favorably of the [19] I should be glad to receive any advice they may be disposed to give in regard to the character of the agent to be designated by this Government, the form of his appointment and the manner most suitable for his fitting out, equipment and travel. It is further worthy of consideration and of conference with the Chinese authorities, whether the representation would favorably be more effective if transmitted exclusively [20] through the good offices of the Chinese Government, and in writing, by a messenger of that government.

Upon these and all other questions bearing upon the subject, your advice is requested. If promptly communicated, it may reach us not much later than the definitive replies to the inquiries which have been heretofore instituted. To guard against possible misapprehension, [21] the President has thought proper that the substance of this dispatch should be made known confidentially to the Western Powers represented in China.

First, Seward was taking a full advantage of the *General Sherman* Incident in 1866 accusing Corea of "a barbarous and inhuman massacre" while fully aware of illegal activities of its crews in violation of both U.S. and international law. Second, upon obtaining full, complete, and reliable investigation, he was setting up a broader picture of how the United States could achieve his vision by officially opening Korea in the following sequences. He identified China as Corea's regent invoking the good offices provision in the treaty Washington signed with Beijing in 1844, the Wangxia Treaty, which disclosed the American stance from the beginning in its encounter with Corea that Washington did not see Corea as an equal partner. This aspect of Corea's being excluded in a matter substantially critical to its own destiny has been the core issue in the Corean Question, which will be discussed fully in the analysis of Commodore Shufeldt's use of the terminology, Corean Question. In fact, as we can clearly see in the contemporary showdown between the United States and North Korea, Washington is clearly aware of China's leverage on Pyeongyang and has taken the same position asking China to play a role of regent in different degrees.

Further, Secretary Seward demanded that his nephew work with the Chinese government to prepare a treaty with Corea which would guarantee indemnity and prevention of incidents like that of the *General Sherman* and favored-nation status for Western powers as well as America. He

Robert Wilson Shufeldt: Foreseeing the Corean Question

implied that Washington should deploy forces in reprisal if Corea refused intercourse.

After an unfortunate first encounter in 1866, American dreams of opening Korea were guided by Secretary Seward's vision of achieving an American century in the Pacific Ocean and Asia, but it was not until 16 years later that Commodore Shufeldt finally brokered the Treaty of Peace, Amity, Commerce, and Navigation with the Joseon dynasty in 1882. With this treaty, the SS Line[7] was finally drawn from Alaska to the Philippines, which in turn contributed to American dominance in this region. This agreement ended millennia of voluntary isolation of the Korean Peninsula and a long tradition of Chinese suzerainty over the Joseon. However, this was just a prelude to the "Corean Question" that has been left unanswered for more than a century and is still reverberating around the Korean Peninsula, on two issues in particular: a showdown between North Korea and the United States around Pyeongyang's nuclear ambitions and provocations and the sandwiching of South Korea between the United States and China.

To the United States, the 1882 treaty was a victory in that Corea weakened its age-old dependency on Sinocentrism. The United States refused China's demands for suzerainty over Corea. Before establishing an official relationship with Corea, however, Commodore Shufeldt raised the Corean question in private correspondence. In the two letters quoted below, he summarizes the Corean question and the thinking that shaped the course of American maneuvers in East Asia. Let's first look at these letters written by Shufeldt to his superior Navy Secretary Ronald Thompson, and consider how the former viewed the Corean question in the context of power competitions among China, Japan, and Russia as well as other European forces from the perspectives of American and Korean national interests. The first letter was addressed by Shufeldt to Thompson on May 29, 1880, two years before a treaty was signed (Shufeldt, 1880).

> U.S. Flagship Ticonderoga
> Special Services
> Yokohama Japan
> May 29th 1880
> No. 15
>
> Hon R.H. Thompson
> Sect'y of the Navy
> Washington, DC

Sir:

Referring to my dispatch to the Department—no. 13—dated April 26th. I have now the honor to submit the following in continuation of and pertinent to the subject of Corea.

On the morning of May 4th the Ticonderoga anchored in the harbor of Fusan—(Chosan) Corea. Immediately communicated with Mr Kondo, Japanese Consul at that port, and delivered to him the letter (copy enclosed in no. 13), addressed him by his Government.

I also handed him my Communication to the King of Corea with the request that this might be forwarded to Seoul the Capital of Corea. It may be well to state here that the Japanese here had for many years a settlement at Fusan, of an extraterritorial character and under the jurisdiction of a consul. Fusan however is a large and commodious bay and has several Corean towns upon its shores.

After the expiration of about 24 hours Mr Kondo informed me of the failure of his mission to the Corean Governor of the District at Torai-Fiu, who refused to forward any Communication from him on the ground that under the Treaty between Japan and Corea—the Consul could not address any communication to the Central Government—his authority being limited to correspondence with the District Governor—and on the further ground that he, the Governor, could (would) not hold intercourse with any foreigners except Japanese.

What transpired while the ship remained at Fusan is substantially told [with] the accompanying slip translated from a Japanese newspaper, and evidently composed by some person cognizant of all the facts. It is enclosed herewith as a part of the dispatch (marked C).

Governed by the peaceful tenor of my orders, and feeling that a collision at this time with the Coreans would render future negotiations impossible, and knowing also that the good Offices of Japan—in giving a simple letter to its Consul at Fusan, had not been exhausted or indeed tendered to the extent due to our Government—I determined to leave for Yokohama with a view to further consultation with our Minister at Tokio.

The Ticonderoga arrived at Yokohama on the 11th [. . .]—after various interviews with our Minister, Mr. Bingham, and HIJ Majesty's Minister for Foreign Affairs, and sundry correspondence—the desirable result has been attained of securing a Communication from HIJM's Minister to the Government of Corea at the Capital—which covers my letter to the King of Corea. Out of deference to the opinion of the Japanese Government, and with the concurrence of Judge Bingham—and to avoid for the present all pretext of hostility I have consented to wait for a reply at Nagasaki for a period of sixty days instead of [. . .] proceeding again to Fusan or any other port in Corea.

I shall accordingly sail on the 31st [. . .] via [. . .] for Nagasaki and there await the time specified, unless something should be developed in the meanwhile to suggest another course.

In this connection I have the honor to acknowledge receipt of Department Communication of April 26th [. . .] and here noted its contents.

The opening of Corea, although at present a matter of little commercial importance, yet it is the only Country in the world from which at the present time, foreigners are excluded. I am satisfied that the European Powers [. . .]—more particularly Russia—are intending to Effect treaties with it, either by persuasion or by force; any complication Especially between Russia and China, would almost [. . .] compel the former to take possession of some of the Corean ports. China is aware of this and, as I have before written, is urging Corea to make treaties with Western Nations.

The Corean question therefore is one of great interest here in the East and it would seem that the prestige—which we acquired by the treaty with Japan should be maintained by being also the first to make a treaty with Corea. If therefore after the present overtures (which are of the most friendly character) are received, that Government should [. . .] to Entertain any proposition—Especially for the protection of Shipwrecked Mariners, and property stranded upon the Corean Coast, it will be for the Government of the United States to decide upon the propriety of using other and perhaps more forcible means.

I think, but do not state it positively, that a display of our naval forces in these Seas, upon the Corean Coast would bring about intercourses at least, and perhaps a treaty, at all [. . .] the Squadron is strong enough to attack and hold any desirable point on the coast.

I have the honor to enclose herewith Copy of my letter to the King of Corea, marked A with Copies of the Correspondence in relation to its transmittal to the Corean Capital, marked B, D, E, F, G, H, I.

I have the honor to be
very respectfully
your obedient servant
Rev. Shufeldt
Commodore U.S. W
on special service

Enclosed
with dispatch No. 15. May 29th 1880, mailed in Yokohama May 30th.
A . . . Copy of letter addressed to King of Corea.
B . . . Consul Kondo's account of his attempt to forward it.
C . . . Slip from "Japanese Herald," May 28th, indicating excitement in Corean local [. . .] during ship's stay at Fusan.
D . . . Copy of letter May 10 to Judge Bingham [. . .]
E . . . Copy of letter from Judge B. May 24th, enclosing copy of his note to Mr. [. . .].

F . . . Copy of Judge B's note May 21 to Mr. S.
G . . . Copy of letter May 26th to Judge B. [. . .] 188. "M."
H . . . Copy of letter May 29th from Judge Bingham, enclosing copy of translation of Mr. S's letter concerning [. . .] to the King
I . . . Copy of translation of Mr. [. . .]'s letter

Included with dispatch No. 15, in a separate envelope marked "confidential," was also a further communication.

Within its quite lengthy contents, this confidential May 31, 1880 letter from Shufeldt to Navy Secretary R. H. Thompson reveals critical information about the main topic of this book, which is the "Corean Question." Shufeldt used the terminology the "Corean Question" for the first time saying, "The Corean Question therefore is one of great interest here in the East and it would seem that the prestige—which we acquired by the treaty with Japan should be maintained by being also the first to make a treaty with Corea." In a literal meaning here, Shufeldt meant "Corean Question" as an attempt to open the last country in East Asia for Western trade and navigational interests. He specified the goals for America and reasons why the United States had to be the first one to open Corea. Here, he also used a very gender-sensitive but obvious word at that period of patriarchal era, "intercourse" meaning opening Corea (Joseon dynasty), which was a reluctant, weak, poor, uncivilized, but necessary country for American hegemony in the Asian market. He made sure that Corea had to be opened to guarantee the protection of shipwrecked mariners and property stranded upon the Corean coast despite little commercial importance to the United States.

The more important reason he advanced for America's opening of Corea, however, was to take the initiative so that Washington might not lose its leading edge in the Asian market because European forces as well as two conventional regional powers, China and Russia, were intending to effect a treaty with Corea. He specifically warned that Russia might take action to control Corea if any complication occurred, which meant serious military commitments for Washington to risk in order to put Corea under its control, first, and to dominate the biggest market and national interest of the United States. Then, he suggested the use of naval forces to bring about at least intercourses, and perhaps a treaty.

In this letter, he alluded to an outline of the Corea Question. His second letter to Secretary Thompson in October 1880, however, quite astoundingly expounded his views and assessments in international politics centering on the issue of opening Corea in East Asia. Let's look at it.

His second letter (Shufeldt, 1880) to Secretary Thompson, on October 13, 1880, reads as follows:

Corea and the American Interests
in the East.
Ticonderoga
at Sea
13 October '80

Hon Thompson
Secretary of Navy
Sir;

I have the honor to transmit herewith a report from Paymaster Thompson on the commercial interests of Corea with a report from Lieut Niles being a brief compilation of its geography and history as far as it is known and at the same time to report some news on Corea and American interests in the East. The acquisition of Alaska and the Aleutian Islands, the treaties with Japan, the [. . .] Islands and Samoa are only [. . .] to the proposition that the Pacific Ocean is to become at no distant day the commercial domain of America. The Atlantic either by force of circumstance or by national indifference has been given over to [. . .], backed by the immense weight of European capital, but under natural law the flow of Commerce—as of Emigration—is from the East towards the West and the geographic position of the U.S. in conformity with this law points to the Pacific Ocean as the main channel of trade and our Country as the source from which the [. . .] people must attain whatever they need in the way of Commercial exchange. In all probability within the next half Century the [. . .] U.S. will find its largest market in Asia rather than in Europe. Thus a treaty with Corea becomes another link in the chain which binds the East with the West and would give to our Country that moral precedence in Corea which is so universally conceded to it in Japan. But the marauding expedition of Europeans and Americans for the purpose of illicit traffic or [. . .] contemptible object of robbing royal graves of suppositions [. . .] golden [. . .], added to the (so considered) unprovoked French Squadron attack in 1866 and the American Squadron in 1870—has naturally led the government and Corea averse to any foreign intercourse. Yet in the [. . .] of events Corea can no longer remain secluded; Japan has already forced a treaty upon her and Russia is silently preparing to appropriate the northern parts; and if any means can now be found to get beyond the "barred gates" and to reach the central government—I am convinced that Corea could be made to understand not only the policy of a treaty with the U.S., but its also late necessity as a protection against the aggression of surrounding powers. Corea would in fact be the battle-ground of any war between China and Russia or Japan in which the [. . .] these natives might confront each other. But to accomplish this treaty needs the same earnestness of purpose that characterized the [. . .] of Commander Perry in Japan. The Commissioner must have some [. . .] and [. . .] sign of the power of his Gov. moral [. . .] with [. . .], and particularly the Coreans who have seen so little of the World, though clothed in the most powerful language, would fail to convince even those willing to believe, unless they saw evidence of the power of the Nation which sought their friendship. Besides in the [. . .] between the United States and Corea, I am not satisfied that Japan has been acting in perfect faith—it is her policy indeed to monopolize the commerce of Corea. She possesses in the country [. . .] rights, and rules the Coreans with an iron rod. Striving to free herself from the obnoxious sway of foreigners on her own soil, she is unwilling to have these foreigners see how she has imposed these same laws in an aggravated force upon her defenceless neighbor. But the "Ticonderoga" has [. . .] a movement in Corea as the [. . .] under Commander [. . .] did in Japan and it only remains for the United States, if it really wishes to extend its influence in the East, to follow up the movement in the Country with a Squadron in the command of a [. . .] officer—as it did in the other—controlled [. . .] so successfully by the [. . .] and wisdom of the Great Commander Perry—otherwise [. . .] shall bestow upon some other nation the prestige of power which of right belongs to ourselves. Moreover it is a duty which we owe to these people to become the pioneers of a more enlightened policy in the East. European power is not employed to "civilize" Orientals—but to subordinate them and to keep them subordinate for the purposes of trade in [. . .]. A distinguished Chinese officer recently said to me "What have European treaties done for China but to force upon her Opium and Missionaries?" The U.S. should take higher grounds while demanding protection for its citizens [and] should ask for nothing more than she is willing to concede. Although as will be seen by Paymaster Thompson report—the foreign goods imported through Japanese hands into Corea as well as those smuggled into its northern territory from Russian territory are of American manufacture yet the commerce is at present unimportant. The Coreans are a poor people, and the Country for the most part rugged and unproductive; a failure of the new crop invariably creates a famine; its mineral wealth of which such fabulous stories have been told is at best apocryphal. The Coreans therefore have had little to sell and therefore little to buy with. The accounts of the French missionaries which are the most authentic indicate that the people are governed most despotically and that their aversion to foreigners [. . .] as much from the fear of their Rulers as from any [. . .] reluctance to have intercourse with them. Judging from the number of Christian converts these missionaries are said to have made, the Coreans must be willing to learn. The conversion has occurred among all classes from the Court to the [. . .] peasant. Indeed it is partially owing to the officious zeal of the priests that much of the aversion of the Corean Government to foreign Government is due. It dreads and perhaps has reason to dread a [. . .] subversion of authority through priestly intrigues with discontented or turbulent subjects. The population of Corea is [. . .] very much exaggerated—the Peninsula is not 600 miles long by 300 broad, and judging by what I have seen myself and from the accounts of others, it cannot possibly contain as estimated 15,000,000 of people or even half of that number. [. . .] by that greed of gain or by that desire of [. . .] which characterizes the [. . .] of foreigners in the East some pretexts have been constantly advanced by them to induce their Governments to "open the Corea" as the last remaining "forbidden land" for the pursuit of trade of the Christian [. . .]. The destruction of the (so-called) American schooner General Sherman and the massacre of its crew in 1866 was the pretext used by English and Americans in China for the forcible entry into Corea by a naval force of the U.S.. The attempt however gallant was fruitless— except [. . .] Coreans against Americans and deferring the prospect of a friendly treaty. Previous [. . .] to this attack, the U.S. ships "Wachusetts" and "Shenandoah" had [. . .] the neighborhood of the [. . .] and a correspondence had ensued between the commanding officers and the Corean officials in which the latter stated distinctly that the massacre was brought about by the impudence and insolence of the people of the schooner—who were made up of several nationalities and which the schooner was ascending the "Ping-Yang [Pyeongyang]" river in defiance of the authorities of Corea and was undoubtedly engaged in illegal traffic. This statement seems to be corroborated by the fact that during the previous year the crew of another American schooner wrecked upon the Corean Coast had been hospitably rec'd and with their effects conducted to the Chinese Boundary whence they safely reached their own Country. But this explanation although forwarded to Washington [. . .] attention and the Naval Expedition in 1871 under Admiral Rodgers accompanying [. . .] the American [. . .] to China, [. . .] Corea apparently in utter ignorance of its existence. On the other hand the French naval expedition in 1866, [. . .] to that country to demand satisfaction for the murder of French missionaries, who had clandestinely entered it and remained there inspired by the pious intention of converting Corea to Christianity. They suffered the martyrdom which they apparently had courted by entering and remaining in a forbidden land. This Naval expedition was still more unfortunate than our own in the loss of life without attaining its object. The People and the Gov. of Corea remember these things to the detriment of friendly relations with Western nations, as well as to exult over the fancied defeat of the powerful naval forces upon their Coast. The object of the "Ticonderoga" was to do away in the first place with this unfavorable reminiscence and the second to endeavor to pave the way to such a treaty as would at least give to the U.S. the right to protect its Citizens and their property if wrecked upon the Corean coast; at present we submit to the humiliation of the protection of the Japanese Gov. the only one which thus far has such right under treaty.

The visit of this ship to Corea however insignificant in its immediate results, has nevertheless attracted the attention of European government and has been followed by the visits of many men-of-war of every nationality represented in the Eastern Seas; it may therefore be regarded as the "first step which is difficult" in the attainment of the purpose. Which acceding to the desire and [. . .] the right of Corea, to remain secluded from the family of Nations, no one I [. . .] will deny to other Countries the prerogative as well as the duty of protecting their citizens wherever found. The Peninsula of Corea juts out into the [. . .] highway of the World; wrecks are liable and indeed often do occur upon her unknown shores. Commerce insists upon the right to trade upon this track and the [. . .] world is justified in demanding its protection. I do not wish to see the U.S. use coercive measures in Corea—or anywhere in the East, yet as I have said before, America is the pioneer of the Pacific, a position she should not only recognize but claim. For this reason—if for no other—I hope she will not resign her place in Corea to other powers both willing and anxious to retard her progress and cripple her prestige in the East.

Rnd. [?]

In this final and quite lengthy letter, Commodore Shufeldt first of all acknowledged that the first and unofficial encounter of 1866 was violent with the tomb-robbing intentions of the *General Sherman* expedition. He clearly found that the burning of the ship and the death of its crew members were the fault of the Westerners, saying, "a correspondence had ensued between the commanding officers and the Corean officials in which the letter stated distinctly that the massacre had been triggered by the insolence of the schooner's crew, which was comprised of several nationalities and while the schooner was ascending the 'Ping-Yang'[8] in defiance of the authorities of Korea, undoubtedly engaged in illegal traffic." He acknowledged the American schooner's illegal and unauthorized behaviors in the critical waterways of Corea. Shockingly, Shufeldt admitted that America's official expedition, the *Shinmiyangyo* which had killed about 400 Coreans in 1871, could have been avoided if this fact had been considered by the American government. In his letter of October, he says, "But this explanation although forwarded to Washington [. . .] attention and the Naval Expedition in 1871 under Admiral Rodgers accompanying [. . .] the American [. . .] to China, [. . .] Corea apparently in utter ignorance of its existence." In other words, the cause of America's attack on Corea in 1871 was faulty judgment, aiming to avenge the destruction of the *General Sherman* and its crew or to use that fact as a pretext for economic gain.

This book argues two points here. First, Shufeldt's acknowledgment of such American blunders in the initial intercourse served later as a successful strategy for persuading a reluctant and doubtful Corea into an official agreement. As this book details elsewhere, Shufeldt withheld the use of military force in his negotiations with Corean and Chinese officials for the treaty and took a very patient but effective course to open the Joseon. Second and ironically, the seeds of mistrust and violence that were planted in 1866 and 1871 have eventually blossomed in the form of the current showdown between Washington and Pyeongyang over North Korea's brinkmanship with its nuclear and ICBM programs. Pyeongyang, in short, argues that it will hold intercourse with Washington only if the United States agrees to incremental negotiations and compensations, while Washington still demands that Pyeongyang give up first.

Why was America so eager to initiate intercourse with a reluctant Corea in the late nineteenth century? Primarily, America was pursuing commercial interests, but Corea was also a perfect midpoint for waystations between Japan and China. In his October letter to Navy of the Secretary, Shufeldt stated that opening Corea would complete America's "acquisition of Alaska, the Aleutian Islands, treaties with Japan, the [. . .] Islands and Samoa are only [. . .] to the proposition that the Pacific Ocean is to become at no distant day the commercial domain of America." He saw the completion of the American commercial sphere, termed the "Great Circle Route" or "Seward-Shufeldt Line" in this book, as critical to American national economic interests in Asia, where he predicted "the largest market" in the world, larger than that of Europe was (Shufeldt, 1880, October 13). Accordingly, America's acquisition of trade and navigation rights in Korea was crucial to America's empire and interest in Asia. Thus, Corea with intrinsically little importance to America's trade interests, was the necessary last stroke in America's SS Line of the Great Circle Route, specifically mentioning the acquisition of Alaska, the Aleutian Islands, Japan, and Samoa to become American territorial boundaries to make the Pacific Ocean an American lake. He was keenly aware of other competitors' prying efforts to gain leverage over Corea despite the fact that Corea was decidedly uninterested in intercourse with the United States, and that was the problem, as Shufeldt expressed in his October letter.

One of the most significant points in his second letter was Shufeldt's understanding of the East Asian international power politics regarding the Corean Peninsula. He was keenly aware of both Russia's and China's tugs of war over dominant accesses to Corea while other European forces were also attempting to sign a treaty with Corea. Schufeldt was determined to have Corea under its control rather than leaving it to either China or Russia. He argued that Washington must not let such an opportunity slip through its fingers. China's traditional suzerainty over Corea was damaged when he successfully refused to include Beijing's demand for its influences on Corea in the treaty he signed in 1882 with Corea. Shufeldt also pointed out that Washington rather trusted Japan for its capabilities to deter both China and Russia, while his experience with the Japanese consul in the Southeastern port city of Busan in his attempts to convey Washington's message for an intercourse with Corea was not at all positive. He sensed Japan's reluctance[9] to help Washington's overture to Corea.

Ultimately, however, the United States decided to ally with Japan considering its willingness to challenge both China and Russia and eagerness to rise as a new hegemon in the region. For Washington, Japan was a perfect card to play it against two powers, without which Washington had to face potential enemies, both China and Russia. There was no better option than to play a Japan-card for Washington's strategic vision, which was to accomplish the Great Circle Route or the SS Line without shedding a drop of American blood.

In this process, the single most important factor should be noted in our discussion on the nature of the Corean Question: that is, the alienation of Corea itself. Krishnan (1984:9) aptly points out the alienation of the main subject in the matter arguing that "The Americans had decided that Korea was no concern of the Koreans. It was the concern of the others; more than anyone else, it was the concern of the United States. The U.S.A sought thus to internationalise the Korean problem."

Here, we need to understand what an internationalization means in the question of Corea. First, it means that the United States chose not to monopolize the ownership of Corea even if Corea was the essential last dot to connect to complete the Great Circle. Why? Because it was too costly for Washington to take monopolistic ownership of the Peninsula. Second, Washington was comfortable having Japan as an agent that would maximize its national interests in the region. Third, Washington chose a policy of regime indifference toward Korea. Here, regime indifference is different from regime denial; Washington did not care what regime was in charge in the Corea and did not intend to change the regime as long as it could keep Corea within its boundary of the Great Circle. Thus, for Washington, it did not matter whether it kept Corea within the SS Line or Theodore-Franklin Line.

These two lines share the exact same geographical boundary of the America's Great Circle linking Alaska, Aleutian Islands, Japan including Kuril Islands, Corea, Philippines, and Samoa. However, there is a drastic and substantial distinction between these two in that Corea became a part of the Great Circle as an independent nation in the former, while Corea's independence evaporated in the latter. That is the essence of the internationalization established in the late nineteenth and early twentieth centuries to the Korean nation. Finally, such American attempts to internationalize the Corean Question ended up driving the destiny of Korea into a cauldron for superpowers' competitions whenever Washington folded its Corean card. Associated with America's folding of the Korean card, there were three decisive moments in the history of Korea which brought about crises for the Korean nation.

The first case was Korea's reduction to the status of a Japanese colony when Theodore Roosevelt yielded Corea to Japan for the Philippines in 1905 through the Katsura-Taft Secret Agreement. Second, President Franklin Roosevelt's decision to put Corea under superpowers' tutelage eventually resulted in the division of the Korean nation in 1945. Third, Secretary of State Dean Acheson's declaration to exclude the Korean Peninsula from the United States' defensive perimeter exacted a heavy price for both the United States and the Republic of Korea. That was the Korean War, which signaled the beginning of the Cold War and has not been finished yet on the Korean Peninsula. Considering the fact that Korea is the only nation currently divided due to an officially expired ideology of communism, historical consequences of Washington's dramatic swing from aggressive zeal to open Corea to an utterly contemptible disregard for Korea are beyond any reasonable scope of understanding.

Korea is not the only nation that is still paying an unfair price due both to America's alliance with the Asian Yankee, Japan, and to the internationalization and alienation of Korea, which was intended to maximize U.S. national interest. However, the United States has also paid grave penalties in the Pacific War against Japan in the Korean War. To make matters worse, China, which has been America's biggest market, is now driving Washington into a potentially catastrophic collision course in the South China Sea. In fact, LaFeber points out that Washington's late nineteenth-century choice of Japan foretold the demises of both China and Corea and brought forth conflicting outcomes for the United States. Currently, China is the biggest enemy to the United States. The loss of China as a friendly nation and, a divided Korea, in addition to Japan as an ally that can't be abandoned will always be a fishbone in Washington's throat.

In his October 1880 letter to the secretary of the Navy, Shufeldt pointed out that Corea was not interested in opening to the United States or other countries, except for Japan, which had forced a treaty on Corea in 1878, and China. He had even considered the use of military force but decided against it. He deployed American naval troops in the harbor near Hanyang, the Joseon capital, to convince the Joseon court to sign a treaty, but without actual use of force. In fact, he wrote in his May letter, "I think, but do not state it positively, that a display of our naval forces in these Seas, upon the Corean Coast would bring about intercourse at least, and perhaps a treaty, at all [. . .] the Squadron is strong enough to attack and hold any desirable point on the coast."

Corea's geopolitical location also was mentioned in Shufeldt's plan for linking the East with the West. His October letter mentions this specifically: "Thus a treaty with Corea becomes another link in the chain which binds the East with the West and would give to our Country that moral precedence in Corea which is so universally conceded to it in Japan."

Shufeldt's ultimate goal in his historic effort to open Corea was to declare American supremacy in the Pacific and Asia, as he wrote in the conclusion to his October letter: Shufeldt went further to criticize European power for its use of military force to subordinate and cultivate colonies in Asian countries. In his October letter, he said, "European power is not employed to 'civilize' Orientals—but to subordinate them and to keep them subordinate for the purposes of trade. A distinguished Chinese officer recently said to me 'What have European treaties done for China but to force upon her Opium and Missionaries?'" Then Shufeldt argued that the United States had to take "higher grounds" while demanding protection for its citizens [and] should ask for nothing more than she is willing to concede. He also expressed "manifest destiny" thinking, according to which, "It is a duty which we owe to these people (Asians) to become the pioneer of a more enlightened policy in the East."

Finally, Shufeldt felt that his attempts to open Corea would be of great benefit to Corea herself, considering that powers around the Peninsula were aiming to place it under their sphere of influence if not colonize it. Shufeldt predicted that "Corea would in fact be the battleground of any war between China and Russia or Japan" (October 1882 letter to Navy Secretary Thompson). Thus, he concluded, "I am convinced that Corea could be made to understand not only the policy of a treaty with the U.S., but its also late necessity as a protection against the aggression of surrounding powers" (October 1882 letter to Secretary Thompson). Looking back on the late nineteenth and early twentieth centuries in East Asian international affairs, Shufeldt was right that Corea would become the battleground for rivalries among superpowers. The rise and fall of new and old powers can be seen in Corea's treaty with the United States and its fall to Japan, respectively, while old powers—both China and Russia—had to wait until World War II ended for their turn.

One big historical turning point that Shufeldt did not anticipate in his ambitions to open Corea, however, was that the United States did not live up to his vision of making Corea America's partner, because President Theodore Roosevelt gave Corea to Japan in exchange for the Philippines and to check Russian expansionism without shedding American blood. Shufeldt's vision for Corea was ultimately reversed by the America's own leadership, resulting in Japanese colonization and leaving the Korean Peninsula open to another war of ideological confrontation during the Cold War era. This is an additional irony of the encounter between the United States and Korea.

INTERNATIONALIZATION OF THE COREAN QUESTION: JAPAN AND GREAT BRITAIN

In the internationalization of the Korean question, the most critical factor that influenced Washington was Japan. The power structure, and power balance, in East Asia was transformed by Japan's victory in two wars in particular: the Sino-Japanese War (1894–1895) and the Russo-Japanese War (1904–1905). The two conventional superpowers in this region—China and Russia—each succumbed to Japan's rise as a new regional power, which cut the Joseon dynasty off from Chinese suzerainty and defeated Russian ambitions on the Peninsula. Left vulnerable to Japan's ambition to rival these conventional powers, Korea began to experience painful estrangement in the relationship it had started building with the United States in 1882. Witnessing the fall of two giants in this region and the emergence and rise of a new hegemon, Japan, President Theodore Roosevelt, in order to maximize national interests, recognized Japan's interest in Korea and traded it for suzerainty over the Philippines.[10]

For Japan, in turn, Great Britain was another potential ally in preventing Russia from preying on the Korean Peninsula. In fact, Great Britain's major interest in East Asia was to maintain its influences on China and to check and balance the Russian expansionism. There were no immediate warnings to Washington on London's stance on Corea either. From that perspective, Japan's attempts to secure an alliance with Great Britain was a welcome addition to Washington's close relationship with Japan. Japan's short-term keen interest in this move was to secure its hegemonic position in the Korean Peninsula.[11]

Wilz (1985:257) documents that "the Japanese determined to bring the Koreans to submission on the matter of a protectorate." That was made manifest in a telegram by Prime Minister Katsura, dated November 6, 1905, instructing the Japanese legation in Washington to advise President Roosevelt in strict confidence that Japan was about to end "once and for all . . . the dangerous and unsatisfactory situation in Corea" by assuming charge of the latter country's external relations. The State Department received a handwritten copy of Katsura's message on November 10. Ultimately, considering this historical evidence, Wilz concludes that the United States betrayed the Korean nation by failing to meet its legal and moral obligations, although its diplomatic dilemma was not uncommon. Griswold (1938:125–6) also confirms that "To assert, as many have done, that the Taft-Katsura Agreement made the United States an '<u>unsigned</u> member' of the Anglo-Japanese Alliance is valid only in that the United States, like Great Britain, had given way before the imperialist ambitions of Japan on the Continent of Asia in order to secure its own imperial Asiatic possessions elsewhere." Yi's (2016) thorough research on the illegalities of Korea-Japan treaties and Wilz's (1985) evidence-based argument point to two clear conclusions—first, that Japan's annexation should have been nullified, and second, that the United States violated its own treaty with Korea and thus bears responsibility for the subsequent 35 years of unprecedented suffering that befell the Korean people.

On the other hand, Great Britain's main objective was to serve as a check and balance against the power of Russia in the region. For that purpose, Great Britain sealed the first Anglo-Japanese Treaty of Alliance on January 30, 1902. As Griswold sharply observes, the treaty's preamble officially stated the independence and territorial integrity of China and Korea. But "the true meaning of the treaty was contained in the clause recognizing the special interests of both countries in China and of Japan in Korea. England had abandoned Korea to Japan" (Griswold, 1938:90–91). Wilz (1985:253) echoes that "Great Britain recognizes the right of Japan to take such measures of guidance, control, and protection in Corea as she may deem proper and necessary to safeguard and advance those interests" (British Foreign Office, British and Foreign State Papers, London, 1905, XCV, 83–84, requoted in Wilz, 1985:253). This treaty implied England's recognition of Japan's "paramount political, military, and economic interests" in Korea and her right to establish a protectorate over that country.

The drastic consequences of the internationalization of the Corean Question were Japan's becoming America's main enemy as a member of the "Rome-Berlin-Tokyo Axis" and American casualties in the Asia-Pacific theatre of World War II, mostly between the United States and Japan, including 111,606 killed or missing in action, 253,142 wounded, and 21,580 prisoners of war, according to the Pacific War Online Encyclopedia. For this partnership with Japan, the United States paid dearly. The price paid by Korea, however, was that of becoming a Japanese colony and remaining divided for 75 years and counting.

Franklin Roosevelt: Completion of the Vacillation

Apparently extending the policies of his cousin Theodore Roosevelt, President Franklin Roosevelt, in his policy and personal perspective on Korea, carried them over by announcing the trusteeship of Korea at the Cairo Conference in 1943 after liberation from Japanese colonial control in 1945. Franklin Roosevelt's idea of placing Korea in his post–World War II American foreign policy as represented in the Cairo Declaration in 1943 was a clear step in the continuation of regime denial of the Korean nation just as his cousin had exercised the policy of ignoring Korean interest. Leaving the destiny of the Korean nation under tutelage or trusteeship of Allied forces for an indefinite time, Franklin repeated Theodore's Korea-bashing even after years of Japanization of the Korean Peninsula. This time, it was done in the name of internationalization on the basis of his perspective that Koreans couldn't govern themselves. Krause (2015:156) aptly summarizes that "The United States championed, for instance, the Cairo Declaration's infamous phrase about independence coming 'in due course,' which in December 1943 delayed Korea's independence indefinitely, due to the widely held belief that the Koreans were incapable of building and safeguarding an independent state. In place of independence, the United States proposed a period of 'tutelage' or 'trusteeship' in which Americans could train the Koreans in the forms of 'self-government."

It is more than ironic, preposterous even, that the two Roosevelts were personally responsible for Korea's falling prey to imperial Japan due to the first Roosevelt and then being divided by the second Roosevelt, both times against its will; Korea was never consulted on these issues that bore crucial relevance to its own destiny. Around the time of this decision so critical to the Korean nation, President Franklin Roosevelt was severely ill and mostly out of hands-on control, leaving his decisions to his closest aides. On the other hand, in his decision to invite the Soviet Union into the Pacific War, President F. Roosevelt informed neither the State Department nor his closest allies, Churchill and Chiang Kai-shek (Hudson, 1955:46). Fenno's observation is startling—that Stalin's terms for entering the Pacific War had already been communicated to Roosevelt before the Yalta Conference in 1943 and that he had already decided to grant them "without giving his official advisers a chance to discuss them—especially in view of the known opinions of Under Secretary Grew, who had been Ambassador to Japan for ten years and had a great knowledge of Far Eastern problems" (Hudson, 1955:46).

In this shocking observation, one thing that stands out is the secrecy involved in the foreign policy of President Franklin Roosevelt's four-term reign. Hurley (1955:55) argues that "secret diplomacy should have no place in a government by the people. In a government by the people, the people cannot make correct conclusions if they are not given all the facts." He (1955:56) furthers claims, "A weak and confused foreign policy after Yalta, and in general after World War II, is the primary cause for every international problem confronting our Nation and for every casualty we have suffered in Korea." Such confusion and weakness originated from two main sources: President Roosevelt's naively optimistic view of the role of the U.S.S.R. at the end of World War II and what it would be afterward, and the Truman administration's confused estimation of the military capability of the already damaged and defeated Japanese forces in the final phase of the Pacific War and of potential American casualties if America acted alone.

President Roosevelt's wishful thinking about the Soviet Union was clearly expressed in a memorandum by his closest advisor, Harry Lloyd Hopkins, six months after the Yalta Conference. President Roosevelt's statement on Russia, bluntly put, was naïve. In this memorandum, Hopkins wrote President Roosevelt thought that:

> we [the U.S. and Russia] are mutually dependent upon each other for economic reasons. We find the Russians as individuals easy to deal with. The Russians undoubtedly like the American people. They like the United States. They trust the United States more than they trust any other power in the world. . . . Above all, they want to main friendly relations with us. (Wilmot, 1955:76)

Roosevelt's personal chief of staff Admiral Leahy provides further critical evidence of this naïve view of President Roosevelt on the Soviet Union: "The President was actuated by the belief that Soviet participation would ensure Russia's sincere co-operation in his dream of a united, peaceful world" (Wilmot, 1955:77). In reality, as history witnessed, Russia had long before transformed itself into the Soviet Union and had begun targeting the United States as its main enemy. Thus, as soon as the U.S. government declared the Acheson Line in January 1950, a proxy war was instigated on the Korean Peninsula.

Claims that the Japanese military was strong enough to produce mass casualties of the U.S. forces if America alone acted to defeat Japan at the end of World War II were unsubstantiated. According to Buckley (1992:6), even in the summer of 1945, not long before Japan's unconditional surrender, "the allied leaders at Potsdam were informed that Japan's military strength exceeded 4,500,000 men." In fact, it was confused and then, later, turned out to be overestimated. Hurley (1955:56) states that "Secretary Acheson tells you that the American people and the American Government feared the final assault on Japan would cost more than a million American casualties." Acheson's unsubstantiated claim was also supported by two of the top military leaders at that time. Both Chiefs of Staff and George Marshall strongly recommended bringing in the Soviet military to end the Pacific War. The problem in Acheson's public statement was that his assertion was seriously disputed by critical members among military officers or government officials.

There were conflicting opinions about the necessity of bringing in the Russian military in response to the American assault against Japan. In July 1944 at Pearl Harbor, both General Douglas MacArthur and Admiral Chester Nimitz briefed President Roosevelt, stating that the United States could win the war against Japan even without invading the Japanese homeland. They both said that "Japan could be forced to accept our terms of surrender by the use of sea and airpowers" (Wilmot, 1995:77). Hurley (1955:57) also ridicules the unsubstantiated claim that we must also believe that the final assault of Japan would cause more casualties than all the battles in Burma, China, the

Atlantic, Africa, Mediterranean, Italy, England, France, Holland, Belgium, and Germany—in other words, [little] less than 1,000,000. In the end, the Joint Chiefs of Staff led by George Marshall in May of 1945 decided that an "early Russian entry into the war . . . is no longer necessary" followed by Admiral Ernest J. King, on June 18, 1945, flatly confirming that the Russians were "not indispensable" and need not be begged "to come in" (LaFeber, 1997:242). Hurley (1955:57) concludes that the United States "cowardly surrendered to him [Stalin] everything that he had signed and we did it secret. President Roosevelt was already a sick man at Yalta." That is why President Truman fearing not only potential casualties as many as 750,000 American soldiers including estimated 250,000 killed but also, at the same time, Russian entry to America's eventual frontline of the Great Circle Route, decided to drop the atomic bomb so that America could show off and demonstrate its overwhelming superiority over Stalin as well as to minimize American loss (LaFeber, 1997:245).

Most importantly, with regard to Washington's Korea policy, President Roosevelt's view of Korea was not substantially different from that held by his cousin, President Theodore Roosevelt. FDR doubled down on the bet that Korea would "need some period of apprenticeship before full independence might be attained, perhaps forty years" (Krishnan, 1984:9). These claims about the self-governing capabilities of the Korean nation, to be sure, had no basis in evidence. Cumings (2011:106) sharply notes that Americans and Europeans unacquainted with Korea's historical background might wonder if Koreans were capable of self-governing. In response, Cumings points out that "Koreans are of an old nation. When the ancestors of northern Europe were wandering in the forests clad in skins and practicing rites, Koreans had government of their own and attained a high degree of civilization" (Cumings, 2011:106).

The Axis Powers in World War II had been Germany, Italy, and Japan. Germany was partitioned by the four Allied forces as punishment for its part in the war. However, such logical reasoning was denied outright in Asia. Rather than partitioning and punishing the aggressor in Asia—that is, Japan—the United States split Korea, which had been suffering in the extraordinarily vicious colonial grip of that Axis power for the last 35 years. Krishnan (1984:9) aptly points out that "The Americans had decided that Korea was no concern of the Koreans. It was the concern of the others; more than anyone else, it was the concern of the United States. The U.S.A sought thus to internationalize the Korean problem." This internalization process was to sacrifice Korean independence and sovereignty for American interests in the Asian market through the internationalization of the Korean affairs.

America's initial desire to pry open isolationist Korea in the late nineteenth century converted into a policy of absolute regime denial in the early twentieth century, but now, its position has changed to one of "concern" in the Peninsula while completely ignoring the voices and desires of the people on that Peninsula. From this perspective, it is no wonder that the Korean nation was halved by the State-War-Navy Co-ordinating Committee (SWNCC) in August 1945, a few days before Koreans were liberated from one of the most brutal colonial experiences to date. First, the destiny of the Korean nation was determined in order to harmonize the political concerns of the United States, to maximize its own sphere of influence in Asia, to check Soviet expansion, but also to placate the Soviet Union and secure its participation in the dismantlement of imperial Japan's World War II forces.

That division, decided by two military figures in less than two hours without consulting any Koreans, has persisted on the Peninsula for nearly a century, and the Korean nation still suffers from that wound. As to the surrender of Japan, Brigadier General John McCloy of the SWNCC ordered two American army colonels, Dean Rusk and Charles Bonesteel, to "retire into an adjoining room and come up with a proposal which could harmonize the political desire to have the U.S. forces receive the surrender as far north as possible and obvious limitations on the ability of the U.S. forces to reach the area" (Dean Rusk's letter of July 12, 1950. See U.S. Department of State, Foreign Relations of the United States, Washington, DC, 1945, vol. 6, p. 1039). Cumings (1973:47) acknowledges that "No sleight of hand can remove the decision on the 38th parallel from the continuum of American thinking on Korea since 1943. Although the decision was taken quickly and rashly in the harried days of mid-August, it was the logical outcome of past planning."

More than the simple fact that Koreans were not consulted on this momentous decision, Koreans were treated as enemies of the United States when the U.S. military launched military occupation operations in the Korean Peninsula in 1945, even though the Korean nation was being liberated from 35 years of the most atrocious form of colonial control under imperial Japan and divided under the control of U.S. General John Reed Hodge, of the Commanding General Armed Forces in Korea (U.S. AFIK). In his directive of September 4, 1945, General Hodge instructed subordinates that "Korea was an enemy of the United States and thus 'subject to the provisions and the terms of surrender.'"[12]

Even if we take the very literalist view that Korea was annexed by Japan, such that Koreans, who had been subjugated by an enemy of the United States, were also enemies of the United States—then all Europeans under German occupation should have been treated as enemies of the Allied forces. Unbelievably, this U.S. military government instigated a vortex of rage among Koreans by continuing to use the Government-General building of the imperial Japanese political institution for its administration. To make matters worse, the head enemy of the Korean nation, the Governor-General Abe Nobuyuki, performed his governance under General Hodge, though only briefly. This demonstrates the extent of the unawareness shown by the U.S. attitude toward the Korean nation.

At first, the United States urgently pushed for official relations with Korea, then completely ditched the treaty it had so ardently pursued, tossing the nation to its former enemy, then treating it as an enemy itself by slicing it in half. Krishnan (1984) sees this as an invasion of Korea by the United States. In describing the American attitude, he (1984:15) also makes a criticism:

> Thus the U.S.A in effect invaded Korea in September 1945 on the plea of accepting the surrender of the Japanese forces south of the 38th parallel. By militarily intervening and forcing a division of Korea, the U.S.A tried to abort Korea's liberation processes initiated by patriotic, democratic, pro-Socialist forces whose mass base, impeccable record of struggle and sacrifice, passion for radical social and economic transformation, and zealous commitment for national independence were beyond doubt.

Thus, Japan—which ought to have been partitioned itself and been required to pay the price for waging one of the most disastrous wars and crimes against humanity—was able to maintain illegitimate control over Korea. In fact, the original document issued by the principal allies resulted from the resolve of the Cairo Conference on December 1, 1943, "Once Japan had been defeated its empire would then be divided." However, the Cairo resolve did not specify how the victors might carry out their occupation beyond the statement that they were fighting "to restrain and punish the aggression of Japan" (Buckley, 1992:8).

In short, even though it did not initiate them, the United States had to fight two big wars in Asia in the mid-twentieth century; the Pacific War from 1941 to 1945 and the Korean War from 1950 to 1953. The former was due to its power competition with Japan, Washington's most trusted partner for Asia policy, over the Chinese market. The latter might probably have been prevented from breaking out if Washington had not declared that the Korean Peninsula was excluded from its defensive perimeter, which corresponded with the original SS Line argued in this book. The war, the largest form of encounter between countries and cultures, first, devastated the whole Korean nation and then resulted in one of the most severe injuries that a conflict could inflict. Its impact forced that nation into starkly contrasting regions: one of the most impoverished and oppressed in the north and one of the most successful in the south in both economic and political aspects. The next section discusses the Korean War and its consequences from the perspective of Diamond's claim on the impacts of encounters between societies and cultures.

WARS AND CONSEQUENCES

Throughout world history, wars have been among the most important causes and consequences of nations' rise and collapse. For the victors, they are indispensable means; for the vanquished, inescapable realities. To powers old and new, however, wars cost dearly in human lives. To honor the sacrifice on all sides, we seek positive outcomes as ground on which to build future insights.

The Peloponnesian War, for example, proved the resilience not only of democratic governance in the Greek city states, which won many important victories contrary to expectations, but also of their alliance against the authoritarian and totalitarian system of Sparta. World Wars I and II witnessed the end of Western colonial imperialism and established what Immanuel Kant would have recognized as a "Pacific Union" among Western democracies. The Vietnam War squelched U.S.-backed French colonialism and triggered political and civic activism in the United States during the 1960s and 1970s. The wars in Iraq and Afghanistan ushered the globe into a new kind of fanatic religious war, challenging us to reconsider the age-old issue of who is "right" in today's context of counterterrorism.

But what byproducts emerged from the Korean War? Many nicknames have been tacked onto it, including "a sour little war" by W. Averell Harriman and "police action" by Harry S. Truman. Republicans called it "the foreign policy blunder of the century." General Omar Bradley said it was "frankly a great military disaster" (Goulden, 1982:xiii). In broad terms, the Korean War was an early signal of the Cold War's approach, the far-front base of U.S.-Soviet conflict and, most famously, "The Forgotten War." Most critically, though, it has become the longest war of the twentieth century, as the 1953 Armistice has not been officially replaced by a peace treaty, giving rise to grave international security issues such as North Korea's nuclear provocations and a collision course in progress between the United States and China.

This forgotten but ongoing war has also dramatically impacted the destinies of the two Koreas in the global context—North Korea, one of the world's most hunger-stricken and isolated countries, versus South Korea, one of the world's most thriving democracies, dramatically transforming from aid-receiving to aid-offering. What could have caused such stark contrasts between these regimes that shared the same culture and political system for more than 5,000 years?[13] How can we explain such disparities between two halves of the same people, separated only by international powers and ideologies?

With a recorded history of five millennia, Korea has maintained its national identity through period after period: the Three Kingdoms Period (57–935 BC) of Goguryeo (37–668 BC), Baekjae (18–660 BC), and Silla (57–935 BC); the Goryeo period (918–1392), which united the Three Kingdoms; and the

Joseon (1392–1910). Moreover, since the early seventh century, the Korean nation has remained relatively homogeneous in terms of its identity, culture, and political community. The Joseon, in particular, was tightly controlled, centralized, and based on the rule of law with a constitution and standing army. Among world dynasties, it was one of the longest (518 years, 1392–1910), outlasted only by the Holy Roman Empire (844 years, AD 962–1806), the Zhou dynasty (790 years, 1046 BC–AD 256) and the Ottoman Empire (724 years, AD 1299–1923). Considering the cohesive and unified nature of their history, the contemporary confrontations between the two Koreas—with such vast discrepancies in their political and economic capabilities—stand out with two seemingly contradictory implications: first, that the current division of the Korean people into two such different nations can be viewed as a temporary phenomenon; and second, that over the long history of Korea, the contemporary impasse between the two halves with backing from superpowers like China and the United States has had only rare historical precedents.

Since the Korean War was the first major war to erupt within the bipolar context of the Cold War system, North Korea was the first state after World War II to invade and seek annexation of another (Clements, Jr., 2016:7). This was not only a Korean civil war between north and south but the first major collision on this scale between China and the United States. In fact, many Korean War veterans clearly remember never having encountered North Korean soldiers. As described by Mr. Benjamin Vincent Arriola, a U.S. veteran of the Korean War interviewed in 2015,[14] the enemies that Americans saw in the Korean War were primarily Chinese.

The first official encounter between the United States and China was the Treaty of Wangxia in 1844. Since then, and until the Chinese Communist movement seized power in 1949, there were no wars between these two countries, aside from the three Taiwan Strait Crises—in 1954–1955, 1958, and 1996—which heightened the chances of military clashes. Indeed, the first real collision between these superpowers was the Korean War. During the Vietnam War, the People's Republic of China (PRC) sided with the North Vietnamese military, while the United States sided with the South. Recently, though it may sound shocking, these two superpowers have been collaborating in the war on terror since the 9/11 attack on the United States in 2001. For fear of losing the strategic benefits of being "frenemies" in the global economy, these two giants, the United States and China, try not to reopen any old wounds; however, when they fail to avoid their differences, the Korean War tends to come up.

As evidence will demonstrate, Korea's late nineteenth-century encounter with the United States not only gave rise to Korea's contemporary situation but also catalyzed a series of outcomes, including the resurgence of international competition for power around the Peninsula, the division of the Korean people, the heightening of North-South confrontations (as well as DPRK-U.S. drama), the continuation of North Korea's isolationism, and the transformation of South Korea into an international economic power and democracy.

Uneven Encounters and Two Koreas

These claims align with Diamond's statement that "The history of interaction among disparate peoples is what shaped the modern world through conquest, epidemics, and genocide. Those collisions sent out reverberations that have still not died down after many centuries, and that are actively continuing in some of the world's most troubled areas today" (1997: 16). Though it may sound like some macro-level grand theory, it is perfectly suitable for the main focus of this book to inquire into how the two Koreas have come to their current state. This refrain will reverberate throughout the passages of this book, which resound with his claim. Besides, cases like the demise of the Aztecs and the Incas, who were brought down by Spanish invasion—echoes from the collisions between Islamic Arab nations and the Christian West, and between Confucian China and Liberal America—are still reverberating around the world and shaking the power balance of world politics. As Diamond (1997: 25) notes, "History followed different courses for different peoples because of differences among peoples' environments, not because of biological differences among peoples themselves." Such claims may sound too reductionist, to some readers, to truly explain differences in wealth, political systems, and culture on such global scale; however, this methodology of closely examining the communication around such moments of pivotal misunderstanding may be the most powerful and macro-level way of conducting historical research on the Korean situation.

To appreciate the nature of Korea's first encounter with the United States, we must first appreciate how radically different these two countries initially were. Like two strangers from vastly different backgrounds crossing paths, they interacted, misunderstood each other, and misinterpreted each other's reactions. On top of that, they were baffled by each other's baggage. The Joseon's baggage included its voluntary submission to Chinese suzerainty, its obstinate faith in and cut-throat guardianship of Confucian doctrines, and its stubborn stance of isolationism toward the West. The United States, under the dual banners of "Manifest Destiny" and exceptionalism, eventually imposed gunboat capitalism and liberal values. Though it could hardly be recognized at the time, seemingly irreconcilable differences between their baggage increased their chances of colliding in due course.

It is not hard to imagine how cultural differences influenced these strangers' initial impressions of and eventual relations with each other until they managed to resolve their differences and normalize relations by agreeing to a treaty in 1882. Rear-Admiral Commodore Robert W. Shufeldt, who brokered this treaty, applied the metaphor of marriage himself to portray the relationship that could develop with Asia.

Introducing Commodore Shufeldt's comment about his view on China, Japan, and Korea, LaFeber (1989: 172) describes the impacts of America's interventions on Eastern power dynamics among China, Japan, and Korea and how each of these nations responded to America's calls to open. To China, American intervention in Korea was a painful reminder of its own demise as center of a Sinocentric world. Japan skillfully adapted to American intervention by choosing to increase its own influence and challenge China while occupying Korea. Korea was subject to competing superpowers then, as now—a dynamic introduced by American intervention.

As cited in Drake's (1984) biography *The Empire of the Seas*, Rear-Admiral Commodore Shufeldt used this overt metaphor[15] of marriage in correspondence:

> The Pacific is the ocean bride of America—China and Japan and Corea—with their innumerable islands, hanging like necklaces about them, are the bridesmaids. California is the nuptial couch, the bridal chamber, where all the wealth of the Orient will be brought to celebrate the wedding. Let us as Americans—let us determine while yet in our power, that no commercial rival or hostile flag can float with impunity over the long swell of the Pacific sea. . . . It is on this ocean that the East and the West have thus come together, reaching the point where search for Empire ceases and human power attains its climax. (116)

Interestingly, in this trope of sexual conquest, Corea is specifically mentioned. It is important to note, though, that while Japan and China had already wedded European grooms, such as Britain, Portugal, and the Netherlands, Corea was a reluctant bride. To be one of the bridegrooms, America did not need to compete much but scavenged nonetheless, marrying one after another—China in 1844 and Japan in 1854. Korea, though, had hoped to maintain fidelity through Confucian marriage. In 1866, when an American blackship demanded relations, Korea refused in what came to be known as "the General Sherman Incident." Ultimately, the United States forced Corea to wed in 1871, through a battle called the *Shinmiyangyo*, one that this book considers as "the first Korean War," since it played such a formative role in U.S.-Korea relations.

While preserving its chastity for China, its Confucian bridegroom, Korea also aimed to stay independent and faithful to itself. In this regard, Griffis (1889: 7–8) aptly observes Korea's long tradition of isolationism. In his book *Corea the Hermit Nation*, he says:

Corea has for centuries successfully carried out the policy of isolation. Instead of a peninsula, her rulers have striven to make her an inaccessible island, and insulate her from the shock of change. She has built not a Great Wall of masonry but a barrier of sea and river-flood, of mountain and devastated land, of palisades and cordons of armed sentinels. Frost and snow, storm and winter, she hails as her allies. Not content with the sea-border she desolates her shores lest they tempt the mariner to land. Between her Chinese neighbor and herself, she has placed a neutral space of unplanted, unoccupied land. This strip of forests and desolated plains, twenty leagues wide, stretches between Corea and Manchuria. To form it, four cities and many villages were suppressed three centuries ago, and left in ruins. The soil of these solitudes is very good, the road easy, and the hills not high. For centuries, only the wild beasts, fugitives from justice, and outlaws from both countries, have inhabited this fertile but forbidden territory. Occasionally, borderers would cultivate portions of it, but gather the produce by night or stealthy by day, venturing on it as prisoners would step over the "dead line." Of late years, the Chinese Government has respected the neutrality of this barrier less and less. . . . Parts of it have been surveyed and staked out by Chinese surveyors, and the Corean Government has been too feeble to prevent the occupation. . . . Chosen [Corea] since acting the hermit policy of ancient Egypt and medieval China, has preserved two loopholes at Fusan [Busan] and Ai-chiu [Eui-ju, a city near the border with China along the Yalu River], the former on the sea toward Japan, and the latter in the northwest, on the Chinese border.

As this quote from an American orientalist strongly indicates, even though Korea viewed itself as the younger brother in a Confucian world system, it also maintained independence from Chinese influence. Chinese suzerainty was evident throughout Korea's history; however, Korea attempted to preserve its own sphere of influence. Korea was different even, as Griffis (1889) noted, from the other Pacific brides: "Corea has always remained Corea, a separate country; and the people are Coreans, more allied to the Japanese than the Chinese, yet in language, politics, and social customs, different from either. As Ireland is not England or Scotland, neither is Cho-sen [Corea] China nor Japan" (9). In terms of culture and trade, China was too attractive to avoid being wooed and ultimately wed by European nations in the early nineteenth century, whereas the bride of Japan was already willing to wed those interested from Europe and America. It was not until Americans soldiers had shed blood in 1866, and Korea had shed blood in 1871, that Korea could be convinced to give her hand. In fact, it was not until 1882 that demands from America finally drove the reluctant bride to marry. This was the same treaty that remained in place until Japan's violation of the marriage in 1905, as there was no formal annulment. Leaders of the Korean independence movement were desperate to appeal to American leadership to deter Japanese action for fear that any treaties may be dropped. The vortex of these interactions among regional and global superpowers serves as a backdrop, then, for the argument we will consider that the contemporary relationships among the United States, North Korea, and South Korea matter for both halves of Korea as well as for America, not to mention America's other "brides."

Corea was soon violated by Japan in the competition for suzerainty over Corea. The United States did little to interfere and even seemed to enjoy Japanese intervention. Until the Japanese became convinced, according to LaFeber, the United States insisted on "creating a Korean vacuum which could be filled at least partially with American commerce and missionaries" (LaFeber, 1998: 57).

The intrinsic differences between the United States and Korea had no chance of being resolved before the partnership was interrupted. Japan had long been eyeing America's new partner, Korea, and divesting the baggage that Korea had once shared with China: strong faith in Confucianism, influence from China, and isolationism. The process of separating China from Korea was painful for both; China was shamefully defeated by Japan, and Korea was sold to Japan by the United States, its former partner. To take this conceit a step further, that is how Korea emerged from the divorce. America's decision to desert Korea by selling it to Japan backfired, though, when Japan bombed Pearl Harbor in 1941, an admittedly separate but nonetheless related betrayal. The Pacific War cost all countries involved very heavily, as the table 1.1 reveals.

The Pacific War waged by imperial Japan left almost 25.4 million civilians dead, 5,873,606 soldiers dead or missing, 3,398,179 wounded, and 240,652 imprisoned, according to *The Pacific War Online Encyclopedia*. The United States lost 111,606 men and women, with 253,142 wounded and 21,580 imprisoned. Arguably, this was the direct byproduct of President Theodore Roosevelt's decision to trust, recognize, and work with Japan in the early twentieth century. Here, naturally, questions arise. What if the United States had not deserted Korea to recognize Japan? And though it may seem hard to ask in light of today's international power politics, would Korea still have fallen under Japanese colonial control, and would there have been so many casualties? Was Theodore Roosevelt's Asia policy, in general, and his faulty pro-Japanese stance, in particular, responsible for such damage to Asian communities and Korea's 35 years of suffering under Japanese exploitation, unprecedented in Western imperial colonial policy? Ultimately, America's decision cannot be entirely blamed on pragmatic international power politics; Korea was responsible for not defending herself. However, President

Table 1.1 Total Casualties of the Pacific War by Nation and Type

Nation	Killed/Missing	Wounded	POWs	Civilian Deaths
Australia	9,470	13,997	21,726	
China	4,000,000	3,000,000		18,000,000
India	6,860	24,200	68,890	2,000,000
Japan	1,740,000	94,000	41,440**	393,400
Dutch East Indies			37,000	4,000,000
Philippines				1,000,000
United Kingdom*	5,670	12,840	50,016	
United States	111,606	253,142	21,580	

Blanks indicate that estimates are unavailable, but the numbers are relatively low.
* Includes only losses in ground combat.
** Prior to August 15, 1945.
Source: The Pacific War Online Encyclopedia, http://pwencycl.kgbudge.com/C/a/Casualties.htm

Roosevelt should not be freed from accountability for the bloodshed caused by Japan.

When Korea and the United States reunited in 1945 after Japan's surrender, it was no happy reunion between equals. In this reluctant rendezvous, the stronger partner chose a path harmful to the weaker—the weaker was chopped in half, forced to undergo severe changes of identity, and take on a heavy burden of baggage. China is now trying to recover its suzerainty over Korea, a tension that has resurfaced as power struggles on the Peninsula between China and the United States go on. Thus, this interaction in the nineteenth century has brought Korea into the same global context as before but with a twist: Korea is now caught in the midst of new interactions with communist China backed by the former Soviet Union for global competition between free capitalism and socialist communism.

As our recurring theme and refrain, this book will summarize the chain of interactions that brought about Korea's situation today—how the Peninsula came to be surrounded, divided and polarized by international superpowers vying for control over it. By delving into the nature, processes, and contemporary outcomes of these interactions, this book finds undeniable evidence of the power struggle between a once debilitated but now resurging China and the defensive hegemon, the United States. Currently, China is challenging U.S. unilateral influence in contemporary international politics around North Korea's nuclear provocations through its own expansionist policy of "One Belt One Road"[16]—two facts that demonstrate the most threatening global power struggles that have stemmed from the unfinished war on the Peninsula.

In the Korean War, the Chinese were the only ones who were fighting not just for their proxies but for themselves as well. When General MacArthur ordered UN forces to march north of the 38th parallel and the Yalu River, which borders on China's Northeast, the PRC feared American pressure along its border with North Korea. The United States certainly did not want to spark another global war by colliding with the world's second-largest communist country, especially so soon after World War II. The stalemate since 1951 in the Korean War ended in armistice in 1953 with both China and the United States signing the longest ceasefire till date. The Korean division cannot be overcome unless these two powers reach an agreement and put their history of military conflict behind them; this is another unbearable legacy of the Korean War especially in the midst of China's rapid rise in global economy and military represented by China's "One Belt One Road" policy, and perhaps the most convincing reason why Washington has not wanted to disrupt the status quo on the Peninsula, which necessarily would involve North Korea and thus break from the policy of regime denial.

Another question is how to explain the current disparities between the North and South, with a totalitarian political system and failing and starving economy on the one hand and the 11th largest economy with a substantive democracy on the other. Is the cause internal, or are external factors at play? In other words, what factors and contexts brought about such stark contrast? Was it due to innate differences between the two Koreas? Perhaps Diamond (1997: 25) is right that "history followed different courses for different peoples because of differences among peoples' environments, not because of biological differences among peoples themselves."

Disparities between North and South

Many wonder why the North failed while the South prospered. Both Koreas proclaimed independent statehood in 1948. Both joined the United Nations on the same day in 1991. Both share the same genes, traditions, and language. If asked to delve into the unique case of the two Koreas, Diamond might ask why they developed such distinct ways of life. As is well known, the North Korean economy, having started out much better after the war, plateaued in the 1970s and began to decline as the South Korean economy skyrocketed in the 1980s and 1990s. Clemens, Jr. (2016: 11) points out that

> [North Korea's] greatest political achievement was to institutionalize and sacralize a ruling dynasty across three generations. By the twenty-first century, the Republic of Korea offered a model of economic dynamism, self-government, educational excellence, and "wired" infrastructure. Its pop culture animated Japan, China, parts of the United States and Europe, and even—underground—North Korea. (2016: 11)

For most North Koreans, the government did little to advance the quality of life. According to the UN Development Programme, infant mortality was nearly eight times higher than in the South: 23 babies died for every 1,000 live births, nearly four times the rate in the United States (6 per 1,000). The UN also reported severe malnutrition and stunting in 28% of North Korean children ages five and under—compared with 9% in China, virtually none in South Korea and Japan, 44% in India, and 69% in Pakistan. The UN reported that the DPRK had a food deficit of 238 calories—high, though only half of Burundi's. Moreover, challenging any expectation of an authoritarian calm, the DPRK homicide rate was 15.2 per 100,000 persons—much higher than in South Korea (2.6) or the United States (4.7) (Simens, Jr., 2016: 12).

Overall, the contrasts between North and South Korea cannot be any clearer than in the figures shown in table 1.2. As mentioned briefly, there was little difference between the 1960s and 1970s in terms of the two Korea's demographic and economic performance (Eichengreen et al., 2015). More specifically, North Korea's exports in 1960 had been $146.9M, more than four times South Korea's $32.8M. Correspondingly, North Korea's per capita income in the early 1960s were estimated to have been twice that of South Korea (Eichengreen et al., 2015: 259).

However, the two Koreas began to take radically different paths with South Korea making waves through a global economic boom and North Korea stuck in the socialist economic bloc that was led by the declining Soviet Union. Such radical juxtaposition of economies offers an ideal opportunity to examine Diamond's hypothesis with the two starkly different Koreas shaped by the histories of their different interactions within the context of the decline of Chinese suzerainty. As we will begin to notice, the reverberations of these interactions are still resounding, as Diamond asserts.

Kim Il-sung's 1960 speech comparing North Korea's economic performance to South Korea's merits some attention here. On August 15, 1945, on the 15th anniversary of Korea's liberation from Japan, Kim Il-sung proposed a scheme for confederation:

> The most urgent problem today is to rebuild the South Korean economy . . . . This problem cannot be solved without economic exchanges between the South and the North. It is a simple truism of economics that no country can develop light industries and agriculture and improve people's lives without the support of heavy industries. In our country, only the northern half has such industries . . . . We also have a plenty of experience with economic development. (Eichengreen et al., 2015: 260)

Such boasting from North Korea's founder about heavy industries and the economy must have placed significant pressure on South Korea's President Park Chung-hee, who had seized power through military coup in 1961. It

Table 1.2 Divergent Paths: South Korea and North Korea, 1960–2010

Year		Population (thousand persons)	Current GDP (US$ billion)	Total Trade (US$ billion)
1960	South Korea	24,989	2.0	376
	North Korea	10,789	1.2	304
	South-North Ratio	2.3	1.7	1.2
1970	South Korea	31,435	8.1	2,819
	North Korea	14,619	4.9	796
	South-North Ratio	2.2	1.7	3.5
1980	South Korea	37,407	64.3	39,797
	North Korea	17,298	9.9	3,451
	South-North Ratio	2.2	6.5	11.5
1990	South Korea	43,390	270.3	134,859
	North Korea	20,000	16.7	4180
	South-North Ratio	2.2	16.2	32.3
2000	South Korea	45,985	533.5	333,174
	North Korea	22,963	10.6	2,394
	South-North Ratio	2.0	50.3	139.2
2010	South Korea	47,991	1,014.3	893,508
	North Korea	24,387	12.3	6,086
	South-North Ratio	2.0	82.5	146.5

Source: Reprinted with permission from Eichengreen et al, *The Korean Economy: From a Miraculous Past to a Sustainable Future*, Cambridge, Massachusetts, London: Harvard University Press (2015).

was not only Kim's boasting about the better economy in North Korea; a renowned British economist, Joan Robinson, who visited North Korea in October 1964 wrote "Korea, 1964: Economic Miracle." Her writing was not about South Korea but its neighbor to the north. According to Eichengreen (2015: 260), Joan (1964) observed that all economic miracles of the postwar world were eclipsed by the economic miracle she witnessed in North Korea. She credited North Korea's well-conceived economic strategy, patriotic rage, and devotion.

Francis Fukuyama, in his 1989 article for *National Interest*, argued that the fall of the U.S.S.R. and consequential end of the Cold War meant that ideological competition could evolve no further. What has happened, he concludes, is "not just . . . the passing of a particular period of post-war history but the end of history as such: that is, the end point of mankind's ideological evolution and the universalization of Western liberal democracy as the final form of human government" (Fukuyama, 1989). Despite the intrinsic problem in arguing for the end of the history, his claim offers the same kind of hint about the evolution of the relationship between the United States and North Korea. Will the current encounter between Washington and Pyongyang bring an end to the relationship—with America demanding that North Korea give up its nuclear arsenal and missile tests and embrace capitalism and free democracy in exchange for normalized relations? Or, will this stalemate end with another Korean War that ushers in another era of devastation and poverty wrapped in bandages by superpowers? Or, will it spark World War III and end history after all?

When the Soviet Union collapsed in 1991, the controlled animosity that had been festering between the United States and North Korea during the Cold War suddenly exploded into hostility, upsetting the bipolar power balance on the Peninsula (Han, 2014a). When Pyeongyang withdrew from the Non-Proliferation Treaty (NPT) in 1993, the Clinton administration considered a surgical strike to destroy the plutonium reprocessing reactor in Yeongbbyeon. At that point, one can reasonably assume, North Korea likely started to feel vulnerable now that its big brother had suddenly disappeared and wanted some means of deterrence against the world's most powerful country—a country that had all but destroyed it 40 years prior. Obviously, China could play some of the roles that its former big brother had once played in the post-Cold War era. However, North Korea's relations with China have not always been so rosy. Compared with the heyday of Kim Il-sung's alliance with the first generation of Chinese Communist Party (CCP) leaders, North Korea's relations with China have been somewhat strained. This was especially so after China normalized diplomatic relations with North Korea's enemy, South Korea, in 1992. North Korea was uncertain about whether China would remain as trustworthy as before. In fact, one of Kim Jong-Il's dying messages to his heir was not to trust China. Also, North Korea knows that it cannot really deter American power. In fact, North Korea is well aware that the United States is the last remaining hegemon that can either ensure its survival and eventual economic recovery or cause its demise (Cumings, 1999, 2005; Han, 2009: 106; Kim, 2010).

Furthermore, North Korea views Washington as the only power capable of stabilizing the region by serving as intermediary in the potentially contentious relations between itself and its neighbors, China, Japan, Russia, and South Korea. Two important events in particular justified North Korea's pursuit of weapons of mass destruction toward the end of the Cold War—the loss of Moscow's nuclear umbrella and the Soviet Union and China's normalization of relations with South Korea (Han, 2014). Cumings (2005: 481) claims that Pyeongyang, by arming itself with "a small state deterrent for a country surrounded by powerful enemies," has played an "ultimate trump card" in order "to keep everyone guessing whether and when the weapons might become available." This point has been demonstrated by North Korea's unwavering pursuit of ICBM and nuclear weapons programs since the early twenty-first century.

NOTES

1. Here, "Yangyo" means the disturbance caused by Westerners.

2. This book uses the word "intercourse" in describing American attempts to open Corea in the nineteenth century mainly because it was used by American leaders in their official and private letters and diplomatic documents. This book will discuss later other implications in the use of this word in detail.

3. The 1882 world map was modified by Ms. Maranda Wilkinson to show the proposed Seward-Shufeldt and Theodore-Franklin Lines as well as the DMZ in detail. The original map may be found in the Library of Congress Geography and Map Division. Call Number G1200 .H37 1882. I want to thank Ms. Wilkinson for her creative thinking and design skills. In addition, I want to also recognize the Library of Congress for its service to the public.

4. Seward's memo to the U.S. minister in Edo, Japan in 1868, two years after the American black ship the *General Sherman* was burned down and the French expedition against Joseon's purge of French missionaries and Korean Catholics, ostensibly disclosed his idea of encounter with Japan. "Not especially religious himself, Seward developed a fixation on proselytizing in, of all places, Japan. Not only were "the simple people of Japan" to be made to respect the institutions of Christianity": their attacks and limitations imposed on Christians were not to be tolerated. He even urged what this biographer termed a "holy war." Japan's attempts to recover its internal harmony by moving against Christians "will only prepare the way for fearful and bloody convulsions" (LaFeber, 1997:27).

5. University of Rochester // February 10, 2020, William Seward Papers, 80: 4, transcribed by Greg Ahlquist. Folder 408 1865–1869 George Frederick Seward to William Henry Seward.

6. As Seward's handwriting is almost illegible and words are crossed out, the author has added notes in parentheses throughout.

7. Both William Seward and Robert Shufeldt shared the same idea and the vision to achieve their American goal by acquiring Corea and completing the SS Line, this book argues, which started to be accomplished with Seward's acquisition of Alaska, naturally linked with the Aleutian Islands and the Kuril Islands through the treaty with Japan, Corea, Philippines, and the Samoan Island in order to make the perfect perimeter for the American era of the Pacific and hegemony in Asian market.

8. Currently, it is Pyeongyang, which is the capital city of North Korea.

9. On the morning of May 4, 1880, Shufeldt and his *Ticonderoga* anchored in Fusan Harbor [Busan] to ask Japanese Consul Kondo for his assistance in arranging negotiations with the Corean government. Consul Kondo's attempts to convey Shufeldt's letter to the king achieved no result, partly due to Mr. Kondo's intentional lack of effort, as Shufeldt wrote in his October letter: "I am not satisfied that Japan has been acting in perfect faith—it is her policy indeed to monopolize the commerce of Corea. She possesses in the country [. . .] rights and rules the Coreans with an iron rod. Striving to free herself from the obnoxious sway of foreigners on her own soil, she is unwilling to have these foreigners see how she has imposed these same laws in an aggravated force upon her defenceless neighbor." Consul Kondo finally conveyed

the Korean governor's intention that Corea "would not hold intercourse with any foreigners except Japanese" (Shufeldt's May letter).

10. In this sense, American exceptionalism faces hard criticism, as Field (2015: 292) aptly notes: American exceptionalism comes in many forms. In U.S. foreign relations, it frequently manifests itself in the belief that the United States has a special mission in world affairs to promote some exalted principle such as liberty, order, or stability, or sometimes an institution such as democracy, international law, or Christianity. That this belief in a special mission carries more than a tinge of self-righteousness has not escaped notice. From European leaders who derided President Woodrow Wilson as a self-styled 'Jesus Christ' at the Versailles Conference in 1919 to Russian leader Vladimir Putin's 2013 editorial in The New York Times denouncing Americans' exceptionalist view of themselves, many foreign statesmen have ridiculed this arrogant aspect of American ideology.

11. While competing heavily with the United Kingdom and the United States in the world economy of the late nineteenth and early twentieth centuries, Japan began to show a desire to march into countries of Northeast and Southeast Asia. However, this was not the first time that Japan revealed ambitions to conquer Korea and expand its influence over the Asian continent. Oliver (1994: 35–36) aptly summarizes it: "In 1590, Hideyoshi, the Napoleon of Japan, embarked on the realization of his dream of creating an Asiatic Empire to comprise Japan, Korea, China, India, Persia, Formosa, and the Philippines. To the rulers of each of them he sent an audacious letter.... 'I am not willing to spend the remaining years of my life in the land of my birth. According to my idea, the nation that I would l create should not be separated by mountains and seas, but should include them all. In starting my conquest, I planned that our forces should proceed to China and compel the people there to adopt our customs and manner. Then that vast country, consisting of more than four hundred provinces, would enjoy our imperial protection and benevolence for millions of years to come—You, King of Korea, are hereby instructed to join us at the head of all your fighting men when we proceed to China.'"

12. This is from Krishnan (1984: 15), requoted from Han-mu Kang, "The United States Military Government in Korea, 1945–1948: An Analysis and Evaluation of its Policy," PhD dissertation, University of Cincinnati, 1970, quoting Hodge's directive of September 4, 1945, pp. 34–35.

13. "While Koreans at times ruled Manchuria, they seldom encroached on their neighbors. On the other hand, outsiders—Chinese, Japanese, Mongols, Manchus, Russians—took turns trying to dominate Korea. As CIA analysts have put it: "Victimized by its strategic location throughout history," Korea has been, and continues to be, "the scene of competition for dominant influence by its powerful neighbors" (Clements, Jr., 2016: 5).

14. Available at http://www.kwvdm.org/ personal_info_detail.php?id=BArriola

15. This metaphor, euphemistic of rape, conflates sexist, racist, and nationalistic views into a single trope. Here, I use the word "veil" with double-meaning, alluding to the wedding veil but also this underlying trope.

16. This very ambitious and challenging policy of the Chinese government was announced by the Communist Party of China General Secretary Xi Jinping on his visit

to Indonesia and Kazakhstan in 2013. It was China's global infrastructure development strategy to revive China's old heyday of the Silk Road as a "Belt" and to link it with sea routes as a "21st Century Maritime Silkroad." This policy was incorporated into the Constitution of the Peoples' Republic of China in 2017. Considered a centerpiece of Xi's global strategy for challenging the United States and other major powers, it aims to build Chinese influence in nearly 70 countries by 2049, the centennial of China's communist revolution.

Chapter 2

Encounter of Isolationist Joseon and Expansionist America

"AUSPICIOUS BEGINNING OF AN ENDURING PARTNERSHIP": SWAPPING KOREA FOR THE PHILIPPINES

Celebrating the 100th anniversary of the Treaty of Peace, Amity, Commerce and Navigation between the United States and Korea in 1882, President Reagan hailed the treaty as having marked "a new chapter in the history of Northeast Asia as the auspicious beginning of an enduring partnership between the United States and Korea," adding that "Americans are proud of the role they have played in Korean history, especially during these last 100 years" (Krishnan, 1984: 3). In fact, among many Western imperialist countries in the late nineteenth century, it was the United States that adopted "the most resolute policy toward Korea while other European powers like Great Britain, France, and Germany did not pay much attention to this small hermit kingdom that had resisted intercourse with others than China" (Kim, 2001: 59). Ironically, this persistent policy of the United States to open the last of the Asian countries was initiated by an incident in which an American merchant ship, the *General Sherman*, in what can only be described as an act of piracy, sparked a battle in the Daedong River near North Korea's current capital of Pyeongyang in 1866.

Even a 68-year history of official U.S.-Korea relations from 1882 to 1950, however, clearly shows that Reagan's statement falls farther afield than most Americans, and Koreans, likely realize. According to Krishnan (1984: 5), whose expertise is in postcolonialism, the speech was "a complete blank and a total and formal break in the official relations between Korea and the U.S.A. as sovereign independent entities from 1905 to 1945." As described earlier, Syngman Rhee, long before becoming first president of South Korea, met with many American leaders urging them to invoke the "good offices" provision of the 1882 treaty as Japan was poised and preparing to declare Joseon its protectorate. LaFeber (1997: 49) reminds us that King Gojong's earnest appeal to the U.S. government was flatly refused by Secretary of State Gresham. He just expressed his wishful thinking that Japan would not wage an unjust war. That same day he told the Japanese privately he had no intention of helping Korea.

In a tense interview with an American ambassador in 1949, Rhee expressed a sense of betrayal, lamenting that "the United States had abandoned Korea on two occasions, in 1905 and again in 1945." In the days leading up to the Korean War, he suspected, and rightly so, that America was about to do so again (Wilz, 1985: 244), as evidence will demonstrate later. Yes, the real bilateral history between the United States and Korea directly contradicts President Reagan's blank reference to the "auspicious beginning" and "an enduring partnership" that began in 1882.

The opening of relations between the United States and Korea had been doggedly pursued and ultimately heralded by Secretary of State William Seward in his service from 1861 to 1869; however, that connection was tragically shattered as a result of Washington's decision to swap its partner with Japan in exchange for the Philippines in 1905.

One thing we must take care to resist in our application of Diamond's theory to the case of the Korean Peninsula is the general temptation to justify current disparities between the South and North and to rationalize U.S. policy toward North Korea. "If we succeed in explaining how some people came to dominate other people," Diamond (1997: 17) says, "may this not seem to justify the domination? Doesn't it suggest that the outcome was inevitable, and that it would thus be futile to try to change the outcome today?" Diamond's argument cautions us not to view South Korea's successful economic development and democratization as justification for America's inconsistent and contradictory interventions in the Korean Peninsula. He concludes, "This objection rests on a common tendency to confuse an explanation of causes with a justification or acceptance of results. What use one makes of a historical explanation is a question separate from the explanation itself. Understanding is more often used to try to alter an outcome than to repeat or perpetuate it" (Diamond 1997: 17). To the question of how Korea would stand today had America not forced it open, surrendered its interest in Korea to Japan, or had not arbitrarily cut the Peninsula in half, we unfortunately have no definitive answer. The point though is that, rather than simply glorifying the South and disparaging the North, we recognize American engagement in the Peninsula as one of the most significant variables in explaining where Korea is now. Adopting Diamond's perspective, the United States serves as the most important factor in Korea's opening and division, with vast disparities between the North and the South.

To discern whether the current disparities between these two truly stem from the ways in which the United States and Joseon encountered each other in the late nineteenth and early twentieth centuries, this book traces the roots of their relationship back through the layers of their history on both sides of their experience.

OVERVIEW OF U.S.-KOREA RELATIONS

1. Early Encounters: The General Sherman Incident (1866)[1] and *Shinmiyangyo*, the First Korean War (1871)
2. Official Treaty between the United States and Joseon (1882)
3. Taft-Katsura Secret Agreement (1905) and Japanese Colonization (1910–1945)
4. Liberation of Korea from Japan (1945) and U.S. Military Administration (1945–1949)
5. The Korean War (1950–1953)
6. Korea's Simultaneous Achievement of Economic Development and Democratization (1962–1990s), rising to world's 11th largest economy and 6th largest exporter
7. North Korea and U.S.-ROK Alliance in the Context of the Thucydides Trap[2]

UNFORTUNATE BEGINNING OF THE ENCOUNTER: THE GENERAL SHERMAN INCIDENT

The General Sherman was an American merchant schooner, owned by Mr. W. B. Preston, who was making a voyage for [hearth: his health]. Consigned to Messrs. Meadow & Co., a British firm in Tientsin, the ship reached that port in July 1866. After her cargo was delivered, an arrangement was made by the firm and owner to load her with goods likely to be saleable in Corea—including cotton cloth, glass, and tin plate—and dispatch her there on an experimental voyage in hopes of thus opening the country for commerce (Griffis, 1889: 391). "In reality," though, as Murray (2011) explains, "the motives behind the expedition were far more dastardly, involving the looting of royal tombs in the vicinity of P'yongyang" (55).

Due to this unfortunate encounter, the first war, Shinmiyangyo, broke out in 1882. It was a very small-scale collision, literally called by Koreans a "disturbance," but it seems to have served as a de facto model for the larger war in 1950. In the estuary of the Han River, gunfire crackled for two days between the United States and the Koreans: about 350 Koreans were killed near Ganghwa Island. Five battleships under the command of Rear-Admiral John Rodgers had entered with 80 cannons and 1,230 crew members bearing swords (Griffis, 1889; Dennett, 1922; Griswold, 1938; Naval Historical Foundation Publication, 1966; LaFeber, 1967; Henderson, 1968; Nahne & Castel, 1968; Swartout, Jr., 1974; Drake, 1984; Kim, 2001; Sterner, 2002; Chang, 2003; Kang, 2005; Murray, 2011). This battle, the *Shinmiyangyo*, was the first real war between the United States and Korea, long before its division in 1945, and although fourteen Medals of Honor were awarded to soldiers from the Navy and Marines, this war is not widely known. Perhaps such forgetting serves as precedent for the Korean War of the 1950s becoming, more famously, "The Forgotten War?"

When President Ulysses S. Grant gave his annual message to Congress in 1871, he noted this small war with Korea, crediting the former State Secretary William Seward and his "Dollar diplomacy" or "Seward Doctrine" (Kim, 2001: 103) for his leadership in opening the nation: "Prompted by a desire to put an end to the barbarous treatment of our shipwrecked sailors on the [C]orean coast, I instructed our minister at Peking to endeavor to conclude a convention with Corea for securing the safety and humane treatment of such marines."[3] By "barbarous treatment," Grant was referring to the burning of a gunboat named *The General Sherman* in 1866 by Koreans in the Daedong River near Pyeongyang, the current capital of North Korea but the second capital in the Joseon dual-capital system. In response to this conflagration, the American government, led by Secretary Seward, sought revenge. In his instructions to his nephew and America's minister in China, George Seward, Secretary Seward said:

> President (Johnson) would be highly grateful if a Corean legation or embassy should arrive here, authorized to give proper satisfaction to the United States for the outrage in question and to enter into a treaty. But should this not occur, the time is thought a propitious one to send a civil agent to Corea for the purpose, first, of procuring a release of any surviving seamen of the General Sherman; secondly, an official explanation . . . with reasonable reparation and indemnity; thirdly, treaty provision for the opening of the ports of Corea to the United States and other nations and for the security of life and property of foreigners in that country. . . . You will endeavor to procure a treaty of amity and commerce as nearly similar in the provisions to those now existing between the United State and Japan, as may be found practicable and expedient. (Kang, 2005: 15–16)

It is worth noting that it was this merchant vessel privately owned by W. B. Preston that happened to serve as justification for America's initial interest in opening and then invading Korea in 1871.[4] Another very critical piece of information that we need to pay special attention to regards how the initial encounter actually took place between the United States and Korea. In fact, there was an earlier contact. Roughly three months before the *General Sherman* was burned down by soldiers and an angry mob near the current capital of North Korea, the American vessel *Surprise* was stranded off the coast of Sonchonpo in northwestern Korea in June of 1866. In this first encounter, shipwrecked American sailors were treated, "after initial inquiry," with an "abundance of good food, tobacco, and even medicines for the sick," and American Charge d'Affaires in Beijing (Kang, 2005: 6) made a detailed report to Secretary of State William Seward that there had been very contrasting reactions among Koreans to the uninvited American visits: the *Surprise* received very surprising treatment from the Koreans but the only reaction possible to the *General Sherman*'s violence was arguably self-protection. The only difference we can presumably tell as to why the Koreans reacted to these two vessels in such opposite ways was that the former had been stranded and had not provoked them with violent or threatening behaviors, whereas the second had used aggression and violence to force the Koreans to trade.

In his report to Secretary Seward, American Charge d'Affaires in Beijing S. Wells William stated that "This consisted of five foreigners (three Americans and two British, one a passenger) and 19 Manilamen, as sailors. I have not been able to learn more than that the *Surprise* had gone over on an experimental trading voyage. The ship had very little, if any, cargo on board" (William, 1867: 414, requoted from Kang, 2005: 6). As shown by this brief report, the main purpose of the *Surprise* was as an experimental trading voyage, according to an American diplomat in China. However, the *General Sherman* was fully loaded with trade items and weapons. In this report, William (1867) also mentioned the *General Sherman*, saying, "If any body from the General Sherman should be given to the authorities there, I hope they will receive better usage" (Williams, 1867: 415, requoted from Kang, 2005: 6).

In this very limited report on the *Surprise* and the *General Sherman*, it is reasonable to posit why these two American vessels were treated differently: Koreans did not want intercourse with Westerners in trade but provided the usual humane treatment for shipwrecked sailors, whereas they reacted fiercely to violent provocations by Americans in the case of the *General Sherman*. The American owner of the General Sherman had dispatched the ship with typical American trade items such as cotton goods, tin sheets, glass, and other items to trade with Korea for paper, rice, gold, ginseng, and leopard skin. The problem in this expedition was that the schooner created a series of protests from local officials, which were met with provocations. By August 16, it reached the capital. After a series of altercations and threats of force from both sides, a skirmish ensued which brought about the destruction of the vessel and death of all crew members on September 2, 1866 (Kang, 2005: 7). Kang adds that the *General Sherman*'s cruise toward Korea's second capital without any prior contact or requests to survey the important waterways was clearly an illegal intrusion. To make matters worse, this intrusion was taking place in the midst of disturbances centering around Korea's persecution of Catholic missionaries and practitioners, and a violent encounter with the French expedition was about to start (Kang, 2005: 7).

Another noteworthy fact for this book in Williams' report to Secretary Seward was that he used the term "intercourse" in this first encounter between Corea and the Westerners—the United States and France. As noted before, Corea's regent Daewongun persecuted French Catholic missionaries and Corean followers in early 1866, which provoked a French expedition in September 1866, a month after the General Sherman Incident. Williams said:

> I hear that the French have already affected a landing in Corea, but nothing more of importance has been learned of their movements. The force now there consists of six ships. I enclose a copy of the notification of blockade, (enclosure C) and shall apprise the department of the operations that are made public. I suppose the expedition will result in throwing open to the western world the last country which now forbids intercourse with other lands, and whose rulers have jealously guarded their subjects from the least acquaintance with their fellow men. It is full time that Corea was introduced into the family of nations. (Williams, 1867: 416, requoted from Kang, 2005: 7)

The illegality and provocative nature of the *General Sherman*'s actions seem to have been well recognized by most of the officials who took responsibility for America's opening of Korea in 1882 through the official treaty brokered by Commodore Shufeldt. In his report to Admiral Bell, who had dispatched him to investigate the General Sherman Incident, Shufeldt wrote that

> the ship was laden with muskets, powder, and other articles which were contraband and had evidently sailed on a marauding expedition. . . . The General Sherman had willfully and under constant protest ascended the Ta Tong River [Daedong River]: that finally the crew landing and behaving in a lawless manner, were attacked and murdered by an enraged mob, which was entirely beyond the control of the authorities. (H.G. Appenzeller, "Opening of Korea," 58–59, requoted in Kang, 2005: 9)

From these multiple sources of official reports, it becomes clear that America should be accountable for the first unfortunate encounter between the two countries, which resulted in an American expedition to Korea in 1871. However, ironically, Shufeldt's recognition of America's initial illegal encounter with "Corea" in 1866 at the same time paved his way to a successful treaty because he made sure to avoid such behaviors when in charge of negotiating the official treaty in 1881 and 1882. Two earlier disastrous interactions served as lessons for Shufeldt, even though he also emphasized and requested, from time to time, a display of American naval power to influence the Korean court whenever negotiations came to a stalemate.

These two intriguing stories of contact between the United States and Korea remind us of Diamond's recounting of how the Incan Empire collapsed due to its encounter with the Spanish Expedition. The fate of the Incan Empire and the Incan emperor, Atahualpa, was determined by their encounter with guns, germs, and steel introduced by Francisco Pizarro and his tiny band of conquistadores, at the Peruvian city of Cajamarca (Diamond, 1999: 28). As Diamond (1999: 25) finds that "history followed different courses for different peoples because of differences among peoples' environments, not because of biological differences among peoples themselves," Confucian and China-centered Koreans were essentially forced to have intercourse with Christian-oriented and commercially motivated expansionist Americans. The second type of intercourse between the United States and Korea, in the form of the General Sherman Incident in 1866, was a collision "between peoples from different continents," which this book designates through "contemporary eyewitness accounts the most dramatic such encounter in history": the opening of isolationist Korea, followed by the *Shinmiyangyo*, the first Korean War, the official opening of Korea by the United States in 1882, and the achieving of independence.

An important point to understand is that, despite its military victory in the Shinmiyangyo and the Low-Rodgers' expedition to Korea, the United States had failed to effectively open Corea. As President Grant concluded in this speech: "the expedition returned, finding it impracticable under the circumstances to conclude the desired convention."[5] There is reason to doubt that President Reagan was aware of President Grant's frustration. It is hard to explain such inconsistencies as America's risking a war to open Korea and then summarily giving it up, unless we consider America's unbridled pursuit of its national interests in the region during the nineteenth century.

The United States ran aground on the shore of the Joseon's faith in China as the center of the world, its attachment to Confucian doctrine in every aspect of society, and its stubborn resistance to Western calls to open. The brief history of happenstance between the United States and "Corea"[6]—or the "land of morning calm" as it was called by Orientalists in the nineteenth century—has caused two opposite situations on the Peninsula: an unprecedentedly successful transformation in the South and an unprecedentedly failed state in the North. This byproduct is of global relevance because the current status of the U.S.-North Korea conflict over Pyeongyang's bold provocations poses serious security threats not only to South Korea but also to neighboring countries.

The next question is why such opposite outcomes emerged from Korea's encounter with the United States. How can they be explained? As mentioned before, this book does not aim to sweepingly lionize the American system and disparage North Korea; however, their starkly different systems and conditions demonstrate this book's puzzle regarding the history of U.S.-Korea relations in the late nineteenth century. Instead, this encounter encourages us to ponder critical questions about the future of human society, in terms of its security, forms of government and ideology, and problems among sovereign states, to name a few. From this perspective, it is crucial to search back through time and discern how such discrepancies between the North and South, according to Diamond (1977), may have begun, how they brought us here, how they might evolve, and what consequences will likely emerge for nations around the Peninsula as well as for Koreans and Americans, especially in light of the 250th commemoration of America's independence in 2026 and the 150th commemoration of U.S.-Korea relations in 2032.

Indeed, after Obama administration's long ignorance of North Korea with its policy of strategic patience, Pyeongyang appears to have become the focus of U.S.-Korea relations again, which justifies the focus on North Korean issues as impetus for this book, since it could also feasibly become the last chapter in the story of their relations, figuratively speaking. The recent narratives and discourse between President Trump and Kim Jong-un on denuclearization certainly seemed to signal a possible end to the whole course of U.S.-Korea relations, but in the least they seem to suggest some closure to the overarching trajectory of the collision course in progress even though the exercise turned out to be another failure.

To retrace the chain of events, it started with the unfortunate burning of America's heavily armed merchant schooner in 1866. And, as symmetry would seem to suggest, may end with a very destructive new turn in U.S.-Korea relations as well. Importantly, though, the Korean War serves as a watershed in the American perspective on Korea in general, with South Korea coming to represent a larger portion of U.S. global politics. All in all, perhaps, American perception of North Korea has not dramatically changed since this first encounter in 1866.

Official relations can be said to have started with Commodore Robert W. Shufeldt's Treaty in 1882; however, if we count the unofficial events of the General Sherman Incident in 1866, then the history of U.S.-ROK relations spans 153 years, a significant portion of America's relatively short history as a nation. If we also exclude Japan's 40-year occupation, then the history is just a century long. Such a short history of bilateral encounters between the two countries, however, has produced one of the most tumultuous regional conflicts with the four main countries of the Korean War involved in what serves to showcase the stark disparities between the models followed by the North and the South.

The United States officially nullified its treaty with the Joseon in 1904, a year before Japan forced Korea to sign the Japan-Korea Treaty of 1905,[7] depriving Korea of diplomatic sovereignty by making it a protectorate of imperial Japan. Then in 1910, Japan annexed Korea, to which the United States tacitly agreed. During these 40 years of Japanese influence, the United States took no interest in Korea. That apathy lasted until Japan rose as an Axis power in World War II. Postwar from 1945 to 1948, the United States treated Korea as a venue for finishing its involvement in World War II and as a buffer against the Soviet Union in the division of the Peninsula. Considering that no action was taken to renullify the Treaty of Peace, Amity, Commerce, and Navigation, official and substantial U.S. involvement in South Korea began when these two signed a mutual defense treaty in 1953, right after the Korean War. This makes bilateral relations less than 70 years old. Considering that North Korea also became the official enemy of the United States in 1953, Washington's current standoff with Pyongyang is equally young.

William Seward, Secretary of State under Presidents Abraham Lincoln and Andrew Johnson, hailed the Pacific Ocean as "chief theater of events in the world's great hereafter" (Murray, 2011: 49). Dennett (1922) credited Secretary Seward as an American political leader on the far-front line for asserting the use of open-door gunboat diplomacy. Chay (1982: 19) argues that American gunboat diplomacy, such as the presence of old warships in Incheon Harbor, with the exception of the 1871 American expedition, aimed "to protect its small interest there and comfort the Korean monarch against his mostly internal foes [i.e., Japan]."[8]

Two military interactions in particular hindered the Americans from opening Korea for layover ports between its bigger customers China and Japan. In light of America's infliction of "more casualties on Asian people than any other U.S. military action until the Philippine uprising of 1899," Korea was not ready for new intercourse with the United States (Murray, 2011). Moreover, even today, the United States still has not realized its dream of opening up the whole of Korea; in fact, the part that resisted its first advances still resists—North Korea. That first war was nicknamed "Our Little War with the Heathens" by *The New York Herald* and referred to as "Speedy and Effective Punishment of the Barbarians" by *The New York Times*.

To comprehend why the American ship the General Sherman was razed by Koreans in 1886, three major historical incidents must be considered, all of which occurred just five years prior. First, America's aggressive interest in opening Korea for trade just so happened to coincide with the Joseon empire's intense policy of isolationism. This policy was led by King

Gojong's father, the Regent Daewongun. In other words, the timing could not have been any worse. Second, Western attempts to dig up, steal, and smuggle objects from royal tombs had tainted Korean perceptions of American efforts to establish trade. Considering that ancestral worship was the *modus vivendi* in the Confucian belief system of the Joseon, it is not hard to imagine how the robbing of ancestral tombs would have been perceived. Nor is it hard to picture how Korean locals and government representatives viewed this blackship bristling with cannons and guns—frankly, as the Western expedition of weaponized graverobbers that it was. Several attempts to smuggle ancient relics were recorded and officially filed.

Third, views on Christianity in Korea underwent major upheavals in 1742 when Pope Benedict XIV outlawed both the veneration of Confucius and the ancestral worship, triggering a series of Catholic purges by the Regent Daewongun. Prior to that, Christianity had not been severely oppressed, though it was not encouraged either. Catholicism posed a threat to the Korean government, however, in two main ways: as a competing ideology and as a weapon of foreign invasion. If the Neo-Confucianists were fearful of the increasing influences of Western thinking among Confucian scholars, they were doubly so of Christian teachings.

As a result, after the Pope officially declared this stance against Confucian values and ancestral worship, the Joseon government lethally purged 300 Catholics, mostly French missionaries and their Korean followers, in 1801. Then, in 1839, a second major persecution left three French missionaries dead. Nonetheless, the Catholic movement there survived and prospered (Swartout, Jr., 1974: 92).

Tensions worsened over the next half-century, and nine French priests were decapitated in 1866.[9] French minister to China Henri de Bellonet aggressively regarded this purge as a chance to open the Joseon and make it a French colony. Sidestepping the chain of command, Minister Bellonet sent an incendiary dispatch to the Chinese Emperor requesting he approve a declaration of war against Korea. However, the Rear-Admiral Pierre Gustav Roze, Commander of the French Far East Squadron, livid over the minister's arrogance, sent a fleet of about 1,000 navy crew members. This French war against the Joseon was called *Byeonginyangyo*,[10] lasting from October 14 to December 17, 1866 (Dennett, 1922; Murray, 2011; Sterner, 2002). It was no puzzle to guess where outsiders might launch their attacks—Ganghwa Island near the Incheon, the harbor and trading city, for easy access to the capital, Hanyang. After two months of fighting, Rear-Admiral Roze withdrew due to a successful attack on November 10 led by Yang Honsu with "a corps of professional hunters in an ambush of the French garrison at Chongdung Temple, slaying thirty-two French soldiers" (Murray, 2011: 53–54).

According to Kim (2001: 24, requoted in Murray, 2011: 54), this defeat was "[o]ne of the few instances in the colonialist history of Europe in which European soldiers were defeated in non-European territory." The failure of Roze's expedition alarmed the French, whose Minister of Foreign Affairs, Lionel, wrote to his minister Bellonet in China: "I am very seriously shocked by your belief that you could carry out any actions which suited your own personal agenda though no such authority had been granted you" (Murray, 2011: 54). One fact relevant here is that Rear-Admiral Roze, despite his failure to avenge the deaths of the French missionaries, brought back intelligence that the General Sherman Incident had occurred in August 1866, prior to the French war against the Joseon.

United States v. Jenkins

Western traders, as it turns out, were in fact attempting to smuggle antiquities out of Korea. The most representative case was *United States v. Jenkins*,[11] arraigned in the U.S. Consular Court, Shanghai, 1868.[12] Lee (2000) summarizes it as follows:

> In June 1867, Earnest Oppert (a German), Feron (a French Catholic priest) and Jenkins (an American) mounted an expedition to rob the grave of a Korean king. The grave-robbers chartered the armed steamer the China and some 100 Chinese and Malay pirates, formerly with the Ever Victorious Army of the Taiping War. They succeeded in partially desecrating the royal tomb but the Korean defenders forced them to retreat. . . . Both incidents of piracy involved Christian missionaries and a handful of miserable Korean converts who were more than willing to sell out their country to foreign devils. The French priest Feron was informed of the "rich" royal grave by his Korean converts and in fact, the Korean traitors willingly led the Chinese crew to the grave site. In the name of God, these Satanic devils attempted to rob a grave. Of these criminals, Oppert was the only one punished by the so-called civilized nations. Oppert served only one year in jail, however. A trial court presided over by George F. Seward,[13] the American Consul-General of Shanghai, cleared Jenkins of any wrongdoing, although it was Jenkins who financed the "expedition." The French simply refused to prosecute Father Feron, and Feron went on "spreading the Gospel."

Two points, here, stand out. First, it is amazing to learn that the American legal justice system operated on foreign soil in the nineteenth century to do justice in this matter, which could easily have been dismissed without trial since it occurred in a country that was small, poor, and primitive. Second, at the same time, blood is thicker than water; Jenkins, who had financed the expedition, was exonerated by virtue of being American.

This legal case was also reported by George F. Seward, U.S. Envoy Extraordinary and Minister Plenipotentiary to China (1876–1880), to Dr. Samuel Wells Williams, a linguist, official, missionary, and Sinologist from the United States in the early nineteenth century:

Mr. G.F. Seward to Mr. Williams
United States Consulate General, Shanghai, July 13, 1868.

Sir: I inclose the supreme court and consular Gazette's report of the trial in the consulate of FHB Jenkins, for setting on foot an expedition to Corea, having for its object to exhume the remains of a dead sovereign, or other person or persons of that country, and to hold the bones for profit. This expedition left Shanghai in April last. There were apparently three leaders: a French priest named Farout, a citizen of Hamburg named Oppert, and our countryman above named. A steamer under the North German flag, named the China, of 648 tons, was chartered for it, and a steam tender of 60 tons, about, also provided. About eight Europeans, 20 Manilas, and 100 Chinese sailors, beyond the complement of the ship, were engaged and embarked. At Nagasaki muskets enough were taken to arm all these. Arrived on the coast of Corea, two small boats were seized, and within a few hours the tender towing them steamed up river about 40 miles. Here the crowd of armed men landed and made their way across the country to a graveyard, where the surrounding hills were covered with Coreans; they went to work to exhume the bones for which they had come. These were contained in a stone or mason work sarcophagus, and having penetrated through the earth to it, they found themselves unable to do more, and returned to the large steamer, having met no opposition which they had not overcome by the simple display of their arms, or by firing them in the air.[14]

In his report to the central government, Kyusu Pak, governor of the province, described the invasion as unprecedented and destructive:

"As soon as the ship arrived in Korean waters, its members made it known to Korean officials that they intended to enter the Daedong River and carry out trade with the city of Pyeongyang, located far up the river. Upon hearing this, the Korean officials notified the foreigners that it was alright for their ships to anchor in the seas off the coast but that the King of Korea had forbidden any foreign vessels to enter the inland waters of the country." . . . The Koreans knew that the river was not safely navigable up to that point for such a large ship. The Koreans had already noticed that the vessel was heavily armed with guns, swords, and cannons. Thus, it would not only be illegal for such a ship to enter inland waters, it would also pose a serious threat to national security. (Swartout, Jr., 1974: 115–116) the foreign vessel . . . [has] plundered provisions from Korean ships, recklessly discharging its guns and killing seven and wounding five Koreans. There has never been such a thing as a foreign vessel entering the inland waters of the country and remaining for a number of days. They say they are going to threaten the Koreans with violence in order to force them to trade . . . so that nothing remained for us but to destroy the vessel. (Yijo Sillok, chapter XXII in Cable, "United States Korean Relations, 1866–1871," 18–20, Swartout, Jr., 1974: 118)

This was not Korea's first clash with the United States. As you might expect, history repeats itself, and the current deadlock between the United States and North Korea can be blamed on unresolved aspects of the Korean War 70 years ago. However, the misunderstandings that developed between these two countries have roots that meander back much further. When Americans first approached the Joseon, it was not North Korea but the Koreans as a people that the Americans engaged, long before Korea got divided into two diametrically opposed nations.

Mishaps in the Wake of the General Sherman Incident

When the U.S. government had endeavored to follow up on the General Sherman Incident of 1866, the first effort simply aimed to follow up on intelligence from French rear-admiral Roze.[15] Based on a report from Anson Burlingame, American minister to China, Admiral Henry H. Bell, Commander of the Asiatic Squadron of the U.S. Navy—encouraged by the State Secretary of William Seward—dispatched Robert W. Shufeldt with the USS *Wachusetts* to investigate. In fact, Secretary Seward approached France proposing to form a joint action in order to obtain from Korea satisfaction for the murders of the Frenchmen and the Americans, even though it was not realized (Kang, 2005: 11). On January 29, 1867, Shufeldt handed a letter to King Gojong but received no clarification regarding the incident and had to withdraw.

The second attempt to follow up on the incident took place in March 1868, when "Yu Wentai, a Chinese national who had abandoned the *General Sherman*, informed a U.S. consul in China that four crewmembers . . . remained alive in Korea" (Murray, 2011: 57). Dispatched by the U.S. Navy, Captain John C. Febiger with the USS *Shenandoah* made some progress with the governor of Hanghae Province, who had been in charge during the incident. Pak Kyusu, who had praised "the moral standards of the United States," expressed Korean bewilderment at American indignation, emphasizing the violent nature of the excursion: "The General Sherman came into our country without permission and caused complications, and now you are blaming us for that incident and we do not understand your intention in doing so" (Kim, 2001: 85, requoted from Murray, 2011: 58). Shufeldt reacted to this report from Captain Febiger, saying that "The letter was so statesman-like in its character and bore such intrinsic evidence of the truth of its statements that both Captain Febiger and I were convinced that the attack on the General Sherman was made by an unauthorized mob under strong provocation" (Kim, 2001: 88, requoted from Murray, 2011: 58).

Finally, the follow-up by George Seward, American minister to China and nephew of State Secretary William Seward, bore no fruit due to his recognition of Jenkins' attempt to rob tombs of ancient Korean relics. Accordingly, Secretary Seward had decided to conclude his efforts to open the last East Asian nation of heathens, Korea, when on July 27, 1868, Admiral Henry H. Bell's proposal of dramatic military intervention finally resulted in the *Shinmiyangyo*, as will be analyzed in chapter 4. In 1871, the U.S. Asiatic Expedition invaded the Joseon, in what came to be called the Shinmiyangyo, to avenge the razing of the *General Sherman*, a boat of pillaging mercenaries.

American Interest in Corea: Commerce and Navigation

After forcibly opening China through the Treaty of Wangxia in 1844 and Japan through the Treaty of Kanagawa in 1854, the United States wanted "the last important Asiatic country"—the Joseon. For thousands of years, it had remained shuttered to all but China (under "ill-defined suzerainty") and a few missionaries (Nahne and Castel, 1968). It was handy for American merchant marine ships to have safe havens in Corea, between China and Japan. Because the Peninsula has long been regarded as a hub of security concerns in Northeast Asia by superpowers like China, Russia, and Japan, it has served not only as a crossroads for commerce but also as a cauldron for war. Many also agree that Korea has been victimized throughout its history due to the strategic appeal of its location, which has made it an object of competition among these superpowers as a springboard to the Asian continent and the Pacific. The Peninsula, moreover, is narrow and readily accessed by three of the most powerful actors on the world stage (Clemens, 2016). In fact, some regard the map of Korea as a dagger toward Japan, China, and Russia.

Congressman Pratt aptly noted Korea's relative insignificance to American economic interests: "On the other hand, the United States could not expect anything like equal advantage from intercourse with Corea" (Swartout, Jr., 1974: 112; Griffis, 1889: 390). Swartout, Jr. (1974: 112) indicates that "Once Japan was open, Korea by herself was not important enough to warrant a special mission," only later did Americans want vengeance for the General Sherman Incident in 1866.

Corea attracted Americans for more than its location. A century earlier, American merchants had taken an interest in Corea for its near monopoly on ginseng, the root of which was the most popular and precious medicine on the Asian market in Beijing and Canton. Among the varieties, Korean ginseng stood out for its quality. According to Griffis (1889):

> America became a commercial rival to Cho-sen [Joseon, i.e., Corea] as early as 1757, when the products of Connecticut and Massachusetts lay side by side with Corean [Korean] imports in the markets of Peking and Canton. Ginseng, the most precious drug in the Chinese pharmacopoeia, had been for ages brought from Manchuria and the neighboring peninsula, where, on the mountains, the oldest and richest roots are found. . . . The sweetish and mucilaginous root, though considered worthless by Europeans, was then occasionally bringing its weight in gold, and usually seven times its weight in silver, at Peking, and the merchants in the annual embassy from Seoul were reaping a rich harvest. (388)

The Dutch traders, immediately noting the great demand for the famed remedy, sought the world over for a supply, and eventually broke the Korean monopoly in the nineteenth century:

> The Hollanders, shipping the bundled roots on their galliots down the Hudson, and thence to Amsterdam and London, sold them to the British East India Company at a profit of five hundred per cent. Landed at Canton, and thence carried to Peking, American ginseng broke the market, forced the price to a shockingly low figure, and dealt a heavy blow to the Corean monopoly. . . . Animated by the spirit of independence, and a laudable ambition, the resolute citizens of the New World declared that "the Americans must have tea, and they seek the most lucrative market for their precious root ginseng. It was ginseng and tea—an exchange of the materials for drink, a barter of tonics—that brought the Americans and Chinese, and finally the Americans and Coreans together. . . . The idea now began to dawn upon some minds that it was high time that Japan and Corea should be opened to American commerce. The first public man who gave this idea official expression was the Honorable Zadoc Pratt, then member of the House of Representatives from the Eleventh (now the Fifteenth) Congressional District of New York. As chairman of the committee on Naval Affairs, he introduced in Congress, February 12, 1845, a proposition for the extension of American commerce by the dispatch of a mission to Japan and Corea as follows: "It is hereby recommended that immediate measures be taken for effecting commercial arrangements with the empire of Japan and the kingdom of Corea," etc. (Congressional Globe, vol. xiv., p. 294) (Griffis, 1889: 388–390)

On February 15, 1845, Congressman Pratt, also as chairman of the Committee on Naval Affairs of the House of Representatives, introduced a resolution calling for a mission to Japan and Korea to establish trade relations. He declared: "The American people will be able to rejoice in the knowledge that the 'star-spangled banner' is recognized as ample passport and protection for all who, of our enterprising countrymen, may be engaged in extending American commerce" (Swartout, Jr., 1974: 111; Kang, 2005: 80). Further, his resolution says:

> Be it therefore resolved, that in furtherance of this object, it is hereby recommended that immediate measures be taken for effecting commercial arrangements with the empire of Japan and Kingdom of Corea. Corea also possesses a large population—estimated at fifteen millions; and assimilates in character to the Chinese Empire, with which it is slightly connected in political relations. The Coreans and Chinese, it may be added, are now nearly the only foreigners with whom the Japanese allow any business intercourse, however, limited. (Kang, 2005: 80)

His initiative and ambition in this resolution proposal failed to pass, however, on the heels of the fiasco in Mexico and amid reports of the failure of Admiral Roze's French expedition to Korea (Kang, 2005: 11).

The commerce which sprang up, not only between the United States and China and Japan but also that carried on in American vessels between Shanghae, Chifu, Tientsin, and Niu-chwang in North China, and the Japanese ports, made the navigation of Corean waters a necessity (Griffis, 1889: 390). This is why the treaty between Joseon and the United States was named "The Treaty of Peace, Amity, Commerce, and Navigation" in 1882. To the Americans, an obvious option was to open the Corean market for their products. Dennett (1922, requoted in Chay, 1982: 19) saw this treaty as "by far the most important action undertaken by the United States in Asia until the occupation of the Philippines" and "the most notable success of the American navy in the peaceful field of diplomacy." Furthermore, Chay (1982: 20) reduces American interests and motives to improving trade and Corean treatment of shipwrecks and argues that Americans knew that Korea was poor with little to no prospect of profiting the United States.

COLLISION: KOREAN ISOLATIONISM VS. U.S. EXPANSIONISM

In 2026, the United States will commemorate the 250th anniversary of independence, which will also be 76th anniversary of the outbreak of the Korean

War. Before delving into the details of this comparison, however, an overview of milestones in U.S. history may be useful. In 1607, the English settled Jamestown, Virginia, where Native Americans had lived for thousands of years. Following suit, other European settlers began to colonize the continent. From 1775 to 1783, the 13 colonies revolted against Great Britain. In 1776, the United States declared independence and ratified the Constitution in 1787 with the Bill of Rights in 1791. In 1861, some states in the South declared themselves separate from the nation and established the Confederate States of America. From 1861 to 1865, America was embroiled in a bloody Civil War. As the war ended, the United States began economic and territorial expansion westward and across the Pacific in the "Gilded Age," which lasted until the late nineteenth century. It was during this era of American expansionism that Korea became the preferred site for waystations between China and Japan.

The General Sherman Incident in 1866 and the official treaty with the Joseon in 1882 coincided with this era of American expansionism and Manifest Destiny in the West. Then, through World Wars I and II, the United States began to join world powers in the early twentieth century. Below is a short summary of the birth and expansion of the United States. America's formation and rise to world power are delineated, for convenience of comparison with Korea, as follows:[16]

1. Incipient stage: first settlement (1607) to Declaration of Independence (1776)
2. State formation: from Independence (1776) to ratification of Constitution (1787) and secession from Union (1861)
3. Civil War: Union vs. Confederate States of America (1861–1865)
4. Domestic expansion to the West: Gilded Age (1865 to late nineteenth century)
5. Rise to world power (early twentieth century to today)

The record of conflicts between the United States and Korea dates back to the late nineteenth century. On several occasions, shipwrecked Westerners were treated hospitably by the Joseon; however, Hamel's[17] account of the Joseon sheds light on its reputation around the world. In one passage, Hamel asks if any foreign nations come to Korea for trade, or whether the Koreans conducted trade anywhere else. He answers as follows: "Nobody carries on trade but this country [Japan], which has a lodge there. The Koreans carry on trade with the northern part of China and Peking" (Hamel, 2011: 38). "Concerning trade with foreign countries as well as among themselves, the only people who do business here are the Japanese from the island of Tsushima, who have a trading post on the Southeast side of the city of Pusan, belonging to the lord of that island" (Hamel, 2011: 68).

So why was Korea so reluctant to sign a treaty with the Americans? Frankly, the last time that the Americans had knocked on their door was in 1866—and that had not gone well. Moreover, Korea already enjoyed easy access to the biggest market in the pre-modern world—China—by land. In Beijing, Koreans could sell special products like ginseng, paper, and porcelain as well as purchase Western and Chinese goods. Indeed, Joseon's heavy dependence on Chinese philosophy, ideology, and culture had enabled them to close their doors to Westerners. The Joseon dynasty was founded in 1392 on strong faith in Neo-Confucianism, not to mention a long history of belief systems derived from Chinese philosophical and cultural schools such as Daoism, Legalism, Mohism, and Buddhism. That the Joseon's governing ideology originated almost entirely in China offers a sense of how Korea's policy on foreign relations evolved. It is shocking to learn how strikingly parochial Joseon's idea of the world was:

> Koreans think there are but twelve countries or kingdoms in the whole world. They claim that once these countries were all subject to the emperor of China and that they had to pay tribute to him. Meaning while all are thought to have liberated themselves since the Tartar took possession of China but could not conquer the other countries. They call the Tartar Taekuksa and Orangkai (Barbarian). They call our country Namban-kuk, which is what the Japanese used to call Portugal. About us, or about Holland, they know nothing. . . . In their old writings it is written that there are 84,000 countries in the world, but they consider this a fiction, saying one ought to count islands, cliffs and rocks among them, for the sun could never in one day shine on so many countries at once. When we mentioned a number of countries they all laughed at us, saying these must be names of cities and villages, because their maps do not reach beyond Siam. (Hamel, 2011: 68–69)

Generally speaking, this is how Koreans envisioned the world—with China as the center and its suzerainty assumed. Also, because Korea is situated between the two biggest Asian powers—China and Japan—its survival has always hinged upon its relationships with them; that is, Koreans have survived "by keeping their country [and culture] closed to almost all outsiders—particularly Westerners" (Bechtol, 2002: 1). Ever since China was forced open in the mid-1800s, its influence on Korea began to wane, leaving the smaller nation vulnerable to Western naval and commercial inroads.

In the early 1860s, the Joseon also faced another challenge—from Christianity. Missionaries from France and a few other countries entered, converting followers by the thousands. In 1866, Chinese suzerainty was declining, and Western influence was increasing when an American merchant schooner, literally out of the blue, ran up against steep resistance from the Joseon.

Dr. Williams, who served as Secretary of the Legation of the United States at Peking and interviewed both Korean and Chinese officials there about the General Sherman Incident, acknowledged America's responsibility for the disastrous outcomes of early encounters between the United States and Korea: "The evidence goes to uphold the presumption that they invoked their sad fate by some rash or violent act toward the natives" (Griffis, 1889: 394). As a result of this unfortunate encounter, Korea developed a general animosity toward American calls to open. As Griffis (1889) observed:

> Certain it is that the national sentiment is that of horror against the disturbance or rifling of sepulchers. Now they had before their eyes a fresh confirmation of their suspicions that the chief purpose of the foreign invaders was to rob the dead and violate the most holy instincts of humanity. The national mind now settled into the conviction that, beyond all doubt, the foreigners were barbarians and many of them thieves and robbers. With such eyes were they ready to look upon the flag and ships of the United States when they came in 1871. (400)

There seems to have been another element, though not overt in its motivation, to the U.S. invasion of the Joseon in 1871—namely, racial prejudice in American perceptions of the Hermit Kingdom, strongly based on its own faith in Manifest Destiny. The Joseon dynasty had been founded on Confucian and Neo-Confucian values, which originated from China. Its foreign origins justified the main principle of the Joseon's foreign policy—*sadae*, literally meaning "serving the great," which was the traditional foreign policy and ideology of serving China, the great.[18] Thus, China was situated firmly at the heart of the Joseon worldview, and the Joseon was determined to uphold Neo-Confucianism and Chinese influence. However, as Catholic and Western influences became inevitable, centering around King Gojong, the Joseon began to violently defend the very foundations of its society and culture. Confucianism greatly valued loyalty and filiality to one's king, parents, teachers, husbands, and seniors. The introduction of Western Catholicism fundamentally challenged that hierarchy, and thus became the direct target of Joseon's Confucian elites. Cumings (2005) aptly describes Daewongun's foreign policy as "no trade, no West, no Catholicism." Heavily and directly involved in the burning of the *General Sherman* in 1866 as well as the Joseon's reaction throughout the *Shinmiyangyo*, Daewongun erected in 1871—the year of the American invasion—about 200 memorial stones around the capital city of Hanyang and major crossroads throughout the nation inscribed with the following verse:

If you don't fight the Western barbarians, that shows your will
to make peace with them. And if you prefer to be friendly,
then that shows your willingness to sell your country.

Such strong anti-Western sentiment, among the Daewongun and Joseon Confucian elites, reflected a fundamental notion of "In-su-dae-byeol," which essentially means "there is great difference between human and beast." This epitomizes the Confucian belief that human nature is flawed and must be refined through proper protocols among human beings. In fact, Oliver (1947: 29–30) aptly compares Korea and the United States in terms of human civilization. He points out that "Koreans, who had practiced self-rule for a period of 4,000 years, and who had been a highly cultivated nation while Russia and the United States were still a savage wilderness, unitedly denounced the trusteeship proposal." Here, Oliver's mention of Korea's trusteeship comes from the superpowers' post–World War II negotiations for the 1943 Cairo Declaration, 1945 Yalta Agreement, and Potsdam Summit.

Also, in the eyes of the Joseon's Confucian population, the adoption of Catholicism represented a direct blow to their worldview. Daewongun's purge of about 200,000 Catholic believers and his reaction to the French and American expeditions in 1866 were natural outcomes of this belief system, being satisfied with China's suzerainty and isolated from the world. Daewongun's isolationist policy and subsequent purge of Western ideas appear to have achieved some continuation in North Korea's ideology of *juche*, self-reliance, and fierce opposition to American imperialism. In response, there may be little to say aside from the fact that this was not the first time that history repeated itself.

Collision with American Expansionism

When the United States declared independence from Great Britain in 1776, the Joseon was just starting its rapid decline. Established in 1392, the dynasty rose to its heyday in the fifteenth century. And after a series of invasions from Japan (1592–1598) and Qing China (1636), one last attempt was made to regain national power. King Gojong (1863–1897) worked to re-energize national power, mostly guided by his father, Heungseon[19] Daewongun, who had served as his regent ever since he first took power at the age of 11. In the mid to late nineteenth century, the Joseon fell prey to Western and Japanese imperialism. Domestically, this critical period of the dynasty gave rise to two major political factions: an isolationist school led by King Gojong's father, the Regent Heungseon Daewongun, and a group of political elites, led by King Gojong's wife, Empress Myeongseong. Daewongun had exerted tremendous influence in the late nineteenth century. His official regency started in 1864 and ended in 1873; however, his power still bore resonance in 1898. China and Japan were also playing tug-of-war with powers in the West. The Joseon had remained, until this time, a proud younger brother from the Sinocentric perspective.

Sinocentrism

Sinocentrism, the prevailing belief system and fundamental philosophy of the Joseon, is a hierarchically organized system of international relations built on the view that Chinese civilization and ethnicity are superior, and that China is the center of not only East Asia but the world. Sinocentrism is an Asian version of international feudalism where peripheral countries such as Korea, Japan, and Vietnam are viewed as vassals to the Chinese Empire. The relationship between China and these vassals is regulated, voluntarily for the most part, by a tributary system whereby peripheral countries offer tribute to the emperor in the center, while China provides protection, at least in theory. Countries outside this tributary system were seen as uncivilized. Clearly nationalism can manifest in all parts of the globe. The Sinocentric system of East Asia was guided by the Confucian code of conduct, morality, and propriety, which dictated a hierarchy of roles that comprised civilization. In this system, the emperor was the only ruler with the mandate of Heaven. Moreover, the succession of power in these tributary countries had to be approved by the center, the Chinese Emperor, the Son of Heaven.

The Joseon, founded on the political principles of Neo-Confucian doctrine, accepted this Sinocentrism proudly. In fact, it served as a major tenet of the international policy until the late nineteenth century, when it was fundamentally challenged by Japan and the West. A quick overview of Joseon's late nineteenth-century international affairs reveals how critical this Sinocentrism was for the foreseeable future of Korea, causing the most atrocious colonial control under Japan from 1910 to 1945. When King Gojong was inaugurated, his father strongly pursued a policy of reasserting national power while remaining a vassal to the Chinese Emperor. Obviously, this reinforced a policy of isolationism with regards to increased calls from France, the United States, Japan, and other nations to open its markets.

ENCOUNTERS BETWEEN STRANGERS: THE UNITED STATES AND THE JOSEON

Secretary Seward deserves a mention, here, in regard to America's open-door blackship diplomacy in Asia. Before the era of William Seward, America's open-door policy largely remained in the mode of scavenger diplomacy, which meant "coming behind the British Lion and taking from Asians whatever the Lion had left behind after its conquests" (LaFeber, 1989: 171). However, Secretary Seward dramatically transformed American tactics by deploying aggressive use of forces and collaborating with European powers to expand Western interests in Asia. To Seward, Korea was a convenient access to the markets and raw materials of Manchuria and northern China. Dennett notes:

> while no political or commercial interest renders such a treaty urgent, it is desirable that the ports of a country so near Japan and China should be opened to our trade and to the convenience of such vessels of our Navy as may be in those waters, and it is hoped that the advantages resulting from the growing and friendly relations between those great empires and the United States will have attracted the attention and awakened the interest of the Korean government. (1922: 461)

The United States forced Japan open in 1854, and Japan launched national reform just fourteen years later, in 1868. Through diplomatic delegations to the United States and Europe, Japan systematically learned Western systems of politics, education, culture, the military, banking, and rail transport. The first was the Iwakura Mission,[20] led by statesman Iwakura (1871–1873), encouraged by influential Dutch advisor to the Meiji government, Guido Verbeck, and modeled after Russia's attempt under Peter the Great (1697–1698) to reform learning from Western Europe (Notehelfer et al., 2004). Until Japan caught up with the imperial system of the West, it was China and Korea that introduced advanced religious, cultural, and political systems and thought to Japan. The Meiji reformation, however, transformed Japan, leading it into imperial competition with the West.

This is when these strangers' relationship turned a corner, as indicated in table 2.1. William Seward's aggressive, though (initially) nonviolent, effort to open Korea through the *Shimiyangyo* in 1871, and Shufeldt's success in establishing an official treaty in 1882, began to give way to a new situation, in which the United States wanted to abandon its commitment to Korea and leave it to Japan. Korea's reaction to American calls for opening was quite extraordinary compared to that of Japan. Korea's faith in Confucian political, economic, and cultural systems made it willing to remain within the suzerainty of China. Tightly controlled by King Gojong's father and the regent Daewongun, Korea resisted Western demands and held fast to its policy of isolationism.[21] The Korean Empire had a chance to learn from Japan's reform efforts but failed to weather the storms of colonialism nonetheless (Huh and Tikhonov, 2005). Table 2.1 spells out the major actors and historic events between the United States and Korea.

KOREA, BETRAYED?

Why is it important for this book to focus on the American betrayal of Korea? A significant time was spent pondering whether the use of the word "betrayal" would be suitable at this point, as it may seem to cast the relationship as an unrequited love affair between unequal partners. However, as this section will demonstrate, the use of the word "betrayal" is no way inappropriate to the task of describing a complete shift from deciding to trade with Corea—which was hailed as an exceptional accomplishment for America in opening the last of the East Asian countries to the outside world—to swapping South Korea for the Philippines. Further, America willfully refused Korean leaders' petitions to trigger the good offices provision of their official treaty in 1882. According to Oxford Languages, the word "betray" means "exposing (one's country, group, or person) to danger by treacherously giving information to an enemy" or according to the Cambridge Dictionary, "often by doing something harmful such as helping their enemies." Literally, this is what the United States did in its secret agreement with Japan in 1905, known as the Taft-Katsura Agreement.

The reason for raising this topic here is not to lay blame but to shed some light on the distinct and contradictory shifts that have occurred in U.S. policy on East Asia, in general, and on Korea, in particular. By so doing, this book substantiates its main argument—that American interactions with Korea have served as the main and enduring factor in bringing about Korea's current situation. Wilz (1985: 244) finds this sense of betrayal by the American government among Korean political leadership: American "geographer Shannon McCune observed in the 1960s that some Korean politicians continue to refer with bitterness to what they perceived to have been an inexcusable lack of American support of Korea in the early years of the twentieth century."

When the United States did nothing to protect Korea from Japanese rule, which was the commitment made by the United States when it signed the treaty with Korea in 1882, did America fail to fulfill the good offices provision? With regards to this question, two issues are often debated: (1) whether the Korean government made a "proper" or "valid" request to the U.S. government to activate and apply "the good offices provision"[22] of the 1882 U.S.-Korea treaty; and (2) whether the U.S. government was aware of the illegalities of the treaties that Korea and Japan had signed leading up to Japan's annexation of Korea.

With regard to the former, some scholars argue that Korea's request for good offices was not proper and valid (Wilz, 1985: 244–247); however, Tyler Dennett and M. Frederick Nelson agree that Korea had approached the U.S. government in a legally correct manner. According to Wilz, Gojong and his associates had made emotional appeals to the U.S. government based on the

Table 2.1 Major Milestones in the History of U.S.-Korea Relations

U.S. History	Relationship	Major History of Korea
1492: Columbus Discovers "The Americas": Lands in the Americas 1630: Massachusetts Bay Colony	No relations	Three Kingdoms: Goguryeo (BC 37–668), Baekje (BC 18–660), Silla (BC 57–935) Goryeo (918–1392) unified Joseon Dynasty (1392–1897) then Korean Empire (1897–1910) with constitution, six ministries, standing army, national civil service exam, *Jikji* iron movable type (1377, before Guttenberg), and Korean alphabet (1444)
1750–1775: Diplomatic Struggles in Colonial Period 1776–1783: Diplomacy and American Republic 1784–1800: Diplomacy of Early Republic 1801–1829: Securing the Republic 1830–1860: Diplomacy and Westward Expansion 1839: First Opium War 1844: U.S.–China Treaty of Wangxia 1854: U.S.–Japan Treaty of Kanagawa 1861–1865: Civil War and International Diplomacy	1776–1865: No relations	Sinocentric worldview and voluntary acceptance of China's suzerainty Korea's strong stance of self-isolationism toward foreign countries other than China and Japan
1866–1898: Continued Expansion of U.S. Interests 1898: Spanish-American War (U.S. Expanding in Asia, Philippines) 1868: Meiji Reformation, Japan 1871–1873: Iwakura Mission (Japan's Learning of the West) State Secretaries: William Seward (1861–1869), Hamilton Fish (1869–1877), Chester Arthur (1881–1885)	U.S. Gunboat Open-Door Policy (aggressive, interested, impatient) vs. Joseon Isolationist Policy (denial of West, disinterest in Western attempts)	1863–1897: King Gojong of Joseon Dynasty, Emperor Gojong (1897–1910) 1864–1898: Daewongun (Father and Regent of King Gojong), Strong Isolationist Policy 1866 (Aug.–Sep.): The General Sherman Incident 1866 (October–December): French expedition (*Byeonginyangyo*) against Korea's Purge of French Missionaries and Korean Catholics 1871 (May–June): Low-Rodgers Expedition, *Shinmiyangyo* (First Korean War vs. US)

Encounter of Isolationist Joseon and Expansionist America

Presidents: Abraham Lincoln (1861–1865), Andrew Johnson (1865–1869), Ulysses S. Grant (1869–1877)	1876: Korea-Japan Treaty 1882: U.S.-Joseon Treaty 1894–1895: Sino-Japanese War (Decline of Chinese Suzerainty) 1895 (Oct. 8): Japan's Assassination of Queen Min of Joseon Dynasty	William Seward vs. Daewongun official intercourse and mutual regime recognition between the United States and Joseon
1899–1913: Defending U.S. International Interests 1894–1895: Sino-Japanese War 1904–1905: Russo-Japanese War 1906–1909: Segregation of Japanese in San Francisco 1906: Nobel Peace Prize for President Roosevelt 1908: Root-Takahira Agreement for Japanese Annexation of Korea *President*: Theodore Roosevelt (1901–1909) *State Secretaries*: John Hay (1898–1905), Elihu Root (1905–1909), Robert Bacon (1909–1912), Willian Taft (War Secretary, 1909–1913)	1902–1903: Anglo-Japanese Alliance 1904: (Jan. 21): Korean Empire Declares Neutrality 1904–1905: Russo-Japanese War 1905: Taft-Katsura Secret Agreement, Japan-Korea Treaty (Protectorate) 1910–1945: Japan's Colonization of Korea 1911: Fall of Qing Dynasty 1919: Korea's Independence Movement and First Korean Congress in Philadelphia 1931: Manchurian Incident	President Roosevelt vacillates from regime recognition to regime desertion and denial of Korea as Japan rises to regional hegemon U.S.-Japan partnership Korea pleads for the United States to intervene against Japanese occupation
1914–1920: WWI and Wilsonian Diplomacy *Woodrow Wilson (1913–1921)* 1921–1936: Interwar Diplomacy 1937–1945: Diplomacy and the Road to WWII 1941 (12/7): Pearl Harbor attack *Franklin D. Roosevelt (1933–1945)*	1943: Cairo Declaration (Nov. 27) 1945: Yalta Summit (Feb. 4–11) and Potsdam Conference (Jul. 17–Aug. 2) 1945: Liberation of Korea from Japan (Aug. 15) 1945: Division of Korea at 38th parallel 1945–1948: U.S. Military Occupation 1949: U.S. Military Forces Withdraw from South Korea	Complete regime disregard No relations, U.S. continuation of disregard for Korea Series of mishaps/failures by the United States on Asia and Korea

(Continued)

Table 2.1 Major Milestones in the History of U.S.-Korea Relations *(Continued)*

U.S. History	Relationship	Major History of Korea
1945–1952: Early Cold War 1945 (Aug. 10): U.S. Divides Korea by 38th Parallel, Authorized by President Truman on Aug. 14 1945 (Aug. 16): U.S. Invites Soviet Union into North Korea Harry Truman (1945–1953)	U.S. reluctant regime recognition of South Korea (1945)	1950–1953: The Korean War 1953: US-ROK Mutual Alliance Treaty
1953–1991: Entrenchment of Bipolar Foreign Policy Dwight Eisenhower (1953–1961), John F. Kennedy (1961–1963)*	U.S. regime recognition of ROK but regime denial of DPRK	1962–1980s: Simultaneous Economic and Democratization (world's 11th largest economy and 6th largest exporter to the United States) Present: DPRK Nuclear and ICBM, and US-ROK alliance in the era of China's challenge against the United States.

* Lyndon Johnson (1963–1969), Richard Nixon (1969–1974), Gerald Ford (1974–1977), Jimmy Carter (197–71981), Ronald Reagan (1981–1989), George H.W. Bush (1989–1993), Bill Clinton (1993–2001), George W. Bush (2001–2009), and Barack Obama (2009–2017).

Source: Created by the author, based on U.S. State Department document, "Milestones in the History of US Foreign Relations," available at https://history.state.gov/milestones/all

1882 U.S.-Korea treaty in the "Far Eastern sense as an elder brother," as mentioned in the previous chapter, asking America "benevolently" to assist. In short, scholars seldom go further than stating that Korea's request for good offices was ineffective. These scholars' claims that Koreans did not understand the legal technicalities, as Wilz (1985: 245) explains, make sense but only if we start splitting hairs.

However, Yi (2016) challenges the legality of the treaties leading up to Japan's annexation of Korea based on his research into the procedures and formalities of the treaties that Japan claims to have ratified with Korea. In general, and in theory, a treaty between two sovereign states involves multiple processes and formalities, ranging from negotiations to final ratification. First, representatives called plenipotentiaries are formally appointed by the heads of the two states. Second, these appointees prepare a proxy statement of the treaty, bearing names, titles, and signs or seals. Third, at the designated location, these representatives enter into negotiations over the proxy statement. Finally, the two heads of state ratify the treaty to put it into effect. These are the procedures and formalities of the treaty-making process under normal circumstances, recognized and enacted by Western countries after the Treaty of Westphalia of 1648 (Yi, 2016: 7). Obvious examples from late nineteenth-century Korea include the Korea–Japan Treaty of Amity, the Ganghwa Treaty (1876), and the Treaty of Peace, Amity, Commerce, and Navigation (1882).

Illegalities of Treaties between Korea and Japan

Japanese efforts to seize Korea started with Japan's war against Russia from 1904 to 1905. By winning this war, Japan gained not only American recognition as a regional power but also access to Korea. In the process, Japan forced Korea to sign four treaties. Soon after Japan assassinated Korean Queen Min on October 8, 1895, the Japanese military withdrew from the Korean palace. King Gojong adopted a series of reforms, and the Joseon dynasty formally became the Korean Empire (Daehan Jeguk, from October 12, 1897, to August 27, 1910). However, those ambitions to strengthen the empire were futile, considering that Japan had fought Russia and won. The incentive for Japan in this war was to achieve a firm hold over the Peninsula by defeating Russian expansionism and forcing Korea to become its protectorate. Japan had stationed its army in the Korean Imperial court and taken steps to sign a series of treaties with Korea under armed threat (Yi, 2016: 12). Under such physical coercion, four treaties were signed: the Japan-Korea Protocol (February 23, 1904); the first Japan-Korea Agreement (August 22, 1904); the second Japan-Korea Agreement, or *Eulsa* Treaty (November 17, 1905); and the Japan-Korea Treaty of 1907 (July 24). The Korean Empire formally fell to Japan on

August 29, 1910, through the Japan-Korea Annexation Treaty. Yi (2016: 12), in explaining the illegality of these treaties based on documentary evidence, concludes that "None of these treaties includes a ratification statement from the Korean Emperor. It is illegal to treat matters relating to national sovereignty in the form of an 'agreement' without a ratification statement from the head of state. Furthermore, the Japanese government frequently forged documents in the process of announcing these forced treaties with Korea to the Western powers."

Controversy: Betrayal or Not

The significant implication of these historical findings is that all of the decisions made between Korea and the United States from the 1882 treaty and up until Japan's annexation in 1905 were heavily influenced by this illegal act of Japan's. Considering the American presence in the Korean Empire,[23] which was proclaimed in 1897, and the closeness of communication between the leaders of the two governments, there is no doubt that the U.S. government knew how the Japanese had secured control over these treaties. Theodore Roosevelt's close relationships with Japanese Prime Minister Katsura and his decision to let his Secretary of War wrap up the secret agreement in 1905 while he met with Syngman Rhee were all based on Japan's bogus treaties with Korea. As a result, the U.S.-Korea treaty of 1882 was essentially nullified when the State Department instructed the minister at Seoul, on November 24, 1905, to close the legation and withdraw from Korea, immediately after Japan forced Korea to become its protectorate. On November 28, 1905, the U.S. legation at Seoul was closed, and all U.S. diplomatic business relating to Korea was subsequently conducted in Tokyo. Finally, the Korean legation in Washington closed on December 28, 1905. Five years later, when Japan annexed Korea on August 29, 1910, the United States ended official relations with Korea (without consulting Korea). Does this answer the question of whether Korea was betrayed?

Nonetheless, it is important to note that Wilz (1985) makes several very controversial observations.[24] First, he notes, "Koreans appeared to have accepted the protocol willingly and without misgiving" (247). In this critically important observation regarding the destiny of the Korean nation, Wilz unreassuringly uses the verb "appeared." Second, Wilz argues that the Korean government "willingly" accepted Japanese demands to surrender sovereignty in its international negotiations with third parties as well as parts of Korean territory, and to accept Japanese intervention in Korean public administrative authority. Immediately after this unfounded criticism of the highly disputed history between Korea and Japan in the early twentieth century, however, Wilz mentions (1985: 247) that U.S. officials were aware that Japan had used heavy military force to ram these treaties through the Korean government:

They knew that contingents of Japanese troops had moved into Korea in recent weeks and, for all practical purposes, were occupying Seoul. In such circumstances, Korea's leaders had been so powerless to turn aside looming menace that they accepted an 'alliance' with Japan and had considerable authority over the government in Tokyo.

It is contradictory to say first that Korea accepted this disdainful and self-defeating treaty "willingly" and then to mention that the United States was aware of Japanese use of force in getting it signed; however, the Korean government had no choice but to accept Japanese demands. The ambiguous meaning and implication of the word "appeared" must be acknowledged in any argument that the Korean government accepted such forceful demands to surrender sovereignty. The U.S. government, according to Wilz (1985), was sympathetic to these Japanese strategies on the Peninsula because the United States was aware of the potential threats that Russia could pose to American interests unless Japan served as a check and balance. More specifically, Wilz (1985) says:

> Those leaders, the President not the least among them, were decidedly sympathetic with Japan in the latter's competition with Russia for supremacy in Northeast Asia. That sympathy was rooted in a variety of considerations. Leaders in Washington, and many other knowledgeable and influential Americans as well, had come to feel profound respect, indeed undisguised admiration, for the ingenuity and industry of the Japanese. They marveled at the way the Japanese had thrown off the restrictions of their feudalist past and projected themselves into the modern world. (247)

It is one thing to marvel at Japan's rise to regional power, but it is quite another to deny that Japan used force to promote its international treaty, which constitutes the last element of the international treaty-making process. Wilz aptly explains the American motivation to fold along the lines of the treaty with Korea in 1882: "While developing respect and admiration for the Japanese, leaders of the United States had concluded that dominance of Korea and Manchuria by Russia would constitute a threat to American interests, mainly commercial, in Northeast Asia" (1985: 247–248).

AMERICA'S STEP BACK FROM SEWARD-SHUFELDT LINE: THEODORE ROOSEVELT

The destiny of modern Korea was deeply shaped by two U.S. presidents, in particular: Theodore Roosevelt and Franklin D. Roosevelt.[25] From distantly related branches of the same family, Theodore Roosevelt was elected in 1901 and ended his second term in 1909, and his fifth cousin Franklin Roosevelt served from 1933 to 1945, which included a third term. These presidents are two of the most respected for the importance of their contributions: Theodore, for America's expansion (both domestically and internationally), and Franklin, for his leadership out of the Great Depression, for ending World War II, and for the United States' rise as a world power. In our exploration of the Roosevelts' political decisions that affected Korea's fate, Theodore Roosevelt's decision to trade Korea in exchange for the Philippines and a better relationship with Japan serves as our foundation. Moreover, it was Franklin Roosevelt following up along the lines of his cousin's decision to desert and betray Korea that ultimately led Korea to be divided, a wound still unhealed after 75 years. Aside from their blood relationship, these presidents shared the same policy toward the Far East. Griswold (1938: 449) observes that "Possibly the most compelling, and certainly the most immediate, reason of all for Franklin Roosevelt's Far Eastern policy was the security of American territorial possessions in the Far East—the selfsame factor that had determined Theodore Roosevelt's policy in 1905 and 1908."

His choice to abandon Corea aimed to maximize U.S. national interests by leaving Corea under Japan's watch, so that the United States could still take advantage of the strategic location of the Peninsula while the traditional suzerain and regional power of China and Russia had been placed in check by his new ally, Japan, the non-white and non-Christian but nonetheless "Yankee" in Asia. For the United States, there was little to lose as long as Washington kept Tokyo as its ally. As emphasized in the Introduction, the SS Line—which Washington wanted to complete by signing a treaty with Corea in order to dominate the Pacific-Asian market—was in fact maintained even through President Theodore Roosevelt's scrapping of the commitment made by State Secretary William Seward and Commodore Robert Shufeldt. The SS Line—starting with the acquisition of Alaska and linkage with the Aleutian and Kuril Islands through treaties with Japan, Corea, Philippines, and the Samoan Islands—remained intact.

The only change from Washington was to sever the relationship with Corea, if there was any. In fact, Washington was more than willing to forsake its treaty with Corea, as discussed in the section above. That decision was a betrayal, for sure, to Corea but just one of many foreign policy decisions to Washington. However, just as the opening of the Pandora's box let loose on world a host of curses and hardships, Washington's policy of turning its back on Korean brought out the century-old problem of the Corean Question. As soon as Japan declared war against the United States on December 7, 1941, however, the SS Line was fundamentally challenged, and Washington had to scrap its policy on Asia again. In this radical turn of Japan from "Asian

Yankee" to principal enemy[26] in World War II, Washington again stuck a knife in Korea by splitting it in two. After 35 years of colonial control under Japan, thanks to Washington's agreement, Korea was divided instead of Japan.

Oliver (1947) heavily criticized President Franklin Roosevelt's decision to divide and rule Korea under superpowers' tutelage so soon after Japan had begun its own U.S.-backed colonization of Korea. And placing it under military occupation of the United States and the U.S.S.R. was critiqued by Oliver, who sees it as an "American sin" toward the Korean nation (1947: 28): "This crime commenced in 1905, when at the conclusion of the Russo-Japanese War, Korea was handed over to Japan, at the treaty conference sponsored by President Theodore Roosevelt in Portsmouth, New Hampshire. It was blackened by a full generation of the foulest kind of individual, political, and economic exploitation of Korea as a slave state by the Japanese." To think that such a highly revered political family of the United States could be responsible for the colonization and 75-year-long division of the nation simply leaves me speechless.

During his first term, President Theodore Roosevelt concentrated his focus mostly on the Caribbean and left the Asian policy to then-secretary of state John Hay (Griswold, 1938: 87). However, when Syngman Rhee arrived in Washington, DC, as leader of the independence movement against Japanese colonial control on December 31, 1904, his goal of appealing to the U.S. government to trigger the "good offices" of their 1882 treaty was of no use. A meeting had already been arranged by the former minister resident and consul general of U.S. Legate in Korea (1887–1890), Hugh A. Dinsmore, between Rhee and then-secretary of state John Hay on February 20, 1905. At that meeting, Rhee had asked Hay to exercise the good offices provision of the treaty that they both had signed in 1882, as that measure alone could protect Korea from imperial Japan. Surprisingly, Hay responded very positively, explaining that "whenever the opportunity presented itself, he would do everything possible to fulfill his government's treaty obligations to Korea" (Wilz, 1985: 251). More specifically, Rhee spoke with President Theodore Roosevelt on August 4, 1905, in the president's New York summer home, asking him to invoke the good offices provision of the 1882 treaty and block Japan's maneuver to acquire Korea. President Roosevelt gave two responses: first, that he would consider Rhee's request, which he had already committed not to do from the start, but second, that the Korean government should present an official petition.

Considering the scholarly research and documents examined above, it is undeniable that President Roosevelt arbitrarily gave Korea as a trophy to the victor of the Russo-Japanese War while also elevating his own international status as a Nobel Peace Prize winner by supervising the Treaty of Portsmouth and serving as a powerful arbitrator in Asia. However, his act in this moment represents an undeniable breach of America's official treaty with Korea, whereby the United States was obligated to, at least, raise the issue with Japan. Notably, this treaty proscribed that "If other powers deal unjustly or oppressively with either government, the other will exert their good offices, on being informed of the case, to bring about an amicable arrangement, thus showing their friendly feelings" (Oliver, 1944: 17). Ultimately, Oliver (1944: 17) concludes that President Roosevelt made an arbitrary trade of Korea to Japan "as a means of settling the Russo-Japanese War in 1905. The United States," he goes on to say, "in supervising the Treaty of Portsmouth, gave its blessing to that award—despite the treaty of mutual assistance we had signed with Korea when we opened its 'closed doors' in 1882."

Despite the rational choice of such a trade, considering that the balance of power would be favorable to the United States in the Far East based on pro-Japanese sentiment, Chay (1982) agrees that President Roosevelt could not possibly have acted otherwise for the Koreans in 1905. However, Chay (1982: 29) argues that President Roosevelt "should and could have listened to Korean complaints about the Japanese and could have made a formal offer of good offices for the Koreans." In addition, Japan violated its own pledges of non-aggression against Korea and commitment to the independence of Korea, which were included in the Treaty of Shimonoseki signed with China in 1895 after the Sino-Japanese War. Specifically, it said, "The two High Contracting Parties [China and Japan] hereby recognize and confirm the complete independence of Korea" (Oliver, 1944: 17). It was not only with China but also in Japan's agreements with Russia, Great Britain, and Korea. Oliver (1944: 17–18) writes:

> In its agreement of 1898 with Russia, Japan approved this opening clause: "Russia and Japan hereby confirm the recognition of Korea's sovereign rights and her complete independence." In the treaty of alliance with Great Britain, Japan stated: "The High Contracting Parties, having mutually recognized the independence of China and Korea, declare themselves to be entirely uninfluenced by an aggressive tendency in either country." In 1904, Japan concluded a Treaty of Defensive and Offensive Alliance with Korea, a document expressly designed to "confirm and uphold the independence of Korea." And in the same year the Emperor of Japan stated in an Imperial Edict: "The independence of Korea is our Empire's real and unfaltering aim and necessity." (Oliver, 1944: 17–18)

These seemingly positive responses from the President and the Secretary of State, however, turned out to be deceitful, since President Theodore Roosevelt had already sent his War Secretary, William Taft, to Tokyo on

July 24, 1905, and authorized him to consent to Japanese Prime Minister Katsura's plan for trading spheres of influence, giving Korea to Japan while the Philippines would fall to the United States. Wilz confirms:

> Roosevelt, only a few days before his meeting with Rhee and Rhee's companion, had given his imprimatur to the proposition that Japan should assume absolute control of the hermit kingdom. He had given his imprimatur when he consented to a secret memorandum drawn up after a conversation in Tokyo in late July 1905 between U.S. Secretary of War William Howard Taft, who was en route to the Philippines, and Japanese prime minister Count Taro Katsura. (Wilz, 1985: 251–252)

In the so-called Taft-Katsura memorandum, the Secretary of War acquiesced in Katsura's outrageous assertion that Korea was to blame for the Russo-Japanese War and that in the interest of peace as well as the security of the Japanese archipelago it was essential that Japan "take some definite step with a view to precluding the possibility of Korea falling back into her former condition and of placing us [Japan] again under the necessity of entering upon another foreign war." Taft thereupon expressed the view that

> the establishment by Japanese troops of a suzerainty over Korea to the extent of requiring that Korea enter into no foreign treaties without the consent of Japan was the logical result of the present war and would directly contribute to permanent peace in the East. The Secretary, in a word, offered unsolicited advice on how Japan might affect the demise of the nation-state whose independence the United States had pledged to support by diplomatic initiative—in the event it was asked to make such an initiative—in the treaty of 1882 [with Korea]. (Wilz, 1985: 252; Griswold, 1938)

Evidence of collusion between the United States and Japan abounds. In "Taft's Telegram to Root, July 29, 1905" by John Gilbert Reid in 1940, President Roosevelt had already confirmed his strong intent not to exert any influence for the plight of the Koreans. According to this telegram, President Roosevelt had already informally advised the Japanese—several months before Taft and Katsura conversed—that he favored Japanese control of Korea. In an interview at the White House, apparently at the end of January 1905, he told the news correspondent Richard Barry that "Japan must hold Port Arthur, and she must hold Korea." President Roosevelt asked Barry to communicate the substance of his remarks to George Kennan, a lecturer and author who was in Tokyo at the time. Kennan in turn was to (and did) pass the views of Roosevelt to "a few men of influence in Japan" (Wilz, 1985: 252; Griswold, 1938: 125).

Like Theodore Roosevelt's public stance against Korea, his personal view of Korea was also clear. This mostly stemmed from his admiration for and fear of Japan. Thus, his disregard for these two Asian countries shaped America's twentieth-century Asian policy. In fact, President Theodore Roosevelt clearly revealed his personal thoughts on why he gave up Korea in favor of Japan, saying:

> [Japan] does not need money. You talk about collecting indemnity. Instead, take Sakhalin, Manchurian railway, Port Arthur, and the coalmine at Lushun. Sooner or later, it will be better for Japan to take Korea. It will be good for the Koreans and Asia. I don't think Japan should take Korea right away, but sooner or later it will be better for [Japan] to take her. (Krishnan, 1984: 5)

President Theodore Roosevelt, by ordering American ministers in Korea to "pack and come home because the annexation of Korea by Japan will be good for Korea as well as Japan" negated America's promise in 1882 of the good offices provision. This bluntly Korea-bashing statement is quoted in confidential documents in Japan's Ministry of Foreign Affairs, which include conversations between Roosevelt and Japanese ambassador Kaneko Kentaro during the Japanese-Russian peace negotiations to settle the Russo-Japanese War.

Hulbert (1906) summarizes this, saying, "we deserted her [Korea] with such celerity, such cold-heartedness and such a refinement of contempt that the blood of every decent American citizen in Korea boiled with indignation. How can we, the American people, prove to the Koreans that we were not accessory to this act, which was so contrary to the principle we have professed to hold?" (426, requoted by Krishnan, 1984: 6).

President Theodore Roosevelt in many instances described Korea as contemptible, weak, and unfit to govern itself. Moreover, he acquiesced to having Chinese suzerainty replaced by Japanese suzerainty. With his keen sense of rising Japanese power and potential threat—not just to America's Far East policy but also to American domestic politics—he had no reservations about forsaking Korea's independence in exchange for peace for America and control of Japan. More specific documents reveal how Roosevelt felt about Korea at that time. Apparently unmoved by obligations that the United States had assumed in the Treaty of Chemulpo, Roosevelt in 1900—a year before he moved into the White House—wrote his German friend Hermann Speck von Sternberg: "I should like to see Japan have Korea. She will be a check upon Russia, and she deserves it for what she has done" (Wilz, 1985: 248). In regard to President Roosevelt's perception of Korea, Wilz says, "Like most other Americans who thought themselves knowledgeable about affairs in the Great East, the president viewed Korea, presided over as it was by a corrupt and hopelessly inept monarchy, as incapable of managing its own affairs. Foreign tutelage of the country was therefore essential" (Wilz 1985: 248).

Wilz's (1985) study entitled "Did the United States Betray Korea in 1905" aptly and unerringly concludes that such accusations of betrayal are more than in order. In the early twentieth century when Japan made clear its intent to occupy Korea, many Korean patriots viewed the United States as a special benefactor or elder brother—a grave misperception. Wilz (1985: 244) attributes such emotional attachment to Korea's long tradition of Confucianism, whose system of ethics suggests that an elder brother must protect his younger brother. In fact, Korean Emperor Gojong believed "(tragically, as it turned out) that Americans were committed to his nation's best interests: independence and protection against Japan and China" (LaFeber, 1997: 47). Gojong, in a conversation with American minister Horace Allen, expressed wishful thinking that the United States would rescue them from Japanese annexation on February 20, 1904:

> shortly after the outbreak of hostilities between Japan and Russia, the distraught emperor told Allen that he was most anxious to secure the assistance of the United States. Fully conscious of the current orientation of the Washington government, the minister avoided the slightest hint of an American diplomatic initiative on behalf of Kojong's ragtag empire. (Wilz, 1985: 249)

In the end, Minister Horace Newton Allen[27] told "Washington that since 'These people [Koreans] cannot govern themselves,' a civilized race like Japan should take over 'these kindly Asiatics for the good of the people and . . . the establishment of order and the development of commerce.'" Of course, Allen was confident Japan would keep Korea "open" to all for "development of commerce" (LaFeber, 1997: 78). He also expressed his honest thoughts on Korea in his letter to his colleague William Rockhill on January 4, 1904, that "Korea should belong to Japan by right of ancient conquest and tradition. I think our Government will make a mistake if it tries to have Japan simply continue this fiction of independence," while he acknowledged that he was "no pro-Japanese enthusiast" (Griswold, 1938: 96–97). Rockhill agreed with him; he thought the annexation of Korea to be "absolutely indicated as the one great and final step westward of the Japanese Empire" and that "it would be better for the Korean people and also for the peace in the Far East when it finally happened" (Griswold, 1938: 97).

Emperor Gojong had also consistently beseeched the U.S. government to protect Korea from Japan. Following up with Emperor Gojong's pleas to the U.S. government, Korean minister in Washington, Chyo Min Hui, had a chance to speak with U.S. State Secretary John Hay. He had been promised an opportunity to speak with President Roosevelt but was given none.

Theodore and Racism

As discussed in his correspondence with friends and other documents, President Theodore Roosevelt's views of both Korea and Japan reveal telltale signs of racist perspectives. While he praises Japan as a non-white and non-Christian Yankee, he does not hesitate to say that Japan should have the more barbarian, uncivilized, and primitive Korea. His comments praising Japan also express his view of Japan as unequal to America or the West in its skin and race as non-Christian. However, Japan was the Asian nation that he thought worthy of American partnership. The racism of President Roosevelt toward Asia was a natural byproduct of his expansionist policy, whereby the United States was following other Western powers' imperialist pursuits of colonies in Asia and Africa. Tikhonov (2012: 31–32) describes the inseparable and innate connection between capitalist expansion and the surface of racism as follows:

> As Immanuel Wallerstein formulated, one of the ideological contradictions of capitalism is that between the supposedly meritocratic nature of the profit system and essentially hereditary belonging to the hierarchically ranged zones of the world economy. The outcome of such a contradiction is the ideology of racism, which legitimizes inequalities in opportunities, power, and wealth on the basis of "hereditary inferiority" of the peripheral Others and denies them any opportunity for social mobility. . . . Racism frequently surfaces when it is needed for certain clear-cut political purposes—such as legitimization of colonial expansion and the extraction of wealth from the colonies, or in cases of intensified interstate rivalry inside the capitalist core—and recedes from the foreground when no longer needed.

Among many aspects of his background, we can conjecture about Theodore's strong racist orientation[28]; however, Professor John Burgess of Columbia Law School seemed to assess Theodore's racist view of the world decisively. According to James Bradley (2009a: 47), Teddy's favorite class, during his Columbia Law school days, was Professor Burgess's political science course. Despite Professor Burgess' fundamental academic contributions to the establishment of modern social science as well as political science, his political worldview was clearly racist. Burgess taught that "the United States Constitution . . . was the modern expression of Anglo-Saxon-Teutonic political genius—a genius which had originated in the black forests of Germany, spread through England and North America and expressed itself in the Magna Carta, the Glorious Revolution and the American Revolution" (Bradley, 2009a: 48).

Thomas Dyer's *Theodore Roosevelt and the Idea of Race* reveals President Roosevelt's undeniably racist way of thinking that world's historical development is essentially based on the superiority of white leadership and intelligence. Dyer writes:

> [Theodore Roosevelt] viewed the entire breadth of the American past through a racial lens. With constant, almost compulsive attention to underlying racial themes, he researched, analyzed, and synthesized the raw materials of history. The force of race in history occupied a singularly important place in Roosevelt's broad intellectual outlook. In fact, race provided him with a window on the past through which he could examine the grand principles of historical development. None of human history really meant much, Roosevelt believed, if racial history were not thoroughly understood first. (Bradley, 2009a: 48)

It is evident that the Western imperialist expansions in the nineteenth century were based on the concept of survival of the fittest, generally misattributed to Charles Darwin and then misapplied as "social Darwinism" in Western imperial policies. In fact, Darwin "did not believe the races to be separate species, understood the 'inferiority of the savages' as a secondary and fully corrigible quality, and regarded their inventive and intellectual powers as basically follies equal to those of 'civilized nations'" (Tikhonov, 2012: 33). Here, the difference needs to be noted between racialism, which is a theory that race determines human traits and capacities and a race-based classificatory scheme applied to the whole of humanity, and racism, which puts some races in a position over others. Teddy Roosevelt's choice to take Japan as the best lower race in Asia for America's Asian policy and to surrender America's initial choice of Korea as its partner was thought to be inevitable in his ambition to make the place of the United States competitive among early Western imperialist countries. Even in the twenty-first century, it is unclear whether America's racist view of nations in Asia and other non-Western countries has ever ceased functioning as Tikhonov (2012: 33) observed—namely, that "It was not easy to combine ardent belief in progress with the conviction that a large part of humanity is genetically blocked from achieving it, although it was equally difficult to abstain from the temptation of ascribing some 'failures of evolution' to certain 'inherited racial qualities.'"

Theodore Revisited

President Theodore Roosevelt's perspective merits special attention here as the most critical factor in U.S. policy toward East Asia, especially on Korea and Japan, in the early twentieth century, particularly because his understanding of American interests in Asia shaped twentieth-century American involvement in the region. Certainly, the strategic importance of Japan served as a basic tenet of his administration; however, it was arguably America's choice of a strategic partnership with Japan that pulled the United States into war with Japan in 1941. "Griswold argues that the President's fear of Japan and, consequently, his uneasiness over the safety of the Philippines grew so intense during the Russo-Japanese War that he first traded Korea for a guarantee of the Philippines in the Taft-Katsura conversation of July, 1905 and finally, in the Root-Takahira agreement of November, 1908, gave Japan a 'free hand' in Manchuria in return for a second guarantee of the Philippines and a promise of co-operation in immigration restriction" (Neu, 1966: 434; Griwold, 1938: 128–130). Griswold adds, on the importance of this second agreement between the United States and Japan, that it "firmly resolved reciprocally to respect the territorial possessions belonging to each other" (Griswold, 1938: 129).

In fact, the power dynamics in East Asia dramatically changed after the successful outcomes of the Meiji Reformation in 1868. In less than 40 years after its modernization policy, Japan was able to vie with Western superpowers. Japan's victory against Russia transformed the power balance in Western competitions in Asia in general as well as in the region, obliterating Russian sea power, driving Russia out of Korea, and securing a stronghold in Manchuria (Griswold, 1938: 121). However, President Roosevelt quickly praised Japan's victory in evicting Russian tyranny from the Far East but was no less quick to perceive in victorious Japan a menace to the Philippines. He in fact feared the complete collapse of Russia and attempted to reestablish the balance of power between Russia and Japan, and thereby prevent further territorial expansion by Japan (Griswold, 1938: 104–105). In fact, President Theodore Roosevelt "sent his directions in code to General Wood, commanding American troops in the Philippines, for defending the islands from a momentarily expected Japanese attack" on July 6, 1907 (Griswold, 1938: 126).

Overall, Roosevelt's policy on Far East was zigzagging from its strong conviction of regional importance to the United States to ceding it to Japan as Washington's Asia regent. Did he have full trust in Japan? Neu (1966) observes otherwise. According to Neu (1966: 437), President Roosevelt was aware of "the danger that Japan would grow too strong, particularly as one Japanese victory followed another in the Russo-Japanese War." However, he knew Russia's Southward expansionism had posed existential threats to Japan and chose to adopt a policy of playing Japan against Russia so that Washington killed two birds with a stone: supporting Japan so that the United States would not have to shed blood in deterrence of Russia. Neu (1966: 437) confirms that: "Roosevelt felt that Japan was 'playing our game' in the Far East, and he looked increasingly to Japan not only to contain Russian imperialism but also to stabilize the Far East and lead China into the circle of 'great civilized powers'" (Neu, 1966: 437). Cautiously and skillfully, however, he did not want Japan too dominant for the United States to deal with in Asia, so he "risked his own personal prestige to end the war [Russo-Japanese War, 1904–1905] and maintain a balance of antagonism in the Far East." However, his naïve wish that "Japan would exercise its power with responsibility and restraint" (Neu, 1966: 435–437) turned out to be disastrously wrong later in the twentieth century.

Theodore Roosevelt was inconsistent and, at times, contradictory in his views and policies on the Far East, LaFeber (1997: 80) explains neatly: "How to avoid the "struggle" haunted Roosevelt during the next four years of his presidency. He failed to find an answer, other than retreating from Asia and leaving it to the Japanese. Not wanting either the "despicable" Russians or the Japanese with their "big head" to triumph, TR hoped "that the two powers will fight until both are fairly well exhausted." The peace terms would then "not mean the creation of either a yellow peril or a Slav peril." For the United States, Japan was simply a timely and convenient player, which was a beginning of the disaster for Korea and the "Corean Question."

CONCLUSION

In light of all the evidence considered, it is no surprise that such Korea bashing or pretermitting attitudes, when combined with a series of mishaps and blunders, led to the outbreak of the Korean War. This book finds that every condition for the first war of the Cold War period was met: the American view of Korea, the foolish invitation of Communist forces to the Peninsula, the 1949 withdrawal of American occupation, and Secretary of State Acheson's inadvertent signal for Stalin, Mao, and Kim Il-sung to start the war in June 1950. The outcomes of the "second" Korean War (i.e., the better-known war of 1950–1953) have been threefold: (1) South Korea survived to become one of the world's top economic powers with substantive democracy; (2) North Korea remained isolationist and has not changed its antagonistic policy toward the United States; and (3) competition among the superpowers still revolves around the Peninsula. The ultimate question is whether, since the war has not yet completed its "due course," the United States and North Korea amid heated exchanges of text with overtures of fury and romance between President Trump and North Korea's Kim will spark another war or finally achieve peaceful resolution. The key to this issue is China—the main enemy of the United States and one of the three signatories to the Ceasefire in 1953, which has not changed for the last 67 years. From this perspective, the current power struggles between the United States and China arose from unresolved aspects of the Korean War.

If the arguments between the United States, China, North Korea, and South Korea over the end of the Korean War—or the insults between President

Trump and Chairman Kim Jong-un in 2018—are any indication, the Cold War clearly is not yet done. Rather, the stark contrast between South Korea's vibrant democracy and global economic power on the one hand and North Korea's failing economy and isolated society on the other suggests that Fukuyama's diagnosis was premature. History did not end with the Soviet Union's collapse in 1991; China has continued to challenge U.S. hegemony not only in the South China Sea but worldwide, and Russia has been clear in its ambition to regain its Cold War influence. In this new phase of unfinished Cold War rivalry, three main issues have taken center stage in international politics—the Korean War, the divided Peninsula, and nuclear negotiations.

As a result of the two Korean Wars, the southern half of the Peninsula has risen from the ashes while the North has remained underdeveloped, isolated, and at odds with the United States. By this point, we can start to assess more fully whether Diamond's questions and argument apply to the two Koreas: "Why did history unfold differently on different continents?" and "Why were those societies the ones that became disproportionately powerful and innovative?" Is the case as Diamond (1997: 10) finds—that the "history of interaction among disparate peoples" is "what shaped the modern world through conquest, epidemics, and genocide?" Indeed, his conclusion seems applicable to North Korea still: "Those collisions created reverberations that have still not died down after many centuries, and that are actively continuing in some of the world's most troubled areas today" (1997: 10).

NOTES

1. Just 100 years after the United States gained independence.

2. Allison Graham's 2017 work conceptualizes the danger of large-scale wars when a rising power challenges the existing hegemon as a "Thucydides Trap," and applies it to the current stalemate and collision course that has formed between the United States and China. China's "One Belt One Road" initiative has directly created visible conflicts with American unilateral hegemony in the early twenty-first century, as witnessed in their military standoff in the South China Sea and the trade war that has been brewing since the inauguration of Trump.

3. Grant, Ulysses S., Third Annual Message to Congress, December 4, 1871, http://millercenter.org/scripps/ archive/speeches/detail/3742, requoted in Murray, 2011: 63. In his annual message to Congress on December 4, 1871, President Ulysses S. Grant fully backed the Low-Rodgers mission and asked Congress to consider further action against Korea, perhaps even war. Congress did not act, and Korea gradually faded from national attention (Chang, 2003: 1359). Also, see Kang (2005: 11–12) on Secretary Seward's reaction to the General Sherman Incident.

4. According to Kang (2005: 2), in a crew of about 24, there were only three American and two British members, and the rest were Malaysian and Chinese.

5. Ibid.

6. Before the modern era, "Corea" was used among Westerners to mean the Joseon dynasty (1392–1910), in particular, and Korea, more broadly. "Corea" is the Romanized spelling and pronunciation of the Goguryeo Kingdom (37–668 BC) during the Three Kingdoms periods: the Silla Kingdom (57–935 BC) and the Baekje Kingdom (18–660 BC). Two eras come later: the Goryeo Kingdom (918–1392) and the Joseon Dynasty (1392–1910, including the Great Han Empire (1897–1910). Regarding the origin of this spelling, Savage-Landor (1895: 22) used it in his seminal book, *Corea or Cho-sen* [Joseon] – *The Land of the Morning Calm* (1895): "The real native name now used is Cho-sen [Joseon], though occasionally in the vernacular the kingdom goes by the name Gori, or antiquated Korai. Here 'Gori' or 'Korai' means Goguryeo Kingdom." He continues: "There is no doubt that the origin of the word Corea is Korai, which is an abbreviation of Ko-Korai, a small kingdom in the mountains of Fuyu, a little further north, whence the brave and warlike people probably descended, who conquered old Cho-sen." In general, this book uses "Corea" when conveying foreigners' perspectives, and "Joseon" or "Korea" when referring to the nation before its division by the United States and the U.S.S.R. in 1945.

7. It is also known as the "Eulsa Treaty," "Eulsa Unwilling Treaty," and "Japan–Korea Protectorate Treaty." Here, Eulsa in Korean means "Year of the Blue Snake" in the Chinese zodiac. This treaty was forced on Korea when Japan declared the Joseon Empire a protectorate of Japan in 1905.

8. Inserted by the author.

9. As mentioned earlier, Joseon's attitude and policy on Christianity were not oppressive at first. In fact, Daewongun was more receptive, but complex power dynamics around the Korean Peninsula at that time triggered an unexpected turn against French Catholic leaders. See, for example, Swartout, Jr. (1974, 93–94): "The immediate cause of the persecutions of 1866 was the appearance of the Russians along the northern Korean border. To counter this new threat, two Catholics, Nam Chong-sam and Hong Pong-ju, proposed to the Daewongun that Korea form an alliance with France and England. The French priests then in Korea, it was thought, could be used as contacts. The Daewongun was at first interested, but the Frenchmen showed little enthusiasm. Later the idea was dropped when the Russian threat seemed to diminish, and it was realized that such an alliance might make China suspicious. In the meantime, the Catholics, against the wishes of the Daewon-gun, made public the news of these events. It began to appear that the Catholics had unusual influence around the throne; and the existence of the foreign missionaries became known by those in government. Soon, increasing pressure was put on the Daewon-gun from the anti-Christian elements in the government to sanction the arrest and trial of missionaries and heretics. Thus the Daewongun had to take a very strong stand against the religion of his friends and his son's nurse, when until that time he had appeared indifferent."

10. "Byeonginyangyo" literally means "Western disturbance in the year of 1866." "Byeongin" is the Korean pronunciation of the Chinese zodiac year of 1866; "yang" means "Western," and "yo" means "disturbance."

11. Also, refer to Kang (2005: 16–19) on Ernst Oppert.

12. *Source: The North-China Herald,* July 11, 1868.
13. The nephew of then Secretary of State William Seward.
14. Mr. Williams to Mr. Seward, No. 19. Legation of the United States, Peking, August 1, 1868. https://history.state.gov/historicaldocuments/frus1868p1/d279
15. Approximately two months after the General Sherman Incident, after a brief survey of the islands in the West Sea, the French Admiral Roze ordered an expedition to avenge Daewongun's brutal purge of missionaries. On October 15, 1866, the French expedition of seven navy ships with a landing force of 600 men began to blockade the Han River by attacking and occupying Ganghwa Island, but when attempts to quell the local populace failed, the French naval forces had no choice but to retreat.
16. Based on U.S. State Department document, "Milestones in the History of U.S. Foreign Relations," available at https://history.state.gov/milestones/all. The history of U.S. foreign relations is broken down as follows:
    1. 1750–1775: Diplomatic Struggles in the Colonial Period
    2. 1776–1783: Diplomacy and the American Republic
    3. 1784–1800: The Diplomacy of the Early Republic
    4. 1801–1829: Securing the Republic
    5. 1830–1860: Diplomacy and Westward Expansion
    6. 1861–1865: The Civil War and International Diplomacy
    7. 1866–1898: The Continued Expansion of U.S. Interests
    8. 1899–1913: Defending U.S. International Interests
    9. 1914–1920: World War I and Wilsonian Diplomacy
    10. 1921–1936: Interwar Diplomacy
    11. 1937–1945: Diplomacy and the Road to Another War
    12. 1945–1952: The Early Cold War
    13. 1953–1960: Entrenchment of a Bipolar Foreign Policy
17. In 1653, Hamel, a Dutch bookkeeper in the East Indies, was aboard *The Sparrowhawk (De Sperwer)* to Japan when he and 35 other crew members were shipwrecked on Jeju Island, south of the Korean Peninsula. During their stay, due to the Joseon's policy of not releasing foreign shipwrecked crews, they were given relative freedom to live normal lives but were not allowed to leave. After spending 13 years in the capital city of Hanyang during the reign of Hyojong (1649–1659), Hamel and 7 other crew members finally escaped from Korea. In Nagasaki, Japan, he wrote a first-hand description of Joseon, reporting that King Hyojong had said to Hamel and his crew that "it was not his way to send strangers away from his land, and that we would have to live there to the end of our days but that he would take care of our support" (Hamel, 2011: 14).
18. It has been heavily criticized as flunkeyism.
19. Heungseon was a title given to Daewongun to honor his contribution to the Joseon's reform policy.
20. The Iwakura Mission followed several such missions that had been sent by the Shogunate, including the Japanese Embassy to the United States in 1860, the First Japanese Embassy to Europe in 1862, and the Second Japanese Embassy to Europe in 1863.

21. Also, we need to recall that America made exceptional, and very persistent, efforts to open Corea, while other European powers had taken little interest in the dynasty. Han (1971: 368) points out that "all of the powers had more important preoccupations elsewhere—Britain in India, Russia, in the Kurile Islands north of Japan, France in Indochina, and the United States with the aftermath of the great Civil War."

22. "If other Powers deal unjustly or oppressively with either Government, the other will exert their good offices, on being informed of the case, to bring about an amicable arrangement, thus showing their friendly feelings" (U.S. Dept. of State, Treaties and Other International Agreements of the U.S.A, 1776–1949, requoted in Wilz, 1985: 244).

23. King Gojong promulgated the "Great Korean Empire" officially terminating the Joseon Dynasty, and declared the new beginning of Gwangmu (Hangul: 광무, Hanja: 光武), which means "warrior of light." Japan was behind this abrupt ending of the Joseon Dynasty. To deter Russian influence and to facilitate its ambition to annex Corea, Japan brutally assassinated Queen Min, leader of pro-Russian reform faction in the court. King Gojong and his son, the Crown Prince, fled to the Russian legation in 1896. Japan's rising influence was a direct outcome of its victory over China in the Sino-Japanese War from 1894 to 1895, which severed Corea from China's suzerainty. King Gojong, after returning from the Russian legation to Gyeonggungung, implemented a new modernization policy and teamed up with new reformist leaders to revamp the ancient regime of the Joseon Dynasty. Reflecting such an ambitious reform policy, and pressured by foreign powers as well as the Independent Association, King Gojong was inaugurated as first emperor of the Great Korean Empire.

24. Born in Fairfield, Illinois in 1930, Dr. John Edward Wilz worked as a lecturer of history at Indiana University from 1958 to 1991. He attended Marquette University in Milwaukee from 1948 to 1950, spent 1950–1951 at the University of Kentucky at Lexington, served in the Army in Korea from 1951 to 1953, and returned to Kentucky for his bachelor's, master's, and doctorate degrees in 1954, 1955, and 1959, respectively. From http://webapp1.dlib. indiana.edu/bfc/view?docId=B10-1996

25. It wasn't just two presidents but also the daughter of Elliott B. Roosevelt and the wife of Franklin D. Roosevelt, Anna Eleanor Roosevelt, who played a role in this family's political fame. In this light, it seems ironic that such devastation to the Korean nation was made possible by one of the most highly revered political families in the United States.

26. LaFeber (1997:65) writes that in the context of Japan's one-sided decision to invade Manchuria after colonizing Corea, Washington began to see a potential war with Japan coming. "By 1912, Japan had sealed off Korea and much of South Manchuria while angry Washington officials vowed to pry open those closed doors. Each began to see the other as a probable enemy in a not-distant war. And for the first time in any significant fashion, questions about the all-important arena of China divided, rather than united, Americans and Japanese" (LaFeber, 1997:65).

27. He is still well known as a good American who established the first modern hospital in Korea and acted as an advocate of the Korean Empire in the late nineteenth and early twentieth centuries in Korea. He arrived as a missionary of America's

Presbyterian church in 1884. It is ironic that even one of the most respected Americans at that time, who in fact did contribute to modernization of hospitals and education, failed to empathize with Korea, arguing for Japanese annexation of Korea as the right path.

28. One source on Theodore Roosevelt's racist orientation is from LaFeber (1997:79–80) "Although heavily racist, and believing that race was a primary determinant in history, TR [Theodore Roosevelt] had little belief in social Darwinism. . . . He preferred Lamarckianism, with its suggestion that superior races could improve the characteristics of the inferior. . . . Certainly Roosevelt considered it unimportant that the "Japanese are of an utterly different race from ourselves and . . . the Russians are of the same race." As he had earlier noted, Russians posed a "more serious problem" to future Americans than did even Germany, while "Russians and Americans . . . have nothing whatsoever in common."

Chapter 3

The Two Korean Wars

Considering the tumultuous record of U.S. relations with Korea, as previous chapters have shown, who could imagine that Korea would become the world's third-largest venue for U.S. military[1] and personnel? America's massive $10.8B garrison in Pyeongtaek—its largest base overseas—after more than a decade of expansion, was completed in 2020. Situated about 45 miles south of the joint command's former headquarters in Seoul, it is expected by 2022 to house nearly 45,000 troops and contractors, with their families, representing the largest peacetime relocation in the history of the Department of Defense.

From a certain perspective, however, such a huge presence of U.S. military forces in South Korea seems ironic after a long history of American vacillation starting with its aggressive attempt to open and leading to abandonment, ignorance, and betrayal. As examined in previous chapters, Korea refused any American presence at first. Then, as a result of America's tacitly agreeing to Japanese control of Korea, Korea was colonized in 1910 and divided in 1945. Decisively, withdrawing American troops in 1949 and its defensive perimeter in 1950 from the Korean Peninsula inadvertently opened the way for the Korean War.

Compared to that history of vacillation, the current scale of American military stationed in Korea demonstrates very opposite outcomes of the vacillating and faithless encounters till the Korean War. General Brooks called such American presence in Pyeongtaek base a "significant investment in the long-term presence of U.S. Forces in Korea," and "living proof of the American commitment to the alliance." According to a Pew survey, also, South Korea is among the world's most pro-American countries, with 75% of Koreans holding a favorable view of the United States in 2017, even though only 17% held a favorable view of President Trump.[2]

It is also surprising to learn how the costs of U.S. military stationing have been supported by South Korea, which also exemplifies epochally transformed reciprocity of allowing American military presence and sharing its cost. It cannot be denied that the encounter resulted in success, even though Korea's contribution to the total cost is just one half. In the fourth round of negotiations over military defense cost-sharing, President Trump demanded that South Korea pay about $5B, roughly five times the current amount, as Hoff (2017) indicates in "Host Nation Cost-Sharing for U.S. Military Bases," which illustrates South Korea's burden sharing contributions compared to Germany and Japan.

Hoff (2017) also tells two contrasting stories in "Funding for U.S. military presence in Korea" from 2008 to 2021. First, it shows that the United States has great interest in the defense of South Korea. Beyond a doubt, our current era represents the high point in America's commitment to the Peninsula. Once the number of U.S. military personnel approached 60,000, a sea change from America's role as antagonist in the past, which included incessant attempts to open Korea, America's first invasion of Korea in the late nineteenth century, and America's division of Korea in 1945, became evident. Second, despite America's dominant contribution to the sharing of costs for U.S. military presence in Korea, Korea's contribution represents a substantial portion of the total, especially considering that Korea was utterly devastated by the Korean War and only began modernization and industrialization in the 1960s.[3]

This is the story of an amazing transformation in the history of U.S.-Korea encounters that emerged from a relationship in which one country crossed the globe to provoke a war, forced a treaty, then secretly scrapped it and pulled away for about a century, only to reluctantly reunite in a manner that caused complete devastation to the Korean nation, though half was resuscitated to spectacular effect in the end. Can any precedent be found in the history of America's foreign involvement where persistent pursuit of a relationship was followed by such abrupt desertion of that commitment? And is there any precedent of such a relationship's being resuscitated with such great success? Isolationist Korea had just become an empire when it was suddenly assailed by violent calls from the West to open, which it did, only to be deserted, then resuscitated and halved. It almost sounds like a poorly rehearsed magic trick gone wrong. So, what does it mean that the North was the site of America's first attempts to coerce the Korean nation into treaties and trade, and that it may also be the site of America's last attempts to conduct intercourse with Korea?

Diamond's (1997) arguments, though cited widely, need to be cited again as they apply to Korea's encounter with America—specifically, though, in terms of how this relationship started, advanced through various stages of intimacy, and eventually led to two seemingly opposite outcomes. After asking why history unfolded differently on different continents and why certain societies became disproportionately powerful and innovative (9–10), Diamond (1997: 16) answers that the inconsistency of development throughout the modern world resulted from interactions among disparate peoples, and "those collisions are still reverberating after many centuries in some of the world's most troubled areas today." This chapter repurposes Diamond's thesis, respectfully reiterating it as follows: Korea's 75-year-old division, with such stark North-South contrast, was shaped and caused by interactions between Americans and Koreans in the late nineteenth century as well as America's contrastingly different relationships with the North and South, through confrontations, wars, and engagements.

Since the General Sherman Incident in 1866, encounters between Korea and the United States have released tremors that still resonate throughout the fractured Peninsula. No other nation compares with South Korea as a staunch ally and North Korea as a fierce enemy—one of "the world's most troubled areas today": a divided nation whose parts hold exactly the opposite positions regarding the United States. The two examples above offer evidence of how interactions between Korea and the United States about 150 years ago contributed to what South Korea is today. Moreover, in the introduction, we investigated how the interactions have generated problems not just between the United States and North Korea but for other stakeholders in regional and global security as well.

Based on this historical reality, this chapter first explores how the two Korean wars—first the *Shinmiyangyo* in 1871 and then the Korean War in 1950—brought the United States and Korea into direct involvement with each another, then analyzes how American motives, perspectives, and policies toward Korea shifted over time.

In many ways, this early war shares some interesting facts with the better-known Korean War of some 79 years later (1950–1953). First, they both broke out in June. Second, the Americans in 1871 invaded through Ganghwa Island, west of Incheon, the same route as General MacArthur's Incheon Landing on September 15, 1950. Third, both expeditions produced Medal of Honor recipients, 14 in 1871 and 145 in the twentieth century. Third, the Shinmiyangyo achieved no clear victory or positive outcome. Similarly, 79 years later, 36,574 U.S. soldiers were killed between June 25, 1950, and July 27, 1953, according to the Department of Defense, and no peace treaty has replaced the Armistice of July 27, 1953. Lastly and most regrettably, these two wars are referred to as forgotten wars.

Few American citizens are aware of the first war between the United States and Korea in 1871. The lack of knowledge among the American public and leaders in regard to Korea had not substantially changed, even by the middle of the twentieth century, when General MacArthur said,

I hope that it can be impressed upon the Department that here we are not dealing with wealthy U.S.-educated Koreans, but with early, poorly trained, and poorly educated Orientals strongly affected by 40 years of Jap [sic] control, who stubbornly and fanatically hold to what they like and dislike, who are definitely influenced by direct propaganda and with whom it is almost impossible to reason. (Kraus, 2015: 157, requoted from Army General Douglas MacArthur to Joint Chiefs of Staff, February 2, 1946, FRU.S., 1946, 8, pp. 629–630)

Thus, for most readers, it is highly surprising that the United States was eager to form a relationship with Korea in the late nineteenth century. Tyler Dennett, in his seminal 1922 work on U.S. diplomacy in East Asia, describes the American effort to engage Korea in the late nineteenth century as the most important political action undertaken by the United States in Asia up until the occupation of the Philippines in 1898. It was also the first time that American ground forces seized territory in Asia and raised the American flag above it, initiating a long and traumatic tradition of U.S. military involvement there (Chang, 2003: 1333–1334). However, such American attempts to open Korea have received shockingly little attention in academia (Dennett, 1922; Chang, 2003: 1332; Swartout, Jr., 1974; Cumings, 1981; Sterner, 2002).

THE FIRST KOREAN WAR, SHINMIYANGYO

Despite William Seward's aggressive interest, all actual attempts to open the Joseon during his term as secretary of state (1861–1869) failed; ironically, it was the new secretary of state, Secretary Hamilton Fish, who garnered recognition for that achievement. In considering the basis of Fish's decision to wage war against the Joseon, Swartout, Jr. explains that Fish had to rely on experts and justify the war on legal bases. Secretary Seward had been the strongest advocate for the opening of Korea, and his nephew, George Seward, served as his agent. Invited back to Washington in early 1870, George Seward consulted with the Department of State. As a direct result, Secretary Fish authorized the American expedition to Korea. Swartout (1974: 107) also analyzed another factor influencing Secretary Fish's decision—his legalistic orientation: "his was a legal mind, well trained, careful in logic, and respectful of tradition. His devotion [was] to the supremacy of law." This legalistic approach, Swartout argues, resulted in the war of 1871, saying "such an outlook would probably place a high value on the necessity for a legally binding treaty between the United States and Korea, especially when an increase of future contacts seemed inevitable. The problem of shipwrecked sailors could thus be handled in an international, legal fashion" (Swartout, Jr., 1974: 107).

America's fundamental attitudes toward the Asian race were the most important factor influencing U.S. policy toward Asia in general and Korea in particular. Americans went to Korea in 1871 not only to establish footholds for help with potential shipwrecks and trade but also to accomplish the American exceptionalistic doctrine of Manifest Destiny. America, with a sense of superiority as a race and civilization no freer from narcissism than any other, clearly despised Korea and the Korean nation as lowly, contemptible, repugnant, and barbarian. On this claim, Chang (2003), Sterner (2002), Dennett (1922), Murrary (2011), and Swartout, Jr. (1974) unanimously agree. Secretary of the Navy George M. Robeson, in America's first war against Korea, aimed to discipline this land of "barbarians." Chang (2003: 1334) specifically argues that the war of 1871 illustrates how ideas about race and civilization shaped the nineteenth-century American approach not just to Korea but to East Asia more broadly. Regardless of their overall ignorance about the Joseon, the U.S. government executed the war plan based primarily on its prejudiced view that America was morally and racially superior to the lowly civilization and racial character of Korea.

> Their attitudes toward Asians as a "race" were an unsystematic mix of ideas about character, behavior, ethics, and intelligence, based on a perceived similarity in physical appearance and a conflation of specific cultures into an "Oriental" type of civilization. And Asians, compared to white Americans and Europeans, were not just different but morally and socially deficient. With these notions, Washington officials, even when there was clearly contradictory evidence, assumed the worst about the Koreans and minimized or discounted information that suggested a more positive characterization of the people and the reasons for their suspicion of westerners. The dominant American attitude, as expressed in official as well as personal records, was that the Koreans were mendacious, backward, and simply barbaric. (Chang, 2003: 1336)

The United States justified its use of force under the banner of its moral duty to force barbarian nations to open for trade and to accept the "superior" religion, culture, economy as well as political and belief systems of American civilization.[4]

Reacting to the Joseon's policy of passive isolationism, American faith in Manifest Destiny[5] was much more aggressive in its notion of converting non-whites in order to civilize them according to America's standards and experience of social Darwinism. Political leaders, including almost all American presidents and secretaries of state during the American collision with the Joseon, were strong believers and activists. The spirit of Manifest Destiny was religious in tenor, and motivated all tiers of leadership in politics, trade, and the church, including missionaries strongly backed by the U.S. Navy.

Though of a personal nature, letters from Captain McLane Tilton, U.S.MC, who was in charge of the U.S. naval expedition to Corea, clearly attest to his faith in Manifest Destiny:

> May 16, 1871
>
> My dear Nannie,
>
> We are really on our way to Korea. . . . , our mission being a peaceful one, and for the purpose only of exacting a reasonable promise from the Korean Govt. that seamen wrecked on their coast may be treated humanely. We have no knowledge of the country, and only very unreliable information in regard to the coast. . . . But you may imagine it is with not great pleasure I anticipate landing with the small force we have, against *a populous country containing 10,000,000 of savages.*[6] (Sterner, 2002, p. 14)
>
> May 26, 1871
>
> My dear Nannie,
>
> When our boats are sailing about & meet native boats, the latter always change their course, *not appearing to desire any communication*; and upon our boats landing on the beach, they get in theirs. (Sterner, 2002, p. 16)
>
> June 21st, 1871
>
> My dearest Nannie,
>
> I am glad to say I am alive still and kicking, although at one time I never expected to see my Wife and baby any more, and if it hadn't been that the Coreans can't shoot true, I never should. It is all over now, and as I expected, *we have failed to make any treaty with the Coreans.* . . . As for me I am quite satisfied, "I have not lost no Coreans," and "I ain't alooking for none neither"—*I want to go home*! (Sterner, 2002, p. 30)

In these letters to his wife, Captain Tilton also expresses a sense of American exceptionalism toward Korea and touches upon several important historical points that U.S.-Korea relations of the twentieth century will later repeat. Korea's reluctance to open relations to the United States has been substantiated in contemporary U.S.-DPRK debacles. Also, Americans wanted to forget about this country at the time, as they would again after the Korean War in 1953.

Admiral Rogers acknowledged in his letter that the United States had failed to shake Corea from its isolationism, saying that "It now remains with the Government to determine what further steps, if any, shall be taken toward requiring from Corea those engagements which it was our purpose in visiting the coast to obtain if we might" (Sterner, 2002: 34).

In the Korean War, history repeated itself yet again. About 1.8 million American soldiers landed in Busan, Incheon, and Yeongdeungpo with essentially zero knowledge of Korea, and found a nation in utter shambles, its people deprived of basic necessities. Even after losing 36,574 soldiers in the twentieth century Korean War, America had achieved no clear victory. In regard to the pain and loss, many simply tried to forget, until eventually that approach became untenable as the legacy of the war became visible again in the South as "the miracle on the Han River"—through the simultaneous achievement of rapid economic growth and democratization, an achievement with no precedent anywhere in the world. That civil war was also the first war between the United States and the People's Republic of China, a memory that lingers around the Peninsula and still haunts bilateral relations between the United States and China in the form of their current trade war.

The Shinmiyangyo: The Course of the War

As touched upon in earlier chapters, this war of 1871 played a crucial role in America's nineteenth-century Asian policy. The U.S. fleet was more than formidable by European standards. It comprised 5 heavily armed warships with 85 cannons manned by 1,230 marines and sailors—the largest Western force to enter Korea before the twentieth century. The French fleet that had arrived 15 years prior, by contrast, had only 600 soldiers. Undoubtedly, the flotilla struck dread into the Korean people[7] with its bristling display of force, provocative use of soundings along the shores to increase pressure on local officials, repeated refusals to meet with low-level representatives, and insistence on communication with only the highest authorities, as had been the case when the U.S. fleet approached Japan to open (Chang, 2003: 1339).

On May 1871, the American expedition, with the *U.S.S. Colorado* as its flagship, left Nagasaki and encountered a few Korean fishing boats in late May. But it was not until May 30 that the fleet finally anchored off a small island in the mouth of the Yeomha River and the estuary of the Han River, Jakyakdo. On the morning of May 24:

> The Palos and four steam-launches were put under the command of Captain Homer C. Blake, to examine the channel beyond Boisee Island [Jakyak-do, south of Gangwha Island and east of Yeongjong-do]. Four days were peaceably spent in this service, a safe return being made on the evening of the 28th. Meanwhile, boat parties had landed and been treated in a friendly manner by the people, with the usual curiosity as to brass buttons, blue cloth, and glass bottles displayed. . . . Approaching the squadron in a junk, some natives made signs of friendship, and came on board without hesitation. . . . They were hospitably treated, shown round the ship, and dined and wined until their good nature broke out in broad grins and redolent visages. (Griffis, 1889: 407)

The first encounter in this American expedition that had aimed to either open or punish Korea was not as disastrous as Griffis writes.

> Strange coincidence! Strange medley of the significant symbols of a Christian land! The first thing given to the Corean was alcohol, beer, and wine. In the picture, plainly appearing, are the empty pale ale bottles, with their trade-mark, the red triangle—"the entering wedge of civilization." But held behind the hands clasping the bottles is a copy of Every Saturday, on the front page of which is a picture of Charles Sumner, the champion of humanity, and of the principle that "nations must act as individuals," with like moral responsibility. (Griffis, 1889: 408)

Such peaceful and seemingly friendly intercourse, however, did not last long. The Coreans fired two hundred guns, which was a total failure of both powder and judgment.[8] In this encounter, Coreans made it clear that they wanted to have a chance to express their unwillingness to engage with foreign intruders. Griffis (1889) provides a description of how Americans reacted to Coreans who waved a white flag to deliver a letter from the Joseon court. Griffis (1889: 412) observes that:

> One of the steam-launches met the junk, and the letter was received. It was translated by Mr. Drew, but as it contained nothing which, in the American eyes, seemed like an apology, the squadron moved on. At 1 o'clock the Monocacy arrived within range of the first fort and opened with her guns, which partly demolished the walls and emptied it in a few seconds.

American ships finally landed in the "mud-flat, in which the men sunk to their knees in the tough slime, losing gaiters, shoes, and even tearing off the legs of their trousers in their efforts to advance. The howitzers sank to their axles in the heavy ooze" (Griffis, 1889: 412).

On Gangwha Island, just 50 miles off the Peninsula, the French navy dropped anchor in October 1866, as General MacArthur would do almost a century later on September 15, 1950. As explored before, the Joseon did not respond to American demands to open and ordered officials in coastal areas to avoid conflicts with Americans. In this first encounter between the United States and Korea, Americans apparently viewed the mission of opening this lowly race as both an honor and a burden for a "superior" people; complimentarily, the Koreans viewed the American blackship as a rude Western barbarian force and refused to make contact with it. Coming from almost opposite economic, political, and cultural backgrounds, these two nations crossed paths. Through provocative threats and military force, the stranger from the West, with a self-image as "civilized" and modern, forced the "savage" Asian stranger to consummate the relationship, despite having different agendas, though it led to Korea's estrangement soon enough.

The report to the State Department by the U.S. Minister in China, Low, clearly reflected such typical American views of the Joseon: "the Korean government would resist' all innovation and intercourse with all the power at its command whether the overtures concerned trade or the humane treatment of shipwrecked sailors." Minister Low states clearly that "The Koreans were simply a 'semi-barbarous and hostile race.'" Future American leaders and citizens would have the same attitudes and judgments toward North Korea. The king of Korea, Rodgers, wrote his wife, "has declared war against a peaceable expedition." In Rodgers' words, this was "premeditated treachery" (Chang, 2003: 1347).

To a certain extent, though, sentiments were mutual. William Elliot Griffis, one of the earliest American scholars on Korea, later argued that the Koreans viewed the American party as "nothing more than a treacherous beginning of war in the face of assurances of peace," adding that, "To enter into their waters seemed to them an invasion of their country." Advancing as the Americans did, after speaking words of "friendship," must have seemed the "basest treachery" to the Koreans (Chang, 2003: 1350).

Unsurprisingly, Western newspapers, including one from America, expressed pro-Western sentiments in their accounts of this first violent encounter, based on expedition reports that had been sent to China. *The Shanghai Evening Courier* in English threw its full support behind the American expedition, saying, "Coreans, with the faithlessness of the barbarian, opened fire on the U.S. flotilla." It went on to emphasize that in this case, "the good of the civilized world must come before the good of a horde of semi-savages," and expected "that now America is about to take her share in opening up the East to the peaceful and beneficent action of western civilization." The newspaper depicted the United States as an ally in advancing a higher moral order, not as a commercial rival. Other Western papers in China, along with those in the United States and Japan, joined in praising the American mission for its bravery, eagerly anticipating an aggressive American response in the name of humanity (Chang, 2003: 1349). Newspapers in the countries that had been opened earlier by Western nations, as well as American outlets, joined the chorus in claiming that civilized races were demonstrating high moral ground by physically forcing the barbarian and backward Korean nation open.

STRANGERS CROSSING PATHS AND OVERRIDING KOREAN VALUES

As touched upon earlier, this war was not Korea's first encounter with the West. Five years earlier, the French navy had attacked the Joseon for purging French Catholic missionaries and their Korean followers. Since then, in fact, the Korean government's isolationism had intensified rather than subsided, especially because the Korean military had defeated the French expedition which included both missionaries and tomb robbers in 1866. The American government was well aware of Korea's stance against Westerners. Importantly, the Korean government had a legitimate and sovereign right to react to American demands to open as well as a natural right to defend its sovereignty from uninvited foreign vessels surveying major waterways near its capital.

For Americans, this should be considered as a legitimate question: if a heavily armed naval fleet from a foreign nation entered a major waterway like the Mississippi River (or closer to the capital, the lower Potomac) without any prior negotiation or approval, how would the United States respond to its demands to open?

After the U.S. naval expedition fleet departed, King Gojong dispatched his own account of the American expedition to China in the obvious hopes of justifying Korea's refusal to open and insisting on maintaining China's favor. His points were simple—that Korea had acted honorably and consistently with past practices—while America had acted with aggression and arrogance.

These conflicting discourses support this book's main argument—that two nations from entirely different backgrounds first encountered each other with vastly different notions but later succeeded in building a relationship in half-success. When America demanded the relationship, Korea initially refused. If Korea had responded smoothly and positively to the American request, as Japan had, then America would not have used force. It was mutual ignorance of each other's ideological, cultural, and socioeconomic backgrounds that caused the first encounter to fail so miserably. Koreans were strangers to Western norms and customs of putting trade as the most important part of their economy, mainly due to Korea's agricultural industry and faith in Confucian China-centered worldviews. It seems clear, though, that Korea's refusal of America's request was justifiable, while the motives of the American expedition were also clear—to trade for economic profit. That, and to loot tombs. Privately, the United States viewed itself as possessing the moral high ground as well as cultural, religious, racial superiority over these contemptible barbarians, as shown in Low's report to the State Department on his Korea expedition.

Criticisms of the U.S. Expedition

The general chorus of support, however, was not without exceptions. Not all Americans accepted such political rationales for aggression, particularly from self-proclaimed "civilized" nations. Edward B. Drew, Low's chief assistant, seems to have privately criticized his superiors' attitude and course of action, and waited more than a decade to reveal his feelings. The Americans, he stated during a public lecture in China, "having trailed their coats before the faces of the Coreans, and having at last persuaded the Coreans to step on them, demanded an apology for the insult." At the time, Horace Greeley's *New York Tribune*, which was generally critical of Grant, condemned the expedition for its pretensions. The paper mocked American claims of superior morality and justice, turning the idea of civilization back upon the United States. Under the sarcastic title "Civilizing the Coreans," an editorial focused on the arrogance of the declaration made by the Low-Rodgers mission that they only wanted to help the Koreans "partake of the sweets of American civilization."

The paper, rather, justified Korean reactions to the Americans' intrusion with armed forces, saying, "What else could be expected but armed clashes when armed foreigners [i.e., the Americans] [went] poking about [the Korean] coast?" And after the Koreans attacked, the paper continued, the American admiral took "such measures as the interests of civilization required: the taking of the Corean forts, guns numberless, and the slaughter of all the natives who did not get to the tall timber." The editorial concludes with rhetorical questions that would be echoed many years later during other American conflicts in Asia: "What right [do] we have in Corean waters, what [are] we to gain by killing these people, how many more are to be killed, and where [is] this fierce diplomacy to land us" (Chang, 2003: 1358–1359).

In addition to Horace Greeley's *New York Tribune* and its antigovernment editorial on American invasion of Korea, there were a few opposition leaders who echoed the tone of the *Tribune*'s report. On April 17, 1878, Senator Aaron A. Sargent, Chairman of Senate Committee on Naval Affairs, questioned American rationales for breaking into a country that wanted no interaction, saying:

> We would not allow any foreign vessel of a nation with which we even might have a treaty to come and survey our James or any other river; but here was a people particularly sensitive to these things, . . . maintaining a rugged independence, isolated from all the world by a policy which it thought necessary in order to maintain itself as a nation at all.

The Koreans guarding the river, as Sargent went on to explain, had "fired for the purpose of warning the invaders of danger. This appears in the records of the Navy Department" (Swartout, Jr., 1974: 141, quoted from Congressional Record, 45 Cong., 2 Sess., April 17, 1878, p. 2601; Kang, 2005: 81).

Neither Low nor Rodgers ever visited Korea again, and both returned to the United States more hostile toward Asians than before. Although Low had been known as governor of California for his somewhat liberal stance on Chinese immigration, he now feared that an East-West conflict, rooted in racial difference and standards of civilization, was inevitable. After returning to the U.S., Low wrote, "The Chinese and the Oriental civilization is as distinct from ours as darkness is from light. There is no similarity in our language or modes of thought." The Chinese, Low testified, were unable to "assimilate, amalgamate, and become part of [this] Government and its people." They, like "negros and Malays," were "incapable" of amalgamation with the "Anglo-Saxon race" (Chang, 2003: 1360). He saw no chance of amalgamation of the Chinese in America without deterioration of the superior race. He, too, now found wisdom in Bret Harte's "The Heathen Chinese," quoting it in correspondence to illustrate the absurdity of Chinese ways. Both he and Admiral Rodgers, after going to war ostensibly to "open" Korea's doors to the West, now endorsed closing America's doors expressly to Asians (Chang, 2003: 1359).

These sources validate the relevance of the main metaphor that this book adopts to explain the first intercourse between these strangers and the transformation of their unruly encounter into something more formal. This continuing rollercoaster ride has resulted in the 67-year-old division of the Korean nation with the North as a failed totalitarian regime and the South as one of the world's most thriving democracies and industrial powerhouses.

No Bond between Strangers

Although Low believed that his expedition had taught Koreans a lesson, the Korean court concluded that Western encroachment had been repelled yet again. Thus, the policy of seclusion was vindicated and officially reaffirmed. Immediately after the Americans' departure, the Korean court ordered the prominent display of special steles throughout the country bearing the Taewon'gun's declaration, "Western barbarians foully attack! Should we not fight, accord must be made! To urge accord is to betray the country!" The court ordered the makers of ink sticks to imprint this declaration on every slab, and showered honors on the fallen and surviving defenders of the Ganghwa forts. To celebrate the victory, the Taewon'gun also composed a flamboyant couplet: "The smoke and dust of the vessels of Westerners cover the world with darkness, but the great light of the East enlightens it throughout eternity." The leaders of the 1871 American expedition to the Joseon were not the only ones guilty of arrogance, though—the Korean court used the successful repulsion of the Americans to elevate its own prestige among the Korean officialdom and intelligentsia. Confucian virtue and moral determination, it seemed to many in the country, had triumphed over the unruly Western barbarians, thereby confirming the validity of the Joseon state's policy. For the next 10 years, the Joseon court held that a state of war existed with America (Chang, 2003: 1361), which ironically reminds us of the contemporary nuclear showdown and principal enemy relations between Pyeongyang and Washington. We wonder if when this antagonistic hatred will end and complete a full circle of Corea-U.S. encounters.

As we reflect again on the nature of America's encounter with Korea in the late nineteenth century, it is useful to note that Diamond (1999) specifically refers to three main ways in which literate societies have collided with each other—through conquest, epidemics, and genocide. Among these three forms of collision, conquest seems best suited for the American-Korean encounter. What drove America to encroach upon Korea's autonomy at that time? The first and most obvious reason was commercial interest, as openly expressed by Secretary Seward and other political and military leaders as well as Frederick Low. At the same time, however, as Low made clear, the 1872 American mission to invade Korea was "of greater importance than mere mercantile advantages" (Chang, 2003: 1364). It was evident that attitudes of American leaders in the 1871 expedition against Korea were based on a claim of the moral and ethnic superiority of American and Western civilization. As expressed in Captain McLane Tilton's letters to his wife, Korea was seen as a country of [10,000,000 savages]. To Washington, its encounter with Korea in the nineteenth century was a clash between a primitive and "barbarian" country and a "superior" civilization with its established systems of international trade, diplomacy, navigation, naval forces, and Christianity. As clearly revealed in the ideology of Manifest Destiny, leaders of the 1871 American expedition harbored deep racial prejudice grown out of powerful international as well as domestic historical sources and implications. Arguing that these ideas strongly influenced the whole conduct of American conquest of Korea, Chang (2003: 1363) writes:

> At each point, Americans' denigration of the Koreans and belief in Korean treachery and barbarism deeply influenced their thinking and helped create a self-fulfilling prophecy: expecting trouble from the Koreans, Low and Rodgers provoked it. . . . Popular prejudices reinforced by assumptions about international relations and natural law encouraged the provocative American behavior.

Another aspect of the American invasion of Korea was in the duality of the Western international system based on inequalities among the nation states. One of the main factors cited by Mr. Low and other leaders of America's conquest of Korea was that Korea's stubborn refusal to open to American requests violated the natural order and trampled the rights of other nations to regularized interaction. The main factor motivating American leaders in this invasion was ostensibly that America had a noble mission for the good of the Korean savages. In other words, the whole team was driven by the belief that their military action was causally related to progress for human civilization.

In his summary report to Secretary of State Fish, Low stressed these high-minded purposes by stating repeatedly that his enterprise had been led by concerns for the good of civilized society (Chang, 2003: 1364).

Counter to Chang's interpretations on these moralistic and racial aspects of the American expedition against Korea, Dennett (1929) interestingly suggests that America's opening of Korea was "an act of absentmindedness" that set Korea adrift in an ocean of intrigue, leading to its eventual absorption by Japan in 1910 (Chay, 1982: 23). Many echoes on "absentmindedness are pointed out by Tyler Dennett, a pioneering scholar on America's nineteenth-century policy on Asia. Battistini also concludes that "The United States had no clearly defined policy or program with which to confront the rivalries of powers in Korea other than the somewhat nebulous tradition of favoring the development of strong and independent states everywhere in the Orient" (Chay, 1982: 24). Moreover, the United States vacillated at decisive moments in the destiny of Korea (Chay, 1982: 25).

In short, absentmindedness, or disregard of Korea other than seeing it as a geographical dot to complete America's Great Circle route, and racist and moral superiority over Korea were critical in the long history of the encounters between the United States and Korea.

THE SECOND KOREAN WAR, 1950–1953

Now, before delving into the similarities and differences between the wars that erupted in 1871 and 1950, let us briefly recall how the United States had come to engage with Korea again after its first unfortunate encounters (in 1866 and 1871), official treaty recognition (in 1882), and Japan's declaration that the Joseon Empire was its protectorate, and the handing over of Korea to Japan (1910–1945). In short, U.S. policy toward Korea during World War II was all about how to end the Pacific War against Japan quickly with the least damage to the United States. In this process, most importantly, Korea was completely left out of American strategies, plans, policies, and considerations, other than the fact that the Korean Peninsula was divided into North and South in order to incentivize the Soviet Union for its participation in America's war against Japan.

In addition, and more importantly, America's greatest concern in the midst of North Korea's invasion of South Korea during its very early period was the protection of Japan for American influence in East Asia. Dulles reported to Secretary Acheson, "it is probable that one of the purposes of the Korean attack was to break up United States planning of a peace treaty for Japan," which, in Dulles' mind, made such planning even more urgent (LaFeber,1997: 285). In a nationwide CBS Radio speech, Dulles declared that if the Soviets held Korea as well as Sakhalin, "Japan would be between the upper and lower jaws of the Russian bear." This means that Washington's whole purpose to engage immediately against the North's attack of South Korea was to deter communist expansion and to keep America's Great Circle route and hegemony in the Asian market by protecting Japan from Stalin's ambition. Thus, fighting for South Korea was essential.

The CIA also echoed that "Soviet military domination of all Korea could turn Japan away from 'future alignment with the U.S.,' and lead to 'neutralizing the usefulness of Japan as an American base'" (LaFeber 1997: 285). Even during North Korea's attack of South Korea, America's fundamental focus and interest lay in defending South Korea not for the sake of South Koreans but for America's strategic interests in defending Japan and America's biggest national interest in Asia.

Ironically, rather than being divided for its sins in World War II, as was the case for Germany, the United States made Japan beholden by allowing the defeated nation to build its economic leap on the bloody back of a war that was killing millions of Koreans just 35 years after the most exploitative colonization imaginable. While the Korean War cost the lives of about 60,000 United Nations troops including 36,574 Americans, Washington gave special U.S. military procurement orders to Japan that accounted for 70% of Japan's exports during the first two years of the Korean War. Japan's once war-devastated economy was suddenly infused with capital and technology transfer, mostly from the United States.

Again, the Korean War was to the rebuilding of Japan as the Marshall Plan was to the rebuilding of Western Europe. It is quite ironic that Japan was enabled to rehabilitate its nuclear-bombed economy at the cost of Korean lives, even after such a long record of atrocities in the late nineteenth century. LaFeber (1997: 295) concludes that "the highest objectives" of the Korean War were "first, to use Japan as the hub of an open, multilateral capitalism in Asia; second, to contain communism; and third, to reassure neighbors by keeping Japan orderly and controlled." At this point, Korea was not a priority in America's costly military intervention but a support bolster for Japan. As usual, the rapid switch from saving the victims of Japanese colonization to subjecting them to massive war casualties left the question of America's true intention and policy toward Korea completely unanswered.

Korea's post–World War II destiny was shaped by the United States without any Korean consultation in the Cairo Declaration, led by President Franklin Roosevelt, in December 1942. It was through this declaration, that Korea was placed under the tutelage or trusteeship of the superpowers, delaying its independence for the foreseeable future to be granted "in due course." Unaware of Korea's 5,000-year history of self-government, Americans may have believed that Korea was incapable of governing itself (Kraus, 2015: 156).

Thus, the idea of putting Korea under a trusteeship after 35 years of Japanese colonial control remained official U.S. policy. In resolving World War II, the Allied powers strangely did not divide Japan, who had been the aggressor, but Korea. Moreover, Korea was excluded from the UN Conference in San Francisco that marked the end of the Pacific War in 1945 (Barry, 2012: 40). However, like a recurring nightmare, or a déjà vu, Korea became the venue for war and suffering, America's frontline against communism for the full duration of the Cold War.

According to State Department expert Charles E. Bohlen, "[i]t was the Korean War and not World War II that made [the U.S.] a world military-political power." The historian John Gaddis has commented that "the real commitment to contain communism everywhere originated in the events surrounding the Korean War" (Kaufman, 1986: vii). The Korean War was also a godsend for Washington to beef up a military that had been radically reduced to a peace system after World War II. By announcing the withdrawal of America's defensive perimeter from the Korean Peninsula, Secretary of State Dean Acheson, who signaled Stalin, Mao, and Kim to execute their plan to attack South Korea also acknowledged that the breakout of the Korean War in fact helped the Truman administration by providing a perfect justification to build up its military budget: "The conflict "prove[d] our thesis" and thus made possible the realization of NSC-68's vast plans to control those and other ocean waves. Or, as he and his assistants concluded, "Korea came along and saved us" (LaFeber, 1997: 283)

Prior to Japan's surrender on August 10, 1945, the whole focus of American leadership in the Pacific War was to defeat the Japanese military as quickly as possible. At that time, U.S. overestimation of Japan's actual capacity in Northern Manchuria and East Asia inadvertently invited Soviet occupation of the Korean Peninsula. Soviet participation, President Roosevelt was convinced, would make Japan's defeat in the Pacific War easy. In early 1945, the Joint Chiefs of Staff recommended that the Soviets be allowed to occupy the Korean Peninsula to prevent Japan from reinforcing its military preparedness on the island prior to the expected American invasion. An obvious historical lesson that was ignored in this decision was to revisit the U.S. alliance with Japan in order to limit Soviet expansionism in 1905 through the Russo-Japanese War. For that purpose, Korea apparently had to be sacrificed again, as had been the case in the 1905 Russo-Japanese War. Thus, it was divided shortly after the end of World War II.

The Swift Choice to Cut Korea in Two

So, to maximize American influence and minimize American casualties in bringing down the Japanese Empire, Korea was halved. Secretary of State

James Byrnes instructed the State-War-Navy Coordinating Committee (SWNCC) to create a plan for the joint Soviet-American occupation of Korea, with the line as far north as possible. Late on the night of August 10, Brig. Gen. George Lincoln, the Army's advisor to the SWNCC,

> took a guess at how far the Soviet could get, and decided on the thirty-eighth parallel, although he was not convinced the Soviets would respect any line. . . . Soon afterwards, he apparently had misgivings. He thought perhaps it should have been the fortieth parallel, if there was any chance the Soviets would respect it. Lincoln then apparently started pondering if he had made a mistake. (Barry, 2012: 44)

Brig. General Lincoln called in Col. Charles H. Bonesteel (later to command UN forces in Korea) and Col. Dean Rusk, giving them just 30 minutes to recommend a better line of division for Korea.

Here again, because Soviet forces had already marched into the north and the closest U.S. troops were in Okinawa, the United States had to make this decision swiftly. The issue for these two army colonels was to design a surrender that the Soviets would accept while at the same time preventing Soviet forces from seizing all of Korea. The only map available was a 1942 *National Geographic* map of "Asia and Adjacent Areas," which did not denote provinces, only latitude and longitude. "Rusk later confided that they had seriously considered drawing the line between Pyongyang and Wonsan, at the narrowest waist of Korea around 39 degrees latitude, but their map's limitations precluded doing so with accuracy. Instead, they chose the 38th parallel" (Barry, 2012: 4). Rusk recounts that:

> During a [SWNCC] meeting on August 14, 1945, Colonel Charles Bonesteel and I retired to an adjacent room late at night and studied intently a map of the Korean peninsula. Working in haste and great pressure, we had a formidable task: to pick a zone for the American occupation. . . . [I]t seemed to us that Seoul, the capital, should be in the American sector. We also knew that the U.S. Army opposed an extensive area of occupation. Using a *National Geographic* map, we looked just north of Seoul for a *convenient* dividing line but could not find a natural geographic line. We saw instead the 38th parallel and decided to recommend that. . . . [SWNCC] accepted it without too much haggling,[9] and surprisingly, so did the Soviets. (Rusk, 1990: 123–124, emphasis added)

There is a reason for emphasizing certain parts of Dean Rusk's revelations above—to highlight how this crucial decision divided the Korean nation and ushered in more than 70 years of military confrontations. First, this decision was made a day before President Truman approved the hastily crafted division plan and ordered Commander of the Pacific War, General MacArthur to cut the Korean Peninsula in half to on August 15, 1945—the day the Korean nation was liberated from 35 years of the most inhumane and vicious colonial exploitation to date. These two Americans were "working in haste and great pressure" for sure, because they had to make this decision for no less than 17 million Korean people. That these colonels studied the map just one day before an entire people was divided attests to America's absolute disregard for, and ignorance of Korea. Moreover, America did not even want the burden of possessing the Peninsula, the strategic location most coveted by the superpowers in East Asia; in fact, the future State Department Secretary Dean Rusk confessed that the "U.S. Army opposed an extensive area of occupation." Again, American leadership made this decision for the sake of "convenience." It was accepted "without too much haggling."

To make America's complete disregard, disrespect, and ignorance of Korea worse, Rusk confessed that with enough background knowledge,[10] the colonels would have had other options for the line of demarcation.

> Remembering those earlier discussions, the Russians might have interpreted our action as acknowledgement of their sphere of influence in Korea north of the thirty-eighth parallel. Any future talk about the agreed-upon reunification of Korea would be seen as mere show. But we were ignorant of all this, and [SWNCC's] choice of the thirty-eighth parallel, recommended by two tired colonels working late at night, proved fateful. (1990: 123–124, requoted in Barry, 2012: 45–46)

In terms of evidence, what more is needed to show that such vacillation of U.S. policy on Asia was based on little more than disinterest and lack of knowledge? Now, the United States has one of its largest and most modern military bases in Korea and has pressured South Korea to join America's fight against their former Korean War enemy, China, despite the fact that China is Korea's largest trading partner and former suzerain. What irony in this story of love and betrayal between two complete strangers!

As mentioned above, just one day before Korea was liberated from Japan, this plan for a divided Korea was signed by President Truman. That decision was communicated to General MacArthur a day later. Part of General Order Number One stated:

> The senior Japanese commanders and all ground, sea, air and auxiliary forces within Manchuria, Korea north of 38 degrees north latitude and Karafuto [Sakhalin] shall surrender to the Commander-in-Chief of Soviet forces in the Far East. The Imperial General Headquarters, its senior commanders, and all ground, sea, air and auxiliary forces in the main islands of Japan, minor islands

adjacent thereto, Korea south of 38 degrees north latitude, and the Philippines shall surrender to the Commander-in-Chief, U.S. Army Forces in the Pacific.[11]

This was how one critical American policy shaped the future of Asia for the rest of the twentieth century and beyond.

Warnings Misfired

As will be discussed more fully later, there were ample signs and symptoms that the Soviet Union was a potential enemy of the American-led free and capitalistic system. These included George Kennan's famous telegram X. If the U.S. government had seriously considered this historic warning about the substantial nature of regimes produced by the Bolshevik Revolution, then the history of the late twentieth century could have taken a drastically different course, avoiding a century of suffering for Korea. Of course, Kennan's warning against Soviet ambition focused on Europe, not Asia or Korea. The fundamental premise of the Marshall Plan in this context had merit. The plan had been that the "United States could safely concentrate on European economic reconstruction, deferring any significant military buildup that would match Soviet capabilities. The bomb would deter the Russians while the Americans revived—and reassured—the European" (Gaddis, 2005: 35).

Kennan's long telegram from Moscow's American Embassy to the State Department on February 22, 1946, was an official warning from a high-level U.S. diplomat about the real nature of the communist political regime with its socialist economic system. Kennan's "long telegram" became the basis for U.S. strategy toward the Soviet Union throughout the rest of the Cold War (Gaddis, 2005: 29) but not toward Korea. Kennan (1947: 575) argued for "long-term, patient but firm and vigilant containment of Russian expansive tendencies."[12] Kennan's warning was that Soviet expansionism would place all European countries in danger.

Despite their awareness of such possible outcomes, U.S. forces completely withdrew from Korea in 1949 with only a few military advisors remaining. Then, on January 12, 1950, Secretary of State Acheson stated to the National Press Club that the Korean Peninsula would be excluded from the U.S. defensive perimeter. Both Joseph Stalin and Kim Il-sung might have executed their plans to attack South Korea even without this speech. In it, though, when Acheson defined the American "defensive perimeter" as running through Japan, the Ryukyus, and the Philippines, he indirectly denied any guarantee of U.S. military protection to Korea and the Republic of China (ROC) on Taiwan (Matray 2002). This post–World War II Asian policy was fundamentally and disproportionately aimed at containing the Soviet Union. As a result of excluding the Peninsula, though, the United States was forced to deal with communist threats for the rest of the twentieth century and still must do so today.

It is obvious to note America's skewed emphasis on Europe, America's home front. The American stateman who designed America's post–World War II and Cold War containment strategy with the highest emphasis on Europe was State Secretary Dean Acheson. Acheson was one of the main designers of the Truman Doctrine, announced in 1947, which was President Truman's request to Congress for aid to Greece and Turkey. In this doctrine, President Truman made clear that the Soviet system of totalitarianism endangered the free West. This doctrine was a reaction to Soviet attempts to expand their system into Eastern Europe and Southwest Asia.

Stalin's ambition to transform Eastern Europe into a buffer zone had been cited by Winston Churchill in his famous "Iron Curtain" speech at Fulton, Missouri, in 1946. The collapse of Albania, Bulgaria, and East Germany in 1945, Romania, Poland, and Hungary in 1947, and Czechoslovakia in 1948 served as warnings of Soviet influence. The collapse of European friends seemed to make the United States' strategic planners neglect Asia in their post–World War II strategy. The Defense Department's strategic planning on Europe was also, most likely, on Acheson's mind. Robert Patterson, Secretary of War, told Truman that "the troops should be redeployed to Europe," while Acheson's own State Department "warned that withdrawal from Korea would lead to a Communist takeover and a severe blow to American prestige in Asia" (Pelz, 1983: 110).

The Wedemeyer Report

A few American decision makers, however, strongly warned that Korea could be a triggering point in the U.S. effort to contain communist expansionism and challenges to the United States. The Report to the President submitted by Lt. General Albert C. Wedemeyer in September of 1947 serves as a clear sign that communist expansion was threatening China and Korea. This "Wedemeyer Report" made comprehensive policy recommendations with wide-ranging surveys on political, economic, and social intelligence from postcolonial Korea. First, in this comprehensive military intelligence report, Lt. General Wedemeyer mentioned that the 1882 Korea-U.S. treaty provision of "good office," examined in chapter 3, had not been properly applied when exiled Koreans appealed to State Department and President Theodore Roosevelt.

When the United States had to decide whether to abandon Korea again in the post–World War II resolution (as it had done by handing Korea to Japan in 1905), President Truman's military aid, interestingly, was mentioned again. Lt. General Wedemeyer invoked this specifically, stating that "The first treaty between the U.S. and Korea, signed in 1882, provided that if other powers dealt *unjustly or oppressively* with either government, the other would exert its good offices to bring about an 'amicable agreement.'" Warning that the Soviet Union and its satellite regime in the North would attack and communize the South in the absence of U.S. forces, his report to President Truman recommended a withdrawal proportional to the Soviet withdrawal, and the provision of strong military and economic aid, warning also of a communist triumph imminent in China and potential threat to South Korea.

Such perspectives on the state of affairs in Korea, and consequential recommendations, could have prevented the outbreak of the Korean War if faithfully adopted; though it may seem they could have reversed the course of the relationship initiated by America in the late nineteenth century as well. His report on the Korean situation accurately reflected South Korea's vulnerability to potential communist attack, due to South Korea's heavy reliance on the North's industrial infrastructure and advanced military capabilities supported by the Soviet Union. Lt. General Wedemeyer was keenly aware of South Korea's strategic importance to America, reporting that:

> The political, social economic and military situations in South Korea are inextricably mingled. A Soviet-dominated Korea would constitute a serious political and psychological threat to Manchuria, North China, the Ryukyus, and Japan, and hence to the United States strategic interests in the Far East. It was therefore in the best interests of the United States to ensure the permanent military neutralization of Korea. Neutralization can only be ensured by its occupation until its future independence as a buffer state is assured. (Wedemeyer 1947: 24)

Sensing the Soviet communization of the entire Peninsula as an imminent danger, he prescribed permanent neutralization of Korea as a defensible buffer state. His report was based on a 1947 visit to Korea after surveying situations in China, in order to assess the military imbalance between the South and the North. He (1947: 26) assessed that "the United States-Soviet Union troop strengths in South and North Korea are approximately equal but the Soviets, assisted by a Soviet-controlled, -equipped and -trained North Korean People's (Communist) Army of 125,000 men, and geographically supported by a contiguous Soviet Siberia, are in an infinitely stronger military position."

He (1947: 25) further emphasized the grave consequences if the United States were to withdraw military support from Korea: "So long as Soviet troops remain in occupation of North Korea, the United States must maintain troops in South Korea or admit before the world an 'ideological retreat.'" The military standing of the United States would decline accordingly, not only throughout the Far East but the world as well. Withdrawal of U.S. occupation forces from Korea would increase unrest among the Japanese due to their uncertainty over the future of U.S. policy in the Far East, and their consequent fears of expanding Soviet influence. This might well increase occupational requirements for Japan. Aware that the United States had to follow Soviet withdrawal from the North, he recommended "proportional withdrawals with as many guarantees as possible to safeguard Korean freedom and independence," "military aid for adequate safeguard," and "continuing to furnish arms and equipment to Korean National Police and Korean Coast Guard."

Specifically, General Wedemeyer foresaw the potential military threat—even then—of a Soviet-inspired invasion of South Korea by troops of the North Korean People's (Communist) Army:

> The withdrawal of American military forces from Korea would, in turn, result in the occupation of South Korea either by Soviet troops, or as seems more likely, by the Korean military units trained under Soviet auspices in North Korea. The end result would be the creation of a Soviet satellite Communist regime in all of Korea. A withdrawal of all American assistance with these results would cost the United States an immense loss in moral prestige among the peoples of Asia; it would probably have serious repercussions in Japan and would more easily permit the infiltration of Communist agents into that country; and it would gain for the Soviet Union prestige in Asia which would be particularly important in the peripheral areas bordering the Soviet Union, thus creating opportunities for further Soviet expansion among nations in close proximity to the Soviet Union. (Wedemeyer, 1947: 13)

In the early twentieth century, the United States, keenly aware of Russian ambition to expand southward into the Peninsula, chose to play Japan against Russia. The result was the Russo-Japanese War from 1904 to 1905, which ended with Korea being awarded as a sort of trophy to Japan. Now, the Japan card was gone, and it was time for the United States either to fold or to make good on its long overdue commitment to Korea. Lt. General Wedemeyer urged the President to create an American-officered South Korean scout force. If that recommendation had been accepted, it could have prevented the Korean War and served as an opportunity to fill the gap of conventional suzerainties retained by China first and then Japan. In fact, Wedemeyer's report mentions:

> During the early period of United States-Korean relations, the United States considered Korea as an independent state for the purpose of fulfilling treaty obligations, although that nation was actually under Chinese suzerainty. Prior to the Sino-Japanese War of 1895, when efforts were made to gain the support of the United States to avert war, the United States took the position that, while it stood for peace, it would do nothing which might cause it to assume responsibility for

settlement of the dispute. Under the treaty ending the war, China relinquished suzerainty over Korea, which was in turn assumed by Japan. Therefore, the United States continued its policy of non-interference in Korean internal affairs and in 1899 denied a Korean request for American initiative in obtaining from the powers an agreement guaranteeing Korea's integrity. (1947: 9)

President Truman not only rejected Wedemeyer's recommendations but also suppressed publication of the report for two years. Thus, the Korean card was folded, again. The United States could enjoy suzerainty over Korea. As predicted, North Korean communists, backed by the Soviet Union, attacked the South, and the United States had to roll back from vacillation and make a firm commitment that fundamentally changed the course of U.S.-Korea relations and of Korea as a nation. The United States was no longer able to take an opportunistic stance at this juncture, because an enemy was created in North Korea that the United States could not dodge, since it directly challenged the core strategic values of American interests in the region.

The first major collision between the United States and communism broke out in the Korean Peninsula, which the United States had deserted long before. Now, the United States had to sacrifice tens of thousands of its own citizens and provide economic aid on a massive scale. "[E]conomic development," Brazinsky (2007: 104) writes, "had also received renewed emphasis during the second Eisenhower administration because academic experts on the subject like Walter Rostow were gaining greater influence in policy circles. Rostow and other prominent scholars maintained that development would be the key to defeating communism in the postcolonial world." The emergence of new enemies—communist North Korea, China, and Soviet Union—forced the United States to significantly alter its attitude toward the half of Korea south of the 38th parallel. The United States had been clear about what to do with Korea: change the regime in the North and recognize the one in the South. The warnings in the Wedemeyer report, however, were set aside and South Korea and the United States were forced to pay the high costs of war, to say nothing of North Korea.

Recommendation from Acting Secretary of State James Webb

This book introduces one more warning signal that fell by the wayside. Chillingly, this communication predicted—almost to the letter—what would happen in Korea if the United States failed to pay attention. Korea is the only area in the world in which democratic and communist principles are being put to the test side by side and in which the United States and the USSR have been, and no doubt in the estimation of the world will continue to be, the sole contenders for the way of life of 30 million people. The entire world, and especially Asia, is watching this contest. To the degree that the Republic succeeds, the people in the still-free nations of Southeast and Southern Asia and Oceania will be persuaded of the practical superiority of democratic principles. To the degree the United States continues to support the efforts of the South Korean people to develop a self-supporting economy and a stable democratic government, the people of this area will be persuaded of the firmness of U.S. determination to support democracy and oppose communism. Weakening on the part of the United States will damage their confidence and undermine the position of the United States.

This letter[13]—written on May 16, 1949, by James Webb, then acting secretary of state to the director of the Bureau of the Budget, Mr. Pace—was top secret. Its main point was not to recommend that the U.S. station troops in Korea but to argue for economic aid when the U.S. military completely withdrew by July 1, 1949, based on the NSC 8/2 Policy Paper. The acting Secretary foretold the fall of Korea under communism or North Korean attack if U.S. economic and military support was not strong enough. As Webb mentioned in this letter, America was pondering whether to abandon Korea or provide limited support.

He did not oppose planned U.S. withdrawal but was making proper financial arrangements to support the NSC decision to pull military resources from Korea and devote them to Europe so that the United States could minimize "to the greatest practicable extent the chances of South Korea's being brought under Communist domination as a consequence of the withdrawal of U.S. armed forces" (Webb, 1949). The U.S. government, Webb argued, must continue to provide political support and economic, technical, military, and other assistance to Korea so that Korea does not suffer a rapid and inevitable collapse once U.S. assistance is withdrawn because he knew that "the only visible source of adequate economic assistance toward a level of self-support is the United States" (Webb, 1949). The acting Secretary was absolutely correct to point out the following:

> It is the only effective foothold of western democracy on Continental Northeast Asia. In the degree to which the Republic with its democratic government flourishes, it will create continuing resistance in the minds of hundreds of millions of people in this area to the acceptance of Communism.

As Webb (1949) predicted, South Korea is still the frontline of the collision between communism and free capitalistic democracy. Moreover, South Korea still suffers from the blunders of that powerful stranger, the United States, to the extent of losing millions of lives, not to mention national morale, from the confrontation between North and South. Webb's prediction was prophetic of Korean destiny, but his insights were tailored toward the interests of the United States:

> Failure of that [i.e., the Korean] government to survive will not only directly affect U.S. interests in the Far East, but will indirectly affect the interest of the U.S. through damaging the prestige and influence of the UN, the support of which is a primary principle of U.S. foreign policy. . . . the interests of the United States will in the long run be best served by planning for a program of relief and economic development of several years' duration, including immediate expenditures for the most essential capital equipment calculated to place the Republic of Korea as rapidly and as nearly as possible on a self-supporting basis.[14] (Webb, 1949)

Despite this prophecy, the United States, which had wanted a formal relationship more than a half-century earlier, suddenly folded, inadvertently bringing about one of the most disastrous and historically epoch-making wars in twentieth-century Asia. There were up to 5 million civilian deaths in the Chinese Civil War, 2.1 million in the Vietnam War, and 800,000 in the Cambodian Civil War. The Korean War had about 2.5 million civilian deaths with 303,212 missing. This decision was also a major blunder in that the U.S. government invited the Soviet Union to halve the Peninsula based on a grave miscalculation. According to military historian Michael Sandusky, U.S. military planners overestimated Soviet military capabilities and ambitions at the end of the Pacific War. Barry argues that:

> the on-the-ground situation on August 15, 1945 in Korea and Manchuria was vastly different from what Washington perceived. Sandusky asserts the Soviets could have been stopped at a line much further north, possibly even at the 40th parallel. He writes: In Korea, the meager Soviet forces were brought to a standstill in Chongjin [about 45 miles south of the Soviet border with Korea]. Few Soviet troops were in Korea and the ones that were there were pinned down by resolute Japanese troops. . . . [T]he Soviets were in no position to expand their presence in Korea. . . . In Korea, Soviet forces were still well above the forty-first parallel [above Kimchaek on the eastern coast].[15] (Barry, 2012: 47–48)

Further, Barry (2012) argues that "given the naval and air transport capabilities that the U.S. had at its disposal, key areas of Korea as far north as Hamhung (below the 40th parallel) could have been secured by U.S. forces had these areas been accorded the appropriate priority" (48). Gaddis (2005: 25) joins Sandusky's reasoning and argues that, "Once it became clear that the Americans possessed such a weapon, the need for Soviet military assistance vanished."[16]

The CIA report also adds credibility to these points. The CIA's Office of Reports and Estimates (ORE) warned that there was high probability of a war breaking out in the Peninsula if U.S. troops withdrew without strengthening South Korean military forces. The ORE report from February 28, 1949 (ORE 3-49), titled "Consequences of U.S. Troop Withdrawal from Korea in Spring, 1949," stated, "In the absence of U.S. troops, it is highly probable that northern Koreans alone, or northern Koreans assisted by other Communists, would invade southern Korea and subsequently call upon the U.S.SR for assistance. Soviet control or occupation of Southern Korea would be the result." The report concluded that "withdrawal of U.S. forces from Korea in the spring of 1949 would probably in time be followed by an invasion, timed to coincide with Communist-led South Korean revolts, by the North Korean People's Army possibly assisted by small battle-trained units from Communist Manchuria."[17]

WASHINGTON VACILLATED

Undoubtedly, there have been blunders in American policy on Korea. This book fundamentally questions the nature of U.S.-Korea relations, and the first matter in that line of questioning was the withdrawal of the U.S. defensive perimeter from the Korean Peninsula, since it served to invite a North Korean attack. Referring to critics[18] of this policy, Matray's (2002: 1) observation on Acheson's exclusion of the Peninsula from America's defensive perimeter and Theodore Roosevelt's exchanging of Korea for control over the Philippines undeniably reinforces this point: "The United States, they bitterly maintain, committed an act of betrayal toward Korea ranking with President Theodore Roosevelt's approval of the Taft-Katsura Agreement in 1905 and President Harry S. Truman's agreement to divide the peninsula forty years later at the end of World War II."

George Kennan's "Long Telegram" from Moscow's American Embassy to the State Department on February 22, 1946, was an official warning from a high-level U.S. diplomat concerning the real nature of the communist political regime with its socialist economic system. Despite such awareness, U.S. forces left Korea in 1949, though a few military advisors stayed behind. When Secretary of State Dean Acheson stated on January 12, 1950, before the National Press Club, that the Korean Peninsula would be excluded from the U.S. defensive perimeter, Joseph Stalin and Kim Il-sung might have already planned to execute an attack on South Korea, but that remains a matter of conjecture.

Stalin read Acheson's declaration carefully and authorized his foreign minister, Molotov, to discuss it with Mao Zedong. The Soviet leader then informed Kim Il-sung that

[a]ccording to information coming from the United States, . . . "[t]he prevailing mood is not to interfere." Kim in turn assured Stalin that "[t]he attack will be swift and the war will be won in three days. Stalin's 'green light' to Kim Il-sung was part of the larger strategy for seizing opportunities in East Asia that he had discussed with the Chinese: shortly after endorsing the invasion of South Korea, he also encouraged Ho Chi Minh to intensify the Viet Minh offensive against the French in Indochina. Victories in both locations would maintain the momentum generated by Mao's victory the previous year. (Gaddis, 2005: 42)

When World War II ended in 1945 with Japan's unconditional surrender, a different kind of war was brewing among allies, the United States, England, and the Soviet Union: proxy wars. They had all learned a fatal lesson—that war among the greatest powers is devastating. According to www.Secondworldwarhistory.com, World War II reached a total death toll of more than 60 million. Among these, Soviet Russia topped with more than 23 million, China with 15 million, Germany 7.7 million, Poland 5.7 million, England 500,000, and the United States 418,000, approximately. Military deaths were approximately as follows: Soviet Union 9.7 million, Germany 5.5 million, China 3.5 million, Japan 2.1 million, the United States 416,000, and England 382,000.

After the official end of World War II, the former allies, the United States and the USSR newly transformed into adversaries, hoped to avoid further confrontations along the first front in Europe, as was apparent in Berlin, Greece, Turkey, Northern Iran, and Eastern Europe. Both the Soviet Union and United States knew that they possessed nuclear bombs by the end of 1949. The United States, because it was geographically isolated, would be able to maintain minimal casualties. However, ICBM technologies with nuclear warheads now render such isolation largely irrelevant. To minimize their own damage and casualties, they used proxies to explore each other's willingness to engage in conventional warfare on a reduced scale and in someone else's territory. This marked the real end of World War II and the start of a new kind of war: the proxy war of the Cold War era.

At the start of his article, Matray (2002) enumerates the scholars and practitioners who attribute North Korea's invasion of South Korea to Acheson's 1950 speech at the National Press Club. However, Matray (2002) shares some counterevidence from archives in Korea and Russia (produced before and during the war) that the North's decision to invade was not swayed by Acheson's speech. Nevertheless evidence of disapproval took multiple forms: Republican senator from Ohio Robert A. Taft's comment on "bungling and inconsistent foreign policy that has provided basic encouragement to the North Korean invasion" (Matray, 2002: 2); presidential candidate General Dwight D. Eisenhower's attribution, in the fall of 1952, of North Korea's attack to the Press Club speech (Matray, 2002: 2); General McArthur's statement in his memoirs that Acheson's policies on Asia were widely condemned in the United States; General Matthew B. Ridgeway's saying Acheson's "clear indication that we had no intention of defending Korea and did nothing to give the enemy even momentary pause"; Robert T. Oliver's comment that "the war came . . . because American authoritative statements indicated that we would not defend Korea"; Claude A. Buss's comment that Acheson's speech was tantamount to inviting communist aggression; Harry Summers' blaming Acheson for "giving their blessing to the North Korean attack and abandoning South Korea"; and Michael Hickey's comment "that Acheson's speech carried enormous weight because it confirmed the United States no longer planned to protect South Korea" (Matray, 2002: 3, 4, 5).

The success of the China's Communist Party's purge of Kuomintang forces from the mainland on December 27, 1949, and the Soviet Union's development of nuclear weapons in November 1949 were the two most important external factors in Stalin and Mao's endorsement of Kim's plan for the war. Maybe Acheson's speech, contrary to Matray's claim, dispelled any reservations that Stalin may have had about endorsing Kim's request for war. One thing that is certain, though, is that Acheson's declaration would have weighed especially heavily toward the outbreak of the Korean War.

Dean Acheson failed to anticipate China's involvement as well. He said, in a nationally televised program on September 10, 1950, "I should think it would be sheer madness for the Chinese to intervene" (LaFeber, 2002: 121). At the same time, the war with China provided an unprecedented opportunity for the U.S. government to rearm the military by appealing to Congress for the passage of huge defense budgets prescribed by the National Security Council report, NSC 68. President Truman submitted a $50B budget, as contrasted with the $13.5B budget, six months earlier. This proposal increased U.S. army personnel by 50% to 3.5 million men and dramatically strengthened the air force, acquiring American bases in foreign countries as well as military alliances with countries in Asia (LaFeber, 2002: 126).

My conclusion in response to the overarching question of why Acheson withdrew the American defensive perimeter from South Korea unfolds into two directions. The first is that Acheson's declaration was an inevitable outcome of the U.S. government's effort to adjust to the post–World War II environment: reduction of defense budget and military size. The Department of State and the Department of Defense did not differ in this major direction for defense cuts. However, there was clear disagreement between the two agencies. Table 3.1 demonstrates the vacillations of U.S. policy on Europe and Asia after World War II. The main reason for such inconsistencies of policy toward Korea, in my opinion, was the stark choice that the United States faced—in the post–World War II mandate for radical reduction of armament—between Europe and Asia. This brings us to my second conclusion regarding the reason for Acheson's exclusion of Korea from America's defensive perimeter. The United States had to make a clear choice about where to allocate more defense resources: Europe or Asia. The timeline below offers an overview of U.S. policy on Korea up until the outbreak of the Korean War, from 1945 to 1950. Table 3.1 shows the "commitments made" by U.S. policymakers to defend the Korean Peninsula as well as the "inconsistencies" in upholding those commitments.

KOREAN WAR VETERANS: THE GENERATION THAT SAVED THE RELATIONSHIP

The main purpose of this book is not to prove right or wrong arguments about chronological aspects of the Korean War by unearthing new historical records and evidence; rather, my aim is to tell the story of the United States' encounter with Korea, to characterize the essence of those events and the relationship that grew from them, and to explain how we reached today's situation. For that purpose, this book also examines the half of Korea in the north, where the whole relationship was first initiated by the United States, asking how we can conceptualize such erratic policy toward Korea, and what lessons we can draw from their major encounters and wars.

The Korean War that began in 1950 differed from earlier encounters in several ways that ultimately led South Korea to rise from the ashes as an Asian model of Western success. The main difference between America's first actual war, the *Shinmiyangyo*, with Korea and the Korean War of 1950 is that the latter had more American casualties—36,574, to offer a relative sense of scale. The commitment was the largest after that made in World War II. Also, the international power dynamics that emerged from this war demonstrated American ideals and the superiority of free, democratic capitalism through the United States' recognition and strong support for the southern half, while the northern half undeniably illustrated an ideology that was wrongheaded and incompetent, as a representative of communism.

In the General Sherman Incident, about 20 crew members were killed, only four of whom were Americans. The 1871 war left three American casualties. That sacrifice has proven to be worth considering as China is still challenging U.S. influence in the South China Sea and around the world with the "One Belt One Road" initiative. China's new expansionist policy is in direct conflict with President Truman's "General Order Number 1" declared in 1945 in which the Acheson Line excluded the Korean Peninsula from American defensive commitment and has shaped American Asian policy since then. It is the evidence that the Korean War has not ended because the contemporary Chinese line of "One Belt One Road" resurrected the 1950 Acheson

Table 3.1   Timeline of U.S. Policy toward Korea Leading up to the Korean War

Dates	Political Leader	Major U.S. Policies, International Affairs, and Inconsistencies
July 9–24, 1866	Secretary of State William Seward	The General Sherman Incident near Pyeongyang.
Oct. 26 to Dec. 17, 1866	Secretary of State William Seward	Byeonginyangyo (French invasion).
June 1–11, 1871	Secretary of State Hamilton Fish	*Shinmiyangyo* (First Korean war between the United States and Joseon).
May 22, 1882	President Chester A. Arthur	Treaty of Peace, Amity, Commerce, and Navigation between the United States and Joseon.
1894–95	President Grover Cleveland	Sino-Japanese War and end of China's suzerainty over Korea.
1904–05	President Theodore Roosevelt	Russo-Japanese War.
July 1905	President Theodore Roosevelt and William Taft	Taft-Katsura Secret Agreement (or Memorandum), President Roosevelt gave War Secretary Taft authority to concede Korea to Japan's Prime Minister in exchange for control of the Philippines.
1905	President Theodore Roosevelt	The United States abandons consulate and treaty with Joseon.
1910	President William Howard Taft	Japan's Annexation of Korea.
1943–45	Presidents Franklin Roosevelt and Harry S. Truman	Multilateral trusteeship of Korea at Cairo Declaration (Nov. 27, 1943), Yalta Conference (Feb. 4–11, 1945), Potsdam Conference (July 17).
1945	President Truman	Surrender of Germany and Japan (May 8 and August 14), USSR enters Pacific War (Aug. 8), nuclear bombs Hiroshima and Nagasaki (Aug. 6 and 9).
Aug. 14, 1945	Colonels Rusk and Bonesteel	Line of division halves the Korean Peninsula: USSR taking the North as the United States takes the South
Feb. 22, 1946	George Kennan	Kennan's "Long Telegram" calls for containment of Soviet expansionism but also U.S. withdrawal from Korea.
Mar. 12, 1947	President Truman	The Truman Doctrine provides economic and military support to keep Greece and Turkey from falling to Soviet sphere; despite such strong commitments to Europe, the U.S. withdraws from Korea.
Apr. 4, 1947	Robert Patterson, Secretary of War	Patterson advises the United States to withdraw from South Korea early, since occupation has drained War Department funds and military resources are needed elsewhere; also, Congress was unlikely to provide $600M for Korea (Acheson, 1971: 2; Cumings, 1983: 20).

(Continued)

Table 3.1 Timeline of U.S. Policy toward Korea Leading up to the Korean War (Continued)

Dates	Political Leader	Major U.S. Policies, International Affairs, and Inconsistencies
May 16, 1949	James E. Webb, Acting Secretary of State	Webb strongly recommends to Director of the Bureau of the Budget, Mr. Pace, that the United States provide economic support to South Korea.
June 1947	George Kennan, Head of PPS	Japan and Korea are the areas outside Europe requiring large-scale economic assistance. Later, he drops first China and then Korea (Cumings, 1983: 21).
June 5, 1947	George C. Marshall	Marshall Plan (for European reconstruction after World War II).
June 7–24, 1947	President Truman	Blockade of Berlin, as a sign of Soviet ambition.
Sept. 9, 1947	Lt. General Albert C. Wedemeyer	The report is delivered to President Truman recommending that the United States provide military and economic support, but the president buries it.
Sept. 24, 1947	George Kennan	"Our policy should be to cut our losses and get out of there as gracefully but promptly as possible" (Cumings, 1983: 24).
Aug. 15, 1948	General Hodge	U.S. military government ends in South Korea.
Nov. 2, 1948	General Election	Republicans lose in Presidential and Congressional elections.
June 10, 1949	Secretary of Defense Louis Johnson	Johnson stimulates NSC 48 deliberations by recommending that the American objective should be to contain communism in Asia (Cumings, 1983: 32).
June 30, 1949	President Truman	Final withdrawal of U.S. troops from South Korea.
Sept. 1949		Soviet Union conducts successful nuclear test.
1949		President Truman limits military budget to roughly $15B for FY1950. Secretary of Defense Louis Johnson commits to cutting defense spending, "demobilization" (Pelz, 1983: 115). The military planners' struggles over budgets, roles, and missions go public in 1949 (Pelz, 1983: 117).
Jan. to May, 1950		Opposite policies between Soviet Union and the United States toward their proxies.*
Dec. 1949		Fall of Chiang K'ai shek and withdrawal to Formosa, a strong sign of China's communist power.
Jan. 12, 1950	Dean Acheson, Secretary of State	Acheson declares the Aleutians (from Japan and Okinawa to the Philippines, Formosa, Korea, Indochina, and Indonesia) excluded from the American perimeter of defense (just five months before Korean War).

(Continued)

Table 3.1 Timeline of U.S. Policy toward Korea Leading up to the Korean War (*Continued*)

Dates	Political Leader	Major U.S. Policies, International Affairs, and Inconsistencies
Jan. 19, 1950	Dean Acheson, Secretary of State	Acheson writes to his daughter, "This has been a tough day not so much by way of work, but by way of troubles. We took a defeat in the House on Korea, which seems to be to have been our own fault. One should not lose by one vote." [The vote was 193 to 192.]
Apr. 7, 1950	NSC68	Calling for increased military force and an end to demobilization, the United States applies force to counteract Soviet expansionism.

* During the first five months of 1950, the Russians gave the North Koreans an offensive force—tactical aircraft, armor, trucks, and artillery. However, Truman and Acheson did nothing to reinforce South Korea with tanks, anti-tank guns, artillery, and planes. Truman had enough ($75M) for aid to the general area of China, approved by Congress in 1950, but Korea was not included (Pelz, 1983: 118).

Source: Created by author.

Line, where these two foreign Korean War antagonists are still figuring out who holds the regional hegemony. China had to surrender its suzerainty over Korea to Japan in the late nineteenth century and had to watch Japan assume its regional hegemonic place when Japan defeated Russia in 1905. The United States was an accomplice in Japan's rising path to the regional power, which meant the end of China's supremacy in the region. Specifically, in 1882, Commodore Shufeldt successfully resisted a Chinese demand to include a provision of China's suzerainty over Korea in the Treaty of Peace, Amity, Commerce, and Navigation with Korea. In 1905, recognizing Japan's sphere of influence in the Korean Peninsula, the United States agreed to acknowledged Japan's control of Korea, meaning China completely lost its control of Korea. However, that game of competition for Korean Peninsula between the United States and China has not finished yet.

These two potential rivals faced each other on the battleground of the Korean War in 1950 in the reencounter between Korea's former suzerain, who had previously been embarrassed but was now freshly equipped with a new ideology of communism, and the Western stranger, who had previously opened and deserted Korea. In the war, the former could have regained its old mastership over Korea and the latter had reluctantly to engage again in Korea, which it had betrayed in 1910. Due to this war, the United States had no choice but to reconnect with its estranged ex-partner. That war of communism versus free capitalism signaled a new era of the Cold War and the Korean Peninsula served as another battleground with significant sacrifices. These two enemies accomplished half successes: each was able to regain its control but only for half of the Peninsula, China over North Korea and the United States over South Korea. That Korean War still serves as the battle line for a new Cold War confrontation between rising China and defending America.

Many people ask why the Korean War is still regarded as "forgotten," despite having such a significant place in twenty-first-century world history, politics, and culture. This raises further questions that are more than merely rhetorical. Why have Korean War veterans received such scant public recognition for their sacrifice and service? What has made the United States and the Republic of Korea some of the strongest allies in the free world, despite all obstacles? Why did it take 35 years to finally form an official organization for Korean War veterans? Is there any link between the galvanizing[19] of these veterans, Korea's rapid recovery from the war, and the people's miraculous simultaneous achievement of economic development and democracy?

We have no quantifiable evidence to causally link the emergence of Korean War veterans' voices with the formation of the Korean War Veterans Association or with Korea's emergence as one of the world's leading economic powers and a model for political development and sustainable development. When the estranged relations of the nineteenth century resurfaced in the twentieth century and the stronger partner finally carried out the good offices provision of the 1882 Treaty of Peace, Amity, Commerce, and Navigation during the Korean War, the abandoned partner called for her own recovery from the past and shifted dramatically from a stance of isolation to a complete embrace of American demands to open in the late nineteenth century. Adopting American principles of free democracy, a liberal political system and capitalism, Korea transformed itself from a scene of devastation into a model of sustainable development for other developing countries, proof of the power, and universality of the American system. By recognizing, supporting, and allying with South Korea, moreover, the United States was able to overcome the shame of not having won the war against Chinese and Soviet backed North Korean forces. Such fluctuation between poles of committing and withdrawing is less likely to be seen again. As a consequence of the blood shed by so many American soldiers, it will not be easy to reverse America's stance. That the bond between these nations was forged by life-and-death struggle this time seems to have made a real difference in the lasting power and enduring nature of their relationship. The fact of their sharing each other's losses and gains, unsurprisingly but thankfully opened spaces for collaborations and understandings to begin to emerge.

So, what made that relationship transform? Before the Korean War, Korea was viewed from a distance as a small, weak, primitive, insignificant, and uncivilized race. To the Korean War veterans, it was a remote area unknown to the American public and still imbued, at least in part, with the backward ways of a traditional and very foreign society. This was a picture very different from the stories they had grown up hearing from their fathers, uncles, and older brothers who had served in World Wars I and II. By contrast, these young Americans had traveled to an unknown country and did not want to talk about their experience when they returned. In addition, there had been no clear victory aside from their enemy's lack of expansion southward. On returning home, many of these veterans were also unsure about what lay ahead for Korea, since there were no positive signs remaining when they left: mountains denuded of vegetation, millions dead, orphans everywhere, and little infrastructure for human life or industrial production. Because the future did not seem bright upon their departure, many Korean War veterans laid those memories to rest.

Eventually, though, some Korean War veterans began to pick up those memories again and honor them by creating an organization platform in 1985. Their first meeting was held that year from July 25 to 27 in Arlington, Virginia. The roster of the original 40 founding members who signed up and paid $10 dues were as follows: Mr. Dale W. Riggs, Mr. William Booker, Mr. Joseph J. Perc, Mr. William F. Mason, Jr., Mr. Robert A. McWatter, Mr. Victor A. Estella, Mr. Arthur T. Patterson, Mr. Donald E. Nelson, Mr. Gabe Lamagna, Mr. Allen M. Smith, Mr. LeRoy M. Stucker, Mr. Richard Winterstein, Mr. John A. Herbert, Mr. Daniel Lucey Jr., Mr. Edward Hoth, Mr. Kenneth Borchardt, Mr. Ralph W. Melcher, Mr. William McCavitt, Mr. C. J. Ritttenhouse, Mr. Thomas C. Harris, Jr., Mr. Wes Worsham, Mr. Harry Wallace, Mr. Herman Vollings, Mr. Charles Ritenour, Mr. Richard Ziemba, Mr. Ralph Lugo, Mr. William T. Norris, Mr. Stanley Hadden, Mr. Herbert Parnow, Mr. Charles Soules, Mr. Jack Cloman, Mr. Mario Scarselletta, Jr., Mr. Howard M. Steele, Jr., Mr. Victor Gerst, Mr. Robert O'Hara, Mr. Joseph Brown, Mr. Joseph P. McCallion, Mr. Herbert Watson, Mr. Milton H. Olazagasti, and Mr. Ralph E. Butler (the first POW to attend the reunion). The men and women of this organizations, Brokaw asserts, developed values of "personal responsibility, duty, honor and faith," the same characteristics that had helped Americans to defeat Hitler, build the American economy, make advances in science, and implement visionary programs like Medicare. According to Brokaw, "[a]t every stage of their lives they were part of historic challenges and achievements of a magnitude the world had never before witnessed."

U.S. COMMITMENT REALIGNED: AID

The Korean War served as a watershed in the history of U.S.-Korea relations in that the American record of folding, ignoring, and betraying Korea, after such dogged pursuit, now turned a corner and the United States reengaged with full force. The catalytic factor was a war that spilled the blood of more than 36,000 American soldiers in efforts to repel communist ambition and protect American interests. The half of Korea in the south had now become undeniably essential to the United States, a type of Maginot Line in terms of the United States' pride and the fundamental battle line against communism. Its enemy was no longer the Axis Powers of Fascism and Nazism but Communism, and the United States had to prove that its commitment to South Korea exemplified its superiority over this new enemy. During the postwar reconstruction of 1953–1960, the United States began to pour both military and economic aid into South Korea. To compare the amount of aid and institutional cooperation for South Korea from 1945 to 1950, the United States is seen to have demonstrated a change of heart, which helped foment South Korea's transformation into a world industrial power, whereas North Korea's partnership with Soviet communism led to a failed state particularly after the USSR fell. South Korea's success served to punish North Korea for resisting the United States. Conversely, North Korea's failure served to signify the American system's superiority. Now, the United States went all-in for the half in the south, partly to save face over its failure to secure complete victory. Post–Korean War U.S. policy toward the North was one of regime denial, as conceptualized in chapter 2, though Washington had been set on regime change. The United States could do little about North Korea during the Cold War competition against the USSR. Thus, America's 1866 encounter with Korea developed into the contemporary division of Korea with regime recognition in the South and regime denial or change in the North.

This book seeks evidence of such a shift in America's attitude to an all-in stance toward Korea from the American blueprint for the post–Korean War reconstruction. Prepared in 1954 for the UN Korean Reconstruction Agency by Robert R. Nathan and Associates, "An Economic Programme for Korean Reconstruction" (1954: v) starts with an overarching vision for rebuilding the nation: "The overwhelming share of the cost and effort of repelling the aggressors was borne by the Korean people. But, without the assistance and active participation by free nations, success could not have been achieved. The same co-operation will be needed for reconstruction."

This program was designed and implemented by the U.S. government, which first became interested in the idea of trusteeship in 1945, divided the Korean nation in less than an hour, withdrew its military, despite clear signs of Soviet ambition toward the Peninsula, and announced the exclusion of the Peninsula from its defensive perimeter. It goes on to say, "What [Koreans] need is help to help themselves. They require more than a generous contribution of goods to provide the bare necessities of life. Rather, they need substantial and sustained assistance over a sufficient period of time to reach the deeply cherished goal of self-support and economic independence" (Nathan, 1954: v-vi). Unequivocally, this indicated that the United States was going all-in for this partner it had so passionately "wooed" in the nineteenth century. Even a decade earlier, when the United States first occupied the Peninsula, the aim was to use it as a battlefield for the Pacific War. The United States committed no more military or economic aid than needed. Nathan (1954: vi) even mentions that "the Republic of Korea's unfortunate legacy of foreign domination, war and inflation must be overcome."

Whereas Captain Tilton, in the American expedition to avenge the *General Sherman*, told his wife that he was entering a country of "savages," Nathan's Korean Reconstruction Programme discusses how it can increase the incomes, GDP, and other sectors of industry for 22,000,000 Koreans. This represents a sea change in American perception of Koreans from a savage horde of subhumans to a population of fellow human beings worthy of concern and empathy. The Programme says, "If miscalculated, such an effort can be economically, let alone politically, explosive. With many of the nations' resources sparse and with the availability of outside aid limited, there is very little margin for error, little room for misallocation or misuse of resources. For this reason, careful and thorough planning is essential" (1954: 50). This further attests to how the Korean War transformed Americans' attitude toward Korea. Specifically, this report (1954: 115) proposed estimates of American economic aid:

> To bring resources into balance with requirements, an arrival of $284 million of net imports will be needed during the current year, $350 million next year, $295 million in 1955–56, $179 million in 1956–57, and $132 million in 1957–58, or about $1,240 million in all. And then How the U.S. would bring its own aids to Korea: The programme has been well launched with the recent authorization of an additional $200 million U.S. aid appropriation. Some $302 million of available funds, including $158 million of ROK foreign exchange holdings, were carried into ROK fiscal year 1953–54, and most of these should result in import arrivals during the year. In addition, current year annual funds now in prospect include $121 million of ROK foreign exchange receipts, a U.S. Army appropriation for civil relief in Korea of $58 million, and an UNKRA programme of $118 million, which has been approved by the UNKRA Advisory Committee but has not been as yet fully subscribed by contributing nations; $149 million of the $200 million emergency appropriation for Korea made by the U.S. Congress in August 1953, and an additional $35 million to be requested when Congress returns in January. The remainder of the $200 million appropriation is for direct support of the ROK military force, and, therefore, lies outside the scope of the present programme.

Such full-scale plans for economic and military aid would be impossible without such a perspective on Korea. Korea was no longer a trophy or bargaining chip for the United States. Again, the Korean War had completely transformed America's stance toward Korea. In fact, the annual average Korean share of American trade between 1894 and 1904 was a little over $200,000, a level ranging between $100 and around $1,000,000. This was less than one-hundredth of 1% of American total foreign trade—a small amount, indeed. In 1948, when the first ROK government was established, United States and Korea signed the ROK-U.S. Agreement on Aid, similar to the ECA program in Western Europe, and about $109M in aid was provided from 1949 to 1953. Kim (1982: 326) points out that Korea was one of the largest recipients of U.S. foreign aid, along with Vietnam and Israel. For the decades of 1945–1976, economic and military aid each reached $12.6B, or roughly $500 per capita (Kim, 1982: 326; Mason et al., 1980: 165). This essentially amounted to settlement from the United States for its long-awaited union after great adversity.

After Korea had been liberated from Japan, the United States essentially invited the Soviet Union to do battle there. Kim (1982: 328) points out that "the early period of U.S. aid (1953–54) was a time for adjustment for Korea, from Japanese colonialism to an independent nation that had undergone a devastating war." And Kim (1982) aptly characterizes such American aid as "unrequited" economic and military aid that sustained the Republic of Korea and its people, as this book sees it. Such unreciprocated American financial aid continued after the Korean War from 1953 to the year before Korea's industrialization policy started, 1961, with a staggering amount of $2.5B. After Korea launched its ambitious Five-Year Economic Plan in 1962, the United States assisted with $200M worth of assistance a year, on average, equivalent to about 10% of the GNP. As a result of such unrequited support for post–Korean War Korea, South Korea recorded for each of the Five-Year Economic Plan periods 30.7% (1962–1966), 48.5% (1967–1971), 34.9% (1972–1976), and 28.9% (1977–1981) growth (Kim, 1982: 328–332).

This is just a facet of the changes in economic and military backing that resulted from U.S.-Korea relations in the wake of the Korean War, representing for America a clear departure from its conventional apathy on Korea. Indeed, the current situation brings prosperity both to America as was wished in the nineteenth century and to Korea. The Korean War served as a milestone for a new partnership in U.S.-Korea relations in the mid-twentieth century. D'Elia's study (1982: 342–346) on the economic relationship between the United States and ROK illustrates how this once estranged but now newly reunited couple became unprecedentedly interdependent. Their economic relationship today is one of mutual benefit, he indicates, with two-way trade rising dramatically to $9.5B in 1980, $4.9B of which was Korean imports from the United States and $4.6B South Korean exports. Here, we should focus not just on the volume of mutual trade but also the items. The United

States takes 35% or more of South Korean electronics, footwear, leather products, games, and machinery exports. Overall, 96% of U.S. purchases from South Korea are manufactured goods, including 25% of American imports of TVs as of 1982. Also, the United States is the second-largest source of equity investment. U.S. equity investment in South Korea between 1962 and 1980 amounted to $252M, representing 23% of Korea's total foreign investment. Finally, the United States was second only to Japan as a source of foreign technology in the 1980s. Throughout that decade, for example, South Korea signed 392 technology import contracts with the United States, representing 23% of their total.

As explained earlier, Korea's unprecedentedly successful recovery from the ruin of war and its rapid rise as an industrial power were largely due to American aid, both military and economic. During the reconstruction (1953–1960), "aid to the military proper started as high as 40% of the total aid volume in the immediate aftermath of the war and never dipped below 20%" (Kim, 2017: 33).

It was the Korean War, this book argues, that fundamentally transformed U.S.-Korea relations. Although America had long offered military aid[20] to its allies, a radical difference can be noted in the level of American commitment to Korea before and after the outbreak of the Korean War. According to Kim:

> The Economic Cooperation Act (ECA) of 1948, which established the Marshall Plan, did virtually nothing except for revealing that "a self-sustaining economy in South Korea per se was never a major goal of American aid programs for South Korea during this period." However, "A drastic change in American aid policy came in the midst of the Korean War as the Truman Administration authorized 7.5 billion U.S.D of foreign military and economic aid under the Mutual Security Act (MSA) of 1951." (Kim, 2017: 38)

And America's "military aid accounted for more than 73% of all economic aid that South Korea received between 1953 and 1961" (Kim, 2017: 38). The contribution of American military aid to South Korean defense expenditure was also "over 80% in the immediate postwar years and then gradually reduced to about 60% by 1960" (Kim, 2017: 45). Even though there is some controversy as to the effect of military aid on the sustained development of the South Korean economy, Kim (2017: 46) concludes that "American military aid helped ease the fiscal burden of South Korean defense spending, facilitating public investments in economic development." American military aid guaranteed the security of South Korea and at the same time significantly contributed to the country's successful industrialization. There is no doubt that the Korean War infused stability into the previously shaky relationship of these two strangers from such vastly different backgrounds. The history of their interaction is what led to the division of Korea at the start of the Korean War and triggered reverberations that have still not died down after one and a half centuries in one of the world's most troubled areas today.

HOW THE KOREAN WAR SHAPED TWENTY-FIRST-CENTURY U.S.-CHINA FRICTIONS

In tracing and analyzing the consequences on U.S.-Korea encounters, three major external factors must be inevitably considered; those are China, Japan, and Russia. For similar but not completely identical reasons, these three countries share a fundamental interest in seizing hegemonic position in the Korean Peninsula and in maintaining the status quo on North Korea's nuclear programs. As a critical ally to Pyongyang, China shed blood in the Korean War and has been the essential factor in Pyeongyang's fortitude in standing up against the world's strongest military power, the United States. In this section, this book will explain how the unfinished inimical status between the United States and China has resurfaced and influenced the contemporary showdown of Washington's firm stance against China's challenge with its "One Belt One Road" policy. Further, this chapter will contemplate how such confrontational Sino-U.S. relations have shaped the connections between two Koreas.

Before it addresses the question, it will examine fundamental and structural dynamics of East Asia power politics on the North Korean question. First, until Japan colonized Corea in 1910, China had maintained its suzerainty over all of Corea mainly due to its cultural influences, which included acceptance of Chinese cultural and philosophical foundations as well as of China's military superiority. Thus, China has maintained its defensive stance to try to hold its hegemonic position over Corea while both Japan and Russia have wanted to gain control over this geopolitically strategic location. For Japan, Corea is a springboard to the Eurasian Continent and serves as a Maginot Line of defense for Japan from China, while, for Russia, it is an object of desire for unfreezing harbors and traditional expansionism toward the South. America's initial aggressive encounter with Corea to open it up in order to complete Washington's Great Circle route was the unsurprising upshot of that rising superpowers' collisions with China, the existing suzerain, and with two other super-neighbors vigilantly awaiting an opportunity to take a control over the Peninsula.

The biggest loser in this collision course among neighboring hegemonies was China swallowing the pains of being detached from its faithful younger brother. However, China was taking a long route to recover its influences over Korea by converting from debilitated Confucian paper tiger to communist empire and demonstrated its long overdue desire to regain sway over the Korean Peninsula in the Korean War, directly colliding with the United States for the first time in its modern history. That war also served as a signal for the beginning of a new international political system, the Cold War, which has not been completely resolved even though the Western version of the Cold War ended with the collapse of the Soviet Union in 1991: in fact, recent policy collisions in China's challenge against the United States represented in Beijing's One Belt One Road and Washington's Pivot to Asia appears to foretell an ominous resurgence of a new Cold War in East Asia. If that comes to pass, it will be the deadliest consequence of America's encounter with Asia as well as Korea.

The current trade war between the United States and China, according to the South China Morning Post, is not just "a mighty tussle over imports and exports" but also

> [is] pitting China against a coterie of Western nations that see it as the gravest threat to their dominance of the existing world order. Slapping on tariffs is just the opening salvo. On the one side, there is the clear goal of slowing down China's seemingly inexorable rise as a superpower. And on the other side is China's determination not to bow to the collective might of the West and forfeit the right to decide its own destiny. (Fong, 2018)

However politically and parochially oriented this remark may sound, the current trade war and tussle between the United States and China should come as no surprise, viewed in historical context. After the Korean War, and up until China became the world's second-largest economy, this collision course has been expected. In fact, it even surfaced in the Obama administration's "pivot to Asia." The Chinese government and pro-communist intellectuals blame this trade dispute on the United States, hegemonic competition in the South China Sea, and the question of Taiwan's autonomy. Wei (2019) claims that "Washington started to regard Beijing as its strategic rival. Before 2010, the United States did not believe China's national strength could pose a threat to it, nor did it think China was a challenge to the U.S.-led international order."

Quoting Director of Policy Planning at the U.S. State Department Kiron Skinner's comment that "China-U.S. competition is a 'clash of civilizations,'" Wei (2019) refutes this argument by explaining that it is actually "a fight with a really different civilization and a different ideology, and the United States hasn't had that before." She adds that "when we think about the Soviet Union and that competition [i.e., the Cold War], in a way, it was a fight within the Western family, but China poses a unique challenge because the regime in Beijing isn't a child of Western philosophy and history." Rather than viewing China as an enemy, though, Wei (2019) concludes that U.S.-China relations are a contemporary struggle between rivals.

Fong (2018) attributes these countries' current frictions to the Korean War. Among many wars in Chinese history, he says, "One that comes immediately to mind is the 1950–53 Korean War, the only occasion when People's Liberation Army 'volunteers' fought American forces directly. In particular, the 1950 Battle of Chosin [Jang Jin] Reservoir seems an apposite case study." As Fong's comment reminds us, Chinese attitudes toward the current trade war may be fed by tensions leftover from the 67-year-old Armistice of the Korean War, "the only occasion" on which the Chinese fought American forces "directly."

A recently created mouthpiece of the Chinese government, *Global Times*, ran an article explaining why China Central Television (CCTV) urgently reshuffled the broadcasting schedule to insert movies on the Korean War.

China's state television aired three classic Chinese films featuring the Chinese army's heroic role in the Korean War (1950–1953) from Thursday to Saturday, replacing the previously scheduled programs, prompting wide discussions online amid the simmering China-U.S. trade war. China Central Television's movie channel CCTV-6 said on its Weibo on Thursday night that the classic war movie *Heroic Sons and Daughters* would air at 8:25 p.m., and the previously scheduled program of the Asian Film and TV Week would be shown at 10:20 p.m. Later, the channel said that on Friday night, it would screen another military film, *Battle on Shangganling Mountain*, depicting a major battle in North Korea. According to the CCTV-6's programming schedule, a third classic film, *A Surprise Attack*, will be aired on Saturday, replacing the scheduled comedy film. All three films featured the war to resist U.S. aggression and to aid Korea, as is accepted in China (*Global Times*, 2019).

The second movie, in particular, was commissioned by Chairman Mao in 1956.

By now it should be clear that the Chinese see the Korean War, in which they fought against Americans for the first time, as the start of a long and continued battle against the United States. Renping (2019) writes that the currently intensifying trade war with the United States is reminiscent of the Korean War. He says:

> The war lasted over three years, and in the latter two years of fighting and talking, our persistence on the battlefield and the continuing gains eventually forced the Americans to bow their heads at the negotiating table. Looking at the current arrogance of the American elites toward a strategic crackdown on China, it's clear that we face a long and almost determined and protracted war regardless of the progress of the trade talks. Regardless of whether a trade deal is signed or not, this game is inevitable. We must carry forward the spirit of the battle on "Shangganling Mountain." A trade war is a great game in which we need to

create and unleash our vitality while maintaining our position and crush the will of the other side with China's growing economic strength.

Evidence of this association is abundant.

China is engaging in trade talks with the U.S. while fighting a trade war. It reminded many Chinese people of a similar situation during the Korean War (1950-53) when China helped North Korea resist the military action of the U.S. . . . Although today's trade war is different from the Korean War, the Chinese people's memories of engaging in talks and fights at the same time remains fresh. It lets Chinese people realize that the trade frictions between China and the U.S. will not end very soon. (Hailin, 2019)

Sheng (2019) explains why these unscheduled Korean War movies were aired so abruptly. Reiterating how the trade war with the United States served as a reminder of the Korean War, he notes that China's state-run CCTV airs Korean War movies each day from Thursday to Sunday. He writes, "CCTV-6 announced Sunday via its official account on China's Twitter-like Sina Weibo social media that it would broadcast a documentary about the 1950 Battle of Chosin [Jang Jin] Reservoir, an important battle that marked the complete withdrawal of U.S.-led UN troops from North Korea." He adds that "because of the demand from the audiences," the channel decided to broadcast China-produced Korean War movies. "We are using movies to echo the current era," CCTV-6 said on its Weibo on Saturday. "We are not afraid of the U.S.," commented one net user who received hundreds of likes, "not in the past, not today. Thumbs-up to CCTV." In May of 2019, Korean War stories plastered the Chinese news and media. "Maybe some in the U.S. believe that the Korean War was a draw, but if you know the history well, you will understand it was a symbolic military victory of China against the U.S.," said a military and history expert at a Beijing Military Academy who asked for anonymity. China "forced" the United States to sign an armistice, he noted, and the United States did not win the war at all. "More importantly, China's military strength at that time was much weaker than America's. It is easy to remind Chinese people of the Korean War these days," he told Global Times. "Because if China could realize such a symbolic victory in a real war with the U.S. in the 1950s when it was weak and poor, then why should China fear a trade war launched by the U.S. today when it has already become a great power of the world?"

Sheng directly links current U.S.-China trade frictions to the Korean War: "Some net users also said that from the historical lessons, they can learn that maybe conflicts are inevitable." One net user commented, "You can only reason with the U.S. and get a fair deal after you prove you cannot be defeated. Otherwise the deal will never be fair." According to his report, the rationale for suddenly airing Korean War movies was as follows: "The history of the

Korean War showed that if China dared not fight, 'you can't let a powerful rival understand your determination and bottom line, and the U.S. won't understand that it will pay for its endless bullying,' said An Gang, a senior research fellow at the Pangoal Institution, a Beijing-based think tank."

A strong lesson can be learned from the Korean War, Sheng indicates, relevant to China's collision course with America: "The trade war is different from a real war like the Korean War that causes huge casualties, but it is getting increasingly obvious that the U.S. is trying to hurt China's interests, including national security and economic development," said Lü Xiang, a research fellow of China-U.S. relations at the Chinese Academy of Social Sciences. It was in this sense that the trade war and the Korean War are similar. Lü continued: "A treasured experience that we gained from the Korean War is that the leadership of the Communist Party of China and the unity of the people were crucial for China to overcome the aggression from the U.S. in the Korean Peninsula. They are also crucial today" (Sheng, 2019).

This coverage of the trade war between the United States and China corroborates findings on how the Korean War has shaped negative narratives of China's policy and attitudes toward the United States. Gries et al. (2009: 437) conducted an experimental case study to investigate how "the valence, source, and nation of historical accounts of the Korean War affect Chinese and U.S. students' beliefs about this shared past, emotions, national self-esteem, and threat perception in the present." This article also validates Sheng's association of the current trade war with the Korean War. Gries et al. (2009) argue that the unfortunate past between the United States and China still haunts them through reverberations in contemporary bilateral affairs. The best example, they claim, is the Korean War. The authors find that:

> While most Americans have largely forgotten the war, many Chinese not only remember it but also draw both pride and strength from that memory. This fortuitous asymmetry of historical relevance mitigates the impact that contending Korean War histories have on U.S.-China relations today. . . . When both parties to a shared contentious past link that past to their self-understandings in the present, there is little room for compromise. (455)

As we find from Chinese depictions of current trade frictions with the United States, the Korean War represents a deep wound and, at the same time, a lesson in Chinese relations with the United States, as in the argument by Gries et al. (2009) that contemporary affairs continue to be shaped by conflicts of the past. They add that "Chinese nationalism today is closely tied with narratives of China's past victimization at the hands of Western and Japanese imperialism, and that national sentiment has an impact on China's foreign policies in general and U.S. policy in particular" (2009: 434).

Even before the current trade conflicts between these two countries, metaphors and direct references to the Korean War appeared in various contexts. According to Gries et al. (2009),

> The People's Daily's reference to the "Korean battleground" is noteworthy. The CCP has long staked claim to nationalist legitimacy partly on the basis of a nationalist narrative in which the CCP led a righteous effort to aid the Korean people and expel the invading U.S. forces from Chinese and Korean soil. Indeed, it has been argued (Gries et al., 2004: 56–61) that in Chinese nationalist narratives, "victory" in Korea over the United States marks the end of the "Century of Humiliation" and thus remains central to both the collective self-esteem of many Chinese nationalists as well as the legitimacy of the CCP today. (Gries et al., 2009: 434)

For the Chinese, the Korean War is a source of national pride, and offers a way to recover from the shameful past of kneeling to Western and Japanese imperialism. Perhaps that is why, whenever China faces problems with countries that have insulted its self-respect, the grizzled specter of the Korean War rears its head.

As indicated by comparative analyses of history textbooks in both countries, current frictions between the United States and China have been shaped by reverberations from the past.

Of greater consequence is the treatment of the Korean War in China's high school history textbooks. Current textbooks continue to refer to the United States as the "enemy" (diren), suggesting that the United States intervened in the "domestic affairs" of Korea without provocation. No mention is made of the North Korean invasion of South Korea. When MacArthur's armies headed toward the Yalu River, the Chinese People's Volunteer (CPV) drove the "invaders" (qinluezhe) back to the 38th parallel, where they were forced to sign the armistice. The CPV had "won" (shengli), and the United States had "lost" (shibai) (see, e.g., People's Education 2006). By contrast, U.S. history textbooks tend to treat Korea as the "Forgotten War." Compared to their much more extensive treatment of the "good war" against German and Japanese fascism during World War II, U.S. textbook treatment of the Korean War is brief. For instance, the 1991 eighth edition of the popular McGraw-Hill textbook *American History: A Survey* devotes 30 pages to World War II but just three to the Korean War. The account begins with the North Korean "invasion" of the South, followed by U.S. intervention to "assist" the overwhelmed South Korean army against "communist forces." It concludes rather ambiguously with a "protracted stalemate" back at the 38th parallel where it had all started (see Brinkley et al., 1991: 844–846).

The current catastrophic stalemate between the United States and North Korea was not the first in their shared history. As this book will detail, the United States' first attempt to open the Joseon dynasty took place on the Daedong River, near the current capital of North Korea. After that, the North had never been an issue in the relationship until Korea's liberation from Japan in 1945, when two superpowers took over the Peninsula. Since then, U.S. policies toward the two Koreas undoubtedly diverged. To shed new light on the main characteristics of American attitudes toward the two Koreas, the next chapter introduces a variation on the conventional notions of regime recognition and regime change—regime denial.

ANOTHER KOREAN WAR?

On July 1, 2021, the Communist Party of China (CPC) held a massive celebration event upon the centenary of the foundation of the CPC, which was established in 1921. Global news and media highlighted a sentence allegedly spoken by China's President Xi Jinping, "Anyone who dares try to do that [bully, oppress, or subjugate China] will have their heads bashed bloody against the Great Wall of Steel forged by over 1.4 billion Chinese people." That was the headline for major news and media. However, that speech in the version that Xi delivered[21] in the Embassy of the People's ROC in the United States of America[22] is quite softer than the one in the news: "Anyone who would attempt to do so will find themselves on a collision course with a great wall of steel forged by over 1.4 billion Chinese people." Regardless of which words are true to Xi's mind, "have their heads bashed bloody against" us "find themselves on a collision course with" the Great Wall of Steel forged by over 1.4 billion Chinese people and 95 million Party members, his message was clear that China will fight against American-led Western bullying and abuse.

President Xi identified two parts of its history as sources of China's humiliations: China's Ancient Regime of semifeudal system and semicolonial exploitations by foreign imperialists. He specifically singled out the Opium War of 1840 and referred unequal treaties imposed on China by foreign powers and all the privileges that imperialist powers enjoyed in China. He finally emphasized that China has to continue its second centenary of national rejuvenation with socialism with Chinese characteristics. The real ominous signs are in his resolute remarks that "We will stay true to the letter and spirit of the principle of One Country, Two Systems, under which the people of Hong Kong administer Hong Kong, and the people of Macao administer Macao, both with a high degree of autonomy" and Taiwan. He said,

> Resolving the Taiwan question and realizing China's complete reunification is a historic mission and an unshakable commitment of the Communist Party of China. . . . We must take resolute action to utterly defeat any attempt toward "Taiwan independence," . . . . No one should underestimate the resolve, the will, and the ability of the Chinese people to defend their national sovereignty and territorial integrity.

In addition to China's Belt and Road initiative, the collision course in Washington's resolute policy of deterring a rejuvenated China is dangerously evolving in the South China Sea. Among many contemporary occasions of Sino-American collisions, one stands out. On Monday, April 26, 2021, an American warship found itself in the middle of a Chinese navy flotilla as it shadowed the group led by China's aircraft carrier Liaoning out of the South China Sea and into the Western Pacific. Satellite images captured the aircraft carrier Liaoning with five People's Liberation Army escort vessels sailing in the Philippine Sea, while a conspicuous U.S. Navy vessel—likely an Arleigh Burke-class destroyer—followed closely behind. This Chinese flotilla was on a return journey to the East China Sea after a month-long deployment in the South China Sea, where it conducted exercises in view of American and Japanese naval assets. Feng (2021) points out that although it is routine for the navies of different countries to observe each other at sea, it was highly unusual for the Arleigh Burke-class destroyer to sail into Liaoning's flotilla unimpeded, said Taipei-based defense analyst Su Tzu-yun.

The Taiwan question raises a portentous warning that not just the U.S.-led alliance of QUAD countries (Quadrilateral Security Dialogue among the United States, Japan, Australia, and India), including Japan but also South Korea with its 25,000 U.S. troops might be dragged into a potential conflict between America and China. The Pentagon has deployed a new strategic concept of "strategic flexibility" of U.S. forces abroad after China has clearly shown its policy of challenging U.S. hegemony in the world while Washington was also embroiled in the quagmire of Middle Eastern conflicts. Sandwiched between Washington and Beijing while heavily dependent upon American military, Seoul has maneuvered a tight-rope dance to maintain its economic market in China and it's a century-long alliance with the United States.

In these contemporary power struggles among major players in Asia, there is an undeniable possibility for a third Korean War to break out. The first Korean War broke out because Corea did not want intercourse with the United States. The second Korean War was a civil war instigated by Moscow and Beijing while Washington also contributed to the breakout with its chronic vacillations toward Korea. As mentioned, it was not only a civil war between North and South Koreas but also the first major war between China and the United States since the Wangxia Treaty in 1844. Now, nineteenth-century imperial forces and bullies toward China, mostly old European imperial countries, have been replaced with the unilateral hegemon of the United States. Their smoldering discontent over their unfinished business from the second Korean War is about to be reignited.

Another detonation can be set off when Pyeongyang achieves its ultimate goal of completing intercontinental ballistic missile technology with multiple nuclear warheads, which can reenter the atmosphere with accuracy. Washington will have to deal with such successes by Pyeongyang because the American continent will theoretically be exposed to North Korea's nuclear bombs. Those two ominous intimations of another world-scale war, this book argues, are the legacy of the second Korean War, which is, again this book argues, the direct outcome of century-long American encounters with Korea.

NOTES

1. The largest deployment is in Japan with 39,345 military personnel. Germany is second with 34,805, and Korea third with 23,468. Italy (12,102), Afghanistan (9,294), and the United Kingdom (8,479) follow close behind. For a list of ranks and numbers of all U.S. military personnel overseas, see Desjardins (2017).

2. Not everyone, however, sees the military presence as benign. Park Jung Eun, for instance, Secretary General of an NGO called the 'People's Solidarity for Participatory Democracy,' says there are "so many problems with the cost and size" of Camp Humphrey, arguing that South Korea's 92% share of the base's $10.8B price tag imposes too great a burden. This year, according to Reuters, under a five-year bilateral cost-sharing arrangement with the United States, South Korea also paid about $857M for the upkeep of U.S. troops. Washington and Seoul are currently negotiating the splitting of costs from 2019 (Hincks, 2018).

3. With regard to the rules governing and protecting U.S. military in South Korea, the United States and South Korea signed the Status of Forces Agreement (SOFA). As Article V of the SOFA stipulates, the United States will bear all costs for maintenance of U.S. troops, except for "all facilities and areas and rights of way" to be borne by South Korea. Since SOFA was signed in 1966, many amendments have been made, and the Special Measures Agreements (SMAs) in 1991 witnessed South Korea sharing a greater portion of the total cost. In February 2019, South Korea agreed for one year to increase its contribution to just under 1.04 trillion *won* ($927M), an increase of about $70.3M from the previous deal. President Trump initially asked South Korea to pay $5B, a fivefold jump, in Trump's words "$5 billion worth of protection." According to a civil organization in South Korea, Korea's contribution has increased to well over 70% of the total cost if we include direct and indirect costs in three categories: personnel costs of South Korean workers hired by U.S. troops, military construction costs such as building facilities within U.S. bases, and military assistance expenses, such as services and materials.

4. Decades earlier, John Quincy Adams made the same argument in support of the British in the Opium War against China in 1840: national exclusivity was selfish and defied natural law by artificially impeding others' pursuit of wealth and happiness. In the 1840s, Adams had persuaded few Americans to support the British, but few Americans by the 1870s denied that the Western international system embodied "natural law" (Chang, 2003: 1353).

5. Manifest Destiny was widely proselytized in the nineteenth-century American expansion westward, primarily to justify imperialist cultural ideology. Later, however, it was also implicated in the imperial cruise to countries in Asia. It epitomized the fundamental mission of the United States to redeem the Old World through the dominance of American civilization and religion. In its pursuit, ethnic superiority over Asians was clearly assumed. In the end, this ideology, among others, justified the genocide of native Americans as well as America's wars in Asia.

6. Italics mine. This is also quoted in Chang (2003: 1344), Dennett (1922), and Swartout, Jr. (1974).

7. The physical presence of the flotilla startled onlookers: The *Colorado* was a steam frigate, with sail and engine, that displaced 4,772 tons, reaching 264 feet at the water line, and carrying 47 cannons, 47 officers, and 571 crewmembers. Three other ships were each at least 250 feet long. The fifth was an iron gunboat measuring 137 feet. When the fleet came into sight off the coast, beacon fires appeared on prominent hilltops near the anchorage. Local residents abandoned villages and took everything they could carry (Chang, 2003: 1343).

8. With regard to the formation of the American expedition, see Griffis' detailed description: "The chastising expedition consisted of the Monocacy, Palos, four steam-launches, and twenty boats, conveying a landing force of six hundred and fifty-one men, of whom one hundred and five were marines. The Benicia, Alaska, and Colorado remained at anchor. The total force detailed for the work of punishing the Coreans was seven hundred and fifty-nine men. These were arranged in ten companies of infantry, with seven pieces of artillery. The Monocacy had, in addition to her regular armament, two of the Colorado's nine-inch guns" (1889: 412).

9. All underlining by the author to highlight how Korean perspectives were ignored by Washington in this momentous decision that dealt permanent suffering to the Korean nation.

10. If he was aware that the Soviet Union would have accepted a higher latitude, like the 39th parallel. As evidence of Soviet acceptance of any suggestion from the U.S. government, Sandusky asserts that the Soviets could have been stopped at a line much further north, possibly even at the 40th parallel, as will be discussed in more detail later. For details, see Barry (2012: 47–48).

11. "General Order No. 1, Military and Naval," quoted in Foreign Relations of the United States, 1945, Vol. VI: British Commonwealth, the Far East, Washington, DC: Government Printing Office, 1969, p. 659. Ibid., p. 86, requoted in Barry (2012: 47).

12. "Stalin ordered his ambassador in Washington, Nikolai Novikov, to prepare a 'telegram' of his own, which he sent to Moscow on September 27, 1946. 'The foreign policy of the United States,' Novikov claimed, 'reflects the imperialistic tendencies of American monopolistic capitalism, [and] is characterized . . . by a striving for world

supremacy.' As a consequence, the United States was increasing its military spending 'colossally,' establishing bases far beyond its borders, and had reached an agreement with Great Britain to divide the world into spheres of influence. . . . It is quite possible that the Near East will become a center of Anglo-American contradictions that will explode the agreements now reached between the United States and England" (Gaddis, 2005: 30).

13. Foreign Relations of the United States, 1949, the Far East and Australasia, Volume VII, Part 2, 895.50 Recovery/5–1649, The Acting Secretary of State to the Director of the Bureau of the Budget (Pace), top secret, [Washington] May 16, 1949.

14. By the author.

15. This city was named after Kim Chaek, the closest comrade of North Korea's founder, Kim Il-sung

16. That is, the nuclear bomb that the United States completed in 1945.

17. The CIA report went on to say, "In the spring and summer of 1950, reports from ORE reaching U.S. military headquarters in Japan and top policymakers in Washington indicated the probability of trouble ahead, although these assessments as before were vague and by no means explicit." On January 13, 1950, the CIA noted "a continuing southward movement of the expanding [North] Korean People's Army toward the thirty-eighth parallel" and their acquisition of heavy equipment and armor but did not see an invasion as imminent. Still, the review contained little information that could conceivably be termed indications or warnings of a pending North Korean attack. ORE's next intelligence estimate specifically on Korea appeared just one week before the invasion. Entitled *Current Capabilities of the Northern Korean Regime*, it declared that North Korea possessed military superiority over the south and was fully capable of pursuing "its main external aim of extending control over southern Korea."

18. That is, the scholars who criticized Secretary of State Dean Acheson's Press Club speech in January 1950 as inviting North Korea's Kim Il-sung's invasion of South Korea.

19. The Korean War Veterans Association was officially founded in 1985, thirty-five years after the outbreak of the Korean War, whereas other war veterans' organizations were quick to form associations, for example, Veterans of the Vietnam War established in 1978, three years after the war ended in 1975.

20. American aid to allies started with the Lend-Lease Act of 1942, which was designed to provide an enormous amount of aid, a total of $50.1B worth of materials, to Allied nations (Kim, 2017: 36).

21. Found at http://www.china-embassy.org/eng/zgyw/t1889022.htm

22. Found at http://www.china-embassy.org/eng/

Chapter 4

North Korean Quagmire
The Last Phase of U.S. Encounter?

THE PLACE OF NORTH KOREA IN U.S.-KOREA RELATIONS

In 2002, Syracuse University initiated a unique nongovernmental program for academic exchange with North Korea's best-known institute of science and technology, Kim Chaek University of Technology.[1] In 2005, however, something unexpected occurred. All preparations had been made to welcome 30 North Korean scholars in Beijing, where they would be learning English and academic skills to advance their involvement in international scholarly platforms. At sunrise on July 5, 2005, as I was about to fly from Seoul to Beijing to host this meeting, I was watching a game of "go" on TV to stay awake when an emergency caption scrolled across the screen: "North Korea fires unconfirmed numbers of missiles"—seven ballistic missiles, to be exact, including a Taepodong-2, a grave concern, especially for the United States, because it was a long-range missile that presumably could reach American territories such as Alaska. Shocked to think how this might nullify Syracuse University's 12 months of preparation for this unexpectedly successful Track II exchange—all operations had been financially supported by several organizations, including the ROK's Ministry of Unification, and positively recognized by the U.S. State Department and other intelligence agencies—I placed a few calls to colleagues who quickly reassured me that the U.S. government would not ask us to cancel the workshop.

To resolve North Korea's brinkmanship with its nuclear and missile tests, Six-Party Talks were initiated in August 2003 between the United States, South Korea, China, Russia, Japan, and North Korea. When these talks wrapped up their fifth round on November 9–11, 2005, North Korea was disciplined for its missile launches by UN Security Council Resolution 1695 in addition to Washington's action to freeze Pyongyang's bank account in Banco Delta Macau Bank; nevertheless, the academic program ended that summer in Beijing successfully. Up until the early twenty-first century, North Korea's provocative missile tests did not pose a sufficient threat to justify cancelling academic exchanges of Track II engagements, mainly because its missiles were not believed to have capacities to reach the American continent.

Just 13 years later, however, the situation took a grave turn for the worse. On May 5, 2019, the North Korean regime test-fired a ballistic missile system (Defence Blog, 2019). According to South Korean defense sources and Defence Blog, it was an indigenously developed model of a Russian-made Iskander-E short-range ballistic missile. What shocked South Korea and its allies, including the United States, about this launch was that it was of a strikingly different caliber from the conventional missiles tested a few years earlier. In 2016, North Korea had test-fired more than 20 missiles, and then a similar number in 2017 (Department of Defense, 2017); however, all had been short-range, mid-range, or Intercontinental Ballistic Missiles (ICBMs) with trajectories conventional enough for South Korea and Japan to intercept. That is why South Korea yielded to U.S. pressure to install the Terminal High-Altitude Area Defense (THAAD) missile system, which became operational on May 2, 2017, despite vehement opposition from the Chinese government.

The reason that North Korea's new Iskander is so threatening is because it is tricky to intercept. According to an article in *National Interest* (2018), "The 9K720 Iskander-M—known in NATO parlance as the SS-26 Stone— . . . was designed to evade missile defenses . . . [and] can maneuver at more than 30g during its terminal phase. It's also equipped with decoys to spoof interceptor missiles."[2] It has also been said that the 9K720 Iskander-M system "has a great potential for modernization, which is happening in terms of armaments and missiles in particular." Aleksandr Dragovalovsky, Deputy Commander of Russia's missile forces, told state-owned Sputnik in November 2015, "A new version of the Iskander would undoubtedly be even more problematic to intercept." It is not known how advanced the North Korean version is at this point; however, the situation is alarming enough to compel South Korea and its allies to seek solutions. In other words, South Korea's current "kill chain"[3] must be significantly modified to protect against North Korea's missile attacks.

Interestingly, amid North Korea's provocations with new missile technologies, the U.S. has shown strong interest in continuing the negotiations on denuclearization initiated by President Trump's threat of "fire and fury" in 2017 in reaction to the North's tests of ICBMs with North Korea's young leader Kim Jong-un. This was followed by the biggest nuclear test to date, and by Chairman Kim's retort that President Trump was "a dotard." The United States. has been consistent in stating that it has no intention of lessening its own sanctions and UN sanctions against North Korea until "final, full, and verifiable denuclearization" (FFVD) of North Korea's nuclear and missile programs, which was a new policy of the Trump administration, as compared to the complete, verifiable, and irreversible denuclearization (CVID) that had been generally agreed to by all parties.

This imperiled both Trump's goal, to stop weapons tests, and his pride in achieving something extraordinary[4] after long negotiations. Ward's (2019) report, on Vox.com, aptly explains what made the situation is so puzzling:

> While it was only a short-range missile that couldn't reach the United States, it shows that North Korean leader Kim Jong Un's patience with negotiations may be wearing thin. The next day, Trump deescalated the situation by tweeting that he remains hopeful that Kim will choose to dismantle his nuclear arsenal, adding, 'He also knows that I am with him.' That's a far cry from Trump's old threats to rain down "fire and fury" and "totally destroy" the country. Then on Sunday [May 6, 2019], Secretary of State Mike Pompeo said North Korea's test didn't end the moratorium on testing because it was not an ICBM that could hit America. In other words, what Kim did wasn't great, but it won't knock Washington and Pyongyang off the diplomatic path.

By contrast, on May 25, 2019, U.S. National Security Advisor John Bolton, on his trip to Japan for President Trump's summit with Japanese prime minister Abe, declared North Korea's ballistic missile launch to be in contravention of UN resolutions (Denyer and Parker, 2019).

Immediately after this official critique of North Korea's breach of the resolution, President Trump tweeted,

> North Korea fired off some small weapons, which disturbed some of my people, and others, but not me. I have confidence that Chairman Kim will keep his promise to me, & also smiled when he called Swampman Joe Biden a low IQ individual, &worse. Perhaps that's sending me a signal?—Donald J. Trump (@realDonaldTrump) May 26, 2019.[5]

According to Denyer and Parker (2019), he "weaponized his friendship with Kim for campaign leverage over Biden, the Democratic presidential candidate on whom Trump and his allies are most focused." In addition to negating his own Treasury's latest round of sanctions, this message directly rebuked his own national security advisor and complicated Bolton's relationship with Japanese prime minister Abe, who wants to punish North Korea for so seriously disrupting Japan's missile defenses.[6]

The UN and the United States have been clear and consistent in executing economic sanctions whenever North Korea breaches a UN resolution;

however, this time, Kim's unconventional and game-changing ballistic missile test smugly evaded triggering sanctions from the UN and the United States. President Trump had too much at stake in his ambitious and mysterious stance with North Korea's Kim, ranging from his personal ambition to win the Nobel Peace Prize to embellishing his political resumé for the 2020 presidential race. After 70 years of apathetic inaction or regime denial of North Korea and 154 years of U.S.-Korea relations, these episodes speak to the current state of bilateral relations between the United States and the DPRK.

As of July 2021, with the Biden administration, there has been no major breakthrough on the current stalemate over Pyongyang's nuclear ambitions and provocations. As mentioned before, America's zeal to open Corea has gone through major historical milestones including opening, colonizing, dividing, and warring since 1866. The biggest success this book finds in this entire course of encounters is South Korea's exemplary successes as a model for rapid but sustainable economic accomplishment as one of the world's economic powers and a resilient and substantive democracy. However, its original vision has not come full circle. Rather, its goal has run aground at the last stop of America's *Odyssey* or Great Circle Adventure launched in 1866 Pyongyang. Chapter 5 here examines historical trajectories of U.S. and Korea encounters and attempts to explain the permanent deadlock of the divided Koreas and the absence of major breakthroughs between Pyongyang and Washington

My swift and intuitive responses on why Washington has been stuck at the last stage of its encounters with Korea go as follows: First, Washington was embarrassed by the ceasefire in the Korean War. Even setting aside the fact that North Korea was backed by both the Soviet Union and communist China, the victor of World War II with the world's biggest military was not able to have a clear victory over a small satellite communist regime. That might have strained America's self-esteem. Second, the North Korean system is contemptuous of the values of American-free capitalistic democracy. North Korea left millions of its own people to suffer either death or widespread and very intense famine as well as very oppressive, totalitarian, and inhuman treatment of its own citizens. This must be so contemptible and despicable that it has driven Washington to think it is not worth dealing with such a failed and brutal regime.

Third, despite all these vulnerabilities on the side of Pyongyang, there is no clear solution for fixing or changing its rule including regime change because any military action from Washington could endanger the safety and security of South Korea and upset the whole East Asian power balance. At the same time, North Korea no longer stands alone but with America's most fearsome foes, China and Russia now. Any move by Washington to change the status quo will automatically bring reactions from Beijing and Moscow. In addition, in order to normalize the relationship with Pyeongyang, Washington has to face South Korea's conservative right-wing political force and Japan's opposition.

The status quo of the power dynamics in the Korean Peninsula is so fixed that any disruption can raise the world's level of conflicts especially in the face of China's economic and military challenges against American power in the region. For all that, Washington cannot swallow North Korea's nuclear status as it did for Pakistan, India, and Israel, which will disrupt America's nuclear policy of nonproliferation and the authority of its nuclear umbrella. Such a decision will encourage proliferation of nuclear armaments in Japan, South Korea, and Taiwan, at least. North Korea is a fish bone in Washington's throat: too big to swallow and too thorny and spiny to leave in. The Pandora's Box of woes opened in the late nineteenth century has never been closed and we don't have any concrete idea when it will be. That's the last point at issue left to the Corean Question raised by William Seward and Robert Shufeldt and vacillated about by Theodore Roosevelt and Franklin Roosevelt. This book predicts there will be a continuation of the vacillations from regime denial to regime change: Why? Because there is no levelheaded option but to continue to ride waves created by the East Asian international logjam.[7] The only detonator for breaking up this century-old status quo will become apparent be when Washington sees that Pyeongyang has nuclear ICBM capacity to target any part of American territory.

Washington and Pyeongyang: "Inadvertently Consistent and Predictably Erratic"[8]

Over the short history of the America's interaction with the Korean Peninsula, the U.S. stance toward North Korea has remained consistent in one main regard—by continually shifting (Han, 2014). North Korea did not prompt much of an agenda to President Reagan, whose policy essentially amounted to regime denial, but it became a focus for the Clinton administration, which initiated a shift to regime recognition or regime change. In his administration, Bush vacillated from the radical policy of regime change, initially branding North Korea as part of the "Axis of Evil" in his 2002 State of the Union, and then he shifted toward a policy of bold negotiation, agreeing to the format of Six-Party Talks in 2003 for the dismantling of North Korea's ICBM and nuclear weapons programs. President Obama veered again, this time to the other extreme of strategic patience led by the then-secretary of state Hillary Clinton, which turned out to be a policy of waiting for North Korea to confess and comply to U.S. demands for denuclearization, an approach I have criticized elsewhere as "a strategic blunder, inaction, and passivity" (2014a).

In his administration, President Trump took a zigzagging path from "fire and fury" to "a big deal," weaponizing Twitter to insult this foreign leader as "a rocket man," to threaten devastation, yet to make overtures of romance. It is possible that the extremely unreliable, almost hysterical and ill-motivated trajectories of his policy would eventually lead them to crash and burn, due partly to his follies in domestic politics leading up to the 2020 presidential election and partly to Pyeongyang's sharp sense of his ultimate fall. In fact, Pyeongyang appears to have been keenly aware that President Trump's style of risk was behind America's complete reversal from harsh economic sanctions to bargaining for a big deal. Moreover, Trump's reputation was in disarray from scandals ranging from collusion with Russia to obstruction of justice as well as many other charges of corruption and fraud, such as campaign finance misuse and embezzlement, tax evasion, and government budget diversions, and so on. North Korea is desperate to shake free from U.S. and UN sanctions but ready to return to playing its own "trump card" (Cumings, 2005: 481) of pursuing the simultaneous development of its economy and nuclear weapons and missiles programs. Such a two-pronged approach from the United States will most likely drive North Korea back to its original stance of continuing nuclear and missile tests while taking a path of voluntarily privation in its already failing economy. As soon as Pyeongyang sees the result of Trump's political scandals, it will likely close off all paths to negotiation and amass nuclear and missile capabilities while adjusting to a new player in Washington, thus returning the Peninsula to a collateral impasse.

With regard to Washington's hostility toward North Korea, the two countries have no mutual understanding or negotiation capital, largely due to their lack of direct (i.e., nonmilitary) civilian contact for most of the nineteenth and twentieth centuries. As shown in table 4.1, American disinterest toward the Peninsula had been pervasive since the late nineteenth century—especially during the Theodore Roosevelt administration, and after the Taft-Katsura Secret Agreement in 1905, which established an understanding between U.S. war secretary William Taft and Japanese prime minister Katsura Taro about Japan's sphere of influence over Korea and non-interference with America's influence over the Philippines.

During the Wilson presidency and until the end of World War II, several decisions[9] and nondecisions by U.S. foreign policymakers led to the outbreak of the Korean War (Henderson, 1968; Cumings, 2005; Bradley, 2009; Han, 2011). America's mostly apathetic and disdainful attitude toward Korea had begun long before and culminated in 35 years of Japanese colonial control (1910–1945). As evidence will show, President Theodore Roosevelt's apathy toward Korea, rooted in racial prejudice, could even be considered one of the main factors in Japan's annexation of Korea. As early as 1900, Vice President Roosevelt had written a friend: "I should like to see Japan have Korea. She will be a check upon Russia, and she deserves it for what she has done [victories over China in 1894 and Russia in 1905]. . . . With their bumbling

Table 4.1 Major Events Surrounding DPRK

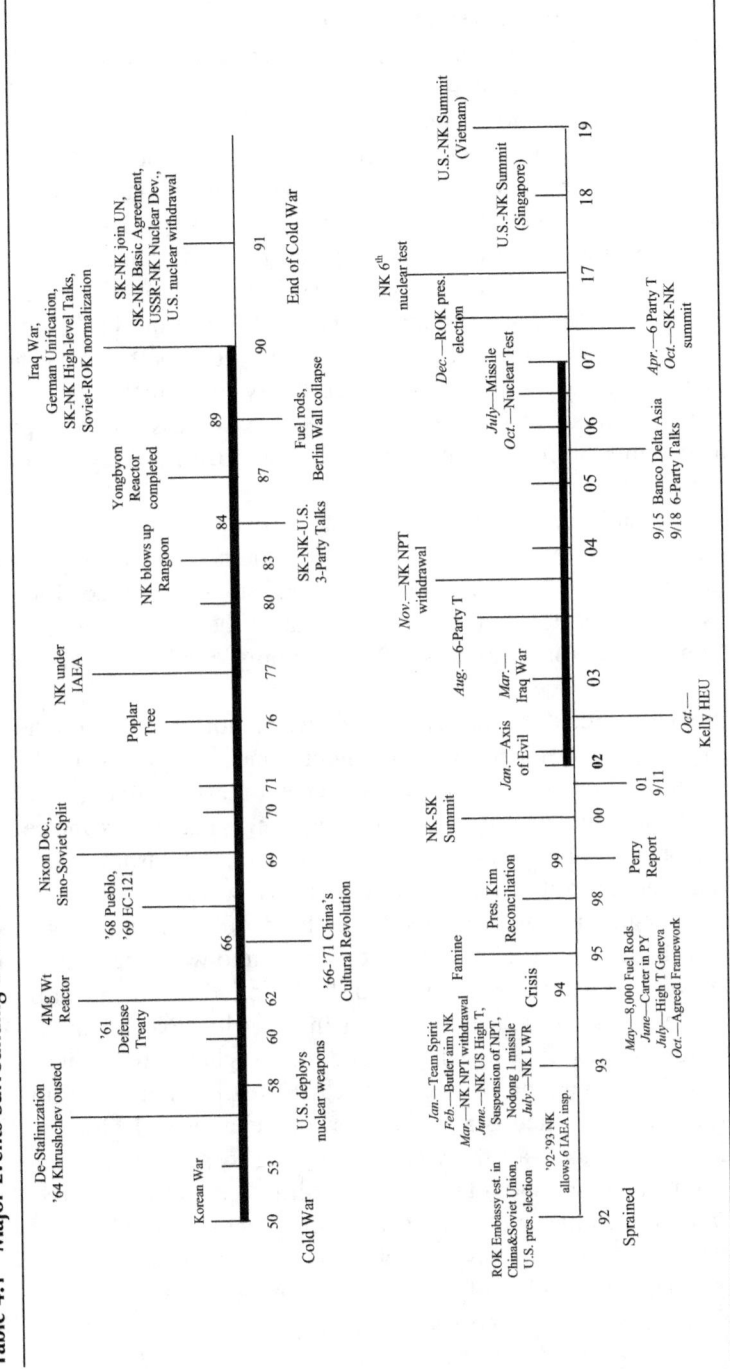

Source: Created by the author.

diplomacy, Roosevelt and Taft had accomplished the seemingly impossible: they gave Korea to Japan" (Bradley, 2009: 322).

As will be examined in detail later, such an attitude would eventually cause the costly error of misleading the Soviet Union and North Korea about the America's willingness to defend Korea from becoming part of the Soviet bloc. As was reflected in Dean Acheson's 1949 withdrawal of the U.S. defensive perimeter from the Peninsula, the United States was the unwitting creator of North Korea, even though Washington perceived the military threat of Moscow clearly and was prepared to counter and defeat Russian forces from 1945 to 1950 (Henderson, 1980; Ross, 1988). When the collapse of the Soviet Union shook the bipolar power balance on the Peninsula, the loss for North Korea was sudden and seismic. For South Korea, however, the collapse became an unexpected opportunity to normalize relations with Russia and communist China. Table 4.1 provides a cross-sectional picture of how the collapse of Soviet Union dramatically drove Pyeongyang to nuclear brinkmanship.[10]

To American leadership, the best way to recover from the failure of unwittingly creating North Korea was to remake South Korea as a country with American democratic and capitalistic values, an Asian model for success. South Korea's prosperity, modeled after that of the United States, stands in direct contrast to North Korea's failed economy, modeled after that of the USSR.

For the past three decades, relations between North Korea and the United States have become much more ambiguous and overtly deceitful, ranging from hostility to exploration of rapprochement and negotiation. Vociferous and pervasive American criticism of Pyeongyang's dangerous and seemingly irrational behavior has focused on its nuclear brinkmanship, human rights violations, and general disregard for its citizens' well-being, as shown by its choice to pursue nuclear weapons while the people starve in a widespread famine. Although both regimes have good reason to work together, establishing a basis for constructive and trustworthy negotiations seems far off, given Washington's globally strategic interest in deterring Pyeongyang's nuclear proliferation versus Pyeongyang's need for a guarantee of its regime's security and economic aid. To date, North Korea has not given up its condemnation of the United States as its sworn enemy and global leader of capitalist imperialism—all the while attempting to normalize relations with Washington. Here, we should note that North Korea's history textbooks constantly reproduce images of American soldiers being burned and destroyed. Moreover, it goes without saying that the parents of these children still have vivid traumatic memories of their wartime experiences. No wonder their images of U.S. soldiers express such hostility.

Acting cautiously, North Korea has taken initial steps to adjust to the changing geopolitical realities of the post–Cold War era. It has revamped its 40-year survival strategy of "muddling through" between the former USSR and China by attempting to consolidate them into one pole as former allies while viewing the United States as a geographically distant, less-threatening, hegemon, as the other. North Korea may be attempting such a "partner swap" in order to survive post–Cold War international politics in a monopolar U.S.-dominated world (Han, 2014). In retrospect, North Korea's entire trajectory of nuclear development since the 1994 crisis invites changed perceptions of North Korea—not as a country led by "irrational xenophobes with a mindless anti-American hatred" (Harrison, 2002: 197) who are "unreliable" (Mazarr, 2007), "aggressive, offensive, and expansionist" (Kang, 1995) but as a boxed-in, would-be junior partner who has pursued a carefully choreographed course toward greater political gains and economic benefits through its nuclear all-in stance toward the United States.

Counter to Pyongyang's expectations, though, the United States has retreated from engagement. According to Sigal (2003), Cumings (2005), Han (2014A), and Harrison (2002), it was not North Korea that failed to implement consistent policy toward the United States, but the opposite. Despite having signed the 1994 Agreed Framework with Pyongyang, former president Clinton—and, later, Bush—followed a policy of engagement that presumed the regime's impending collapse. Mazarr (2007: 76) and Noland (1997) aptly argue that Washington's North Korea policy has been characterized as "erratic" (Moon, 2005), "zigzag" (Cha, 2002: 80), and a "strategic muddle."

As illustrated above, the Korean Peninsula is currently witnessing the formation of a status quo in which there seems to be no solution to the 75-year-old division. Moreover, North Korea's programs of nuclear weapons pose existential threats to Japan, South Korea and potentially the United States, increasing the chances that China, as it rises, will collide with Japan and the United States. How can we possibly explain such a deadlock, and what is the most responsible way to prevent it? What variables offer insights into this situation? In working toward answers, this book argues that it was the United States that opened Korea, forcibly at first in 1866 and 1871, and diplomatically later through the 1882 treaty. Moreover, the United States separated China from Korea by riding the Japanese wave in the early twentieth century, yielding Korea to Japan in 1905, ignoring it at the end of World War II, and sundering the Peninsula. By inviting its enemy into the Peninsula in 1945, the United States. inadvertently gave China the opportunity to regain suzerainty over the north, the factor that has served as the single greatest stumbling block to the resolution of the Korean question today.

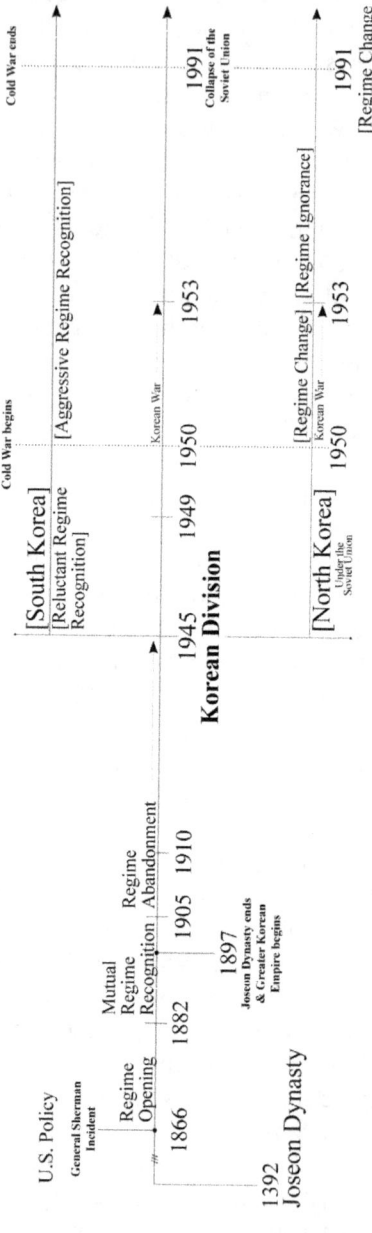

Figure 4.1 Conceptualization of U.S. Korea Policy: Regime Change, Regime Denial, and Regime Recognition. *Source:* Created by the author.

In this attempt to explain the current stalemate on the Peninsula, let us turn again to Diamond's hypothesis about the history of interactions among disparate peoples accounting for today's conflicts and collisions. America's involvement in the Peninsula, over roughly one and a half centuries, has decisively shaped the destiny of the Korean nation as well as East Asian power politics more broadly. Does the United States have a clear policy for dealing with these problems, normalizing relations with North Korea, and replacing the armistice with a peace treaty? The U.S. government in the early twenty-first century seems to have tried but ended up with conflicting policy implementations. For example, the Bush administration in 2002 dramatically vacillated from regime change to initiating Six-Party Talks. Then, without producing any concrete resolution, the Obama administration made no great efforts to shift from the status quo. Its policy of "strategic patience" ultimately meant doing nothing but waiting for Pyongyang to renounce its nuclear ambitions and come clean. On June 12, 2018, however, the 67-year stalemate between the United States and North Korea was dramatically shaken up. The whole world was watching to see if the first summit between the United States and North Korea would bring progress when instead it spawned a spate of cosplay-style texts between Mr. Trump and North Korea's Kim.

Such inconsistency, though, conceptualized as regime denial in this study, appears to have deep historical roots. The Obama administration's "strategic patience" was another version of the regime denial that has been immanent in U.S. perception of North Korea since the early twentieth century. As stated before, the two countries lacked direct civilian contact for most of the nineteenth and twentieth centuries. As illustrated in figure 0.1, American apathy toward North Korea has been pervasive since the late nineteenth and early twentieth centuries, especially during the Theodore Roosevelt administration. The United States' largely apathetic and disdainful attitude toward Korea had begun long before, but President Theodore Roosevelt's apathy toward Korea could be considered as one of the factors contributing to Japan's annexation of Korea. Figure 4.1 shows a series of major transformations in America's policy toward the Korean Peninsula.

Again, an attitude such as this would later mislead the Soviet Union and North Korea about America's willingness to defend Korea from being absorbed into the Soviet bloc. As reflected in Dean Acheson's 1949 withdrawal of the U.S. defensive perimeter from the Korean Peninsula, the United States was the unwitting creator of North Korea, even though Washington perceived the military threat of the Soviet Union clearly and was prepared to counter and defeat Russian forces from 1945 to 1950 (Henderson, 1980; Ross, 1988).

For the past three decades, relations between the United States and North Korea have swung much more visibly from hostility to ambiguous exploration of rapprochement or negotiation. Pervasive and vociferous American criticism of North Korea's inexplicably self-destructive behavior has focused on Pyeongyang's persistent disregard for the good of its citizens in exposing them to the horrors of preemptive or retaliatory nuclear strikes, loss of human rights, and starvation. Setting a foundation for useful discussion and sound approaches would seem to be necessary for dismantling the barriers to proper relations, yet neither side appears willing to give an inch, for each side sees the need to do away with the other's nuclear menace. Moreover, Pyeongyang needs to ensure economic aid from Washington, as it perceives the United States as the last remaining superpower capable of ensuring its economic recovery and survival.

Some readers may object to the idea that North Korea is aware of the America's capacity to either destroy or save it, due to North Korea's heavy dependence on trade with China. Indeed, table 4.2 shows a clear reliance upon Beijing in Pyeongyang's exports and imports. In fact, China continued to expand its trade and invest in North Korea even after North Korea's second nuclear test in 2009, which worried South Korea, leading it to believe that North Korea had become China's fourth Northeastern province (Eichengreen et al., 2015: 282). However, China is also subject to enormous international financial sanctions from the United States. Once China's banks or other financial institutions are sanctioned by U.S.-led global financial regimes and networks—due to China's favorable economic dealings with North Korea against both U.S. and UN sanctions—then North Korea's reliance on China becomes an Achilles heel. In other words, China cannot help North Korea if it is against the will of Washington. Thus, Pyeongyang is aware that the United States ultimately has the potential to end its poverty as well as ensure

Table 4.2 North Korea's Exports and Imports, 2007–2012 (US$ million)

	2007	2008	2009	2010	2011	2012
North Korea's Exports To						
China	582	754	793	1,188	2,464	2,485
Japan	0	0	0	0	0	0
Russia	34	14	21	27	13	11
South Korea	765	932	934	1,044	914	1,074
Total	1,685	2,062	1,994	2,554	3,704	3,945
North Korea's Imports from						
China	1,392	2,033	1,888	2,278	3,165	3,528
Japan	9	8	3	0	0	0
Russia	126	97	41	84	100	65
South Korea	1,033	888	745	868	800	897
Total	3,053	3,578	3,095	3,528	4,330	4,827

Source: Reprinted with permission from Eichengreen et al., *The Korean Economy: From a Miraculous Past to a Sustainable Future*, Cambridge, Massachusetts, London: Harvard University Press (2015).

its survival. Despite this fact, however, North Korea has never given up its propaganda condemning the United States as a sworn enemy and global leader of capitalist imperialism while nonetheless striving to normalize relations with Washington. Table 4.2 offers an overview of North Korea's heavy reliance on China and South Korea, and demonstrates why its normalization with the United States, if realized, could disrupt contemporary power balances in the region.

From this perspective, Pyeongyang's move to go all-in with its nuclear weapons program can be viewed as a risky but necessary attempt to win Washington's attention and force negotiations. After nearly half a century of diplomacy with Moscow and Beijing best characterized as "tightrope dancing" and "muddling through" (Chung, 1978; Kun, 1967), the DPRK faced a new environment that called for a new stance toward the United States. This need became especially urgent when South Korea established embassies in Beijing and Moscow in 1992. Seeing its protectorate system at this point significantly strained and no longer securely in place within a bipolar system (French, 2007: 197; Kang, 1995: 262; Eberstadt, 1999: 49; Park, 1998), Pyeongyang's all-in strategy of playing the nuclear card for U.S. recognition can be seen as a strategy to extricate itself from dysfunctional alliances and team up with a new big brother—the United States (Gallucci, 2006; Sigal, 2003; Harrison, 2002: 201; Han, 2014A, 2014a).

When the action was on in October 2002, however, rather than continue to negotiate, the United States raised the stakes. Neoconservative strategy, in general, and former president Bush's characterization of North Korea as one of the "Axis of Evil" countries, in particular (followed by preemptive strikes against Afghanistan and Iraq), clearly signaled Washington's desire for regime change and its intention to simply wait for the demise of the current regime (Niksch, 2003; Eberstadt, 2005, 2007). According to Cumings (2007: 1), Vice President Cheney's blunt statement "We don't negotiate with evil; we defeat it" epitomizes U.S. strategy at that time. In early spring 2002, as this strong no-negotiation message was being broadcasted by Bush administration hardliners, rapprochement advocates within the government simultaneously began to send signals suggesting that Pyeongyang would be recognized and receive desperately needed economic aid if it denuclearized and joined the world community (Mazarr, 2007: 82). The offer was to be presented by Kelly, but it never was presented at all, due to deep dissent within the Bush administration. Instead, Kelly revealed the Highly Enriched Uranium (HEU) program, dramatically raising the stakes (Cumings, 2007; Wit et al., 2005; 371, 378). Cha (2002: 81) characterized this sort of vacillation in U.S. policy as "hawk engagement." Mazarr (2007: 92) similarly criticized U.S. policy toward Pyeongyang as misguided and "alternately fragmented, bitterly ideological, and impelled by top-down, instinct-driven mandates." Kissinger (2006), noting the contradictory nature of U.S. policy, advised the Bush administration that "focusing on regime change as the road to denuclearization confuses the issue," recommending diplomacy instead.

For most of the Bush administration, initial U.S. policy toward Pyeongyang was based on both poor conceptual strategies and inconsistent decision-making, most recently demonstrated in the Bush administration's shift toward a policy of engagement, as signaled by actions like sending the New York Philharmonic to Pyeongyang in early 2008 (Wakin, 2007). Eberstadt (2007), like others, advocated Washington's "no-negotiation-but-wait" policy and noted that, ironically, "the Bush team . . . embraced the very approach it had once mocked as weak-kneed and 'Clintonesque.'"

Historical Origins of Mutual Apathy and Hostility

As stated before, the roots of the mutual hostility and apathy[11] between these two countries run deep through the layers of their bilateral history. For North Korea, it all seems to stem from the utter devastation they experienced at the hands of the U.S. military. Berlinger (2017) aptly describes how, in just three years, the war claimed the lives of millions and forever changed the Peninsula: "We went over there and fought the war and eventually burned down every town in North Korea anyway, some way or another, and some in South Korea, too," said former U.S. Air Force Commander Gen. Curtis LeMay in 1988, in an interview for an Air Force military history volume (Berlinger, 2017). The war's level of casualties was also astonishing. "By the time the armistice was signed on July 27, 1953, North Korea—which began the war with a population of 9.6 million—had suffered an estimated 1.3 million civilian and military casualties, according to figures cited by the U.S. Air Force. South Korea, meanwhile, suffered up to 3 million civilian and 225,000 military casualties, from a total population of around 20.2 million in 1950" (Berlinger, 2017). During a congressional hearing in 1951, General MacArthur said he had never seen such devastation. "I shrink with horror that I cannot express in words–at this continuous slaughter of men in Korea," MacArthur said. "I have seen, I guess, as much blood and disaster as any living man, and it just curdled my stomach the last time I was there." About 37,000 Americans were killed, while about 600,000 Chinese were left dead or missing. However, the impacts of such brutality left indelible scars on North Korea with its whole infrastructure decimated and its towns and cities obliterated, while the Chinese and Americans could go home to the luxury of forgetting. The U.S. government banned Americans from traveling to North Korea. "The bombing is treated as the American original sin in the (North Korean) propaganda and it certainly was savage,"[12] according to Robert E. Kelly. For the North Korean regime, the legacy of destruction still remains a key focus of propaganda:

For North Koreans, destruction came from above. The conflict is seen as the first large-scale air campaign conducted by the U.S. Air Force. American planes dropped approximately 635,000 tons of explosives on North Korea (that's more in three years than during the entire Pacific theater of World War II), including 32,000 tons of napalm, according to historian Charles Armstrong. That continued fear of deadly U.S. military airstrikes helps the North Korean government to portray Americans as a far-away caricature, a faceless enemy that leveled their country and could do so again. As Kelly a professor of political science at South Korea's Pusan National University points out. "It's become a political tool to justify the permanent emergency state. Japanese colonization is used the same." (Berlinger, 2017)

Renowned Australian war correspondent Wilfred G. Burchett (1968), who covered the Korean War and the Panmunjeom truce talk for the Paris-based journal *Ce Soir* and met North Korea's founder, Kim Il-sung, in Pyeongyang, describes how "Everything the Korean people had inherited over the millennia from their ancestors was destroyed":

> everything they had been able to salvage after 35 years of Japanese occupation; everything they had been able to build up in the five years of peace between the defeat of Japan and the start of the war. All was destroyed under the flag of the world's most universal peace-keeping organization. Although Hitler sometimes killed a higher proportion of people in the countries he occupied, he never managed anything like the total destruction of North Korea. (Burchett, 1968: 66)

Taking advantage of such unprecedentedly brutal annihilation of their land, the North Korean regime has consistently fostered a visceral hatred for the United States. Kindergarteners draw anti-American images, and news media release videos of U.S. soldiers in flames. The Korean War anniversary on June 25 is "the day of struggle against U.S. imperialism." And the national ideology of *juche*, meaning "self-reliance," has steadily permeated the minds of North Koreans since Kim first introduced it in the 1950s, to replace the notion of *sadae* or flunkeyism,[13] which he saw as the Joseon's habit of serving the great, as they served China. This ideology was repurposed to help liberate Korea from Japanese colonial control, then conveniently extended to U.S. imperialism. Works of propaganda like "Sea of Blood"—and the fact that it is nearly impossible for those inside the country to obtain information from the world outside—help reinforce the underdog survivor mentality at the heart of *juche*, which is often translated in English as "self-reliance."[14]

America's hostility toward North Korea was described by Gregory Henderson (1980), renowned scholar on Korean history and politics, and a career diplomat long stationed in Korea, as "unprecedented" in U.S. history. The U.S. government's animosity toward Korea, he notes, was "longer-lasting" than that expressed toward "George III's England, the Kaiser's and Hitler's Germany, Ho Chi Minh's Vietminh, Stalin and Castro." McCormack (1993) goes further to say, "The pressure resulting from this confrontation, and the continuing fear of renewed conflict, leading possibly to nuclear annihilation, helped to sustain the monolithic unity of the regime and state" (41). Ironically, the mutual hatred has only helped to legitimize the illegitimate regime in North Korea while bringing Washington not even a step closer to resolving one of the most imminent nuclear confrontations of this century. How can we explain Washington's unswerving reluctance to address and change its hostile relationship with North Korea? Why the United States appears to have no intention of resolving the North Korean issue is a real puzzle to scholars of international politics, intellectuals, and liberal Koreans. Is it because doing so would reawaken the shame of having won no clear victory in the Korean War? Or, would engaging with Pyongyang feel like a sin to Washington? Is North Korea too small and poor for anything good to come out of it for American economic interests? Or, is it because there is no easy way to solve this problem due to the safety concerns of China, Russia, and South Korea?

Ultimately, despite such unparalleled attempts by the American military toward the end of the Korean War, General MacArthur and U.S. Air Force Commander General Lemay, who were directly responsible for the scale of the air bombing, confessed that even they were appalled (Berlinger, 2017) by the lack of a clear victory. It must have been a real blow to the self-respect of the United States, who had led the push in World War II against the Axis powers and rose to become the world's most powerful nation. The post–World War II era of the Pax Americana in fact commenced with a great sense of frustration that the United States did not want to mention; the United States might have preferred to forget rather than to aggravate that scar. Fortunately, under the bipolar system of the Cold War headed by the United States and Soviet Union, North Korea, under the auspices of America's rival, the Soviet Union, would pose no threat to the United States during the Cold War period, other than the three military incidents mentioned earlier. Even if there were cases in which North Korea caused the United States to lose face, the United States seemed to have few options for addressing its vitiated authority. When the fall of the USSR began to unsettle the power equilibrium of the Cold War bipolar system, however, North Korea became an issue. At the grim prospect of standing alone in a new era of unilateral American power, North Korea must have recalled America's destructive force in the Korean War and, for the sake of its survival, accelerated its development of an asymmetric weapons system in order to play its own trump card against the United States. As mentioned in the previous chapter, North Korea's brinkmanship did not pose any real threat to the United States and its allies in the region until North Korea successfully tested nuclear weapons and became capable of deploying ICBMs. Now, the U.S. government and its allies are no longer able to ignore Pyongyang's provocations and brinkmanship, because it seems to have real capacity to target the far-west portion of America, U.S. military bases in the West Pacific, as well as key allies Japan and South Korea, as confirmed by former national security advisor McMaster to President Trump, on June 1, 2019, with "Axios on HBO." General McMaster admitted, "North Korea could directly threaten the United States, China, Japan, the world with its nuclear arsenal and could also engage in nuclear blackmail.... This regime could say [if U.S. forces] don't go off the Korean Peninsula, we're going to threaten the use of nuclear weapons, for example." McMaster also raised the prospect of nuclear proliferation if North Korea were to sell its nuclear secrets, or weapons, noting that Pyongyang "was developing a nuclear weapons program for the Assad regime in Syria." He also cited the risk of inciting nuclear armament among U.S. allies Japan, South Korea and beyond, asking: "If North Korea gets a weapon, who doesn't?" (Lawler, 2019). He concluded this interview by warning that the United States needs to "prepare for at least the option of the use of military force" to convince Kim to denuclearize. This policy change of considering the use of military force in response to Pyongyang's refusal to denuclearize ended the United States' tradition of regime denial toward North Korea and launched a new chapter in the history of U.S.-Korea relations.

Contrary to popular opinion, though, U.S. hostility toward North Korea is not based solely on the rogue state's nuclear weapons. Pyongyang's attempt to develop and possess nuclear weapons and ICBMs clearly challenges the U.S.-led nuclear nonproliferation regime, despite the fact that countries such as Iran, Syria, Algeria, and Saudi Arabia have constantly sought opportunities to declare themselves nuclear states as well. Now, with ICBM capabilities, though limited, North Korea does pose a credible threat to the United States and its allies in East Asia. In reality, it was not North Korea but Pakistan that declared itself nuclear in 1990 and transferred nuclear weapons technology to "Axis of Evil" countries, including Iran, presumably Saudi Arabia and Libya as well as North Korea. Ironically, though, Pakistan did not become a target of U.S. hostility for strategic geopolitical reasons, such as forming a containment alliance against China. Instead, Pakistan became one of the United States' most important allies in the Middle East, as exemplified in the 2015 Joint Statement by President Obama and Prime Minister Nawaz Sharif of Pakistan despite the potential threat of proliferation.

The United States' hostility, this book argues, is deeply rooted in the history of U.S. policy toward the Korean Peninsula, including its first attempt to breach the Korean market in 1871, its costly failure to deter the outbreak of the Korean War, and its apathy on all issues related to North Korea until the early 1990s.

American hostility toward North Korea started with general apathy toward the Peninsula as a whole. A short survey of U.S. involvement in Asia, with unsuccessful attempts in the late nineteenth century clearly indicates a lack of American interest in the Peninsula from the early twentieth century until the end of Japanese occupation in 1945, despite an initial interest in opening Korea for trade and way stations. Again, the Taft-Katsura Secret Agreement, signed by the United States and Japan in 1905, attests to this disinterest.

Such disinterest toward Korea and recognition of communist expansionism and challenge from the USSR and China, respectively, led U.S. foreign policy to prize an alliance with Japan as the prime interest in the region. That is one of the reasons why the United States did not push for Japan to be divided as was done with Germany in the wake of World War II. Instead, the Korean Peninsula—which had just been suffering under Japanese colonial occupancy—was, itself, divided. This is indeed an absurd reality and serves as a clear sign that Korean interests and voices were utterly disregarded, if not disdained. As stated in the previous chapter, Dean Rusk, one of those responsible for drawing the line of division, chose the 38th parallel on a map from an issue of *National Geographic*. Looking back to the military and political circumstances of that moment, one cannot help but conclude that Korea's interests were no real concern for America; rather, its location met the needs of American interests in preserving peaceful relations with Japan and in containing communism. Thus, urgency, convenience, and minimal commitment were the principles that guided considerations for halving this nation. According to Fry (2013):

Future U.S. secretary of state Dean Rusk, then a colonel on General George Marshall's staff, and fellow Army staffer Col. Charles "Tic" Bonesteel were assigned the task of identifying a line of control to which the United States and the Soviets would both agree. In this decision, time was of the essence: the Soviets had just entered the war against Japan, and American officials feared that Russia would rush in to occupy the entire Peninsula before the United States—whose nearest troops were still 600 miles (966 km) away on Okinawa—could establish a presence of its own on the mainland. Rusk knew that the 38th parallel "made no sense economically or geographically"—Korea, in fact, had enjoyed unity and a high degree of geographic continuity for the better part of a millennium—but this was the Cold War. "Military expediency" had to rule the day. Korea, it was thought, would be divided only temporarily.

In his 1991 memoir, *As I Saw It*, Rusk later recalled how hurried and stressful the experience was. On the night of a meeting on August 14, 1945, the same day as the Japanese surrender, he and Bonesteel intently studied a map of the Korean Peninsula in a nearby room. Their daunting task was to zero in on the United States' occupation zone. Though neither of them was a Korea expert, they recognized that the American sector must include Seoul, the capital. They were also aware of the U.S. Army's opposition to an overly widespread area. With these requirements in mind, they consulted a National Geographic map for a convenient place to mark the division of Korea but failed to find a naturally occurring line in that topography. Instead, as soon as they noticed the 38th parallel, their decision was made. They recommended it. "[Our commanders] accepted it without too much haggling, and surprisingly, so did the Soviets."

That this is how a nation's destiny was determined is almost laughable. Two U.S. colonels were ordered to find the most convenient line for the permanent division of a people, completely overlooking any views of the people whose lives they were changing. For this decision that should have involved at least some consultation with Korean leaders, there was none—a clear sign of disinterest as well as disdain. Except for the benevolent consideration of keeping Seoul on America's side, this essentially amounted to a stance of regime denial.

In this choice of policy that would divide the Korean people for generations and counting, Japan's security and prosperity became, by far, the most important national interest of the United States while Korea became the frontline for its military confrontation against the communist Soviet Union, with China as a buffer zone. The importance of Japan to U.S. national interest in the region even led to the formation of "The Chrysanthemum Club," mostly composed of high-level pro-Japanese decision makers in U.S. government and business. Alternately, Korea could serve as a convenient scapegoat, and serve American interests in protecting Japan.

As many declassified documents from the National Archive confirm, in addition to prioritizing Japan over Korea when weighing its national interests in East Asia, and thus confirming its traditional disregard and disdain for Korea, the United States' unrelenting hostility toward North Korea can only be explained by considering other contexts. Most obviously, North Korea's current image as a totalitarian and repressive regime that persecutes political prisoners and neglects millions dying of hunger is the antithesis of the values that America represents. This contrast offers a convincing rationale for Washington's decision to designate North Korea as one of the "Axis of Evil" countries. Second, U.S. apathy toward Korea lasted through the 35 years of Japanese colonial control and ultimately caused the costly error of misleading the Soviet Union and North Korea about American willingness to defend Korea, as shown by Acheson's withdrawal of the defensive perimeter from the Peninsula in 1949. According to Henderson, "The United States was the unwitting creator of North Korea, as of few other nations besides the Philippines, America itself, and South Korea." America's apathy and negligence caused the costly mistake of inviting North Korea's attack against South Korea, with the two Koreas still technically at war. Third, domestically, the Korean War became highly unpopular, because the call for another draft arose before the trauma of World War II had even begun to fade from American minds. Thus, the Korean Peninsula became a source of many problems.

The best way to recover, it seemed, was to remake South Korea—with American democratic and capitalistic qualities—as an Asian model for success. Ironically, though, South Korea's success resulted instead in the reinforcement of American antagonism against North Korea, as South Korea's prosperity offered glaring contrast to the failure of North Korea's centrally planned communist economy and the family dictatorship of *Kimilsungism*, which were based on the ideology of *juche*. Therefore, the success of South Korea (modeled after the United States) and the failure of North Korea (modeled after the USSR, America's Cold War rival) provided the United States with ostensible justification for increased hostility toward the North rather than working toward conflict resolution and reconciliation. Another important factor contributing to the solidification of U.S. hatred toward North Korea was that South Korea and North Korea engaged in severe regime competition, using state propaganda to demonize each other as prime enemies, which in turn has validated the hostility of South Korea's patron, the United States, and its strongly anticommunist stance. As many critics have noticed, due to the strong stance of President Moon and the South Korean government toward normalization and rapprochement with North Korea, cracks have begun to appear in the structure of U.S.-ROK relations.

REASONS FOR STALEMATE

The current escalation of tensions between North Korea and the United States over the nuclear weapons and ICBM programs may be a necessary step on the way to the building of trust, and might continue for some time, given the short history of direct engagement. One thing, however, is clear: neither Washington nor Pyongyang can afford to start over, meaning we cannot afford for these two political regimes to take as long to untangle this knot as it took to create it.

Doyle (1983), in his renowned articles "Kant, Liberal Legacies, and Foreign Affairs" and "Liberalism and World Politics," points to the *entente* between liberal France and Britain on the one side and illiberal pre–World War I Germany on the other as evidence of "a significant predisposition against warfare between liberal states" (213). However, warfare between these two countries had been constant before they peacefully coexisted and formed an alliance. It took eight centuries for these two countries to form a "Pacific Union" (Doyle, 1983, 1986), with wars in every century since the Norman Conquest of 1066 till the French Revolutionary Wars and the Napoleonic Wars (1792–1815). Another century was needed to extend the Pacific Union to the former illiberal Germany through two world wars, considering the determined stance of German contrition over World War II as evidence of a "Pacific Union" among these three superpowers in Europe. Taking into account the common denominators in political, economic, religious, and cultural proximity among these European countries, Doyle's observation cannot be overemphasized: "when it comes to acquiring the techniques of peaceable interaction, nations appear to be slow, or at least erratic, learners" (1983: 220–221).

When the United States first engaged with East Asia in the early nineteenth and twentieth centuries, the DPRK did not exist. Pyeongyang became the prime enemy at the outbreak of the Korean War (1950–1953), and is still technically at war with the United States. The main military confrontation between Pyeongyang and Washington erupted three years after the collapse of Pyeongyang's big brother (the USSR) over North Korea's nuclear weapons program. As Doyle (1983) points out, military technology often sparks military conflicts. In this case, North Korea's nuclear weapons program sparked the conflict and, at the same time, created the first opportunity to explore the potential for normalization between these two countries in 1994 when the Clinton administration was on the brink of striking North Korea's plutonium reprocessing facility at Yongbyon. What made this confrontation so perilous was that these countries shared none of Doyle's other elements (1983: 220) that, with prudence, could lead to peace: "experience, geography, expectations of cooperation and belief patterns, and the differing payoffs to cooperation (peace)." This study identifies Doyle's point as "capital for peaceful negotiation and trustworthy relations." The collapse of the USSR unsettled the Cold War balance of power between the United States and the DPRK, though it was asymmetrical in that Washington dealt with Pyeongyang's boss, not Pyeongyang. The Six-Party Talks after North Korea's withdrawal from the Non-Proliferation Treaty in 2003 seemed an internationally concerted effort to deal with the complete absence of "effective standards of mutual toleration" (Doyle, 1983: 221) between Washington and Pyeongyang.

Another fixation of the stereotypic image of the North Korean regime is that Pyeongyang has not addressed the economic plight of the people, which caused the deaths of millions in the mid-1990s. In the sudden absence of economic aid from the Soviet Union, and severely damaged by droughts and floods from 1994 to 1999, the Pyeongyang regime faced the "Arduous

March" in the mid-1990s, which left millions of North Koreans dead from starvation. In a desperate measure to survive as the economy failed, informal economic activities skyrocketed in North Korea in the late 1990s, and North Korea's regime eventually had no choice but to introduce limited capitalistic market principles into the centrally planned communist economy in July 2002. Fearing that these informal economic activities might gain uncontrollable power in the market, Pyongyang executed a currency change on November 30, 2009, to quell the rising influence of any market mechanisms. However, the regime decided to allow limited market activities again, since the currency change had failed to repress informal market economic activities but rather had prompted new hardships and unrest, according to *The New York Times* on February 3, 2010 (Choe, 2010). Assuming that contemporary changes in the economic system have already reached the point of no return, the coexisted and North Korea may be shifting from mutual hostility to mutually agreeable or tolerable negotiations.

Another contribution that may come from greater engagement like the nongovernmental Track II dialogue is in exchanges of personnel. As the examples of Deng Xiaoping and Alexander Yakovlev illustrate, extended exchanges of young future leaders can have great impact for closed societies. From October 1919, Deng Xiaoping spent six years in France attending middle school as a part of the work-study program in which 4,001 Chinese would participate by 1927 working in a steel and iron plant in Renault and participating in a Chinese communist Youth League in Europe. His experience as a young man in France is said to have greatly shaped his later conciliatory diplomacy with Western countries and his modernization policy as well as the opening of the Chinese economy. Similarly, Alexander Yakovlev, the so-called godfather of "Glasnost" and ardent supporter of "Perestroika" during Gorbachev's reign, attended Columbia University on exchange in 1958. His exposure to political leaders and thinkers there certainly played a role in his later criticisms of the Soviet Union and its transformation from communism to the current Russia.

As mentioned at the start of this chapter, Washington's policy toward North Korea has lacked consistency since the end of the Cold War (Cumings, 1999, 2005; Han, 2009; Hecker, 2010; Joel & Town, 2011; Laney & Shaplen, 2003; Sigal, 2003; Wit & Town, 2011). Over the course of the Bush I, Clinton, Bush II, and Obama administrations, Washington has been unable to commit to regime change or regime recognition. Such fuzziness was branded by the Obama administration as "strategic patience," and involved "essentially, waiting for North Korea to confess and change its bad behavior before engaging with it in nuclear negotiations" (Joel & Town, 2011).

This policy was heavily criticized by the hardliner, former Ambassador to the UN, John Bolton as "deliberate silence and near-palpable lack of interest" (2011). The diplomatic engagement school of thought also viewed Obama's strategic patience as a "strategic blunder" (Joel & Town, 2011) and "strategic passivity" (Goodby & Gross, 2010): "like a poker player who can't choose whether to call, raise, or fold" (Han, 2009: 109). Since the Soviet Union's collapse, the United States has vacillated between regime change (early Clinton administration and most of Bush II administration) and bold negotiation (i.e., Clinton's Agreed Framework in 1994 and Bush II's bold bargaining in 2006). Despite President Obama's campaign promises, no major policy toward North Korea was implemented from 2009 onward, when he took charge of U.S. foreign policy. In addition, President Trump's eye-opening approach to North Korean leader Kim Jong-un has also failed to move negotiations even an inch forward. The North Korean issue had become a complete stalemate as of late 2020.

In oscillating from regime change to bold bargaining, Washington's policy toward North Korea has relied on the assumption that the Pyeongyang regime would soon collapse, leading to a policy of eventual change of regimes without grand U.S. intervention. In reality, judging from these preconditions, one can notice conflicting evidence of regime change and engagement policies originating from Washington. This leaves the current relationship between Washington and Pyeongyang in a state of mutual denial, prolonging the nuclear standoff that has been in place since the end of the Clinton administration.

Consequently, the ambiguous and vacillating stances toward North Korea in the late twentieth century can be best explained by employing a new concept— "regime denial." In this study, the U.S. policy of regime denial consists of three elements: (1) historically rooted American disinterest and hostility toward North Korea; (2) an unwillingness to break from the status quo on the Peninsula, based on false assumptions and a liberal stance; and (3) strategic reasons to maintain the status quo and not normalize relations with Pyeongyang.

In order to explain and apply the concept of regime denial to the current nuclear standoff between Washington and Pyeongyang, this study explores the core concepts of regime change, regime promotion, and regime containment throughout the general history of U.S. foreign policy and evaluates the current literature on America's North Korea policy from the perspective of pragmatism. To explain the motivation for regime denial toward Pyeongyang, and to further appreciate the prolonged stalemate in relations, this chapter traces back the historical roots of Washington's unprecedented hostility toward Pyeongyang and examines alternative explanations for U.S. inaction toward North Korea. Ultimately, it also explores the geopolitical and structural reasons behind Washington's denial of the Pyeongyang regime, which, this study argues, aims to maintain the status quo on the Peninsula and East Asian international politics from a pragmatic perspective. Finally, reevaluating Washington's policy toward Pyeongyang as "regime denial," and reviewing the criteria that classify the approach under this new concept, offers the opportunity to assess whether Washington has exhausted all possible policy options. The chapter concludes that the current nuclear standoff, in fact, provides the first-ever opportunity to bring these antagonists to the negotiating table and transform this mutual denial into mutual recognition.

REGIME CHANGE AND CONTAINMENT IN U.S. FOREIGN POLICY

Regime change has generally been viewed as an important U.S. foreign policy tool for removing possible threats to national security and replacing troubled regimes with U.S.-friendly political systems and ideologies (Gasiorowski, 1996; Waltz, 2000; Owen, 2010). Gasiorowski defines a "political regime" as the system of national political institutions that "set rules, procedures, and understandings governing political participation" (1996: 470). Similarly, Owen (2010: 1) defines "regime change" as the "alteration of a country's fundamental political institutions" by "the coercion of outside powers." Its goals are clear: to remove potential threats to national security, to liberate the oppressed, and to control faraway places vital to the material prosperity of the capitalist, free-market system (Kinzer, 2006). In this respect, any action that aims to alter the fundamental rules of major political institutions and governing procedures in a country—whether active or passive, direct or indirect, overt or covert—can be viewed as regime change.

Foreign policy in the twentieth century provides numerous examples of regime change: either active and overt or passive and covert. The former was undertaken through the use of widescale military force. The United States can be seen as a regime-changer in World War II and the fight against Hitler's Germany as a defensive measure that later imposed a democratic system consistent with American values in West Germany. Compared to the regime change of Hitler's Nazi Germany, there have also been many cases of covert and indirect regime change where small-scale military operations or economic sanctions were involved in the regime changes of Latin American, Caribbean, and Asian countries. Examples from this period abound—Cuba in 1906 and 1917; Nicaragua in 1910, 1912, and 1925–1933; Honduras in 1911 and 1924; the Dominican Republic in 1912 and 1916; Iran in 1953 and from 2005 to till date; Guatemala in 1954; Cuba in 1959; Iraq in 1960–1963, 1992–1996, and 2002–2003; the Dominican Republic in 1961; Brazil in 1964; Chile in 1970–1973; Nicaragua in 1981–1990; and Panama in 1983—deploying into these countries either U.S. Marine, covert CIA, or other military operations (Owen, 2010: 165; Kinzer, 2006).

If we understand the notion of regime change as forcible intervention into one political regime by another, then political intervention in the opposite direction (i.e., to maintain the current regime) can be understood as regime promotion. Regime promotion usually occurs when two or more countries are in antagonistic regime competition. Superpowers, especially the United States and the Soviet Union during the bipolar international politics of the Cold War, have promoted one regime against another "to extend or preserve one's sphere of influence and to arrest the spread of the other's sphere" (Owen, 2010: 182) without changing the regime(s) and without directly confronting rival superpowers if the object of regime change is under its protection. In most cases of American regime promotion, Washington's intention was to support the authoritarian regimes in power so that the United States could contain Soviet expansionism and maximize its own influence. Such Cold War rivalry of regime promotion between Washington and Moscow has extended to the current rivalry between Beijing's backing of the Pyeongyang regime and Washington's support for South Korea.

U.S. foreign policy throughout the Cold War period is customarily categorized as one of three policy stances—regime change, regime promotion, or containment—however, these concepts seem to explain neither the prolonged confrontation after the Korean War nor the current nuclear standoff between the United States and North Korea. On the world stage, the U.S. failed in its attempt to defeat the North Korean regime on September 15, 1953, when UN forces marched into the North Korean region in their first offensive after the successful Incheon landing. Since then, Washington has remained passive regarding the status quo around the 38th parallel, even up until now. The Truman administration's policy of regime change was the reactionary fallout after UN forces had changed their stance from defensive to offensive, successfully clearing the North Korean military from the southern Peninsula by the end of September 1950. Initially after World War II, the United States did not favor a policy of regime change toward North Korea. North Korea had been under Soviet control and had not drawn the attention of Washington for direct talks or contact. Instead, Washington aggressively adopted a policy of regime promotion in South Korea. Yet, none of these three categories—regime change, containment, or promotion—can completely explain the U.S. stance against North Korea since the end of the Korean War, however, especially from the late 1990s on, when Washington had to deal with a nuclear North Korea in the post–Cold War era. Specific reasons as to why these concepts evade explanation will be covered in sections to come.

North Korea has been uniquely positioned in the Cold War rivalry between Washington and Moscow, which has recently been complicated by new post–Cold War power dynamics in East Asia—with North Korea being forced to play the role of a check against the United States and, at the same time, to compromise in order to sustain its economic modernization.

Historical Background for Regime Denial

In the eyes of North Korea, as stated before, the United States is the last remaining superpower that can either determine its survival and eventual economic recovery or bring it to a brutal end (Cumings, 1999, 2005; Han, 2009: 106; Kim, 2010). Moreover, in Pyeongyang's view, only Washington is capable of stabilizing the region by serving as an intermediary in potentially contentious relations between the DPRK, on the one hand, and China, Japan, Russia, and the ROK, on the other (Han, 2009; Kim, 2010). In the wake of the Cold War, two important events took place that seemed to motivate Pyeongyang's pursuit of nuclear weapons: first, its loss of Moscow's nuclear umbrella; and second, the Soviet Union and China's normalization of relations with South Korea in 1991. Cumings (2005: 481) argues that Pyeongyang chose to play an "ultimate trump card" by arming itself with "a small-state deterrent for a country surrounded by powerful enemies" to "keep everyone guessing whether and when the weapons might become available" by initiating a nuclear weapons program. By contrast, Washington has vacillated between regime change and engagement, between denunciation and a bold approach, moving back then forward (Han, 2009). This chapter attempts to conceptualize such inconsistency as a phenomenon of America's overarching policy of regime denial.

Since the end of the Cold War, the circumstances of Washington's policy options have become much more complex. Experts have split over how the United States should address North Korea's nuclear proliferation. Scholars and experts are of two camps: proliferation determinists and proliferation pragmatists (Montgomery, 2005: 153–154). Although opinions diverge regarding how to resolve nuclear development in North Korea, they generally concur that Washington's overall stance toward Pyeongyang has been one of regime change in underlying intention, even when the Clinton administration signed the Agreed Framework in 1994 and the Bush administration engaged in Six-Party Talks until 2007 (Hass, 2005; Montgomery, 2005; Kang 2003; Waltz, 2000). According to Montgomery (2005: 155), a proliferation determinist (PD) argument of regime change must meet several conditions: the regime must be part of an "axis of evil" (e.g., Iran, Iraq, North Korea), it must be "dead set on proliferating," and proliferation networks for technology transfer must be widespread and decentralized such that rogue states can achieve nuclear armament despite objections from the international community.

Proliferation pragmatists refute the PD argument on the basis that tacit knowledge of nuclear weapon development is too difficult to obtain since "nuclear proliferation networks are highly centralized and are much less effective than determinists claim" (Montgomery, 2005: 156). Furthermore, Montgomery (2005: 156) argues that "proliferators can be persuaded to talk or roll back their programs," suggesting that the threat of proliferation is easily addressed. The strong stance taken by proliferation determinists regarding the threat level of proliferator states' (as well as Washington's) seemingly irrevocable rhetoric has inadvertently convinced rogue countries that the United States is a nonnegotiating state (Montgomery, 2005: 154). Instead, rogue countries often perceive the United States as being determined "not to uphold any settlement short of regime change," which has only bolstered Pyongyang's resolve to pursue its own interests over mutual interests that they share with Washington (Montgomery, 2005: 154).

Examples of regime change policy abound throughout America's short history, providing rogue states with justification in the eyes of their own citizenry and, sometimes, of regional partners. For instance, a month after the United States declared war on Iraq (The War on Terror) on March 20, 2003, a secret memorandum by Secretary of Defense Donald Rumsfeld was leaked, stating that the United States should call for regime change in another rogue country—North Korea (Rennie, 2003; Montgomery, 2005: 163). Possibly in a concerted effort to rally behind Rumsfeld's memo, Eberstadt (2004) explained that the Bush administration would be repeating the "talk—or [bribe]" mistakes of previous administrations if Bush continued to negotiate with North Korea, and suggested instituting regime change from the State Department instead. According to Rumsfeld's analysis, the U.S. policy of bribery toward North Korea had been achieving miserable results for 15 years. With regard to the role of the nonproliferation regime, hawkish neoconservatives in the Bush administration did not consider the main problem to be nuclear weapons per se. Rather, they understood that—unlike Israel, Pakistan, or India—"rogue states" such as Iran, Iraq, and North Korea, could not be deterred or contained as proliferation determinists argue. Thus, the only option, from the American perspective, was for their leaders to be removed (Perkovich, 2003: 3–4; Wu, 2005; Cumings, 2005; Eberstadt, 2004; Fly, 2010; Harris, 2002; Hass, 2005: 67; Rennie, 2003). In short, regime change of North Korea must have been a consistent goal; in reality, though, Washington was unable to take that path.

While promoting regime change, Bush's hawkish advisors recognized that "talk of military action against North Korea is unrealistic, given the country's huge conventional arsenals aimed at South Korea" (Rennie, 2003). However, after then-president Bush approved a carrot-and-stick approach against hardliners' arguments for regime change, represented by Secretary Rumsfeld and other neoconservatives, his administration in 2003 was divided over its North Korea policy. In fact, the leaking of Rumsfeld's memo disclosed an overall ideological split as well as internal foreign policy disputes among top-level national security advisors. Thus, U.S. policy was neither regime change nor regime recognition.

This split is essentially what has led to Washington's policy of regime denial, which arose in the wake of the Soviet Union's collapse. Meandering between stances of regime change and regime recognition, Washington seems to have become confused and gotten lost, causing it to choose neither option but to wander instead the unprecedented path of regime denial.

Realist Perspective: Promotion of South Korea and Denial of North Korea

While Washington's North Korean policy cannot entirely be equated with either regime change or regime containment, the notion of regime promotion seems to offer a new angle into the U.S. policy of regime denial toward North Korea. The USSR and the United States as regents both—for the most part—avoided the mutually destructive path of seeking to directly change each other's satellite regimes and adopted instead an approach of indirect competition through regime promotion of their proxies: starting in 1953 in Korea, 1954 in Indochina, the 1960s in the Arab world, and the 1990s in the Caribbean and Latin America. In fact, Washington has been involved in as many as 68 cases of regime promotion (Owen, 2010: 199). Since regime change was defined earlier as the "alteration of a country's fundamental political institutions," regime promotion can be seen as "an effort by a regent to preserve proxies' fundamental political institutions" and keep them in accordance with those of the regent. The most forcible regime promotions were conducted under transnational ideological polarization after World War II between Soviet communism and U.S. liberal democracy and capitalism. Moreover, the Korean War (1950–1953) signaled the fierce competition of regime promotion in Asia between these rivals. As a result of the Korean War, this transnational rivalry of ideological competition between the two poles also lined up most of the Southeast Asian countries for a bipolar confrontation once France departed from Indochina in 1954.

Kissinger (2011: 131) saw U.S. intervention in Korea as a passive approach to defeating aggression from the North: "the United States had no military plan for Korea when the war broke out" and wanted "a return to the status quo along the 38th parallel." However, when President Truman authorized U.S. forces to cross the 38th parallel into North Korea after the successful Incheon landing on September 15, 1950, and advance northward to the Yalu

River by October, the U.S. counter-intervention shifted from regime promotion of South Korea to regime change of North Korea, thereby posing a threat to communist China. Kissinger (2011: 131) said that "the Truman administration opted for continuing military operations until Korea was reunified," which strengthened his commitment to regime change in North Korea.

In the end, Washington's policies of regime containment toward the USSR and regime promotion of South Korea resulted in a lack of specific policy toward North Korea in the Cold War era. Aside from a few military collisions with Pyongyang—North Korea's seizure of the U.S. Navy intelligence ship the USS *Pueblo* in 1968, the downing of the U.S. spy airplane the *EC-121* in 1969, and the Poplar Tree Ax incident in the demilitarized zone (DMZ) in 1976—there was no need for Washington to deal directly with Pyongyang. Instead, Washington focused on regime promotion in South Korea to demonstrate the benefits of democracy and capitalism while ignoring the existence of North Korea's communist regime in terms of direct contact.

The most important factor, however, in Washington's denial of the Pyongyang regime is that the post–Cold War environment has continued in East Asia: China's presence as a new quasi-regent of North Korea has created a context only slightly different from that of the bipolar era of the Cold War. On the other hand, this East Asian context differs radically from that of other regions where Washington has pursued regime change both overtly and covertly, as in Central and South America and the Middle East. As Waltz (2000) argues, the Cold War may have seen changes in East Asia but not more broadly.

While some critique realism's core concepts of anarchy, self-reliance, and power balancing as being irrelevant in the changed context of the post–Cold War, Waltz (2000: 5) argues that big changes after the Cold War—such as global democratization, deepening interdependence among economies, and strong demands for peace and nuclear nonproliferation—have not reached the level of constituting "changes of the system" in international power politics. Though the Cold War ended nearly three decades ago, the realist notion of balancing powers remains pervasive in East Asia. Under the unipolar system led by the United States, there are three possible scenarios for balancing power in East Asia: a U.S.-led alliance with South Korea and Japan against China, or an alliance of China, South Korea, and Japan, at one extreme, against America, or a U.S. alliance with Japan against China and Korea in the middle. While most scholars and experts focus on the former scenario, some have begun to recognize the possibility of the latter while Korea's position in between the United States and China is currently going more and more adrift due to South Korea's heavy dependence on the Chinese market and pro–North Korea appeasement stance. Kang (2003: 72), for example, argues that the question remains unanswered as to whether Asian countries fear or support China's growing presence in their realms; thus, they rely on the U.S. military, whose presence in Asia has been consistent. Contrary to the general belief that historically rooted animosity among three East Asian countries—China, Japan, and South Korea—would hamper harmonious relations among them, there is evidence of other countries bandwagoning with a rising China (Kang, 2003: 70–82; Alagappa, 2003: 571–606; Waltz, 2000) mostly due to their skepticism about the American nuclear umbrella and the shared legacy of China-led cultural heritage in the region (Kang, 2003: 72).

While this study recognizes the possibility of a new alliance forming around China, it argues that the presence of North Korea as a significant nuclear proliferator and military power has markedly hindered that alliance and contributed to the maintenance of U.S.-led traditional power balancing against China. Additionally, lingering Cold War tensions between China and the United States have continued even though a major difference is noticeable from the era of bipolar competition between the United States and the USSR: the United States is more interdependent with China in the global economy than it was with the USSR before. The world is watching the tug-of-war between Washington and Beijing to see how the Biden administration's trade and military policy, mostly in continuation of the former, to curb China's expansions would work, either bringing China down or enabling China to weather American approaches toward containment.

Until the early twenty-first century, the threat of North Korea has provided justification for U.S. military presence without directly confronting or irritating China. In 1991, following the collapse of the Soviet Union, when General Colin Powell commented, "I'm running out of demons. I'm running out of enemies. I'm down to Castro and Kim Il Sung" (Waltz, 2000: 29), he indirectly explained why Washington still needs the Kim regime. As an extremist provocateur of international problems, North Korea is a dwindling, much-needed resource that provides Washington with the justification to keep counterbalancing Chinese military presence along China's coastal borders. For instance, in the immediate aftermath of the *Cheonan* sinking on March 26, 2010, and North Korea's bombing of South Korea's Yeonpyeong Island in November 2010, the United States' 7th Fleet was moved directly under China's nose in the West Sea. Another example is the joint military exercise Key Resolve, which takes place between the ROK and the United States each year. As Waltz (2000: 29) says, "Constancy of threat produces constancy of policy." Indeed, Washington needs a rogue state in order to maintain its strategic interest of being the hegemon in East Asia, and the Pyongyang regime serves that purpose. Now, with the pivot to the Asia-Pacific, justification for the presence of the 7th Fleet in Asia and the Pacific Ocean, and for the expansion of a global missile defense system, is vital and creates a stronger foundation for pursuing regime denial rather than regime change or recognition.

Nevertheless, with the ongoing Cold War–like competition between the United States and China, a resolution with North Korea may be impossible without first overcoming major obstacles or making a breakthrough in U.S.-China relations.

CONCLUSION

The Obama administration did not exhaust all options to advance beyond the North Korean policy of the previous two administrations. In fact, North Korea was the only enemy that President Obama took no action toward after promising to engage. Washington's vacillating behavior, as this book reveals, originates from its denial of the Pyeongyang regime. Conversely, Pyeongyang has gone "all in" (Han, 2009) to become a nuclear power, not as an end in itself but to gain bargaining power for negotiations with Washington, which it continues to perceive as a nonnegotiating power. Viewed in this light, going nuclear, which seems like an expression of hostility, may actually be a tactic for prodding the United States into engagement. It may also be intended to help North Korea extricate itself from its dysfunctional alliance with China and align with the United States to maximize the benefits in the middle—indeed, this would be a more reliable path to regime preservation than living under the shaky roof of Chinese economic support.

Once its motives and strategy are understood, the Pyeongyang regime appears a lot less like an irrational xenophobe possessed by anti-American sentiment and more like a boxed-in, would-be junior partner who has pursued a nuclear all-in strategy in order to maximize its domestic political stability and gain normalization and economic aid from the United States. Through the various lenses of America's North Korean policy, contrary to the generally accepted perception about North Korea, this study argues that Pyeongyang adopts agendas such as normalization of relations with the United States for its own survival, while Washington has good reason not to disrupt the status quo of power dynamics around the Peninsula or recognize a regime that left millions to die of hunger.

Ironically, it is Pyeongyang's nuclear weapons program that recently brought these antagonists to the negotiating table and is now providing them, for the first time in their relationship, with the rare opportunity to engage in dialogues on denuclearization, which remained largely in impasse during the Obama administration. A dramatic shift in U.S. policy toward Pyeongyang is desperately needed, however, from the perspective of political realism, that may not be feasible until Washington comes to terms with China.

In fact, President Trump's top-down approach to the North Korean problem attracted global attention when he met with North Korean chairman Kim

Jong-un twice, which was the first time in the relationship history between North Korea and the United States. Until 2018, no state heads of these two countries had ever met, with the exception of former president Carter, who met with Kim Il-sung in 1994 to ease tensions that had been caused by North Korea's withdrawal from the NPT in 1993 and America's threat to bomb the Yongbyon nuclear reactor site. From that perspective, President Trump was willing, regardless of his main motivations including his own political ambition for reelection and Nobel Peace Prize, to meet with the head of the regime that the United States has denied or tried to topple.

On June 12, 2018, at the Capella Hotel, Sentosa, Singapore, the heads of the United States and DPRK had their first face-to-face meeting, known as "The 2018 North Korea–United States Singapore Summit." A historic joint statement was produced with major agreements such as security guarantees for North Korea, new peaceful relations, the denuclearization of the Korean Peninsula, recovery of soldiers' remains, and follow-up negotiations between high-level officials. To demonstrate Washington's willingness to break the 70-year stalemate, the Trump administration announced a series of surprising policies such as temporarily pausing the provocative U.S.-South Korea joint military drills and, more surprisingly, bringing U.S. forces back home. Reacting to President Trump's unarranged announcement to Congress with regards to the status of the U.S. military in South Korea, on August 1, 2018, the U.S. Senate passed the military budget bill for 2019, forbidding the reduction of active U.S. Forces Korea (USFK) personnel below 22,000. Interestingly, significant removal of U.S. forces is considered a nonnegotiable item in denuclearization talks with the North. Despite the U.S. Senate's swift decision to prevent the Trump administration's efforts to reduce the level of U.S. forces in South Korea, it was a shock not only to South Korea but also to the international community that United States was willing to yield to North Korea's demands, even after a period of heightened conflict that included North Korea's successfully testing what it claims to be its first hydrogen bomb and the Hwasong-15 ICBM in late 2017. To expedite the agreed upon list of mutual actions from the first Singapore summit, the two leaders met again in February 2019 in Vietnam for the Hanoi Summit, which exposed their opposite views of each other. North Korea demanded a tit-for-tat approach of incremental denuclearization measures immediately followed by American indemnifications such as security guarantees, easing of economic sanctions, and ultimately regime recognition. By contrast, the United States demanded North Korea's "Final Fully Verifiable Denuclearization (FFVD)." Due to such directly opposing attitudes and policy differences, suddenly exposed just before the summit, the second Hanoi summit was cut short with no agreement being reached.

Regardless of recent efforts to normalize the relationship between North Korea and the United States, the concept of regime denial explains the asymmetric power relationship between a superpower (the United States) and a small antagonist (North Korea) that has its own regent (China). The applicability of this concept is limited, though, as it is hard to find similar configurations where two superpowers are competing, as are their proxies. Together, the two Koreas are the only nation still divided by Cold War ideology.

Sadly, Washington's vitriolic stance of unprecedented hatred toward an "Axis of Evil" composed of "rogue states" has simply fed the legitimacy of North Korea's troubled regime without moving Washington a step closer to preventing nuclear proliferation or ending the 67-year-old armistice on the Peninsula. Washington's disengagement since the inauguration of President Obama may even have worked against U.S. interests by giving Pyongyang more time to advance its nuclear development and ballistic missile technologies.[15] Thus, Washington's inaction, stemming from regime denial, is provoking and exacerbating a grand threat to its own national security. With no breakthrough in either multilateral (e.g., Six-Party Talks) or bilateral negotiations, the likelihood of North Korea's becoming a nuclear state will only increase. As mentioned above, the most recent attempt by the former Trump administration to cut through the Gordian knot also ended with no concrete results aside from the allegedly ever-increasing capabilities of North Korea's nuclear and ICBM technologies.

NOTES

1. This university was named after Mr. Kim Chaek, Kim Il-sung's closest comrade in the guerrilla resistance against Japanese colonists. His real name was Kim Hong-gye. After joining the anti-Japanese resistance in 1927, he fought alongside Kim Il-sung in Manchuria in the 1930s. When the Soviet Union occupied the north of the Peninsula, he came along with Kim Il-sung and was appointed vice chairman of the Workers' Party of Korea. In the end, he was purged for his alleged failure in dealing with General MacArthur's Incheon Landing.

2. Thrust vector control (TVC), during the boost phase, is accomplished by graphite vanes similar in layout to the V-2 and SCUD series tactical ballistic missiles. According to rumor, the missile follows a quasi-ballistic path in flight, performing evasive maneuvers and releasing decoys in the terminal phase to penetrate missile defense systems. The missile never leaves the atmosphere as it follows a relatively flat trajectory. Throughout its flight, it is controlled by gas-dynamic and aerodynamic control surfaces. It uses small fins to reduce its radar signature, according to Russian source Ракетная техника http://rbase.new-factoria.ru/missile/wobb/iscander/iscander.shtml.

3. A system for performing a preemptive strike against Pyeongyang's nuclear and missile facilities, the kill chain is composed of three main elements: (1) the preemptive strike system, (2) the Korean Air and Missile Defense (KAMD), which tracks and intercepts typical ballistic missiles, and (3) the Korea Massive Punishment and Retaliation (KMPR) plan. Here, North Korea's test of a new Russian Iskander-type missile may render South Korea's KAMD ineffective. The KMPR would be used to retaliate against North Korea if it were to strike South Korea.

4. With regard to the underlying motivations of Mr. Trump in his unusually strong efforts to make a deal with North Korean leader Kim, there have been some speculations, including his ambitions to build his towers in North Korea. President Trump said North Korea is "located between Russia and China on one side, and South Korea on the other. It's all waterfront property. It's a great location, as we used to say in the real estate business," according to *The New York Times* reporters Parker and Denyer (2019, May 27).

5. At the joint news conference with Japan's Prime Minister Shinzo Abe, President Trump directly contradicted his own national security advisor, John Bolton, as well as his host, by arguing that Pyeongyang had not launched ballistic missiles that month nor violated UN Security Council resolutions: "My people think it could have been a violation, I view it differently." However, Prime Minister Abe pointed out in that same conference that it was short-range ballistic missiles that constitute a violation of the UN Security Council's resolution, making clear that "this is quite a regrettable act" (Parker and Denyer, 2019, May 27).

6. The official Korean Central News Agency (KCNA) slammed U.S. National Security Advisor John Bolton, who developed various "provocative policies" against the North after the Bush administration designated it as part of the "Axis of Evil" along with Iran and Iraq in 2002, on Monday (May 27, 2019), calling him a "war maniac," "war monger," and "human defect [with a different mental structure from ordinary people]." The statement came just minutes after President Trump—on a visit to Japan—said there was "great respect" between the U.S. and North Korea and predicted "lots of good things" https://vaalweekblad.com/afp/733273/north-korea-slams-human-defect-bolton/.

7. In general, scholars have used the term, quagmire to depict deadlock of the status quo in the power dynamics in the Korean Peninsula and following Korean Question. However, I rather see a different metaphor, a logjam, fit better than the former in deciphering those realities. A quagmire is a kind of swamp with many hidden and barely seen dangers from sunken trees, rocks, and animals. It is easy to get stuck in the thick water. Getting through it requires sharp eyes and ears to detect dangers. The crew usually poles through, feeling for menaces under the water. Second, a logjam, is a tangled collection of logs blocking a river. When it comes apart, the logs fall in every direction endangering all that is in the river and even on its banks. The way I see it, the logjam is the more apt metaphor for the concept for the intrinsic nature of the Korean Question. That blockage makes progress on the river impossible. The crew may portage the boat by land around the barrier in order to relaunch when they see free flowing water. On the other hand, they may carefully dismantle the logjam so as to avoid being crushed as the logs shift and crash. That sounds like the problem

in the Korean Question. All the resentments and the negative status of relations form the barrier to reaching the goal of a productive relationship. Thus America and all interested parties may seek a way to get around these obstacles and/or demolish the logjam doing all possible to control against further destruction, wait for the river to calm down, and then continue the journey toward the goal.

8. This section is mostly from the author's 2009 article, "North Korea's Diplomacy to Engage the United States," in *Australian Journal of International Affairs* (Vol. 63, No. 1). The main reason for adopting this article in this book is that there have been no real and substantive changes either in the will of Washington nor in the power dynamics in East Asia. In fact, there are more reasons for Washington to maintain its conventional options swinging from regime change, regime recognition, to regime denial.

9. These are the three that most critically shaped the destiny of Korea around the end of World War II: on November 27, 1943, the Cairo Declaration, in which President Roosevelt, Prime Minister Winston Churchill, and China's President Chiang Kai-shek discussed Korea's liberation in "due course" from Japanese colonial control; on 1945 February, President Roosevelt, Prime Minister Churchill, and the Soviet Union's Stalin met at the Yalta Conference in the Crimea on the Black Sea, in which Korean division was briefly discussed; and on July 26, 1945, President Harry Truman, Prime Minister Churchill, and China's President Chiang discussed Japan's surrender, which included the future of Korea.

10. Syracuse University's academic exchange with North Korea's Kim Chaek University of Technology was launched in 2002, during the Six-Party Talks, and lasted until 2010 with the university's chancellor visiting for the last exchange. This exchange program, which is evaluated as the most successful Track II trust-building measure to date between the two countries, was not only an academic exchange in communications and information technologies but also a litmus test to see if the United States would lift its technology sanctions—The Wassenaar Arrangement—against Pyongyang. As a result of these academic exchanges, Syracuse University proposed to construct Twin Labs in North Korea's technological university, modeled after the Global Collaboration of the Maxwell School of Citizenship and Public Affairs with state-of-the-art communications and information technologies and equipment. However, Syracuse University's request for technology and equipment export to North Korea was blocked in the final stages. As a result of this Track II exchange, though, North Korea's first-ever digital library was completed in 2005 at Kim Chaek University of Technology.

11. Greek ἀπάθεια (apatheia), a state of indifference or an absence of passion.

12. The same word was also used to describe U.S. impressions of Corea, when America's first expeditionary forces invaded the Joseon Dynasty in 1871.

13. Here, *sadae* means toadyism or flunkeyism, which denotes an attitude of serving or worshipping the powerful. North Korea has frequently used this term to criticize South Korea's servile attitude toward American military power or Joseon's ancient regime of upholding China as a big brother, while Pyongyang has been heavily dependent upon Beijing's guarantee of its survival both economically and in terms of security.

14. Interestingly, this ideology seems in many ways to align with the transcendental views in R.W. Emerson's essay "On Self-Reliance."

15. When it comes to renunciation of nuclear and missile programs, Pyeongyang has not forgotten the case of Libya. A North Korean delegation to Syracuse University that included the DPRK's representatives to the UN Mission once commented that Moammar Gadhafi's regime simply disappeared from the map. Once Gadhafi gave up his pursuit of nuclear weapons in exchange for security guarantees and sanctions relief, he was ousted and assassinated. This case reinforced the strong belief that nuclear weapons facilitate a regime's survival.

Chapter 5

Upshots of Encounters

HALF-SUCCESS IN SOUTH KOREA

The Introduction examined U.S. relations with Korea in general and North Korea in particular. This chapter completes that story by looking to the south. According to interviews with Korean War veterans from all 22 countries that participated in the war, virtually nothing was left standing by the end—Korea was utterly devastated. So, how did South Korea transform itself into one of the world's most powerful countries in about 30 years of industrialization? Since 1962, the first year of President Park's "Five-Year Economic Development Plan," South Korea broke world records with the highest economic growth rate of 7.1% for 1962–1966, by encouraging the development of light industries for export. And, despite criticisms from world-renowned economists that it was unrealistic, the target was exceeded with an economic growth rate averaging 8.9%, propelling South Korea to rapid industrialization.

In Seoul during the 1960s, the catchphrase "export war" was being propagandized in the news media and movies. As a result of the nation's ambitious drive for exports, South Korea recorded 29% growth, 15% manufacturing per a year. The Korean government implemented a policy focus during its Second Five-Year Economic Development Plan (1967–1971), attracting direct foreign investment and improving basic infrastructure. The third plan (1972–1976) served as a turning point by restructuring the Korean economy from light to heavy industries and production of capital goods. Such dramatic shifts in Korea's economic bases from primary industries to highly value-added electronics and heavy industries are well documented in table 5.1. For roughly 30 years, these five-year plans enabled the Republic of Korea to join the ranks of the world's strongest economies, rising from the ashes in what came to be called the "Miracle of the Han River." In the last Five-Year

Table 5.1 Top 10 Korean Exports, Progress from 1967 to 2009

	Series Name	Amount (US$ million)	Ratio (%)
1967			
1	Prepared text. fibers; fabrics	59.96	18.73
2	Wearing apparel, except fur	51.72	16.16
3	Plywood, particle board, and other	35.87	11.20
4	Preserved fish and fish products	25.91	8.09
5	Other misc. manuf. Articles	25.42	7.97
6	Nonferrous metal ores, exe. nucl.	15.99	4.99
7	Vegetables, horticult. spec.	9.89	3.09
8	Cereals and other crops n.e.c.	9.84	3.07
9	Footwear	8.52	2.66
10	Iron ores	5.61	1.75
	Total	320.13	
1987			
1	Wearing apparel, except fur	5,582.42	11.83
2	TV and radio receivers, record	4,438.03	9.40
3	Prepared textiles, fibers, fabrics	3,316.68	7.03
4	Motor vehicles	3,120.87	6.61
5	Footwear	2,850.89	6.04
6	Electronic valves and tubes	2,393.39	5.07
7	Manuf. basic iron and steel	2,316.73	4.91
8	Office and computing machinery	1,704.45	3.61
9	Knitted fabrics and articles	1,614.79	3.42
10	Preserved fish and fish products	1,397.56	2.96
	Total	47,206.59	
2009			
1	Building and repairing of ships	38,180.71	10.50
2	Electronic valves and tubes	32,101.99	8.83
3	Motor vehicles	29,589.04	8.14
4	TV and radio transmitters & tel.	26,927.80	7.41
5	Optical instr. and photo equip.	26,172.11	7.20
6	Refined petroleum products	22,840.41	6.28
7	Manuf. basic iron and steel	17,878.37	4.92
8	Basic chemicals, exe. fertile	15,738.41	4.33
9	Plastics and synthetic rubber	15,318.54	4.21
10	TV and radio receivers, record	12,285.75	3.38
	Total	363,470.55	

* Ratio is percentage of total exports.
Source: Reprinted with permission from Eichengreen et al., *The Korean Economy: From a Miraculous Past to a Sustainable Future*, Cambridge, Massachusetts, London: Harvard University Press (2015).

Economic Development Plan (1992–1996), South Korea completed its transition from being an aid-receiving country to an aid-offering country. In 2010, South Korea hosted the G20 in Seoul, an international forum for the governments and central banks of 19 countries and the European Union. As mentioned earlier, the South Korean economy is now the world's 11th largest and is projected to rank 7th in 2030.

The most important aspect of South Korea's rapid economic development can be found in its relations with the United States. Now, South Korea is no longer known as "Corea" or "land of morning calm." This country whose destiny was in the hands of the United States in the 1950s has now become the United States' seventh largest trading partner, which increasingly matters to the American economy and national security. Indeed, hundreds and thousands of U.S. Korean War veterans who have joined the Korean government's "Revisit Program" and witnessed Korea's achievements tear up on witnessing the prosperity of Korea today, an achievement that seemed beyond all possibility when these soldiers left in the 1950s. Table 5.2 captures the most important aspects of these nations' political economic relations.

As shown in tables 5.3 and Table 5.4, U.S. exports of goods to South Korea in 2012 were valued at roughly $43B, an increase of 92% from 2002. South Korea's exports of goods to the United States were worth over $58B in 2012, up 79% from 2002. The total value of U.S.-ROK two-way trade of goods and services exceeds $125B annually. South Korea had a trade surplus in goods with the United States totaling $16B in 2012, while the United States had a trade surplus in services with South Korea totaling $8B. In 2012, U.S. trade with South Korea ($2,023 per Korean) was higher than with China ($397 per Chinese) and Japan ($1,696 per Japanese) when adjusted for population (EWC & AIPS, p. 8). Keep in mind that almost 90% of the Korean government's annual budget in the late 1950s and early 1960s was appropriated through sales of the surplus rice that the U.S. government had provided as economic aid.

Major U.S. goods exported to Korea as of 2011 included agricultural products ($7B), electrical machinery ($6B), mechanical machinery ($6B), optical and medical instruments ($3B), aircraft ($3B), mineral fuel and oil ($3B), and other ($16B) (EWC & AIPS, p. 8). On the other hand, major Korean goods exported to the United States included electrical machinery ($16B), vehicles

Table 5.2 Major Indicators, the United States and the ROK

Indicators (2012)	United States	South Korea
Population	316 million	50.2 million
GDP (current USD)	15.7T	1.2T
GDP Growth (annual %)	2.2	2.0
Trade as % of GDP	32%	110%
	(2nd largest exporter)	(7th largest exporter)
FDI, Net inflows (BoP, current USD)	$206B	$5B
Military Expenditure (% of GDP)	4.4%	2.8%
Internet Users (% of population)	81%	84%

Source: Reprinted from *Korea Matters for America/America Matters for Korea*, 2018, p. 6, with permission from the East-West Center in Washington, DC.

Table 5.3 Top Export Partners for U.S. Goods, 2012 (in billions)

Rank	Country	Exports (US$)	Share (%)
1	Canada	292.4	19
2	Mexico	216.3	14
3	China	110.6	7
4	Japan	70	5
5	United Kingdom	54.8	4
6	Germany	48.8	3
7	Brazil	43.7	3
8	South Korea	42.3	3
9	Netherlands	40.7	3
10	Hong Kong	37.5	2
Total	All countries	1,547	

Source: Reprinted from *Korea Matters for America/America Matters for Korea*, 2018, p. 9, with permission from the East-West Center in Washington, DC.

($12B), machinery ($10B), mineral fuel and oil ($3B), iron and steel ($2B), and other ($14B) (EWC & AIPS, p. 9). Exports to South Korea supported more than 119,000 jobs across the United States in 2012, an increase of 28% since 2002. These exports supported at least 1,000 jobs in 29 states and at least 3,000 jobs in another 8 states (EWC & AIPS, p. 12).

Table 5.5 shows how many Korean War veterans came from states that had sent over 40,000 soldiers; this number includes Korean War era veterans who were not in the Korean theater but elsewhere. These numbers roughly indicate which states provided soldiers for the Korean War. California far exceeded the others with a total of 203,300. Texas sent the second most with 143,200. Florida ranked third with 196,900, New York fourth with 112,700, Pennsylvania fifth with 108,700, and other states provided less than 100,000.

Table 5.4 Korea's Goods Export Partners, 2012

Rank	Country	Exports (US$)	Share (%)
1	China	134.3	25
2	United States	58.6	11
3	Japan	38.8	7
4	Hong Kong	32.6	6
5	Singapore	22.9	4
6	Vietnam	15.9	3
7	Taiwan	14.8	3
8	Indonesia	14	3
9	Russia	11.1	2
10	Saudi Arabia	9.1	2
Total	All Countries	547.9	

Source: Reprinted from *Korea Matters for America/America Matters for Korea*, 2018, p. 9, with permission from the East-West Center in Washington, DC.

Table 5.5 Korean War Veterans Dispatched by State (over 40,000)

State	Total Veteran Population	Gulf War Veterans	Vietnam Veterans	Korean War Veterans	WWII Veterans
Washington	626,500	178,000	220,600	56,500	40,900
California	1,918,100	517,300	621,300	205,300	157,800
Colorado	417,800	119,600	149,900	36,700	24,800
Arizona	551,300	143,200	178,700	65,200	48,200
Texas	1,683,200	541,100	556,700	143,200	102,800
Minnesota	371,900	70,900	137,600	42,100	29,800
Missouri	496,700	123,800	169,100	51,200	36,800
Michigan	684,500	141,400	243,900	72,100	56,700
Wisconsin	407,600	90,200	138,800	43,400	32,200
Illinois	762,500	196,400	244,900	77,600	62,000
Indiana	482,100	115,300	163,400	46,700	34,600
Tennessee	489,100	130,100	172,700	46,300	31,400
Ohio	867,200	199,000	296,100	87,800	71,000
Georgia	773,300	250,500	257,400	58,900	37,600
Florida	1,617,200	412,100	504,300	196,900	161,800
New York	913,500	180,700	297,300	112,700	92,600
Massachusetts	378,600	70,900	125,400	48,700	41,000
Pennsylvania	933,400	189,000	312,900	108,700	94,200
New Jersey	423,300	80,100	134,800	55,900	47,200
Virginia	823,300	311,300	255,900	59,700	40,100
Totals	15,621,100	4,060,900	5,181,700	1,615,600	1,243,500

Source: Department of Veterans Affairs, the United States.

Tables 5.5 and 5.6 show how the states that sent the most veterans roughly coincide with those having the highest trade volumes with South Korea. Most of these veterans, understandably, at the time of their dispatch, could not have found Korea on a map. Now, however, trade with South Korea has come to represent a significant portion of their states' economic scales. Could any of these soldiers ever have imagined that their state would ultimately be conducting business with this country for which they once fought and then simply hoped to forget?

An additional 10 states increased exports to South Korea by at least 50% during this period. Twenty-five states export more than $500M a year to South Korea. Of South Korea's 16 provinces and independent municipalities, 11 more than doubled their exports to the United States between 2002 and 2012. Three cities and two provinces in Korea each exported more than $5B to the United States in 2012. There are no official statistics on whether any of these states have traded with North Korea since the end of the Korean War in 1953 (EWC & AIPS, 2013, p. 10). Table 5.6 also shows mutual interdependencies between Korea and ten major American states that export to Korea.

South Korean investment in the United States increased from $3B to more than $24B. During the same period, U.S. investment in South Korea increased from $10B to $35B. This investment supported more than 32,000 U.S. jobs. For example, South Korean auto manufacturing—like the Hyundai plant in Montgomery, Alabama and the Kia plant in West Point, Georgia—created about 8,000 jobs for Americans (EWC & AIPS, 2013, p. 14), as seen in table 5.7, which shows how the economic partnership with Korea created jobs in principal states that dispatched most Korean War veterans. New investment flowed into the United States in 2012 totaling $161B. Europe accounted for $105B, Canada $22B, and other countries $1B. Countries in the Asian Pacific accounted for $32B. Among these, Japan

Table 5.6 Top 10 States (Goods Exporters to Korea, 2012)

Rank	State	US$
1	California	7.9B
2	Texas	7.8B
3	Washington	2.5B
4	New York	1.3B
5	New Jersey	1.0B
6	Illinois	1.0B
7	Massachusetts	1.0B
8	Michigan	1.0B
9	Ohio	932M
10	Pennsylvania	892M

Source: Reprinted from *Korea Matters for America/America Matters for Korea*, 2018, p. 11, with permission from the East-West Center in Washington, DC.

Table 5.7 Top 10 States (Jobs from U.S. Exports to Korea, per 100,000 Residents, 2012)

State	Jobs
Alaska	412
Idaho	146
North Dakota	116
Washington	102
Nebraska	102
Vermont	86
West Virginia	86
Montana	85
Texas	79
South Dakota	74

Source: Reprinted from *Korea Matters for America/America Matters for Korea*, 2018, p. 13, with permission from the East-West Center in Washington, DC.

contributed the largest share with $19B, and South Korea next with $5B, followed by Singapore $3B, Australia $1.6B, Hong Kong $1.5B, China $1.4B, Taiwan $500M, and India $400M (EWC & AIPS, 2013, p. 15).

South Korea is the third-largest source of foreign students in the United States, while the United States is the sixth-largest source of foreign students in Korea. The number of South Korean students in the United States increased sharply over the past decade, rising by more than 40% from 51,500 in the 2001/02 academic year to more than 72,000 in 2012/13. Only China and India have more students in the United States than South Korea does (EWC & AIPS, 2013, p. 18). In 2002, Koreans represented 8.4% of all international students in the United States; in 2009, they reached 11.2% (EWC & AIPS, 2013, p. 16). Koreans are the ninth-largest group of visitors to the United States, spending $6B in 2011. Conversely, Americans are the third-largest group of visitors to South Korea, and the number of Americans traveling there has risen by 63% since 2001. American and Korean carriers offer regular nonstop flights from 11 U.S. cities to destinations in South Korea, 10 of which are served daily (EWC & AIPS, 2013, p. 20). Koreans comprise 9% of the Asian American population. Nearly 62% of Korean Americans are foreign-born. Koreans are the fifth-largest Asian American community after Chinese, Indians, Filipinos, and Vietnamese. Many Koreans attain U.S. citizenship, ranking twelfth in their share of all U.S. naturalizations in 2012 and fifth among Asians [Source: U.S. Census Bureau; U.S. Department of Homeland Security] (EWC & AIPS, 2013, p. 22). These indicators demonstrate the extent to which encounters between the United States and Korea shifted the balance of power surrounding the Peninsula.

The 1953 Mutual Defense Treaty, which has guaranteed peace and stability on the Peninsula for more than 60 years, remains the cornerstone of the two countries' relationship. Currently, the United States maintains about 28,500 military personnel in the Republic of Korea. The Combined Forces Command, established in 1978, remains the centerpiece of the ROK-U.S. Alliance. Joint sessions of the U.S. Congress have been addressed by six Korean presidents: Syngman Rhee on July 28, 1954, Tae-woo Roh on October 18, 1989, Young-sam Kim on July 6, 1995, Dae-jung Kim on June 10, 1998, Myung-bak Lee on October 13, 2011, and Geun-hye Park on May 8, 2013 (p. 27). This is the most by any Asian nation, topped only by addresses from the president of Mexico and prime ministers of the United Kingdom. Recent United States and Korean cooperative military efforts around the world have included Iraq (Operation Iraqi Freedom), Lebanon (UN Peacekeeping Mission), the Persian Gulf (Operation Desert Storm), Afghanistan (Operation Enduring Freedom), the Gulf of Aden (Operation Dawn of Gulf of Aden), Somalia (UN Peacekeeping Mission), and Haiti (UN Humanitarian Mission) (EWC & AIPS, 2013, p. 26).

Undoubtedly, U.S.-ROK relations have come to possess global importance. Together, the two countries fund nearly 30% of the total budget for UN Peacekeeping Operations. They are both members of the G20 and the Nuclear Security Summit (NSS), which was initiated by President Obama in 2010. Seoul successfully hosted the G20 in 2010 and the NSS meeting in 2012. South Korea also achieved the distinction of becoming the first country to transition from being a recipient of development assistance (ODA) to being a member of the OECD's Development Assistance Committee (EWC & AIPS, 2013, p. 28).

Table 5.8 shows the 10 Congressional districts with the most exports to South Korea; CA-17, five districts in Texas, the state of Alaska, and WA-2 demonstrate greatly increased trade relations as well as economic interdependence with other countries. Table 6.8 shows where an official 2.2 million Korean Americans are concentrated in the United States. Despite poor political representation in these districts, the Korean American community has great potential for civic engagement relating to domestic political affairs. Finally, table 5.9 demonstrates the mutual interdependency is not just confined to the economic sphere but also arises from exchanges of people.

While America's encounter with South Korea has produced remarkable progress, notably in the shift from initial stances of apathy and hostility to mutual interdependence, its relationship with the DPRK has preserved the initial hostility and produced negative outcomes, as with the contemporary impasse. One major difference is that the Joseon ideology of isolationism has been subsumed by North Korea's modern stance toward the outside world, *juche*, which has even exacerbated that isolationism through approaches such as nuclear deterrence and brinkmanship.

A survey of how these two countries became so interdependent and arrived at a more equal footing than a century earlier accounts for the dramatic

Table 5.8 Congressional District Exports to Korea (137 U.S. Congressional districts exporting more than $100M to Korea)

Rank	District	Export (US$)	Note
1	CA-17	892,112,268	
2	AK	691,382,318	
3	WA-2	625,980,052	
4	TX-32	575,604,523	12 districts in Texas total $2.5B, and 32nd district leads this trend
5	TX-14	509,058,497	
6	TX-10	505,238,654	
7	TX-36	486,795,284	
8	TX-24	482,242,922	
9	WA-9	474,173,551	
10	WV-3	423,376,752	West Virginia leads in U.S. exports to Korea in the East

Source: Goods exports (2012) are estimated by the Trade Partnership (Washington, DC) from the US Bureau of the Census, US Department of Agriculture, and Moody's Analytics data.

transformation of the southern half of the Peninsula. Despite the history of betrayal, as well as the partly sparse roots of Korea's democracy, Korea became a world economic power and democracy largely as a result of its interaction with the United States. Moreover, by accomplishing industrialization so rapidly, South Korea reversed to a certain extent some negative trends in its intercourse with the United States, in terms of inequality, racism, and intrinsic disregard.

KILROY RESURRECTED

Besides Korea's capability to transform from the poorest aid-recipient to the 11th largest aid-offering economy, and aside from its strategic geopolitical

Table 5.9 Top 10 Districts of Korean American Community

Rank	District	Population
1	NY-5	47,972
2	CA-33	42,280
3	CA-40	40,034
4	NJ-9	38,090
5	HI-1	33,811
6	VA-11	33,474
7	CA-48	27,403
8	CA-31	25,304
9	CA-42	24,323
10	GA-7	23,277

Source: US Census Bureau, 2010, 113th Congressional districts.

value to the United States, and the decisive effects of U.S. economic and military aid after the Korean War, what other factors might have led the United States to commit rather than to fold as before? This chapter cites the loss of American lives in the Korean War as support for Diamond's thesis that dramatic transformation emerged from such "collisions between different peoples from different continents." Through layers of collisions and interactions, as acting Secretary of State Webb predicted in 1949, Korea has become

> the only area in the world in which democratic and communist principles are being put to the test side by side and in which the U.S. and the former U.S.S.R (currently known as the Russian Federation) have been, and no doubt in the estimation of the world, will continue to be, the sole contenders for the way of life of 30,000,000 people. The entire world and especially Asia is watching this contest." (Webb, 1949: 2)

Indeed, South Korea's post–Korean War interaction with the United States has demonstrated Webb's prediction:

> To the degree that the "Republic succeeds, the people in the still free nations of Southeast and Southern Asia and Oceania will be persuaded of the practical superiority of democratic principles. To the degree the United States continues to support the efforts of the South Korean people to develop a self-supporting economy and a stable democratic government the people of this area will be persuaded of the firmness of U.S. determination to support Democracy and oppose Communism. Weakening on the part of the United States will damage their confidence and undermine the position of the United States. (Webb, 1949: 2)

As Webb argued, "The only visible source of adequate economic assistance toward a level of self-support is the United States," which was expounded in chapter 3. He did not, however, foresee such a heavy loss of American lives. This book specifically places that part of the history up front.

In his article "Kilroy is Back: Images of American Soldiers in Korea, 1950–1953," Huebner (2004) uses the term Kilroy[1], originally coined to designate GIs (Government Issues) during World War II, to distinguish veterans of the European war from veterans of the war in Korea. Whereas the former had taken place in an area that was familiar and even a source of pride, the latter had occurred in an area no one recognized or liked, and was quickly forgotten. When the message that "Kilroy was here" started popping up throughout Europe in the wake of World War II, the tone was jubilant, victorious, and spirited. When it appeared in Korea, however, the sense was disheartened, demoralized, and desolate (Huebner, 2004).

Such images were aptly captured by David Douglas Duncan, one of "the indispensable photojournalists of the 20th century" (Cosgrove, 2012). "It was forty below zero during the retreat from *Jangjin*[2] Reservoir," Duncan recalls of one especially appalling battle in the winter of 1950. "And the wind chill! The wind was barreling down from Manchuria and must have made it closer to 50 or 60 degrees below zero. It was so damn cold that my film was brittle—it just snapped, like a pretzel. But I managed to unload and load the camera under my gear and get some film in there, and I got some usable shots" (Cosgrove, 2012).[3] This firsthand account of events from late November to December 1950 captures the horrific conditions faced by U.S. Marines who came to find that the enemy forces outmanned them by a factor or two.

Those Kilroys' horrified expressions, which had frozen in place during the Korean War, were later resuscitated and brought back to life, no longer sad but proud of what South Korea had become as a result of the war they fought. Despite such a dramatic reversal, however, the other half of the country was kept from prospering. More than half a million North Koreans died of hunger in the Arduous March from 1995 to 1999.

The Korean War Legacy Foundation[4] has conducted and archived almost 1,200 interviews with Korean War veterans in their mid to late 80s, capturing firsthand accounts of the war they fought and the country they experienced in the early 1950s. The country that they left behind was utterly in shambles. Many describe the capital of Korea as utterly leveled. The mountains had few trees, if any. After 35 years of devastating colonial control by Japan, the Korean economy was in dire straits, because Japan's colonial policy had been predatory and exploitative with designs toward its own economic and military expansionism. According to Oxford Research Encyclopedia, Korea, at its founding in 1948, was "one of the world's poorest states." Then, "Twelve years later, in 1960, it remained so with a per capita income of about the same as Haiti."

The country that young American soldiers saw when they arrived in Busan in the early 1950s (the biggest port, in the southeast) or Incheon (second-biggest port, in the west, near the 38th parallel) is now completely transformed. These young Americans, many as young as 16, had arrived in Korea expecting barbarians. In interviews with 1,100 Korean War veterans not just from America but from all participating countries, many confessed having known nothing about Korean history or culture, and even having been unable to locate Korea on a map before their military service. And this wasn't just the veterans themselves. When American veterans returned from their service in the Korean theater, friends commonly asked where they had been. Almost none of the Korean War veterans whose uncles or fathers had served as missionaries before the outbreak of the Korean War, or in the military that occupied the Peninsula from 1945 to 1948, had known where Korea was located on a world map. Almost none had been taught about Korea in middle or high school. Basically, Korea was a kind of *Alice's Adventures in Wonderland* of the worst possible sort, according to interviews with veterans from the digital archive of the KWLF.

Such negative images of Korea completely changed, however, when these veterans were invited back to Korea in their mid to late 80s to witness how the nation had transformed into the world's 11th largest economy, according to *The Economist*,[5] and the 6th largest exporter, according to *Statista*.[6] When these veterans landed in the world's top international airport in Incheon in these days, their eyes bulged as they took in the view. Approaching Seoul, they were shocked to see so many buildings standing tall, one of the world's 10 biggest metropolises. When the bus took the highway along the Han River, their fingers almost automatically started counting bridges. There was only one bridge in the 1950, almost destroyed. Now there are 31. Tears of gratitude and victory were not uncommon.

Finally, they could take a deep breath, feel some closure, and set down their burden—the legacy of the formerly forgotten war now complete. In fact, according to interviews in the KWLF digital archive, they are the ones who wanted to forget the war they had fought. They fought in a country they had not known at all and under miserable conditions. Compared to their uncles' and fathers' experiences of battle in World War II, their own experience was hot and cold and life-devouring to an unprecedented degree, as will be discussed in the next section. They achieved no clear victory either. By contrast, World War II was a huge win to celebrate, and Europe was the ancestral home of most Americans. The whole nation mobilized to win this well-known war with a noble cause. Everyone paid attention to spirited news from our "Kilroys" abroad.

LEGACY OF U.S.-KOREA RELATIONS

In order to better discern how the contemporary successes and failures of Korea came about, a long gestaltic and holistic survey of U.S.-Korea relations has been attempted. The fundamental questions were how North and South Korea have taken such drastically different paths of socioeconomic and political development as well as why Korean issues have never been resolved but rather have intensified in step with North Korea's nuclear provocations, which are threatening regional and global security with Sino-U.S. confrontations along the Acheson Line in the South China Sea.

Are Koreans, overall, happy about this intercourse with America? Yes and no. Was their encounter painful? Yes, certainly. Relations between the United States and Korea have led to two wars: the *Shinmiyangyo* in 1871, which had no concrete outcomes, and the 1950 Korean War, which led to massive killings of civilians and soldiers as well as eventual spectacular developments for the South and extreme isolation, a failed economy, and a totalitarian dictatorship for the North. The latter has worsened since that first encounter with the *General Sherman* in 1866. Are Koreans happy with the United States now? Yes and no. Could South Korea independently have become what the Republic of Korea is now? No. Have the United States and Korea overcome their racist views toward each other? In some senses, prejudice has significantly subsided, due both to South Korea's unprecedentedly rapid industrialization and assimilation of American sociocultural system and to America's globalization, self-education, and amazement at Korea's success.

Has the United States changed its approach to North Korea after the stalemate in the Korean War? Not really. The United States has attempted a policy of regime change toward North Korea with no concrete outcome other than a souring relationship. During the Cold War, the United States did not need to do anything, and now the United States is in deep denial of North Korea, because the rogue nation has nuclear and possibly ICBM capabilities that hamper United States attempts to perform a surgical strike on its nuclear facilities for fear of sparking World War III or incurring massive human casualties, not just in South Korea but in Japan as well. Sandwiched between its increasingly heavy reliance on exports to China and its traditional alliance with the United States, South Korea cannot move an inch forward in its relations with North Korea. Economic sanctions from the UN and the United States make South Korea's moves for economic cooperation with North Korea risky in terms of its international position and alliance with the United States.

Evidence abounds for the vulnerabilities caused by Korea's dependence on China and the United States. A good example is Korea's heavy dependence on the economic power of the United States and China, especially in the midst of their ongoing trade war. A new model by economists at Pictet Asset Management lists countries that would be most economically damaged by trade war escalation. In Selby-Green's (2018) evaluation of countries' integration into the global value chain of raw materials and supplies in the production of goods for export, South Korea ranked sixth. Besides European countries, Korea is second only to Taiwan. One more example aptly illustrates South Korea's exposed position between vying superpowers who fought each other in the Korean War. South Korea suffered about a 41% loss in Chinese tourism (Yonghap News Agency, 2019) since July 2016 when the United States almost forced its ally to accept the installation of a THAAD (Terminal High Altitude Area Defense) missile system in South Korea. Its official purpose, Koreans were told, was to deter and intercept nuclear missile attacks from North Korea. However, its real purpose was to monitor and threaten Beijing, because its functions were not originally designed for short-range missile attacks. Reacting vehemently to South Korea's decision to accept THAAD, China ordered all state and private tour organizations related to China's overseas tourism not to visit Korea. According to Federation of Korean Industries quoted by Yonhap News Agency (2019), a total of 4.79 million Chinese visited South Korea in 2018, down 40.6% from the 8.07 million who had visited just two years earlier.

Diamond (1997) explained the unequal and uneven fates of human societies among different peoples and nations in his book, *Guns, Germs, and Steel*. Having attempted to account for the dual fates of the Korean nation in the context of its intercourse with the United States, it is now time to ask what this relationship between the United States and Korea might produce and where it might lead.

WHAT LIES AHEAD FOR KOREA: KOREA DISREGARDED

In 1905, Alice Roosevelt and Willian Taft, the then-secretary of war and future president of America, embarked on an Asian voyage from San Francisco, first to Japan and then to the Philippines, China, and Korea. It was a critical time for each of these countries: President Roosevelt favored Japan over Russia in negotiations for a peace treaty in the Russo-Japanese War, and thus had given Japan control over Korea in exchange for continued control over the Philippines. Bradley (2009) called this trip "The Imperial Cruise." Alice Roosevelt's visit to Korea was critical to the Joseon emperor. "In the summer of 1905, the world was a scary place for Korea. The Russo-Japanese War had recently ended but Korea was still occupied by Japanese troops and pressure from the Japanese government was increasing almost daily." And "It was perhaps the emperor's hope that he could favorably impress her and thus ensure her father's aid with the Japanese" (Neff, 2014).

On September 19, Alice and her entourage arrived at Jemulpo (today's Incheon) and proceeded to Seoul on a special train decorated with American, Korean, and Japanese flags. According to one observer, "Most of the houses in the city had been decorated with Korean and American flags, some of the latter lacking an occasional star or stripe, or showing somewhat of a variety of color, but all bearing evidence of a uniform desire to honor the nation's guest" (Neff, 2014). After receiving a wonderful reception from Japan, Alice[7] had a pretty clear sense that American understanding of Korea had been backward and reported immediately sensing that "Korea, reluctant and helpless, was sliding into the grasp of Japan" (Furgurson, 2015).

The emperor had no choice but to bestow on the president's daughter the highest honor at his command. On September 20, Emperor Gojong held a luncheon[8] for Roosevelt and her entourage at Deoksu Palace and treated her with "more consideration than [had] ever been shown to visiting royalty before" (Neff, 2014). After that luncheon, the emperor specially arranged an excursion to the tomb of his former queen, Queen Minbi, in the capital's outskirts. In this specially arranged trip that itself was based on the hopeless expectation of somehow influencing Alice to entreat her father to honor his commitment to Korea's destiny, an incident occurred that revealed America's attitudes, which may reveal contempt toward Korea at that time. In fact, the emperor did not waste this opportunity "to urge the senator [Senator Francis G. Newman] to speak favorably to the American president concerning Korea's situation in regard to Japan. The senator advised the Korean government to hire a lawyer to make a formal appeal citing the good offices clause of the U.S.-Korea treaty" (Neff, 2014). However, Alice's pompous and inobservant behaviors in her excursion to the tomb of emperor's former queen Min seems to indirectly reveal America's indifference and contempt of Korea. Keat (1909) describes this incident in her 1909 article for the *San Francisco Call*:[9]

> At their head rode a dashing young horsewoman clad in a scarlet riding habit, beneath the lower extremities of which peeped tight fitting red riding breeches stuck into glittering boot. In her hand she brandished a riding whip, in her mouth was a cigar. It was Alice Roosevelt. We were flabbergasted. We had expected a different sort of appearance. The Rough Rider's daughter seemed to think it all a Joke. She was mainly interested in the colossal figures of gods and the mammoth stone images, of animals, which watch over the graves of departed rulers of Koreans. Sighting a stone elephant, Alice hurled off her horse and in a flash was astride the elephant, shouting to Longworth to snapshot her. Our suite was paralyzed with horror and astonishment. Such a sacrilegious scene was without parallel in Korean history.

Neff (2014) also confirms that the incident of Alice's disdainful attitude occurred in one of the most sacred places in Korea at that time:

> She recalled that Roosevelt arrived at the party in a cloud of dust on horseback with a large escort of men. She was clad in a scarlet riding habit, beneath the lower extremities of which peeped tight-fitting red riding breeches stuck into glittering boots. In her hand, she brandished a riding whip; "in her mouth was a cigar . . . everybody was bowing and scraping in the most approved Korean Court fashion, but the Rough Rider's daughter seemed to think it all a joke." She apparently paid little attention to those around her but was fascinated with

the stone statues that guarded the tomb. "Spying a stone elephant, which seemed particularly to strike her fancy, Alice hurtled off her horse and in a flash was astride the elephant, shouting to Mr. Longworth [her fiancé] to snapshot her. Our suite was paralyzed with horror and astonishment. Such a sacrilegious scene at so holy a spot was without parallel in Korean history. It required indeed 'American ways' to produce it." After a short chat with the American legation staff and bravely partaking of the champagne, she suddenly "gave orders of the saddling of her horse, and galloped away with her male escorts like a Buffalo Bill." Many denied the event ever took place—including Alice's father-in-law who declared Kroebel was "either drunk or crazy, or both." The denials went on for some time but no one could or would provide the proof that was needed to finally put the matter to rest.

The American delegation departed Seoul by train for Busan on September 29. American vice-consul Willard Straight was quick to note in his correspondence that

> the Japanese had done everything they could to disrupt the visit . . . [The Japanese] were principally afraid of the effect that the visit would have on the Koreans. [The Koreans] are seeking for straws just now and the Roosevelt trip looked like a life preserver to their jaundiced imaginations. This the Japanese tried to get around by appearing to be doing the entertaining themselves.

As this anecdotal evidence from 1905 indicates, loosely speaking, the U.S. did not give damn about Korea. Has that changed? Of course, Korea's relative importance to America's economy and national strategic interest has affected America's esteem for Korea; however, such changes seem only relative. A racially oriented American attitude specifically on Korea is unknown because most American citizens are largely unaware of their government's long history of international relations, so Korea's place in the minds of Americans remains as prejudiced as their views of other Asian nations.

The long history of the Korean nation bore witness to countless foreign attacks, but Korea rarely invaded other nations. The history of Korea's encounter with the United States clearly raises some critical questions. Can the Korean nation become independent from the superpowers surrounding it? Can it avoid future attacks from China, Russia, and Japan? Can it maintain economic independence from China, the United States, and Japan? Can Korea declare permanent neutrality to all superpowers' interests so that it can be free from them? In fact, Emperor Gojong endeavored to avoid Japanese interference by declaring the Korean Empire a permanently neutral country before Japan's protectorate in 1905. He declared it on January 21, 1904. The Korean government "instructed its British Chief Commissioner of Korean

Customs, John McLeavy Brown (1835–1926), to draw up a memorandum to the British Foreign Office to this extent. In addition, it sent one of Gojong's most trusted courtiers, French-speaking Hyón Sanggón (Translation Bureau, Ministry of the Court), to St. Petersburg to discuss the matter with the Russian government and used private channels to express similar intentions to Tokyo. It even published a formal neutrality declaration on January 21, 1904, on the eve of the commencement of hostilities" (Tikhonov, 2012, 38). And as we now know, his efforts were in vain.

WHERE THIS HISTORY LEADS IN AMERICA'S ASIAN POLICY

My overarching concern in writing this book was whether I was adopting an overly parochial—or Korea-centered—perspective in criticizing America's policy on the nation of my upbringing and heritage. If Korea had become the rising power in the region or the world in the late nineteenth and early twentieth centuries, would Korea have followed the same trajectory, taking opportunistic stances to play certain countries against others? As the United States played Japan against Korea, could Korea, for example, have played the United States against Taiwan? The only way to overcome that hurdle was to trace back the history of America's Asian policy in general and to explore directions for future policy.

A brief but holistic and gestaltic view of the United States' position can now serve as our point of departure for reassessing the story of how the United States and Korea have treated each other. The United States is at serious odds with Asia's biggest giant, China, as its "frenemy": U.S. consumers, as well as the American industry system and its structures, are heavily dependent on cheap bulk products from China. The United States has fallen into a Thucydides Trap with China, along the same lines as the Acheson Line, which excluded Korea from the U.S. defensive perimeter in 1950, colliding with China's contemporary "One Belt One Road" initiative as discussed in earlier chapters. Japan, which was favored by President Theodore Roosevelt in 1905, is now strongly aligned with the United States, despite its attack on Pearl Harbor in 1941, the first foreign invasion of American territory. Japan's declaration of war in December of 1941 explained its position quite clearly: "It is a fact of history that the countries of East Asia have been compelled for the past hundred years or more to observe the status quo under the Anglo-American policy of imperialistic exploitation and to sacrifice themselves to the prosperity of the two nations [the U.S. and the U.K.]. The Japanese government cannot tolerate the perpetuation of such a situation" (Bradley, 2009). Ironically, Franklin Roosevelt's confidence in Japan's military capability to launch a surprise attack boomeranged against the United States. And the American president's support emboldened Japan to increase its military might and imperial ambitions. In December 1941, the consequences of Theodore Roosevelt's recklessness would become clear to the few who knew of his secret dealings. "No one else—including my father on Iwo Jima—realized just how well Japan had indeed played what President Roosevelt called 'our game'" (Bradley, 2009 b).[10]

Korea and Japan host the most U.S. military bases, with Germany and NATO coming in second. According to the IMF's World Economic Outlook (WEO) Database, April 2019, the total GDP of China, Japan, and Korea accounts for more than one-third of the whole world's. From the perspective of other superpowers, these three countries have fortunately not fully recovered from their scars. According to mass surveys, the Chinese and Koreans have a lower opinion of Japan than of North Korea. Japan's imperial invasions and mass killings of Chinese, Koreans, and other nations in Southeast Asia engendered great distrust toward Japan. Interestingly, China, Japan, and Korea share the most fundamental cultural and religious roots of Chinese civilization: Confucianism, Chinese characters, Buddhism, and many branches of philosophy. For example, there is a group of intellectuals from these three countries who try to bridge contemporary animosities by promoting their shared cultural heritage, that is, 800 shared Chinese characters. Imagine these three countries overcoming the scars of their unfortunate histories and being reborn as allies to form a trilateral alliance? How would that impact world politics and the United States? Undoubtedly, we all stand to learn from the blunders caused by the United States' opportunistic stance and blatant disregard of the broader historical context of U.S.-Korea relations.

Deep Roots of American Racial Prejudice

U.S. policy on Korea can be said to have started with America's greatest visionary on Asia, Secretary of State William Seward. His ambition was simple—to force Korea open—as the United States had already opened China and Japan, the giants of the region. Opening these nations had not cost the United States much. However, to open Korea, the United States ironically had to pay some tolls, such as the razing of the *General Sherman* in 1866 and the first battle with Korea in 1871. Indeed, after Korea was officially opened through the 1882 Treaty of Peace, Amity, Commerce, and Navigation, the United States first folded on its commitment by abandoning Korea but reengaged later, though reluctantly. Many strategic blunders also followed this major watershed in the relationship, resulting in the Korean War.

One of the major problems with America's policy on Asia and Korea, this book concludes, stems from its deep racism against Asians and Asian nations.

This, in turn, led to the lack of coherent and consistent policies toward Asia, as numerous scholars and policymakers have noted (Dennett, 1922; Neu, 1966; Henderson, 1968; Cumings, 1973 & 1983; Swartout, 1974; Krishnan, 1984; LaFeber, 1989 & 1997; Lee, 2000; Sterner, 2002; Chang, 2003; Bradley, 2009; Murray, 2011). From this perspective, this book regrets the necessity of having to challenge one of the greatest political leaders in U.S. presidential history, President Theodore Roosevelt.

Roosevelt's favoritism for Japan was also based on his fear and dislike of Japan as one of the Orientals. Burton's (1973) comprehensive study "Theodore Roosevelt and His English Correspondents: A Special Relationship of Friends" reveals the president's deep-seated prejudice against Asians. Objecting to mass immigration from Japan to the United States, he wrote to George O. Trevelyan in 1905 that "There should be no immigration in mass of Orientals where the English-speaking peoples now form or will form the populations of the future" (Burton, 1973: 33). The ban against Japanese laborers, he stressed, should be "a complete cessation" (Burton, 1973: 33).

President Roosevelt was not only against Orientals but also no fan of the Russians. In his letter to his dear British friend Spring Rice in 1896, he freely acknowledged his feelings of utmost dislike among Western white nations for the Russian menace: "They [the Russians] are below the Germans just as the Germans are below us; the space between the German and the Russian may be greater than that between the Englishman and the German, but that is all" (Burton, 1973: 29). "Indeed Russia is a problem very appalling," he said, and went further to add, "All other nations of European blood, if they develop at all, seem inclined to develop on much the same line; but Russia seems bound to develop in her own way, and on lines that run directly counter to what we are accustomed to consider as progress. If she ever does take possession of Northern China and drill at the North Chinese to serve as her Army, she will indeed be a formidable power" (Burton, 1973: 28). Bradley (2009 b) adds, "No human beings, black, yellow or white, could be quite as untruthful, as insincere, as arrogant—in short, as untrustworthy in every way—as the Russians," he wrote in August 1905, near the end of the Russo-Japanese War. Despite his stated opposition to Japanese immigration, he declared that the Japanese, on the other hand, were "a wonderful and civilized people," Roosevelt wrote, "entitled to stand on an absolute equality with all the other peoples of the civilized world" (Bradley, 2009 b). As discussed, Roosevelt was well aware that Japan coveted the Korean Peninsula as a springboard to its expansion to the Asian continent. Here, Roosevelt "preferred to balance an emerging Japan against an established Russia, partly because he feared an all-powerful Japan as a threat to the United States in the Far East" (Burton, 1973: 45).

In June of 1905, President Roosevelt made world headlines when he invited the two nations to negotiate an end to their war. His private letter to his son told another story:

> I have of course concealed from everyone—literally everyone—the fact that I acted in the first place on Japan's suggestion . . . Remember that you are to let no one know that in this matter of the peace negotiations I have acted at the request of Japan and that each step has been taken with Japan's foreknowledge, and not merely with her approval but with her expressed desire.

In his letter to his dear British friend Spring Rice in late 1904, in the midst of the Russo-Japanese War, he wrote that "It is always possible that Japan and Russia may come to terms of agreement. . . . My policy must of necessity be somewhat opportunist," which seems natural and reasonable to the American national interest. However, his opportunistic patriotism led him to use Korea a sort of scapegoat.

THE LEGACY OF THE KOREAN WAR

As mentioned earlier, it was the Korean War from 1950 to 1953 that fundamentally transformed relations between the United States and Korea in the south. It was not just between the United States and Korea but also for America's post–World War II global strategy. LaFeber (2002: 111) argues that "Indeed, although the war was limited to Korea, Truman and Acheson used the war as the opportunity to develop new American policies around the globe. Because of these American initiatives, the six months between June and December 1950 rank among the most important of the Cold War era." Despite such critical importance of the Korean War in the post–World War II Cold War history, it has basically been forgotten, in terms of not only Korean suffering from the 67-year-old division, confrontations, and hatred but also the sacrifice of American men and women who shed their blood and gave their lives. However, other far-reaching, critical issues remain unresolved, critical not just to Korea but to powers around the Peninsula in the East Asian context as well—issues such as the 67-year-old division of the Peninsula, North Korea's weapons program, potential Sino-American conflicts over the South China Sea, U.S. deployment of THAAD, and Russia's challenge to Western power. Yet, the war has also demonstrated some historically important points—the superiority of capitalist democracy over communism, and the sustainability of the simultaneous rapid economic development and democratization accomplished in South Korea from the 1960s to the 1980s.

To my amazement, the bilateral history of the relationship in 1866, the sinking of the *General Sherman*, is echoed in many respects: the *Shinmiyangyo* in 1871 in America's occupation of Kwanghwado, close to the Wolmido and Silmido, two main targets of U.S. operation of the Incheon Landing on September 15, 1950. The *General Sherman*, American schooner, razed in 1866 and the *Pueblo*, seized in 1968. The United States fought for South Korea in 1950 and the *Pueblo* was captured by North Korea at the same location in the Daedong River near Pyeongyang. The radical difference is that the part of Korea that America originally encountered was the part that President Bush in 2002 branded as belonging to the "Axis of Evil."

Another outcome was that the Korean War reshaped the countries' perspectives and relationship with one another. As the United States broke Korea from its isolationism and joined the last wave of Western imperialism, Korea was seen as merely a colony to toss to Japan in exchange for the Philippines. Even earlier, Korea was seen as a mere way station for American merchant ships seeking to replenish their logistical supplies. President Franklin Roosevelt wanted to take this nation, recently liberated from 35 years of Japanese colonial rule, and place it under the tutelage of the superpowers in 1945. However, during and after the Korean War, such a lopsided relationship took a quick but serious turn. These two countries not only fought side by side—including U.S. aid to Koreans during the Korean War and South Korean aid to Americans during the Vietnam War—they also became heavily interdependent in trade, culture, human exchange, and the promotion the superiority of free capitalistic democracy over socialist communism.

Ultimately, Korea's unprecedentedly simultaneous achievement of economic development and democratization in the 1980s was another legacy of the Korean War. This included (1) the most successful involvement of the United States in a war after World War II; (2) Korea's success in representing an alternative indigenous model of sustainable development; and (3) the two countries' successful transformation from strangers, antagonists, and enemies into likeminded and mutually assimilated allies through 150 years of interaction. Furthermore, from the U.S. perspective, the legacy of the Korean War proved the value of U.S. democracy and capitalism in the context of Cold War competition.

The first phase of interaction between the two countries, however, did not begin so well. They first met as complete strangers with opposite mindsets and economic modes of production and exchange. This phase began with the United States joining the Western imperial shift toward Asia and the Joseon containing its regime within the old notion of China as the center of its cosmic system. Breaking from a century of isolationism himself, President Theodore Roosevelt initiated a new era of U.S. expansion, while King Gojong of the Joseon Empire, which was administered by Premier Daewongun, opposed any interaction outside the Sinocentric international system. The unfortunate encounter between U.S. expansionism and Korean isolationism was a clash between center (rising America) and periphery (Joseon).

One obvious outcome of such a collision was a disturbance, according to the Korean view, in 1871, the year of Shinmi. What is striking about this first encounter, which has not been officially recognized as a war, is that it bore great resemblance to the so-called "Korean War" that broke out 79 years later. The U.S. Marines landed in Incheon, causing a disturbance that resulted in 15 Medals of Honor for the United States. The Incheon Landing on September 15, 1950, the second intervention, produced 146 Medals of Honor. The main difference between the two wars is that the United States fought North Korea in the second but was fighting the whole of Korea in the first. Viewed from this perspective, this book argues that the Korean War we know is actually the second Korean War, and strongly resembles the first.

This second phase of the encounter between the center and periphery was followed by America's long absence from the Peninsula due to the Taft-Katsura Secret Agreement with Japan, which arranged for the Philippines to fall to America as the Joseon fell to Japan, and which this book sees as a policy of utter disregard.

However, with Japan's unconditional surrender once atom bombs fell on Hiroshima and Nagasaki in August of 1945, the United States reluctantly engaged with Korea again, and the outcome was the division of the Peninsula and the second Korean War. Yet, despite the many successes and failures that resulted from this war, it has largely been forgotten. The Kilroy that once symbolized American support for World War II returned from Korea with a different story: "desolate, horrified, cold, disheartened, sorrowful, demoralized." From this perspective, the forgotten nature of the Korean War seems somewhat natural: Korean War Kilroys wanted to forget this horrible war that lacked a clear victory. The next phase witnessed fundamental changes to this relationship between the center and periphery: the center gained a foothold in the South, demonstrating the superiority of its political and economic systems and material base; the North, however, represented the opposite of American ideology in the bipolar system of global competition. More critically, the unfinished second Korean War coincided with the start of the Cold War and is now contributing to a new Cold War, driving the United States into a possible East Asian Thucydides trap, as a rising China challenges U.S. hegemony.

A CENTURY-OLD STATUS QUO AMONG THREE EAST ASIAN COUNTRIES

China's rise as a global economic power and its aim to challenge American hegemony also make the century-old power competition among China, Japan, and Korea more complicated than it was in the late nineteenth and early twentieth centuries. This new development has not relieved any tensions on the Korean Peninsula. More specifically, Japan's rise as a new regional power in East Asia during the nineteenth and twentieth centuries successfully extricated Korea from China's suzerainty, and the United States served as an accomplice in this process. Now, China's ambitions to regain influence over the two Koreas and challenge the U.S.-Japan alliance in the region are undisguised. Considering contemporary situations in the South China Sea, it is also no surprise to see military face-offs between these two forces, which will again sandwich South Korea between these conventional foes unless China, Japan, and Korea can achieve Immanuel Kant's Pacific Union in the near future.

Immanuel Kant's concept of a "Pacific Union," as mentioned in the Introduction, was a lesson learned from the devastating destruction that took place through two world wars of imperial colonial competition that killed 10 million soldiers and 60 million civilians. The lesson they learned was that they could establish a permanently peaceful relationship if several conditions were met. These included replacing the ancient European dynastic political systems with republics and promoting international trade.

In this shift from all-in wars to a Pacific Union among these Western countries, two points stand out. First, these Western European countries share the religious and cultural heritage of Christianity and Hellenism, with the exception of a few members at each pole, and associated powers such as Japan, India, and the Ottoman Empire, which was also the case in World War II. Despite common denominations in terms of religion and culture, the level of mutual annihilation in these wars was unprecedented. Second, as Karl Marx predicted, the highest stage of capitalism was imperialistic in the competition for colonies, and the two world wars ended the era of nineteenth-century colonialism, at least officially.

Through a brief consensus among Allied forces in World War II, humanity faced a new era in the form of the bipolar international system of the Cold War. The world split along the lines of the confrontation between communist socialism and democratic capitalism. With the collapse of the Soviet Union in 1991, however, the world confronted the clash that Samuel Huntington foresaw in his book *The Clash of Civilizations and the Remaking of World Order* in 1996. In this book, Huntington, in fact, took the liberty of suggesting that Western capitalist democracies should play two of the most belligerent civilizations against each other—Confucian China and Islamic fundamentalist countries—so that the West would not have to fight them in order to maintain power over the world. Huntington's projection that these two civilizations should collide with each other was not fully realized. Instead, China is now challenging American unilateral hegemony, and the clash between Western Christianity and Islam is currently represented by Iran's nuclear ambition.

220   Chapter 5

In the twenty-first-century global politics, a new Sino-American clash has subtle implications for the relationships among three East Asian and Confucian countries: China, Japan, and Korea. Historians generally agree that there are nine civilizations: Mesopotamian, Persian, Islamic, Egyptian, South Asian, East Asian, Western, Mesoamerican, and Andean. What countries belong to each category? According to Worldometer.com, there are 195 countries in the contemporary world, most of which belong to one of these civilizations. Among these are 50 Muslim-majority countries, 30 countries and territories in the Western hemisphere, 9 South Asian countries, 11 South East Asian countries, and 8 East Asian countries (China, Japan, Mongolia, Hong Kong, Macau, Taiwan, North Korea, and South Korea). East Asia's place among these nine civilizations deserves special attention in terms of its populations, contributions to the global economy, and portions of their military budgets in world military competitions. The irony is that the three most prominent East Asian countries—China, Japan, and Korea—are at odds with each other.

East Asian Potential

Table 5.10 captures the performance of these three East Asian countries in each of these categories. The population of China is 1,439,323,776, which accounts for 18.5% of the world population with a territory of 9,388,211 km². Japan has 126,476,461 people, which is 1.62% of the world total, with a size of 364,555 km², while South Korea has 51,269,185 people, representing 0.66% of the world total, with a territory of 100,210 km². North Korea has 25,778,816 people, representing 0.33% of the world total, and Taiwan has 23,816,775, representing 0.31%. Altogether, the Confucian-oriented countries of China, Japan, and Korea account for 20.78%, slightly more than one-fifth, of the world's population, and 24.16% of world's GDP ($86,599B).

All of these similarities matter, but the commonality that is most fundamental is language. Chinese, Japanese, and Korean culture all make use of Chinese characters. Both Japanese and Koreans use Chinese characters in written documents. The only difference is in pronunciation, which varies, but vocabulary and pronunciation are highly similar.

In addition to their disproportionately large representations in the GDP and populations, their languages are increasingly favored by U.S. university students as a second language while conventionally popular languages such as French, German, Italian, and Spanish are seeing a sharp downturn. According to the Modern Language Association, Korean recorded a sharp increase of 95% in learners of selected languages at U.S. universities between 2006 and 2016 with a 5.2% increase in Japanese and 3.3% in Chinese. Western languages recorded sharp decreases among American college students, with

Table 5.10 East Asian Countries' Potential

	United States	China	Japan	S. Korea	N. Korea	Taiwan
Population	331,002,651	1,439,323,776	126,476,461	51,269,185	25,778,816	23,816,775
	(4.2%)	(18.5%)	(1.62%)	(0.66%)	(0.33%)	(0.31%)
	3rd	1st	11th	28th	54th	57th
Land Size	9,372,610	9,706,961	377,930	100,210	120,538	36,193
	(6.1%)	(6.3%)	(0.2%)	(0.1%)	(0.1%)	(0.0%)
GDP (GUSD$)	21,439.45	14,140.16	5,154.48	1,629.53	18.00	586.10
	(24.7%)	(16.9%)	(5.98%)	(12, 1.8%)	(0.01%)	(21,0.67%)
	1st	2nd	3rd	12th		21st
Language	English	Chinese	Japanese	Korean	Korean	Chinese
(millions)	379	918	128	77.3		
(% of world population)	(4.922%)	(11.922%)	(1.662%)	(1.004%)		
Military Expenditures (US$B)	732.0	261.0	47.6	43.9	4.0	
(% of GDP)	(3.4)	(1.9)	(0.9)	(2.7)	(23%)	

Sources: Created by author using data from International Monetary Fund's *World Economic Outlook* (October 2019), 2019 Nominal in billions of US Dollars (ranks, percentage); Ethnologue (2019, 22nd edition); The Stockholm International Peace Research Institute, 2020 *Fact Sheet* (for 2019); US State Department's 2018 World Military Expenditures and Arms Transfers report; and Worldometer (worldometer.com)

a 27.4% decrease in Italian, 17.9% in Russian, 14.7% in French, 14.4% in German, and 13.3% in Spanish.

Quoting the IMF research forecast, Kreppmeier and Ankel (2019, Business Insider Deutschland) cite eight countries that will dominate global growth in 2024. In this report, three East Asian countries lead with China ranked first, Japan sharing seventh with Germany and Turkey, and South Korea ranked in the top 20. Another indicator to consider in regard to the prospects of these three East Asian countries that will be competing for economic dominance in the near future is their global leadership in economic, managerial, and high-tech innovation. According to the latest Bloomberg Innovation Index, Germany has broken South Korea's six-year streak as the "the most innovative nation in the world," as South Korea now ranks second in the world and the U.S. ranks 9th, with Japan and China at 12th and 15th, respectively. South Korea relies heavily on tech-oriented firms, such as Samsung Electronics, Hyundai Motors, and LG Electronics. To rate a country's innovative capabilities, the Bloomberg Innovation Index uses criteria for R&D spending, manufacturing capability, and concentration of high-tech public companies.

Mutual Interdependence: No Getting Away from It

According to the Japan Tourist Bureau, China and South Korea accounted for almost half of the tourists who visited Japan in 2019. China was the largest, recording 9,594,394 tourists, accounting for 30.1%, while South Korea ranked second with 5,584,597 visitors, accounting for 17.5%. With Taiwan (15.3%) and Hong Kong (7.2%), East Asian countries comprised 70.1% of tourists to Japan in 2019.

As data on Korea-inbound tourism also shows, these three East Asian countries are their own biggest mutual beneficiaries in tourism. According to the Korea Tourism Organization, the total number of visitors to Korea[11] from January to June 2019 was 8,439,214. Among those, China accounted for the largest portion with 33.2% and a total of 2,802,486, while Japan comprised the second-largest with 19.6% and a total of 1,653,686. American tourists reached 508,481, representing only 6%.[12] Statista.com data on Chinese tourism in 2018 shows that Korea and Japan were first and second with 4,193,000 Korean and 2,691,000 Japanese visitors, accounting for 17.6% and 11.3%, respectively, of the 23,807,000 total.[13]

Most importantly, let's look at interdependences among China, Japan, and Korea in terms of mutual trade. Created by the International Business Center and the Eli Broad College of Business at Michigan State University (IBC), globalEDGE reports that China was Korea's largest export country with $162B, while the United States was second with $73B. After Vietnam and Hong Kong, Japan ranked fifth with nearly $46B. Again, China was the largest importer of Korean goods and Japan was third largest.[14] The case of Japan was not much different in that both China and South Korea were each other's largest trading partners, too. The same data source states that Japan's largest total of exports went to China with $144B, the United States with $140B, and South Korea with $52B. Japan imported the most from China with $173B in imports. The United States was the second largest with $83B, and South Korea was fifth largest with $32B after Australia and Saudi Arabia, the two biggest exporters of iron and oil.[15] Lastly, according to the Observatory of Economic Complexity (OEC), China's biggest exporting country in 2018[16] was the United States with 19.3% of China's total export of $2.59 trillion, Hong Kong with 10.9% as the second, Japan third with 6.01%, and South Korea fourth with 4.14%. China's imports have become even more dependent upon its neighbors, with the most coming from Korea (9.93%), Japan (8.6%,) Germany (6.79%), and Taiwan (6.05%) out of a total $1.61T in imports in 2018.

Not only do such exchanges of personnel and trade make China, Japan, and Korea bilaterally and multilaterally interdependent, but these countries have shared philosophical, cultural, and dialectical orientations since their very early history as well. With the exception of a few aboriginal belief systems, such as shamanism in Korea and Shintoism in Japan, these countries are strongly linked by influences of Confucian cultural, socioeconomic, and political principles and institutions, Buddhist religion, and language. As mentioned, they share a vast amount of vocabulary. Even though Korean and Japanese have different pronunciations and alphabet systems, they both use many original Chinese characters, as the pages of this book attest.[17]

They are also geographically close to each other. A two-hour flight from Incheon Airport will bring you to Beijing, the capital of China, while a two-and-a-half-hour flight will take you to Tokyo, the capital of Japan. Only 110 km separate Korea's biggest harbor, Busan, from Japan's Tsushima of Nagasaki Prefecture. Tourists from these countries find their East Asian neighbors convenient, reliable, and knowledgeable in their travels for pleasure. They are structurally inseparable in their geographical proximity, cultural and historical foundations, and economic interdependence. Clearly, they can be the best of friends and form cohesive communities and alliances.

Despite such given conditions for peaceful coexistence, these three countries have significantly suffered from their own unfortunate rivalries. First, their disastrous past has been both a regional and global stumbling block, which is still reverberating in this region. It would be hard to estimate the opportunities lost to such deadlock. To make matters worse, South Korea is being torn apart again due to the "Thucydides Trap," where a rising China has recently challenged the only hegemon, the United States, over navigation routes in the South and East China Seas, which Graham Allison warns may spark a large-scale war, as he found by examining trends from the Greek City State era to the current day. American reactions to China's challenges have brought Japan to the point of what feels like a déjà vu of its war against China. South Korea is stuck in the tug-of-war between China on the one side and the United States and Japan on the other. With the brinkmanship of nuclear and ICBM provocations from North Korea, contemporary East Asian rivalries can light the fuse of another destructive war, if not World War III. Caught in the jaws of such a status quo, we cannot move ahead an inch.

Frenemies

We have looked at the potentials that these three East Asian countries have cultivated and will exert in the near future in terms of their territorial and population sizes, their GDPs accounting for at least one-fifth of the world's total GDP, and finally their military expenditures. On top of possessing such powers, their cultures share a foundation in Confucianism and Buddhism, and their languages all make use of Chinese characters with the same meanings and similar pronunciations. However, their history tells us the opposite—namely, that they have become each other's principal enemies. According to figure 5.1, which is based on the Pew Research Center's "Global Attitudes & Trends" poll, updated in March 2020 with polling data from the Spring 2019 Global Attitudes survey, South Korea and Japan reported the most negative views on China. Japanese responses were 14% positive to the question "Do you have a favorable or unfavorable view of China?" while South Koreans were 34% positive and Americans were 26%. Russians were most favorable toward China with 71% positive. The same survey in 2018 found that Japan's view of China had worsened. Japan and China share a complicated history that has resulted in immensely negative perceptions across the East China Sea. In 2018, 78% of Japanese held an unfavorable view of China, by far the most negative response across all countries surveyed. Just 17% had a favorable view of China.

As shown in figure 5.1, hatred and hostility are mutual between Japan and China. China holds a much more favorable view of South Korea than Japan does.

In fact, their unfavorable views of each other take a downward turn, as shown in figure 5.2, as is also the case in the diagram below.

The key to understanding such mutual animosity can be found by looking into the past—specifically, Japan's invasion of China. Most Chinese strongly maintain that Japan has not committed to serious and meaningful contrition regarding its war crimes in World War II, as shown in figure 5.3. However, the Japanese view of this topic is quite opposite, as shown in figure 5.4.

VIEWS OF ▶ VIEWS IN:	Japan	China	India	South Korea
Australia	79%	52	53	55
India	44	31	—	30
China	14	—	26	55
Japan	—	11	54	27

Figure 5.1 How Asia-Pacific Nations See Each Other. *Source:* Spring 2016 Global Attitudes Survey, Pew Research Center.

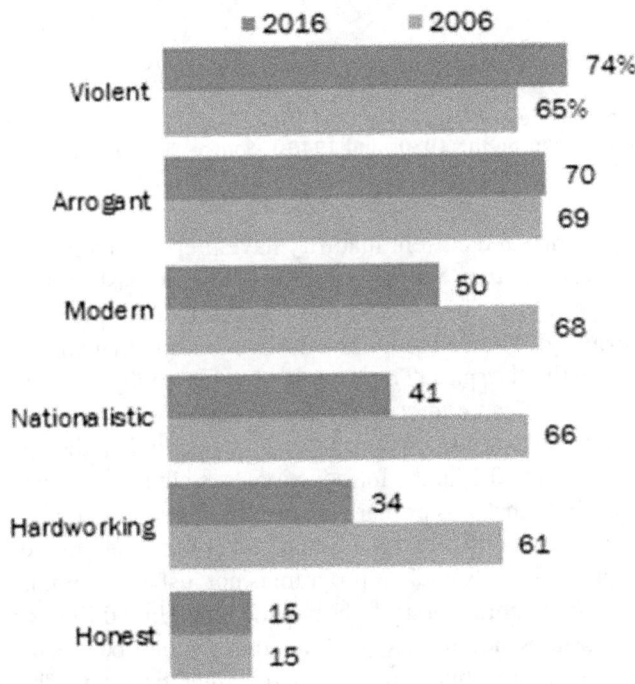

Figure 5.2 Changes in Chinese Views of Japanese (% Chinese Who Associate __ with Japanese). *Source:* Spring 2016 Global Attitudes Survey, Pew Research Center.

The Road Ahead

For final and complete reversal of such mutual hatred and animosity among these three East Asian countries, we need to build a foundation strong enough to sustain the recovery of neighborly relations. One thing that is clear is that

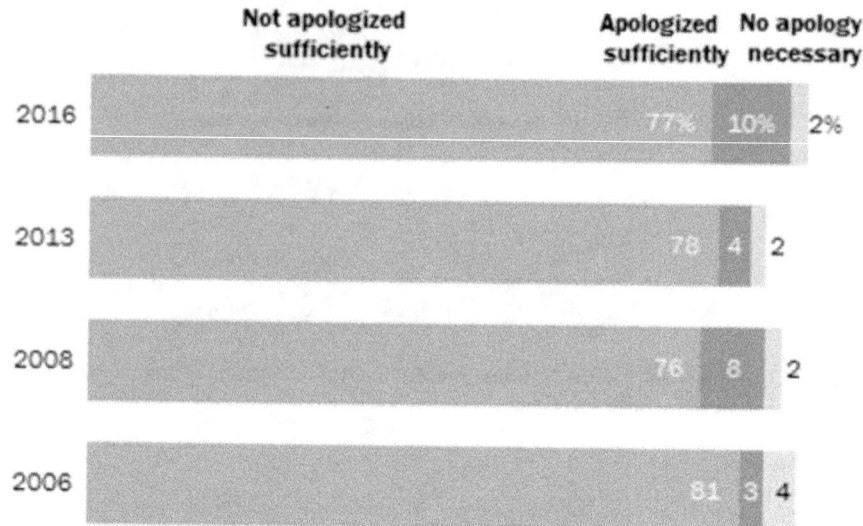

Figure 5.3   Chinese Views on Japanese Contrition (% Chinese Saying Japan Has __ for Its Military Actions during the 1930s and 1940s). *Source:* Spring 2016 Global Attitudes Survey, Pew Research Center.

their past experience and current maturity have prepared them to take up this challenge. Otherwise, they will remain buried by the past, unable to escape this trap of unfortunate history, and this has become an unending source of embedded hostility. We need to build a new generation that can clear itself of this mutually destructive past. Thus, we need to learn why we became mutual enemies and how we can overcome this status quo.

For that purpose, we need to have a future-oriented look at that past, which is the Pacific War. Figure 0.1, in the Introduction, lays out how many killings took place during this war that was primarily driven by Japan's imperial ambitions.

The contemporary confrontational impasse between the United States and North Korea on the latter's nuclear program is not just a bilateral issue but has been entangled in a century-long fight between the United States and China. This confrontation is not limited to bilateral tensions between the United States and North Korea but stems from the fight between China and the United States. Our past of World War II and the Korean War has driven us to a complex world entangled with war, hatred, animosity, and rivalry between the East and the West, such that we must now consider the present-day dangerous encounters of Japan's siding with the United States while Korea tries to free itself from its age-old plight of being bullied by superpowers. This century-long record of mutual hatred and destruction makes the U.S.-Korea relationship much more complex.

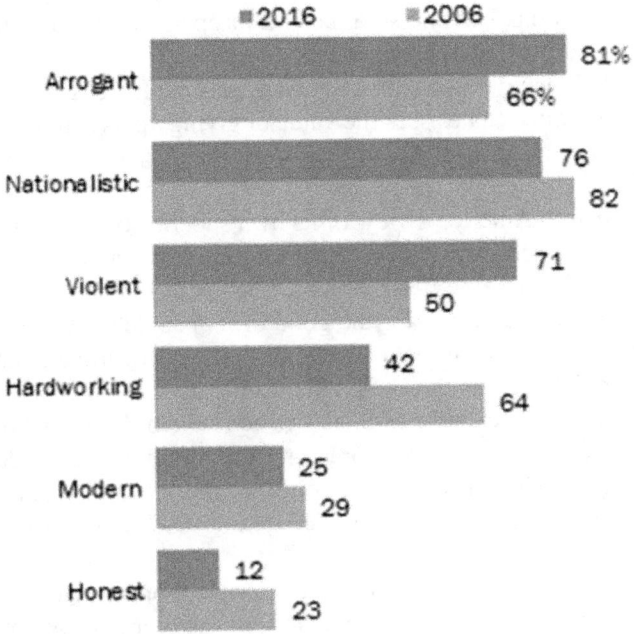

Figure 5.4 Japanese Views of Chinese Turn More Negative over the Past Decade (% Japanese Who Associate __ with Chinese). *Source*: Spring 2016 Global Attitudes Survey, Pew Research Center.

AT THE CROSSROADS OF THIS RELATIONSHIP

The Republic of Korea and the United States are now two of the closest allies in the world. To describe the traditional and strategic relationship between North Korea and the People's Republic of China, a Chinese idiom of four characters is often used: 唇亡齒寒 (순망치한, *sun mang chi han*), meaning "teeth hurt without lips." Now, it can also be applied to the relationship between the United States and Korea. There are many differences between these two countries, in addition to their geography. They have two different cultures; from the start, South Korea's Confucian, Buddhist, and collectivist culture clashed with America's Liberal, Christian, and Hellenic orientations. Race was another characteristic that set these two nations apart. However, these two countries fought alongside each other in the Vietnam War and are still fighting together in Afghanistan and against Ebola in Africa. Numerous statistics in economy, politics, and culture in both countries indicate that they think, live, and act alike. The beginning of their relationship presented vast differences in the late nineteenth century, as noted above, however. So, how did these two nations become so alike and inseparable, despite such radical differences at their original encounter?

Can the relationship between the United States and Korea evolve to such an extent that the United States sees the value of giving up its original policy and leaves Korea detached from America and neutral? Apparently, the powerless had to suffer the strength of the powerful; Korea had to suffer wars and devastation partly due to America's view of its own superiority as an advanced and more "civilized" race, religion, political system, and economic system. But did Koreans really deserve death and destruction at the hands of those who claimed to be opening Korea for the good of its people? Ultimately, can we recognize the differences in belief systems and ways of life among different nations and societies? Can the United States overcome its exceptionalism and uphold American values, as was done by the few Americans who criticized America's failed policy toward Korea and supported Korean independence movements in the United States: "not only for the sake of Korea but for the good of the United States." As Fields (2015: 296–297) expresses:

> We the friends of Korea believe that the principle of equal right to live and develop in freedom for weak and strong alike, should be upheld by America, as we fought [in World War I] for that purpose . . . as Christians we feel it to be our moral duty to inject ourselves into the issue; for reasons of Christianity and humanity. The American public must make its voice manifest upon the great principles involved, for failing to do so will be shirking our duties.

Can the United States and South Korea together lead North Korea toward peaceful regime change and finally reunify the Peninsula? Will Korea finally be able to shed the role it has been pigeonholed to play, and stop being viewed as a quagmire, tinderbox, or powder keg?[18] If so, could such dishonorable labels for the Korean War as "sour little war," "police action," "foreign policy blunder of the century," and "a great military disaster" (Goulden, 1982: xiii) finally be removed? Then, perhaps the Korean War, which was an early signal of the Cold War, the far-front base of U.S.-Soviet conflict and, most famously "The Forgotten War," could finally regain its proper place in the twenty-first-century society. These are the important questions that the history of U.S.-Korea relations now calls on us to answer.

NOTES

1. Even though it became associated with GIs in the 1940s, Kilroy was the name of a real person, James J. Kilroy (1902–1962). *The New York Times* in 1946 indicated J.J. Kilroy as the origin, an American shipyard inspector in Fore River Shipyard,

Massachusetts. Kilroy had marked the ships as they were being built, as a note to himself that he had inspected a compartment. In short, Kilroy symbolized citizens committed to doing their part in winning the good war.

2. Originally, the location name was Chosin, which was the Japanese phonetic spelling of the Chinese characters, "長津." In Korean, it is "장진."

3. Cosgrove quotes from Duncan's 1951 photo narrative *This Is the War!*

4. www.koreanwarlegacy.org

5. https://worldinfigures.com/rankings/ topic/8

6. https://www.statista.com/statistics/ 264623/leading-export-countries-worldwide/

7. Even though they remained a voice in the wilderness, some Americans recognized the United States' hypocrisy in dealing with Korea's independence movement in the early twentieth century. Field (2015) examines lobbying activity from 1919 to 1922 of Korean independence activists in the United States from the perspective of three Americans who became supporters of the Korean cause. Field (2015: 293) argues that "Most Americans who became advocates of Korean independence did so not due to previous ties to Korea but due to the importance of the questions that the Korean independence activists raised. Was the United States fulfilling its national destiny in world affairs? Were its actions abroad in keeping with American ideals? These activists argued persuasively that, at least with respect to Korea, they were not. They challenged Americans to pressure their government to repudiate Roosevelt's acquiescence to Japanese annexation of Korea and to observe the U.S. government's obligations under the 1882 treaty (Fields, 2015: 293).

8. According to Willard Straight (American Vice-Consul): "At the first luncheon, the Emperor brought Miss Roosevelt in on his arm and sat at the same table with her. The Crown Prince also officiated at a plate and another Imperial figurehead, Yi Yong, was among those present. The rest of us were at smaller tables sandwiched in with prominent Korean officials, many of whom had, by special order of the Emperor, got themselves into European clothes for the first time and who certainly did look, and from their appearance feel, like Hell. Their clothes were long and short and anything but what they should have been. It was a strange and wonderful sight to see Miss Roosevelt on the Emperor's arm, or rather he on hers, as they came into the banqueting hall which looked more like a boarding house parlor than anything else" (Neff, 2014).

9. Keat wrote this article when Fraulein Emma Kroebel, a German who was chief mistress of ceremonies at the court of the Korean Emperor in 1905, published a book in 1909 entitled *Wie ich an den koreanischen Kaiserhof kam* that contained sections dealing with Alice Roosevelt's visit to Korea that year.

10. According to Bradley (2009 b), "In planning the attack on Pearl Harbor, Adm. Isoroku Yamamoto was specifically thinking of how, 37 years earlier, the Japanese had surprised the Russian Navy at Port Arthur in Manchuria and, as he wrote, 'favorable opportunities were gained by opening the war with a sudden attack on the main enemy fleet.' At the time, the indignant Russians called it a violation of international law. But Theodore Roosevelt, confident that he could influence events in North Asia from afar, wrote to his son, 'I was thoroughly well pleased with the Japanese victory, for Japan is playing our game.'"

11. With regards to Korea-inbound cases since 2017, we need to take two factors into consideration. First, Chinese tourists drastically decreased by order of the Chinese government, which vehemently opposed the deployment of the American THAAD missile system in Korea in 2017, and Japanese tourists also decreased due to the trade conflicts between Japan and Korea in 2019 when the Japanese government barred Korea from access to three major technologies needed in the production of semiconductor chips.

12. On Korea-inbound statistics, this refers to data from the Korea Tourism Organization 2019, from https://www.news1.kr/articles/?3677707

13. Source: Statista.com, https://www.statista.com/statistics/234149/tourists-in-china-by-country-of-origin/

14. Source: https://globaledge.msu.edu/countries/south-korea/tradestats

15. Source: https://globaledge.msu.edu/countries/japan/tradestats

16. Source: https://oec.world/en/resources/about

17. In this perspective, it is ludicrous that Samuel Huntington categorized Japan as a civilization, when its language, main religion, and cultural orientation, along with so many other elements, either originated from or were transmitted through China.

18. Oliver (1944: 16) sees the place of Korea in the international power struggles of East Asia "as a buffer state that for centuries limited the expansion possibilities of Russia, China, and Japan; and as the sacrificial victim ceded to Japan's 'protection' in 1905 to appease the Nipponese militarists. It seemed then a cheap means of satisfying Japan's expansive urge."

Chapter 6

The Corean Question Revisited

The United States has been involved in the many major wars and military operations since the Korean War, including the Cuba invasion (1961), Vietnam War (1961–1973), military operations in the Dominican Republic (1965), Peacekeeping operation in Lebanon (1982), Grenada invasion (1983), Panama invasion (1989), Gulf War (Kuwait and Iraq, 1991), military operations in Somalia (1993), the Haiti invasion (1994), military operations in Bosnia (1994–1995), military intervention in Kosovo (1999), Afghanistan War (2001 to present), Iraq War (2003–2010), military intervention in Libya (2011), War with ISIL (2012–2019), and military operations in Syria (2017 to present). Among these 16 military involvements by the United States, major and conventional warfare has been conducted in only 5, including the Korean War. Even among those five wars that meet the conventional definition of wars, the Korean and Vietnam wars are the major ones.

Interestingly, only the Korean War resulted in the establishment of a bilateral defense treaty. Defense treaties that the United States signed since World War II include the Inter-American Treaty of Mutual Assistance (Rio Treaty, 1947) and the treaties with NATO (1949), the Philippines (1951), Australia and New Zealand (1951), the Republic of Korea (1953), Southeast Asian countries (1954), the UK[1] (1958), and Japan (1960).

According to the U.S. Collective Defense Arrangements by the Department of State,[2] among the mutual defense treaties that the United States has with other countries, there have been only four cases of bilateral defense treaties (the Philippines, South Korea, the UK, and Japan) while all other treaties were collective defense arrangements. Except for the UK, the remaining three countries are within the Seward-Shufeldt Line or the Great Circle Route, which exemplifies the importance of the Asia and its market to the United States.

In addition, it is noteworthy that, among these four mutual defense treaties, the treaty with South Korea has basically been permanent, whereas the treaties with the Philippines and Japan are reassessed every 10 years. The treaty with the UK, in which is written "The Agreement [between the U.S. and the UK] . . . shall remain in force until terminated by agreement of both Parties" does not have a regular renewal provision like those of the Philippines and Japan. There is no provision in any of the treaties that the United States has signed with any country like Article VI of the mutual defense treaty between the United States and South Korea, which says "This Treaty shall remain in force indefinitely" even though there is a nominal termination provision, saying "Either Party may terminate it one year after notice has been given to the other Party."

The first interesting observation that can be made is that among these four "mutual" defense treaties that the United States signed, three are with Asian countries, while one is with its old Anglo-Saxon frenemy, the United Kingdom. It is noteworthy that the majority of Washington's defense commitments went to countries in Asia, fitting the vision of nineteenth-century American leaders such as William Seward and Commodore Shufeldt. This may be because Washington did not need more mutual defense treaties with Western countries of similar ethnic and cultural and historical roots and mainly because the treaty with NATO already covered most of the Western countries.

The fact that Washington had mutual bilateral defense treaties with three Asian countries shows how important Asia has been to America's global strategy of containing communism and maintaining its hegemonic leadership in the free world. The Korean Peninsula was critical in this American strategy because it borders on America's principal enemies of China and Russia and could serve as a buffer state in relations with Japan. Such geopolitical and strategic significance of the Korean Peninsula to the United States seems well reflected in a very unequal and unfair provision of the mutual defense treaty between the United States and the ROK, namely, Article IV: "The Republic of Korea grants, and the United States of America accepts, the right to dispose United States land, air and sea forces in and about the territory of the Republic of Korea as determined by mutual agreement." According to this article, Washington has almost absolute rights to deploy its military forces in any part of Korean territory "indefinitely" while treaties with the Philippines and Japan do not allow such unilateral decisions to deploy American military forces into their territories.

One of the most striking changes brought forth by the U.S.-Korea mutual defense treaty was that it served as a tripwire for the communist North, which had the world's largest communist countries behind it, the Soviet Union and China. The preamble of the mutual treaty made clear that the United States would not remain neutral when South Korea was attacked by an aggressor in the Pacific area: "Desiring to declare publicly and formally their common determination to defend themselves against external armed attack so that no potential aggressor could be under the illusion that either of them stands alone in the Pacific area." Article III made clear that a mutual tripwire would take effect in that:

> Each Party recognizes that an armed attack in the Pacific area on either of the Parties in territories now under their respective administrative control, or hereafter recognized by one of the Parties as lawfully brought under the administrative control of the other, would be dangerous to its own peace and safety and declares that it would act to meet the common danger in accordance with its constitutional processes.

This is a noteworthy commitment from Washington after a series of vacillations of opening, deserting, ignoring, and dividing Korea throughout its encounters. Even more significant is that the good offices in the 1882 U.S.-Corea treaty, which was rejected as worthless in the face of Japan's absorption of the Korean Empire, both in 1905 and 1910, is now resurrected as Article III, an automatic tripwire provision.

Such a dramatic reversal in America's Korea policy must be understood from expensive lessons learned from the following points, this book argues. First, and repeatedly, Korea's strategic geopolitical location is essential in America's hegemony not only in East Asia but also in Asia in general. As an ally, Washington would not want to give up such a strategic location at any cost as historically confirmed even in the vacillation from the Seward-Shufeldt Line to the Theodore-Franklin Line. Washington would not rescind its influence on the Korean Peninsula for its global strategic national interest even though it be under Japan's direct control as long as Washington keeps the line, as this book discusses. Second, the United States cannot entrust Korea to Japan as President Theodore Roosevelt did in 1905 for the following reasons: Japan no longer wants to have Korea under its influence unless it wants war to break out against the will of Washington and South Korea. The Republic of Korea has become a global economic and military power. Japan is no longer an option to Washington for the tutelage of Korea.

Furthermore, the Korean nation's hatred against Japan's 35 years of colonial control has become more entrenched, which will force any attempt by Washington to promote Japan's influence over Korea to be fundamentally faced with vehement resistance from both Korea and China. Third, the United States paid heavy tolls over the Korean War including its 36,547 soldiers killed in action, many POWs, and still thousands missing in action. Finally, South Korea can be regarded as the apple of America's eye with many reasons for Washington to be proud of its commitments both in blood and in treasure, among them: South Korea's standing as the 10th largest economy in the world with heavy interdependence upon mutual markets and technology, and a strong military alliance with its commitments to answer Washington's call for international military missions.

For these reasons, since the end of the Korean War, there has been no interruption in U.S. military presence in the Korean Peninsula, with U.S. Forces Korea (USFK) ranging from roughly 23,000 to 70,000. Simply put, the USFK has played the role of tripwire triggering automatic intervention of U.S. Forces against aggressors, as prescribed in the mutual defense treaty. The official triggering mechanism in this bilateral defense treaty between the United States and the ROK can be the USFK's DEFCON (Defense Readiness Condition), an alert system developed and used by U.S. Armed Forces. It was, for example, triggered on August 18, 1976, when UN Command officers were axed to death by North Korean soldiers. Captain Arthur Bonifas and platoon leader First Lieutenant Mark Barrett went to the Korean side of the demilitarized zone to trim a poplar tree that was blocking the view. All American troops in South Korea raised their defense readiness levels to DEFCON 3 as fighter jets, helicopters, and bombers flew in from Guam, and another 12,000 troops were ordered to South Korea. Parties of the defense treaty were ready not just to trim the poplar tree but to cut it down, which was named as Operation Paul Bunyan. South Korean special forces were also involved, including the unit of the 19th South Korean president Moon Jae-in. The work was assigned to the second Engineer Battalion, according to Li (2020).

During Operation Paul Bunyan, about 200 North Korean troops with machine guns and assault rifles were set up but held still for the entire process of cutting the poplar tree. Nuclear war was one gunshot away, according to Li (2020). Since the Korean War, DEFCON 4, which means that no military conflicts were involved, has continually been on and several cases of DEFCON 3 have triggered command control by the Combined Forces Command, not the Korean military. The first was the poplar tree case, and the second was in 1982 when Korean government officials were killed by an explosion detonated by North Korea in Rangoon, Burma, and the 1999 skirmish near Yeonpyeong Island.[3]

Compared to America's Korea policy ranging from the *General Sherman* incident in 1866 to the withdrawal of U.S. forces from the Peninsula in 1949, the first Korean War of 1871, the 1882 treaty, the 1905 abandonment of Corea to Japan, the 1945 Korean partition, and the 1950 exclusion of the Peninsula from America's defensive perimeter, tripwires set up by Washington in the Korean Peninsula resulted from the bilateral defense treaty, which was the direct outcome of the Korean War. The role of the Korean War, in the encounters between the United States. and Korea, has been that of fundamentally transforming America's attitudes and policies toward the Korean Peninsula: from the Theodore-Franklin policy of abandoning and ignoring Korea to returning to the Seward-Shufeldt vision of engaging with Korea to strengthen its own dominance in Asia.

This book concludes that there are three main reasons for this reversal from viewing Korea as only a coveted strategic location to seeing it as a sovereign country that Washington should include in its regular international affairs. The first reason lay in Japan's fall. Japan, Theodore Roosevelt's strategic partner in Asia—by defeating China and Russia and colonizing Korea—had become Franklin Roosevelt's principal enemy. At the end of World War II, Korea was no longer an object of Japan's control. Washington had to come to a decision on how it would deal with an independent Korea. Here, Washington made a series of critical mistakes, first, by inviting the Soviet Union to divide and rule the Korean Peninsula. The best metaphor to explain this first mistake would be for Washington to ask Moscow, its soon-to-be principal threat, to team up as accomplices in banditry.

The second and most crucial reason was that with the Acheson line, which had carelessly paved the way for the communist invasion of South Korea, the United States was shooting itself in the foot. Corea was the last piece of the puzzle, completing the century of Pax Americana in Asia. The Corean Question was America's effort to rival European dominance in the Atlantic Ocean in the late nineteenth century. By voluntarily excluding the Korean Peninsula from its sphere of influence on January 12, 1950, Washington eventually gave up Korea again in the advent of the new world system that was overshadowing twentieth-century international politics. Thus, President Truman's decision to undo the Acheson declaration and intervene in the war was a checkmate move. If Washington did not commit, it might lose the most strategically critical geopolitical point, the Korean Peninsula, not to mention its ownership over the Pacific Ocean. Ultimately, Francis Fukuyama's argument on the end of history likely would not have manifested so strikingly if Moscow had achieved control over the Korean Peninsula. If Washington had not been negligent about multiple signs of what the Soviet Union was to become in the post–World War II world, had not voluntarily called the Soviet Union to occupy half of Korea, and had not voluntarily withdrawn from Korea, the 70-year-old war could have been avoided, at least.

This book finds that there is no way for Washington to be exempted from responsibility for the Korean division, millions of deaths, and the current impasse with North Korea. Even China's rise as world economic powerhouse might not have posed such a threat to the United States, if Washington had not shot itself in the foot. It was Washington that opened the Pandora's Box releasing many bitter woes that must be resolved in order to bring closure to the Corean Question.

The third reason for the fundamental change in Washington's view, this book argues, is South Korea's dramatic rise as a world economic power and a democracy. In fact, it is almost impossible to find a country that can catch the two rabbits of economic development and democratization at the same time; however, South Korea was the exception. This well-known post–World War II simultaneous accomplishment in the late twentieth-century history of Korea was also triggered as an outcome of the Korean War, and serious financial aid was offered by the United States to a totally devastated Korea. In fact, it was not the first time that Washington had made a financial commitment to South Korea. Washington ran a military administration in Korea and provided aid from 1945 to 1949, beginning with Korea's liberation from Japanese colonial control in 1945. However, the main purpose of that commitment was not to boost the Korean economy but to run the American military administration, which aimed to wrap up post-Japanese control of Korea and rule the divided nation until the U.S. withdrew from South Korea in 1949.

Even before the mutual defense treaty was signed on October 1, 1953, on August 8 of that same year, however, the *Chosun Ilbo*[4] featured an editorial which discussed the Eisenhower administration's decision to provide $200M in post–Korean War reconstruction funds and introduced President Eisenhower's special envoy, Dr. Henry Tasca, who had hinted that the $200M was just the start of American aid to help Korea recover from the devastation of the Korean War when President Rhee of the Republic of Korea and U.S. secretary of state Dulles were discussing the two most important changes made as a direct result of the Korean War: the ROK-U.S. Mutual Defense Agreement and U.S. economic aid for reconstruction.

The scale of economic and military aid all together from 1946 to 1960 amounted to $4.2B; the Korean War had done far more damage to Koreans than the World War II had to the Europeans and Americans. President Eisenhower acted swiftly on July 27, 1953, two days after the armistice was signed, asking Congress to spend $200M on reconstruction in Korea. President Eisenhower's memo on July 31, 1953, to the Secretaries of State Dulles and Defense Wilson went far further emphasizing that the Eighth Army under General Maxwell Taylor had a golden opportunity to rebuild South Korea (Han, 2014: 12). The memo says

> something almost unique in history. It is the opportunity of an army in a foreign land to contribute directly and effectively to the repairing of the damages of war; to rebuild and revive a nation, to give to itself the satisfaction of constructive and challenging work, dedicated to the preservation and enhancement rather than to the destruction of human values. (Callow, 1995: 16)

Here, the phrase we should note is "a golden opportunity to rebuild South Korea." It more or less reminds us of the views and policies of State Secretary William Seward and Commodore Robert Shufeldt having considered Corea as a regular party to sign the treaty, which was necessary to accomplish the goal of American supremacy in the Pacific and Asian regions, not only as a location or means of a country to be exploited. President Eisenhower's phrase of "a golden opportunity to rebuild South Korea" in his memo to General Taylor is likely to set Washington on the return path to the Seward-Shufeldt policy while breaking away from the Line of Theodore-Franklin on the Korean Peninsula.

Here, we must raise a very important question, that is, to what extent did U.S. economic and military aid contribute to Korea's rapid economic development, which is also critical to the main question of this book: what really caused the change of heart in U.S.-Korea relations? To be sure, American economic aid to Korea from 1946 to 1960 can only be interpreted as having "created the preconditions that made Korea's economic miracle possible" (Han, 2014:12; Callow, 1995:2; SaKong and Koh, 2010). Nonetheless, we must also note that the Korean economy did not take off until after this period. One more important aspect to note on this subject is that not all of those countries that received economic aid from the United States produced such rapid and simultaneous economic development and democratization; such countries as Somalia, Zaire, Egypt, Liberia, and Sudan, which were top recipients of American economic aid (Blackadar & Kreckel, 2005: 8), did not achieve the same outcomes as South Korea.

With regard to South Korea's simultaneous democratization and economic development, we need to refer to research on the causal relationship between foreign economic aid from advanced Western countries and the formation of a long-term and self-sufficient economy and mature democracy in newly independent countries after World War II (Easterly, 2003: 30; Han 2014: 12). According to Easterly (2003: 30), "Clearly, the empirical links from aid to economic growth are far more fragile than the drumbeat of media and development agency reference to the Burnside and Dollar (2000) paper suggested . . . the result that aid boosts growth in good policy environments is fragile to defining growth, aid and policy over a sufficiently short period" (Han, 2014: 12).

Let's consider what Burnside and Dollar's well-known article "Aid, Policies, and Growth" in *American Economic Review* argued in 2000: "aid has positive correlations with the economic growth of developing countries that have good fiscal, monetary, and trade policies but has little effect on those that have poor policies" (Han, 2014: 13). As this epoch-making article finds, American aid to South Korea took place from 1946 to 1960 when post–Korean War Korea, regardless of being North or South, suffered worse than many poor countries at that time. We know there were no fiscal and industrial bases and no records of trade immediately after the war, in which the Korean Peninsula had suffered far more devastation than Europe and America had in the World War II. Even America's initial aid programs in most cases, including South Korea, were politically oriented to serve the national strategic interests of the United States and thus had been developed as "a tool for containing the spread of communism; in order to win leaders to its side" (Blackadar & Kreckel, 2005: 8).

There is another important study that should be applied to South Korea's simultaneous achievement of substantial democracy. Generally speaking, foreign economic aid can positively affect democratization in recipient countries in several ways: by improving the technological infrastructure of electoral processes, by assisting the functions of legislature and judiciaries against administrative power, by promoting civil society, by supporting education, and by bolstering per capita income (Han, 2014: 12). Yet, some argue that economic aid, instead, undermines the accountability processes essential for sound democratic institutions or creates corruption and bribery. In order to assess which of these views is best supported by the data, World Bank analyst Stephen Knack (2004) conducted a multivariate analysis of the impact of aid on democratization in a large sample of recipient nations from 1975 to 2000 and found no evidence of a causal connection between aid and democratization (Han, 2014: 13).

Thus, based on our research on the causal relationship between foreign aid and the processes of economic growth and democratization in aid-recipient countries, this book argues that no generalizations should be made and that there should instead be diverse perspectives for analyzing how post–Korean War South Korea was able to achieve both economic and political development in an unprecedentedly rapid and simultaneous way. My book *Power, Place, and State-Society Relations in Korea: Neo-Confucian and Geomantic Reconstruction of Developmental State and Democratization* (2014) attempts to articulate the state-society relations, which are key to understanding how South Korea's achievements were possible.

In this book, I have focused instead on how South Korea's rapid rise as a regional and global economic power and democracy impacted Washington's perspectives and attitudes regarding Korea in general. To Washington, there is no better evidence that American democracy and capitalism are superior to Soviet communism and to its centrally planned and commanded socialist economic system. South Korea's post–Korean War achievements glow even more brightly against the backdrop of North Korea's failing economy with its isolated totalitarian dictatorship and collapsed ideology of communism. South Korea exemplifies the primacy of Pax-Americana and best serves Washington's political purpose in its global leadership both during the Cold

War rivalry and post–Cold War era of American unilateralism. South Korea undoubtedly confirms and reinforces what the American system represents as the right path for all countries. The rise of South Korea should be sufficient reason for Washington to withdraw from the policy of the Theodore-Franklin line that this book formulates.

Two major global issues discussed in the Introduction, both of which stemmed from the Korean War, have emerged to test the changed nature of South Korea's alliance with the United States. The first issue is the rise of China, which has complicated the stance of South Korea with relation to the United States. Heavy dependence on bilateral trade with China and China's clear intention to defy American military power have tugged Seoul back and forth between Beijing and Washington, because Beijing has leveraged not just economic influences critical to the South Korean economy but also the military threat it poses to the region and control over Pyeongyang, which even Washington recognizes as the most critical power in resolving Washington's headaches over North Korea.

The key question is how Washington will ultimately resolve issues with Pyeongyang: 70-year-old mutual hostility and potential normalization of bilateral relations, the nuclear and ICBM powers of North Korea, and North Korea's alliance with China. As mentioned before, a renowned scholar on Korea and a career diplomat long stationed in Korea, Gregory Henderson, (1980) pointed out that Washington's animosity toward North Korea is unprecedented in U.S. history and "longer-lasting" even than that expressed toward "George III's England, the Kaiser's and Hitler's Germany, Ho Chi Minh's Vietminh, Stalin, and Castro." At present, Washington's denial of Pyeongyang is also incongruous, especially considering that it recognizes Non-NPT nuclear powers such as Pakistan. As McCormack (1993: 41) argues, Washington's disengaged and disdainful attitude toward Pyeongyang in fact has inadvertently legitimated that communist dictatorship: "The pressure resulting from this confrontation, and the continuing fear of renewed conflict, leading possibly to nuclear annihilation, helped to sustain the monolithic unity of the regime and state."

The ultimate question is what options Washington has: normalizing relations with Pyeongyang by either recognizing North Korea as a nuclear power, or succeeding in dismantling weapons of mass destruction, or maintaining the status quo of the Obama administration's strategic patience. The first option will finally bring closure to the General Sherman Incident of 1866 and possibly pave the way for reunification of the Peninsula; the last option will likely be to forever fixate on the contemporary division, antagonism, and insecurity.

The most critical issue in the Korean Question was the exploitative alienation of Korea in American attempts to press for encounter. Washington excised and ignored the main subject in its question on Korea so thoroughly that Korea seemed nonexistent till the Korean War in 1950. Rather, America concerned itself with other matters such as America's transient partnership with Japan, or Washington's failure with Beijing, which were all about what matters to the United States. Without a firm stance about its initiatives toward Corea, Washington had unsuccessfully internationalized the Korean Question about the Korean Peninsula and paid a hefty price in the Korean War.

That Korean War has served as a watershed in America's issues with the Korean Peninsula. South Korea has become an essential ally to Washington: Shufeldt's notion of Corea as a bridesmaid in its Pacific bride seems to have been completely dropped. South Korea's vibrant economy and democracy have been widely adopted as a sustainable model to other developing countries, which, in turn, serves as a symbol of American superiority in its free democracy and capitalistic economic system. It took a long journey for the 1866 U.S.-Korea encounter to finally arrive at a mutually beneficial relationship. However, that half success has been juxtaposed with gravely worse situations, which are stalemate, showdown on North Korea's nuclear provocation, failure to feed its own people, and the rapidly rising communist challenge of China. These are the actual two communist countries remaining out of the Soviet Union's collapse in 1991.

The second Korean War, as the eventual outcome of American zigzagging encounters with Corea, hasn't played out its role in the history of twentieth-century human civilization. Rather, its place has metamorphosed into one of the gravest threats to global peace and prosperity. The Corean Question has become a question of humanity now that the current confrontations between the triangular alliances of North Korea-China-Russia on the one hand and the U.S.-ROK-Japan on the other can ignite another world-scale war or bring closure to the twentieth-century Cold War rivalry and to the end-of-history debate brought forth by Francis Fukuyama: The Corean Question's becoming the question of the end-of-history.

If the relationship between the United States and North Korea is normalized, we will witness the Stars and Stripes waving on the North Korea and China border. It can be compared to the sale of Alaska to Washington. I wonder what William Seward and Robert Shufeldt would say to that? Had they ever imagined that their historical judgments and policy executions would turn out this way today? What about Theodore Roosevelt and Franklin Roosevelt: would they still justify their Korea-bashing and Japan-first policies now that Japan, with its debilitated, defense-only military and the Peace Constitution under the sway of Washington?

A key issue in the Korean Question raised in this book is about who has the right to hold control over the Korean Peninsula, although it may sound very illogical that any nation other than a Korean one must have the ultimate sovereignty. The problem with this point is that Korea was too weak to resist the advances of opportunistic superpowers once Korea's old suzerain was stripped of its power and control as the regional hegemon. Thus, Korea's sovereign voice was lost in this process of internationalization of the Korean Peninsula issues. The core aspect of such an internationalization of the Korean affairs was America's policy and its actions to significantly weaken China's prolonged suzerainty over Korea through the 1882 Treaty of Peace, Amity, Commerce, and Navigation between the United States and the Joseon Dynasty, and to involve Japan in the governance of the Korean Peninsula. The process of ending World War II brought those old players of both China and the Soviet Union equipped with communist ideology back to the Peninsula and resulted in the division and a devastating war there. That structure of an ideologically divided nation has endured more than a half-century.

We don't know how this Korean Question is to be resolved, meaning a series of resolutions needs to be taking place regarding North Korea's nuclear provocations, normalization of the United States and North Korea relationship, and international agreement for peaceful reunification of the divided Korean nation. In talking about an ultimate resolution of the Korean Question, I see that a Korean proverb which says, "the one who has tied the knot is the one who can untie it," is well suited to the resolution of the Korean Question. To me, it is the United States that encountered and opened Corea and played a central role in the internationalization of the Korean Question and as the one who tied the knot of the Korean Question ought to be the one to untie it. The United States is the only hegemon that actually can untangle this knot that began to be tied in the late nineteenth century by Washington. The Gordian Knot seems pertinently applicable to this case as a metaphor for an intractable problem (untying an impossibly tangled knot) solved easily by finding an approach to the problem that renders the perceived constraints of the problem moot ("cutting the Gordian knot"). According to Andrews (2016), an oracle at Telmissus (the ancient capital of Lycia) decreed that the next man to enter the city driving an oxcart should become the king among the Phrygians who were without a monarch. Gordias, a farmer, drove into town on an ox-cart and was immediately declared king. Out of gratitude, his son Midas dedicated the oxcart to the Phrygian god Sabazios (whom the Greeks identified with Zeus) and tied it to a post with an intricate knot of cornel bark (Cornus mas). The knot was later described by Roman historian Quintus Curtius Rufus as comprising "several knots all so tightly entangled that it was impossible to see how they were fastened." To Koreans, the knot that divided the nation drove the nation into a civil war and a permanent structure of the division is an intractable task. The divided nation alone does not seem to have any means to untie the knot.

Here comes the other part of the story on the Gordian Knot on how it was eventually resolved. Andrews (2016) goes on to say:

The oxcart still stood in the palace of the former kings of Phrygia at Gordium in the fourth century BC when Alexander the Great arrived, at which point Phrygia had been reduced to a satrapy, or province, of the Persian Empire. An oracle had declared that any man who could unravel its elaborate knot was destined to become ruler of all of Asia. Alexander the Great wanted to untie the knot but struggled to do so. He then reasoned that it would make no difference how the knot was loosed, so he drew his sword and sliced it in half with a single stroke. In an alternative version of the story, Alexander the Great loosed the knot by pulling the linchpin from the yoke.

The contemporary deadlock on the Korean Peninsula needs a figure like Alexander the Great, who can make a revolutionary decision to untangle the knot. Without hesitation, this book argues that it is the United States, with both assertiveness and adroitness, that can usher in a Copernican transformation on the Korean Question, which does not appear to promise such a change in the near future.

The Corean Question is still reverberating in Asia and is now bringing up a bigger question of how this centuries-old series of switches between respites and unfortunate, sometimes disastrous, encounters between America and Corea will evolve into a broader and more significant question of whether the encounters between East and West, respectively, represented by China and the United States will be recast as the Pacific Union, catalyzed and mediated by the Korean Question.

A SHORT SUMMARY

This book, in its survey of U.S.-Korea relations, has adopted a holistic approach. It follows the meandering route of this relationship from the moment that America's open-door gunboat diplomacy ran up against Korea's isolationism: the *General Sherman* Incident in 1866, *Shinmiyangyo* in 1871, and the long-overdue treaty in 1882, followed by American abandonment in 1905 of the treaty they had so doggedly pursued, reluctant reunion in 1945 with a newly divided Korea, the Korean War in 1950, and finally Korea divided but reborn in the South as a model of sustainable economic development and democracy in contrast to the communist totalitarian state with its failed economy in the North. To explain how these two Koreas developed such contrasting realities, retracing the salient aspects of these developments and drawing more insights from the inter-relatedness of their parts, repeated overviews of that history's outline are helpful.

The case of Korea is unique because this one nation—divided along the lines of Cold War ideology into halves backed by superpowers from opposing poles—illustrates the shortcomings of totalitarianism and communism as well as the virtues of democracy and capitalism. This bears relevance beyond the failure or success of just one nation and has grave consequences for world peace as well since North Korea's nuclear weapons program with ICBM capability has been cited as having the potential to spark World War III. In addition, along the lines of the old Acheson Line, China's "One Belt One Road" initiative has placed the United States and Japan on course for a collision with China. According to Allison's Thucydides Trap, when a rising power challenges an existing hegemon, there is a 75% chance of large-scale war, according to his study of wars since the Peloponnesian War. The United States and China were enemies in the Korean War and are colliding again along those lines now. Furthermore, North Korea's nuclear brinkmanship automatically makes China's influence one of the most important aspects of these issues. China and the United States have competed for suzerainty over the Peninsula at different times—China as the original suzerain and the United States now in the South. China did not hesitate to battle the United States, first, in order to protect its Northeastern border with North Korea, and then, to regain suzerainty over the North. As in a déjà vu of the same parties that fought in the Korean War 75 years ago, their animosity has never gone away but merely resurfaces in the form of bigger problems. Borrowing Diamond's claim (1999), the pain of the unfortunate interaction in 1866 between the United States and Korea with almost opposite ideas on economic, political, cultural, and ideological systems led not just to collisions but to a permanent division of the Korean nation, none of which has died down even after one and half centuries of relations.

As discussed, America's first battle with Korea broke out in 1866 near the current capital of North Korea, Pyeongyang, which has now become a global emblem of anti-American sentiment. Thus, the current deadlock between the United States and North Korea is more than a century old. North Korea is no match for the United States, the unilateral hegemon of the world, in terms of either state power or capacity. However, during the Cold War period from 1950 to 1991, America could not, nor did it need to, do anything against its former enemy of the Korean War, North Korea, due to U.S. rivalry with the Soviet Union. North Korea was under the complete control of the head of the communist bloc. After the Soviet Union's collapse in 1991, the unilateral presence of its former enemy got under Pyeongyang's skin, as it lacked a kingpin of its own, driving North Korea to build asymmetric weapons of mass destruction and hold South Korea and Japan hostage. Now, North Korea's ICBM capability with possibly nuclear warheads may have become an existential threat to the United States.

America's encounter with Korea produced stark contrasts between North and South, creating one of the world's most volatile powder kegs. From this perspective, this book argues that contemporary Korea mirrors the United States, both in its successes and failures. A history of Korea-U.S. relations shows how U.S. interactions with East Asia, in general, and with Korea, in particular, have shaped international power dynamics in the region. The United States chose Japan as its strategic partner in the late nineteenth and early twentieth centuries, gave Korea to Japan, and challenged China's influence. However, America's choice gravely backfired in 1941 when Japan attacked Pearl Harbor, which ended with the United States dropping the first nuclear bombs on Japan in 1945.

Viewed in this light, it is undeniable that the intercourse which the United States insisted on having with Korea in the nineteenth century produced one of the most ironic outcomes in the world's history of encounters among disparate peoples and ideas. Regardless of the current status of the U.S.-ROK military alliance and economic and cultural interdependence, the United States is primarily responsible for the permanent division and suffering of the Korean War as George McCune, in charge of the Korea Desk at the State Department in 1945 and one of the earliest American Korea experts with field knowledge of old Korea,[5] unhesitatingly concludes in his book *Korea Today*: "the United States unwittingly made Korea the tragic victim of far-reaching international rivalries" in settling on the phrase "in due course." He even recognizes, and criticizes, the paternalistic nature of U.S. policy toward Korea, stating that the nation "is still looked upon as a stepchild in high government circles in Washington" (Kraus, 2015: 159, George M. McCune, "Occupation Politics in Korea," Far Eastern Survey, 15, 3, February, 1946). Another American pioneer in the study of Korea-U.S. relations echoes McCune's critique of U.S. policy toward Korea. A more critical view blames the U.S. for a policy of drift and vacillation, of oversight and blunder. Gregory Henderson put it succinctly:

> No division of a nation in the present world is so astonishing in its origin as the division of Korea; none is so unrelated to conditions of sentiment within the nation itself at the time the division was effected; none to this day so unexplained; in none does blunder and planning oversight appear to have played so large a role. Finally, there is no division for which the U.S. government bears so heavy a share of the responsibility as it bears for the division of Korea. (Henderson, 1968: 34)

A more common criticism is offered by historian Charles M. Dobbs:

> The confusions of wartime diplomacy would continue [in American policy toward Korea throughout the 1940s]; the hasty and sometimes incomplete decision-making process would reoccur. American officials would still find Korea

of little strategic significance. . . . Of course, as the confusion continued, policymaking vacillated, and the situation would worsen or suddenly change. . . . In almost every case, policy would be made only for the short-term. . . . [T]he Soviets deserved the lion's share of the blame for the ensuing controversy; but the U.S. government also deserves criticism for its failure to gain control of the situation, to plan ahead, to be prepared to act when the moment called for action. American officials should have recognized that. . . . the peninsula would demand not just idle musings but serious, step-by-step planning. (Barry, 2012: 50)

In this history of relations between the United States and Korea, George McCune aptly concludes "almost no thought at all was given to Korea as a nation of more than 26 million persons." Barry (2012: 50–51) follows McCune's point that "the division of Korea into occupation zones was a decision made by military staffs without political considerations and was presented as a *fait accompli* to the State Department."

After 40 years of American silence starting from Theodore Roosevelt's decision not to pursue the "good offices" provision of the 1882 Korea-U.S. treaty but rather to give Korea to Japan in 1905 till the liberation of Korea from Japanese colonial control, another early American Korea expert and the closest advisor to the first president of the Republic of Korea Syngman Rhee, Robert T. Oliver, examined the painful impacts of America's arbitrary division of the Peninsula as follows:

> The net result of this arbitrary division of Korea into two tightly-closed zones is that the country is economically and politically bleeding to death. Despite the savage rigor of the Japanese rule of Korea, many Koreans assured me during my visit to their country last summer that they are worse off today under the joint Russian-American rule than they had been even under the Japanese. . . . The first error Americans made in regard to Korea was in the Yalta deal, inviting the Russians in. The second error has been in leaving southern Korea in the Japanese administrative area. This means that every restriction we apply against the Japanese as a punishment for their war guilt is automatically applied also against the Koreans. One of these restrictions is a refusal to permit their currency to be established on the international exchange.[6] (Oliver, 1947: 31–32)

Such holistic approaches to the history of U.S.-Korea relations reveal the tumultuous nature of their interactions, without which we can fall into a distorted sense of America's place in Korean history. For example, Koreans unaware of the early history of U.S.-Korea relations—that is, before the Korean War—tend to regard the United States as a savior or beneficent big brother. Korea's scars made Japanese colonial control unforgettable, not to mention America's reluctance to intervene at the end of World War

II, liberating Korea from Japan and making the most catastrophic decision for Korea by chopping the Peninsula in two. However, if Koreans were to recall how the nation was halved, America's place in Korean minds would take a radical downturn from savior to villain. To make matters worse, if they understood how the United States responded when Japan wanted Korea as a colony—essentially swapping it with Japan for the Philippines—then America's place in Koreans' minds would fall from savior to Satan's accomplice. What really makes matters worst of all, though, is that it was the United States, not Korea, that so aggressively pursued the establishment of an official relationship with Korea in the first place. Korea was doggedly courted then ditched,[7] occupied then split with outcomes that were completely mixed.

Yet, it would still be hasty to conclude what the eventual consequences of this century and a half of interactions will be, because, as mentioned before, it has brought about two contrasting outcomes. Some knowledge of world history is required to discern how these contemporary Korean issues may evolve. Can South Korea escape the vortex of competition among superpowers? Can the free world peacefully resolve North Korea's nuclear brinkmanship? Can the United States and China come to reasonable terms in their economic and military competition? And can South Korea's capitalist economy and democracy defeat North Korea's totalitarian dictatorship and achieve reunification when the status quo on the Peninsula is so deeply entrenched? If so, what positive role can the United States play in this process?

The place of the United States in Korean history has shifted radically, and is likely to become positive again, but no certain indicators are present as to when. As argued, Diamond's (1997, 28) thesis is relevant to Korea's encounter with the U.S.

> collisions between peoples from different continents, by retelling through contemporary eyewitness accounts the most dramatic such encounter in history: the capture of the last independent Incan emperor, Atahuallpa, in the presence of his whole army, by Francisco Pizarro and his tiny band of conquistadores, at the Peruvian city of Cajamarca.

Diamond's observation can be paraphrased for the Korean case as follows: to pull world peace from a potential powder keg, one must start at the division of Korea with a failed state in the North and a model state in the South, and search back through the various misunderstandings and understandings that make up the early history of U.S.-Korea relations.

A series of mishaps, and finally war, started with the *General Sherman* in 1866 and the war in 1950 between the United States and North Korea has eventually led to the nuclear and ICBM showdown, which has become the most explosive powder keg in the world. So far, Pyeongyang's demand of tit for tat, meaning incremental denuclearization and reciprocal economic compensations, has met with an American ultimatum for "full, final, irreversible denuclearization" (FFID) on the North Korean side first, then to be followed by corresponsive economic reparation. Ultimately, this showdown will only be resolved when there is a high enough level of mutual trust in the transparency of North Korea's nuclear and ICBM capabilities and in Washington's solid confirmation of giving up its policy of regime change in Pyeongyang. Meanwhile, Washington and Seoul have to meet a new challenge that South Korea's economic dependence upon China's rising power may reconfigure the relationship that was recovered through massive sacrifice during the Korean War. After a tumultuous one and a half-century affair full of love and hatred, China is taking full advantage of its economic leverages against Korea to weaken Korea's dependence on Washington. I wonder how this whole story of extreme rivalries around the Korean Peninsula and Korea's fearsome and undetachable destiny with these neighbors will end, if it ever ends.

EPILOGUE: A PETITION TO END THE KOREAN WAR BY THE VOICES OF KOREAN WAR VETERANS

Aside from the Six-Party Talks in early twenty-first century on the denuclearization of North Korea, few attempts have been made to resolve the Korean Question. Many voices have been raised to end the Korean War and replace the armistice with a peace treaty, but those voices have not changed the surrounding superpowers' stakes in maintaining the status quo in the Peninsula. Marshall (2015: 208) aptly summarizes the strong incentives for this status quo among China, the United States, and Japan:

> The Chinese do not want to fight on behalf of North Korea; nor do they want a united Korea containing American bases near their border. The U.S. does not want to fight for South Korea, but neither can it afford to be seen as giving up on a friend. The Japanese, with their long history of involvement in the Peninsula, must be seen to tread lightly, knowing that whatever happens will likely involve them.

Thus, it behooves us to disentangle the conflicting interests of these superpowers and petition the United Nations to end the Korean War and replace it with a peace treaty.

In 2015, I had a chance to interview many Korean War veterans in Honolulu, Hawaii and met a renowned scholar on the Korean War, Korean War veteran and Professor Emeritus of the University of Hawaii, Dr. Glenn D. Paige. His book *The Korean Decision, June 24–30, 1950* examines President Truman's decision-making process and how the United States mobilized the United Nations to intervene in the Korean War. Dr. Paige also established the Center for Global Nonkilling.[8] During my interview with him for the Korean War Veterans Digital Memorial,[9] Dr. Paige explained why he created the CGNK: "I killed many in the Korean War and had to do it because I was there for it." Based on his experience in the Korean War, Dr. Paige launched, in the year of the Seoul Olympics, the Center of Global Nonkilling, an international non-profit promoting changes toward the measurable goal of a killing-free world. In a discussion about how the unfinished aspects of the Korean War can finally be resolved, Paige shared his lifelong dream of ending the Korean War with a treaty for peace. His rationale was simple—that the UN had declared the war against the North's invasion of South Korea and signed the armistice, and thus is uniquely situated to replace that armistice with a peace treaty. Together, we decided to solicit support from those who had actually fought in the Korean War and send this petition to the UN secretary-general in 2015 in commemoration of the 65th Anniversary of the outbreak of the Korean War. The petition was designed to explain why the UN was the most suitable institution for initiating the end of the Korean War and obtaining signatures from Korean War veterans around the world. This was done in the hopes that the breakthrough would take place in the same international regime that initiated the Allied forces' intervention into the communist invasion of South Korea—the United Nations. As the Korean adage says, "the one who has tied the knot is the one who can untie it."

ENDING THE KOREAN WAR: A PETITION TO THE UNITED NATIONS BY ALLIANCE OF KOREAN WAR VETERANS AND GLOBAL CITIZENS TO END THE KOREAN WAR ORGANIZED BY THE KOREAN WAR LEGACY FOUNDATION & THE CENTER FOR GLOBAL NONKILLING

Preamble

The Korean War began June 25, 1950, and, although combat ended July 27, 1953, an outdated armistice has perpetuated a state of war on the Peninsula to this day. This war that killed millions of soldiers and civilians over a period of three years and left the Korean Peninsula utterly devastated continues politically as a result of an armistice signed 67 years ago. In the history of modern civilization, no war has lasted more than a half-century after a ceasefire. This represents an unnecessary failure on the part of humanity—we believe—to develop, practice, and promote peaceful coexistence.

Due to the unprecedented military confrontation that has centered around the demilitarized zone on the 38th parallel, more than two million Korean youths, with enormous government backing, are compelled by the insecurity in the region to serve in their military. To make matters worse, North Korea's all-in stance for nuclear weapons and ICBMs has been threatening to drag the Peninsula back into a vortex of competition among superpowers. Amidst such ever-increasing armament regimes, brothers and sisters, divided by politics and diplomatic missteps of past generations, continually aim bullets at each other, preventing hundreds of thousands of relatives from ever sharing the same space and homes again.

The hostility that has sadly crystalized around North Korea and South Korea has outlasted even the Cold War itself, which dissolved in 1991. Periodically, the parties reiterate negotiations that perpetuate the stalemate between North and South Korea and between North Korea and the United States; however, the Korean division remains the most overdue peace agenda in the world.

What we owe to this unresolved tragedy of the last century is to officially end the war and mutually recognize a treaty of peace among all parties involved. Sharing the belief that North Korea's nuclear program poses the most dangerous threat to peace on the Peninsula, we argue that continued failure to end this war after so many years is unjustified. Specifically, the Armistice Agreement envisioned "an appropriate agreement for a peaceful settlement at a political level between both sides" (Art. V, Sec. 62), a commitment that has not been upheld. More importantly, President Moon Jae-in of the Republic of Korea recently reinforced the political and symbolic significance of ending the Korean War, saying "The end-of-war declaration will, indeed, open the door to complete denuclearization and a permanent peace regime on the Korean Peninsula" during his video address to the 75th Session of the UN General Assembly on September 23, 2020.

Petition

As a Korean proverb says, "The one who tied the knot untie it." It is time to begin a transition from 70 years of war hostilities to final closure and peace on this, the 67th anniversary of the Armistice Agreement. We, the Korean War veterans of all participant countries, joined by peace-seeking global citizens, and led by the Center for Global Nonkilling, urge the United Nations with the support of major powers around the Korean Peninsula (the United States, China, Japan, and Russia), to convene a "UN Korean Peace Settlement Conference to End the War." As survivors who fought for peace in the Korean War, representing ourselves and those who sacrificed their precious lives, we feel we have a legitimate claim to urge UN leaders to conclude peace before we die. Our average age is 89.

The rationale for UN action includes the following:

1. President Truman engaged the United States in the Korean War for world peace under the auspices of the UN (UNSC Res. 82, 83, 84), saying "We can't let the UN down!" (Glenn D. Paige, *The Korean Decision: June 24-30, 1950*, p. 125; also pp. 188, 211, 243).
2. Subsequently, 21 UN members (16 combatants and 5 humanitarian participants) joined to support the UN Command.
3. The July 27, 1953, Armistice Agreement was signed by the UN Command Delegation, the Delegation of the Korean People's Army, and the Chinese People's Volunteer Army.
4. Now all Korean War combatants and humanitarian participants, including the two Koreas and their allies, are UN members.
5. In the historic Inter-Korean Summit meeting held on April 27, 2018, at the "Peace House" at Panmunjom, Kim Jong-un, chairman of the State Affairs Commission of the Democratic People's Republic of Korea, and Moon Jae-in, president of the Republic of Korea, agreed to end the current armistice and establish a firm peace regime on the Korean Peninsula. This historic mission must not be delayed any further. The two sides agreed to declare an end to the war this year, which marks the 65th anniversary of the armistice, and pursue trilateral meetings involving the DPRK, the ROK, and the United States, or quadrilateral meetings involving these parties and China, with a view to replacing the armistice with a peace agreement and establishing a solid and lasting peace.
6. Based on the ceasefire agreement in 1953 and the two Korean leaders' declaration on April 27, 2018, the current UN secretary-general, António Guterres, with deep understanding of Korea, can bring the absence of a Korean Peace Settlement to the attention of the Security Council as a "matter which may threaten the maintenance of international peace and security" under Article 99 of the UN Charter.
7. Security Council members China and Russia both support seeking a Peace Settlement to end the Korean War armistice.

We hereby petition the United Nations to:

1. Seek a UN-initiated Korean Peace Settlement as a comprehensive approach for achieving peaceful inter-Korean relations, denuclearization of the Korean Peninsula, relaxation of regional tensions, and strengthening of peace and security in Asia and worldwide.
2. Establish within the Security Council a Standing Committee for Ending the Korean War.
3. Commission the International Academic Community to assess political, military, economic, social, and cultural costs/benefits of Korean peace

for all parties involved, including the two Koreas, the United States, China, Japan, Russia, and all countries of the Asia-Pacific region.
4. Convene a Korean War Peace Settlement Conference chaired by the secretary-general as directed by the Security Council Standing Committee to End and Replace the Korean War with a peace treaty.
5. In the spirit of "commitment for commitment, action for action," the Petition calls attention to the steps agreed in the 9/19 Joint Communique of the Six-Party Talks:
   1) The DPRK committed to abandoning all nuclear weapons and existing nuclear programs and returning at an early date to the Non-Proliferation Treaty (NPT) and International Atomic Energy Agency (IAEA) safeguards.
   2) The DPRK, the United States, and Japan take steps to normalize relations subject to their respective bilateral policies.
   3) The six parties undertook to promote economic cooperation in the fields of energy, trade and investment, bilaterally and/or multilaterally.
   4) Committed to joint efforts for lasting peace and stability in northeast Asia.

NOTES

1. The official title of the treaty is "Agreement between the Government of the United States of America and the Government of the United Kingdom of Great Britain and Northern Ireland for Cooperation on the uses of Atomic Energy for Mutual Defense Purposes."
2. https://2009-2017.state.gov/s/l/treaty/collectivedefense//index.htm
3. DEFCON3 was considered on December 19, 2011, when North Korean leader Kim Jong-il was reported dead.
4. One of South Korea's most influential daily newspapers of all time.
5. He was born in Pyeongyang, as the son of American Presbyterian educational missionaries Helen (McAfee) and George Shannon McCune, and worked in Korea until it became a protectorate of Japan's in 1905.
6. In his field study, Oliver (1047: 31–32) noted the disruptive economic impacts of America's hasty and largely arbitrary division of the Korean Peninsula: "This effectively freezes every Korean asset and renders them helpless to aid themselves. Another restriction is a total prohibition of any imports. Since Korean manufacturing resources are all in the north, this ban leaves them completely stripped of consumers goods. As a result, inflation has hit them hard. I paid $26 last summer to get a pair of shoes half-soled. Rice, when I landed in Korea last June, was selling on the black market for 2,400 Yen a bushel (with college professors receiving a salary of 2,000 Yen a month). When I left in August the price had risen to 4,750 Yen a bushel. A further effect of our restrictions upon Korea is that it is not allowed any form of government

of its own. This means that it has absolutely no official spokesmen by whom its case can be pleaded before the bar of world opinion. With all their mistreatment, Koreans are not even allowed the privilege of speaking out on their own behalf."

7. Robert T. Oliver investigates one of many instances when U.S. leaders ignored Korean leaders' appeals for help in protecting Korean independence from Japan: "However, the peace-makers at Paris, considering that Japan had given at least nominal support to the Allied cause in the war, refused to consider the Korean claim of independence. When Japanese delegates threatened to withdraw from the Peace Conference if the Korean Question were raised, President Woodrow Wilson acquiesced in keeping it completely off the agenda. Dr. Syngman Rhee, who sought to go to Paris to plead his country's case, was refused a passport by the State Department in Washington" (Oliver, 1944: 48).

8. See CGNK, https://nonkilling.org/center/
9. See www.kwvdm.org, www.koreanwarlegacy.org

Bibliography

Acheson, Dean. 1971. *The Korean War.* New York: W.W. Norton & Company, Inc.
Alagappa, M. 2003. *Asian Security Order: Instrumental and Normative Features.* Stanford, CA: Stanford University Press.
American Foreign Policy. May 27, 2019. North Korea slams 'human defect' Bolton. https://vaalweekblad.com/afp/733273/north-korea-slams-human-defect-bolton/
Andrews, Evan. 2016, February 3. "What was the Gordian Knot?" *History.*
Armacost, M. 1996. *Friends or Rivals? The Insider's Account of U.S.-Japan Relations.* New York: Columbia University Press.
Barry, P. Mark. 2012. The U.S. and the 1945 Division of Korea: Mismanaging the Big Decisions. *International Journal on World Peace*, 29(4): 37–59.
BBC News. 2009, December 12. Thailand Seizes 'Arms Plane Flying from North Korea'. http://news.bbc.co.uk/2/hi/asia-pacific/8410042.stm (accessed on December 12, 2009).
Bechtol Jr., Bruce E. 2002. Avenging the General Sherman: The 1871 Battle of Kang Hwa Do. Master Thesis submitted to Marine Corps University.
Benedict, R. 1946. *The Chrysanthemum and the Sword.* Boston, MA: Houghton Mifflin Company.
Berlinger, Joshua. 2017, July 28. Why North Korea still hates the United States: The legacy of the Korean War. *CNN.*
Blackadar, Andy and Sarah Kreckel. 2005. Dilemmas of Foreign Aid: Debating U.S. Priorities, Policies, and Practices. The Choices for the 21st Century Education Program. Providence, RI: Watson Institute for International Studies, Brown University.
Blair, D. 2010. Annual Threat Assessment of the US Intelligence Community for the Senate Select Committee on Intelligence, February 2.
Blue, A. D. 1973. Early Steamships in China. *Journal of the Hong Kong Branch of the Royal Asiatic Society*, 13: 45–57.

Bolton, J. 2011. 'BOLTON: North Korea Edges Toward Next Nuke Test'. *The Washington Times*, July 14. http://www.washingtontimes.com/news/2011/jul/14/north-korea-edges-toward-next-nuke-test/ (accessed on 10 September 2012).

Bradley, James. 2009a. *The Imperial Cruise*. New York, Boston, London: Back Bay Books/Little, Brown and Company.

Bradley, James. 2009b, December 5. Diplomacy That Will Live in Infamy. *New York Times*. https://www.nytimes.com/2009/12/06/opinion/06bradley.html?referringSource=articleShare

Brazinsky, Gregg. 2007. *Nation Building in South Korea: Koreans, Americans, and the Making of a Democracy*. Chapel Hill, NC: The University of North Caroline Press.

Brokaw, T. 2001. *The Greatest Generation*. Random House.

Buckley, Roger. 1992. *US-Japan Alliance Diplomacy, 1945-1990*. New York and Oakleigh: Cambridge University Press.

Burchett, Wilfred G. 1968. *Again Korea*. New York: International Publishers.

Burnside, C. and Dollar, D. 2000. Aid, Policies, and Growth. *American Economic Review*, 90(4): 847–868.

Burton, David H. 1973. Theodore Roosevelt and His English Correspondents: A Special Relationship of Friends. *Transactions of the American Philosophical Society*, 63(2): 1–70.

Callow, T. 1995. Nationbuilding in Korea, A Research Report submitted to the Faculty in Fulfillment of the Curriculum Requirement of Air War College, U.S.A.

Carlin, R. 2011, March 1. Testimony Before the Senate Foreign Relations Committee. http://www.foreign.senate.gov/imo/media/doc/Carlin_Testimony.pdf.

Cha, Victor. 2002. Korea's Place in the Axis. *Foreign Affairs*, 81(3): 79–92.

Chang, Gordon H. 1990. *Friends and Enemies: The United States, China, and the Soviet Union, 1948-1972*. Stanford, CA: Stanford University Press.

Chang, Gordon H. 2003. Whose "Barbarism"? Whose "Treachery"? Race and Civilization in the Unknown United States-Korea War of 1871. *The Journal of American History*, 89(4): 1331–1365.

Chappelle, Howard I. 1982. *The History of American Sailing Ships, 1935*. New York: Bonanza Books.

Chay, John. 1982. The First Three Decades of American-Korean Relations, 1882-1910: Reassessments and Reflections. In Kwak, Tae-Hwan, Chay, John, Cho, Soon Sung, and McCune, Shannon (eds.), *U.S.-Korean Relations 1882-1982*. Seoul: The Institute for Far Eastern Studies, Kyungnam University.

Cho, Soon Sung. 1967. *Korea in World Politics, 1940-1950*. Berkeley and Los Angeles: University of California Press.

Choe, Sang-Hun. 2010. "Economic Measures by North Korea Prompt New Hardships and Unrest." *New York Times*. http://www.nytimes.com/2010/02/04/world/asia/04korea.html?scp=1&sq=north%20korean%20economy&st=cse.

Chowdhuri, S. R. 2004. *Nuclear Politics: Toward a Safer World*. USA, UK, India: New Dawn Press, Inc.

Chung, Chin O. 1978. *P'yongyang between Peking and Moscow: North Korea's Involvement in the Sino-Soviet Dispute, 1958-1975*. Alabama: The University of Alabama Press.

CIA. The Korean War Controversy: An Intelligence Success or Failure?. https://www.cia.gov/news-information/featured-story-archive/2015-featured-story-archive/korean-war-intelligence-success-or-failure.html

Clapper, J. 2011. Statement for the Record on the Worldwide Threat Assessment of the U.S. Intelligence Community for the House Permanent Select Committee on Intelligence. February 10. http://www.dtic.mil/cgi-bin/GetTRDoc?Location=U2&doc=GetTRDoc.pdf&AD=ADA536770.

Clemens Jr., Walter C. 2016. *North Korea and the World: Human Rights, Arms Control, and Strategies for Negotiation.* Lexington, KY: The University Press of Kentucky.

Congressional Research Service by Mark E. Manyin, Emma Chanlett-Avery, Mary Beth D. Nikitin, Brock R. Williams, Jonathan R. Corrado. 2017, May 23. U.S.-South Korea Relations, https://fas.org/sgp/crs/row/R41481.pdf

Connally, Tom. 1950, May 5. World Policy and Bipartisanship: An Interview with Senator Tom Connally, *U.S. News & World Report*, re-appeared in Regarding U.S. Policy in Korea, Memorandum by the Assistant Secretary of State for Far Eastern Affairs (Rusk) to the Under Secretary of State (Webb), Foreign Relations of the United States, 1950, Korea, Volume VII, 611.95/5–250.

Cook, Harold F. 1982. On the Centenary of America's First Treaty with Korea. *Transactions of The Royal Asiatic Society, Korea Branch*, 57: 11–28.

Cosbrove, Ben. 2012. Korean War: Classic Photos by David Douglas Duncan. *Time*, June 22. http://time.com/3667583/korean-war-photos-david-douglas-duncan/

Cumings, Bruce. 1973. American Policy towards Korean Liberation. In Frank Baldwin (ed.), *Without Parallel: The American-Korean Relationship since 1945*. New York: Pantheon Books.

Cuming, Bruce. Ed. 1983. *Child of Conflict: The Korean-American Relationship, 1943-1953.* Seattle and London: University of Washington Press.

Cumings, Bruce. 1983. Introduction: The Course of Korean-American Relations, 1943-1953. In Cuming, Bruce (ed.), *Child of Conflict: The Korean-American Relationship, 1943-1953.* Seattle and London: University of Washington Press.

Cumings, Bruce. 1999. *Parallax Visions: Making Sense of American East Asian Relations at the End of the Century.* Durham and London: Duke University Press.

Cumings, Bruce. 2004. *North Korea: Another Country.* New York and London: The New Press.

Cumings, Bruce. 2005. *Korea's Place in the Sun: A Modern History.* New York and London: W.W. Norton & Company.

Cumings, Bruce. 2007. Kim Jong Il Confronts Bush--and Wins: A New Page in North-South Korean Relations. *Japan Focus*, October 9. http://www.japanfocus.org/products/details/2539

Cumings, Bruce. 2011. *The Origins of the Korean War.* New York: Modern Library.

Cumings, Bruce, Abrahamian, E. and Ma'o, M. 2004. *Inventing the Axis of Evil: The Truth about North Korea, Iran, and Syria.* New York and London: The New Press.

D'Elia, Thomas A. 1982. U.S.-ROK Economic Interdependence. In Kwak, Tae-Hwan, Chay, John, Cho, Soon Sung, and McCune, Shannon (ed.), *U.S.-Korean Relations 1882-1982.* Seoul: The Institute for Far Eastern Studies, Kyungnam University.

Defence Blog. 2019, May 5. North Korea Launches Ballistic Missile Similar to Russian Iskander. https://defence-blog.com/news/north-korea-launches-ballistic-missile-similar-to-russian-iskander.html

Dennett, Tyler. 1922. *Americans in Eastern Asia: A Critical Study of the Policy of the United States with Reference to China, Japan and Korea in the 19th Century*. New York: The MacMillan Company.

Denyer, Simon and Parker, Ashley. 2019, May 25. Trump Appears to Contradict Bolton on North Korea, Expresses 'Confidence' in Kim. *New York Times*.

Department of Defense. 2017. Military and Security Development Involving the Democratic Peoples' Republic of Korea 2017: A Report to Congress Pursuant to the National Defense Authorization Act for Fiscal Year 2012.

Department of Defense. 2019, June 1. The Indo-Pacific Strategy Report. https://media.defense.gov/2019/Jul/01/2002152311/-1/-1/1/DEPARTMENT-OF-DEFENSE-INDO-PACIFIC-STRATEGY-REPORT-2019.PDF

Desjardins, Jeff. 2017, March 18. U.S. Military Personnel Deployments by Country. *Visual Capitalist*. https://www.visualcapitalist.com/u-s-military-personnel-deployments-country/

Diamond, Jared. 1997. *Guns, Germs, and Steel: The Fates of Human Societies*. New York and London: W.W. Norton & Company.

Doyle, Michael W. 1983. Kant, Liberal Legacies, and Foreign Affairs. *Philosophy and Public Affairs*, 12(3): 205–235.

Doyle, Michael W. 1986. Liberalism and World Politics. *The American Political Science Review*, 80(4): 1151–1169.

Drake, Frederick G. 1984. *The Empire of the Seas: A Biography of Rear-Admiral Robert Wilson Shufeldt*. Honolulu, HI: The University of Hawaii Press.

Duncan, David Douglas. 1951. *This is the War!: A Photo-Narrative of the Korean War*. New York: Harper & Brothers.

Easterly, W. 2003. Can Foreign Aid Buy Growth? *Journal of Economic Perspectives*, 17(3): 23–48.

East-West Center & The Asan Institute for Policy Studies. 2013. Korea Matters for America Matters for Korea, Honolulu and Seoul: East-West Center & The Asan Institute for Policy Studies.

Eberstadt, N. 2004. Tear down This Tyranny: A Korea Strategy for Bush's Second Term. *The Weekly Standard*, 2910 (11). http://www.weeklystandard.com/Content/Public/Articles/000/000/004/951szxxd.asp.

Eberstadt, Nicholas. 1999. The Most Dangerous Country. *The National Interest*, 57: 45–54.

Eberstadt, Nicholas. 2005, September 2. A Skeptical View. *Wall Street Journal*, A-26.

Eberstadt, Nicholas. 2007, February 5. Talking Only Makes It Worse. *Time International*, 169(4).

Ebrey, Patricia Buckley. ed. 1981. *Chinese Civilization and Society: A Sourcebook*. New York: Free Press.

Eichengreen, Barry, Lim, Wonhyuk, Park, Yung Chul, and Perkins, Dwight H. 2015. *The Korean Economy: From a Miraculous Past to a Sustainable Future*. Cambridge, MA and London: Harvard University Press.

Encyclopedia.com. Maritime Technology. https://www.encyclopedia.com/history/encyclopedias-almanacs-transcripts-and-maps/maritime-technology

Feng, John. 2021, April 28. U.S. Warship Shadows China's Aircraft Carrier on Journey Home. *Newsweek*. https://www.newsweek.com/us-warship-shadows-chinas-aircraft-carrier-journey-home-1587114

Fenno, Jr., Richard. F. ed. 1955. *The Yalta Conference*. Boston, MA: D.C. Heath and Company.

Field, David P. 2015. The Rabbi, the Lawyer, and the Prophet: American Exceptionalism and the Question of Korean Independence, 1919-1922. *Journal of American-East Asian Relations*, 22: 291–314.

Finch, Michael. 1996. German Diplomatic Documents on the 1905 Japan-Korea Protectorate Treaty. *Korean Studies*, 20: 51–63.

Fly, J. 2010. 'Regime change is the only way to solve the North Korean security challenge'. *The Foreign Policy Initiative*, November 24. http://www.foreignpolicyi.org/content/regime-change-only-way-solve-north-korean-security-challenge-says-fpi-executive-director-jam.

Fong, Leslie. 2018, September 29. Korean War to trade war, China has a Trump card against US: resilience. *South China Morning Post* (SCMP.COM).

Fontenrose, Kirsten. 2020, May 23. The Real Reason U.S. Patriot Missile Defense Batteries Are Leaving Saudi Arabia. *The National Interest*. https://nationalinterest.org/print/blog/buzz/real-reason-us-patriot-missile-defense-batteries-are-leaving-saudi-arabia-157426

Foster-Carter, A. 1987. Korea: From Dependency to Democracy. *Capital & Class*, 33: 7–19.

Fowler, William M., Jr. 1984. *Jack Tars and Commodores: The American Navy, 1783–1815*. Boston, MA: Houghton Mifflin.

French, Paul. 2007. *North Korea: The Paranoid Peninsula*. London and New York: ZED Books.

Fry, Michael. 2013, August 4. National Geographic, Korea, and the 38th Parallel: How a National Geographic map helped divide Korea. https://news.nationalgeographic.com/news/2013/08/130805-korean-war-dmz-armistice-38-parallel-geography/

Fukuyama, Francis. 1989. The End of History? *The National Interest*, 16: 3–18.

Furgurson, Ernest B. 2015, September 17. Global Diplomacy Was in Theodore Roosevelt's Hands, But His Daughter Stole the Show. *Smithsonianmag.com*. https://www.smithsonianmag.com/smithsonian-institution/global-diplomacy-theodore-roosevelt-hands-daughter-stole-show-180956578/

Gaddis, J. Lewis. 2005. *The Cold War: A New History*. Penguin Books.

Gallucci, Robert. 2006. Nuclear Shockwaves: Ramifications of the North Korean Nuclear Test. *Arms Control Today*, 36(9): 6.

Gardner, Lloyd. 1983. Commentary. In Cuming, Bruce (ed.), *Child of Conflict: The Korean-American Relationship, 1943-1953*. Seattle and London: University of Washington Press.

Gasiorowski, M. 1996. An Overview of the Political Regime Change Dataset. *Comparative Political Studies*, 29(4): 469–483.

Global Times. 2019, May 17. Netizens praise state TV for airing war films against US. *Global Times*. http://www.globaltimes.cn/content/1150362.shtml

Goodby, J. and Gross, D. 2010. Strategic Patience Has Become Strategic Passivity. *Brookings.* http://www.brookings.edu/articles/2010/1222_korea_engagement_goodby.aspx?p=1.

Gordon, Michael R. and Gordon Lubold. 2020, July 17. Trump Administration Weighs Troop Cut in South Korea. *Wall Street Journal.* https://www.wsj.com/articles/trump-administration-weighs-troop-cut-in-south-korea-11595005050

Goulden, Joseph C. 1982. *Korea: The Untold Story of the War.* New York: Times Books.

Graham, Allison. 2017. *Destined for War: Can America and China Escape Thucydides's Trap?* Boston and New York: Houghton Mifflin Harcourt.

Gries, Peter Hays, Jennifer L. Prewitt-Freilino, Luz-Eugenia Cox-Fuenzalida, and Qingmin Zhang. 2009. Contentious Histories and the Perception of Threat: China, the United States, and the Korean War—An Experimental Analysis. *Journal of East Asian Studies,* 9(3): 433–465.

Griffis, William Elliot. 1889 (1882, 1888). *Corea: The Hermit Nation.* New York: Charles Scribner's Sons.

Griswold, Whitney. 1938. *The Far Eastern Policy of the United States.* New York: Harcourt, Brace, and Company.

Ha, Tae Hyung. 1970. Maxims and Proverbs of Old Korea. Seoul, Korea: Yonsei University Press.

Hailin, Xu. 2019, May 19. Concurrent Trade War and Talks will Become New Norm. *Global Times.*

Hamel, Hendrik. 2011, 1994, 1998. *Hamel's Journal and a Description of the Kingdom of Korea, 1653-1666* (translation from the Dutch Manuscript in 1668, Jean-Paul Buys). Seoul: The Royal Asiatic Society.

Han, Jongwoo and Jung, Tae-Hern. 2014. *Understanding North Korea: Indigenous Perspectives.* Lanham, Boulder, New York, Toronto, Plymouth, UK: Lexington Books.

Han, Jongwoo. 2009. North Korea's Diplomacy to Engage the United States. *Australian Journal of International Affairs,* 63(1): 105–120.

Han, Jongwoo. 2011. The Road Not Taken, from The Korean War Veterans Digital Memorial (www.kwvdm.org).

Han, Jongwoo. 2012. *Networked Information Technologies, Elections, and Politics: Korea and the United States.* Lexington Books, Lanham, Boulder, New York, Toronto, Plymouth, UK: Lexington Books.

Han, Jongwoo. 2014. *Power, Place, and State-Society Relations in Korea: Neo-Confucian and Geomantic Reconstruction of Developmental States and Democratization.* Lanham, Boulder, New York, Toronto, Plymouth, UK: Lexington Books.

Han, Jongwoo. 2014a. The Irony of US Policy Toward North Korea: Regime Denial between Regime Change and Containment. In Han, Jongwoo and Jung, Tae-Hern (eds.), *Understanding North Korea: Indigenous Perspectives.* Lanham, Boulder, New York, Toronto, Plymouth, UK: Lexington Books.

Han, Jongwoo. 2014b. Is US Policy Toward North Korea Actually Beneficial to the United States?: On the Significance of Introducing South Korean Scholarship on

North Korea to Anglophone readers. In Han, Jongwoo and Jung, Tae-Hern (eds.), *Understanding North Korea: Indigenous Perspectives*. Lanham, Boulder, New York, Toronto, Plymouth, UK: Lexington Books.

Han, Jongwoo. 2014c. North Korean Economy in Transition: Market Feudalism. In Han, Jongwoo and Jung, Tae-Hern (eds.), *Understanding North Korea: Indigenous Perspectives*. Lanham, Boulder, New York, Toronto, Plymouth, UK: Lexington Books.

Han, Woo-keun. 1971. *The History of Korea*, translated by Lee, Kyung-shik. Honolulu, HI: University of Hawaii Press.

Harden, Blaine. 2009, December 2. North Korea Revalues Currency, Destroying Personal Savings. *Washington Post*. http://www.washingtonpost.com/wp-dyn/content/article/2009/12/01/AR2009120101841.html (accessed on December 9, 2009).

Harrison, S. 2005. Did North Korea Cheat? *Foreign Affairs*, 84(1): 99–110.

Harrison, Selig. 2002. *Korean Endgame: A Strategy for Reunification and U.S. Disengagement*. Princeton and Oxford: Princeton University Press.

Hass, R. 2005. Regime Changes and Its Limits. *Foreign Affairs*, 84(4): 66–78.

Hecker, S. 2010. A Return Trip to North Korea's Yongbyon Nuclear Complex. http://iis-db.stanford.edu/pubs/23035/HeckerYongbyon.pdf.

Henderson, G. 1968. *Korea, the Politics of the Vortex*. Cambridge: Harvard University Press.

Henderson, G. 1980, March 19. North Korea: A Need for Reappraisal. *Christian Science Monitor*. http://www.csmonitor.com/1980/0319/031929.html (accessed on December 10, 2009)

Hernandez, Javier C. 2018, March 31. A Hong Kong Newspaper on a Mission to Promote China's Soft Power. *New York Times*.

Hincks, Joseph. 2018, July 12. Inside Camp Humphreys, South Korea: America's Largest Overseas Military Base. *Time Magazine*. http://time.com/5324575/us-camp-humphreys-south-korea-largest-military-base/

Hoff, Rachel. 2017, November 1. Burden-Sharing with Allies: Examining the Budgetary Realities. *American Action Forum*. https://www.americanactionforum.org/research/burden-sharing-allies-examining-budgetary-realities/

Hudson, G. F. 1955. The Lesson of Yalta. In Fenno, Jr., Richard. F. (ed.), *The Yalta Conference*. Boston, MA: D.C. Heath and Company.

Huebner, Andrew J. 2004. Kilroy is Back: Images of American Soldiers in Korea, 1950-1953. *American Studies*, 45(1): 103–129.

Huh, Donghyun Huh and Vladimir Tikhonov. 2005. The Korean Courtiers' Observation Mission's Views on Meiji Japan and Projects of Modern State Building. *Korean Studies*, 29: 30–54.

Hulbert, Homer B. 1906. *The Passing of Korea*. New York: Doubleday, Page & Company.

Hunt, Michael. 2007. *The American Ascendancy: How the United States Gained and Wielded Global Dominance*. Chapel Hill, NC: The University of North Carolina Press.

Hurley, Patrick J. 1995. Testimony on the Military Situation in the Far East. In Fenno, Jr., Richard. F. (ed.), *The Yalta Conference*. Boston: D.C. Heath and Company.

ITAR-TASS News Agency. 2009, December 11. North Korea Reports Progress with US on Six Party Talks Resumption. http://www.itar-tass.com/eng/level2.html?NewsID=14629272&PageNum=0 (accessed on December 12, 2009).

Jamrisko, Michelle and Lu, Wei. 2020, January 18. Germany Breaks Korea's Six-Year Streak as Most Innovative Nation. *Bloomberg Innovation Index*. https://www.bloomberg.com/news/articles/2020-01-18/germany-breaks-korea-s-six-year-streak-as-most-innovative-nation

Jones, F. C. 1968. The Tragedy of Korea. *Pacific Affairs*, 41(1): 86–89.

Kang, D. 2003. Getting Asia Wrong: The Need for New Analytical Frameworks. *International Security*, 27(4): 57–85.

Kang, Woong Joe. 2005. *The Korean Struggle for International Identity in the Foreground of the Shufeldt Negotiation, 1866-1882*. Lanham and Oxford: University Press of America.

Kaufman, Burton I. 1986. *The Korean War: Challenges in Crisis, Credibility, and Command*. New York: Alfred A Knopf.

Keat, Wes. 1909, November 17. Alice Roosevelt's Welcome to Korea. *San Francisco Call*, Volume 106, Number 170. https://cdnc.ucr.edu/?a=d&d=SFC19091117.2.13&e=-------en--20--1--txt-txIN--------1

Kennan, George F. 1947. "X," The Sources of Soviet Conduct. *Foreign Affairs*, 25, July.

Khanna, Parag. 2014, September 26. Dismantling Empires Through Devolution. *The Atlantic*, http://www.theatlantic.com/international/archive/2014/09/dismantling-empires-through-devolution/380774/

Kim, Dae Jung. 2010. *Autobiography of Kim Dae Jung*, vol. 2. Seoul: Samin.

Kim, Ki-Hoon. 1982. The Development of Contemporary U.S.-ROK Economic Relations. In Kwak, Tae-Hwan, Chay, John, Cho, Soon Sung, and McCune, Shannon (eds.), *U.S.-Korean Relations 1882-1982*. Seoul: The Institute for Far Eastern Studies, Kyungnam University.

Kim, Pil Ho. 2017. Guns over Rice: The Impact of US Military Aid on South Korean Economic Reconstruction. *International Development and Cooperation Review*, 9(1): 33–50.

Kim, Yongkoo. 2001. *The Five Years' Crisis, 1866-1871: Korea in the Maelstrom of Western Imperialism*. Inchon: Circle.

Kim, Young-sik. 2003, May 15. A Brief History of the US-Korea Relations Prior to 1945. A paper presented at the University of Oregon, sponsored by 'MeetKorea in Eugene'

Kinzer, S. 2006. *Overthrow: America's Century of Regime Change from Hawaii to Iraq*. New York: Times Book.

Kissinger, H. 2011. *On China*. New York: The Penguin Press.

Kissinger, Henry A. 2006. A Nuclear Test for Diplomacy. *Washington Post*, May 16, A17. http://www.washingtonpost.com/wp-dyn/content/article/2006/05/15/AR2006051501200.html [accessed on September 20, 2007].

Korean War Educator. Participating Nations: Their Contributions to the Korean War Efforts. http://www.koreanwar-educator.org/topics/united_nations/p_un_involve.htm

Kraus, Charles. 2015. American Orientalism in Korea. *Journal of American-East Asian Relations*, 22: 147–165.

Kreppmeier, Lea and Ankel, Sophia. 2019, October 30. These 8 Countries will Dominate Global Growth in 2024, Says the IMF. *Business Insider Deutschland*. https://www.businessinsider.com/ these-8-countries-will-dominate-global-growth-2024-imf-says-2019-10?r=US&IR=T

Krishnan, R. R. 1984. Early History of U.S. Imperialism in Korea. *Social Scientist*, 12(11): 3–18.

Kun, Joseph C. 1967. North Korea: Between Moscow and Peking. *China Quarterly*, 31: 48–58.

Kwak, Tae-Hwan, Chay, John, Cho, Soon Sung, and McCune, Shannon. (ed.). 1982. *U.S.-Korean Relations 1882-1982*. Seoul: The Institute for Far Eastern Studies, Kyungnam University.

Labaree, Benjamin W., et al. 1998. *America and the Sea: A Maritime History*. Mystic, CT: Mystic Seaport Museum.

LaFeber, Walter. 1967. *The New Empire: An Interpretation of American Expansion 1860-1898*. Ithaca and London: Cornell University Press.

LaFeber, Walter. 1989. *The American Age: United States Foreign Policy at Home and Abroad since 1750*. New York and London: W.W. Norton & Company.

LaFeber, Walter. 1997. *The Clash: U.S. – Japanese Relations throughout History*. New York and London: W.W. Norton & Company.

LaFeber, Walter. 2002. *America, Russia, and the Cold War, 1945-2002*. Ithaca: Cornel University Press.

Laney, J. and Shaplen, J. 2003. 'How to Deal with North Korea'. *Foreign Affairs*, 82(2): 16–30.

Larsen, Kirk W. 2008. Treaties and Troops: Bringing Multilateral Imperialism to Korea. In *Tradition, Treaties and Trade: Qing Imperialism and Chosŏn Korea, 1850–1910*. Harvard University Asian Center, pp. 72–94.

Lawler, Dave. 2019, June 1. Global Hotspots: North Korea and Iran. *Axios*. https://www.axios.com/global-hotspots-north-korea-iran-99c8094c-2974-4cc7-9922-708ed49f8cff.html

Lee, Ki-baik. 1984. trans. by Wagner, E. W. and Shultz, E. J. *A New History of Korea*. Cambridge, MA and London: Harvard University Press.

Lee, Suk, and Duol Kim. 2011. *Comparing Long-term Economic Trends between South and North Korea and Implications for North Korea Policy*. Seoul: Korea Development Institute (in Korean).

Lee, Wha Rang. 2000, May 27. Ernst Oppert's Kingdom of Corea: Grave-Robbing in the Name of God. https://groups.google.com/forum/#!topic/alt.politics.korea/ZpPAm0JHbm0

Li, Qizhen. 2020, May 29. How a Tree Almost Started a War: When 2 American Soldiers were Axed to Death. *Medium.com*. https://medium.com/history-of-yester-day/korean-axe-murder-incident-48f3e16e47b6

Marshall, Tim. 2015. *Prisoners of Geography: Ten Maps That Explain Everything About the World*. New York, London, Toronto, Sydney, New Delhi: Scribner.

Mason, Edward S. et al. 1980. *The Economic and Social Modernization of the Republic of Korea*. Cambridge, MA: Harvard University Press.

Matray, James I. 2002. Dean Acheson's Press Club Speech Reexamined. *Journal of Conflict Studies*, XXII(1): 28–55.

Mazarr, Michael J. 2007. The Long Road to Pyongyang. *Foreign Affairs*, 86(5): 75–94.

McCormack, Gavan. 1993. Kim Country: Hard Times in North Korea. *New Left Review*, I/198: 21–48.

McCune, George M. 1950. *Korea Today*. Cambridge, MA: Harvard University Press.

McLellan, David S. 1968. Dean Acheson and the Korean War. *Political Science Quarterly*, 83(1): 16–39.

Montgomery, A. 2005. 'Ringing in Proliferation How to Dismantle an Atomic Bomb Network'. *International Security*, 30(2): 153–187.

Moon, Chung-in. 2005. North Korean Foreign Policy in Comparative and Theoretical Perspective. In Byung Chul Koh (ed.), *North Korea and the World: Explaining Pyongyang's Foreign Policy*. Seoul: Kyungnam University Press.

Murray, Ian. 2011. Seward's True Folly: American Diplomacy and Strategy During "Our Little War with the Heathens," Korea, 1871. *Penn History Review*, 18(2): 43–68.

Nahne, Andrew C. and Castel, Albert. 1968. Our Little War with the Heathen. *American Heritage*, 19(3).

Nathan, Robert R. (Associates, INC). 1954. An Economic Programme for Korean Reconstruction, prepared for the United Nations Korean Reconstruction Agency, March 1954.

Naval Historical Foundation Publication. 1966. *Marine Amphibious Landing in Korea, 1871*, compiled by Miss Carolyn A. Tyson, Historical branch, G-3 Division Headquarters, U.S. Marine Corps. http://www.navyhistory.org/marine-amphibious-landing-in-korea-1871/

Neff, Robert. 2014, July 2. Alice Roosevelt's Visit to Joseon Korea In 1905, 10Magazine. https://10mag.com/alice-roosevelts-visit-to-joseon-korea/

Neu, Charles E. 1966. Theodore Roosevelt and American Involvement in the Far East, 1901-1909. *Pacific Historical Review*, 35(4): 433–449.

Niksch, Larry. 2003, July 17. Bush Ponders a Military Option. *Far Eastern Economic Review*, 166(28).

Noland, Marcus. 1997. Why North Korea will Muddle Through. *Foreign Affairs*, 76(4).

Norris, William T. 2003. The Forming of the Korean War Veterans Association. *The Graybeards*, vol. 17, No. 2, March-April, 2003. http://kwva.org/graybeards/gb_03/gb_0304_final.pdf

Notehelfer, F. G., Saveliev, Igor, and Walle, W. F. Vande. 2004. An Extraordinary Odyssey: The Iwakura Embassy Translated. *Monumenta Nipponica*, 59(1): 83–119.

Oliver, Robert T. 1944. *Korea: Forgotten Nation*. Washington D.C.: Public Affairs Press (The Monumental Printing Company).

Oliver, Robert T. 1947. The Tragedy of Korea. *World Affairs*, 110(1): 27–34.

Owen, J. 2010. *The Clash of Ideas in World Politics: Transnational Networks, States, and Regime Change*. Princeton, NJ: Princeton University Press.

Oxford Research Encyclopedias, http://oxfordre.com/asianhistory/view/10.1093/acrefore/9780190277727.001.0001/acrefore-9780190277727-e-271

Paige, Glenn D. 1968. *The Korean Decision, June 24-30, 1950*. New York: Free Press.

Paik, L. George. 1935. trans. The Korean Record on Captain Basil Hall's Voyage of Discovery to the West Coast of Korea. *Transactions of the Korea Branch of the Royal Asiatic Society*, XXIV: 15–19.

Park, Dong Whan. 1998. The Washington-Seoul-Pyongyang Triangle and the Future of the Korean Peninsula. In Dong Whan Park (ed.), *The U.S. and the Two Koreas: A New Triangle*. Boulder and London: Lynne Rienner Publishers.

Parker, Ashley and Denyer, Simon. 2019, May 27. Still angling for a deal, Trump backs Kim Jong Un over Biden, Bolton and Japan. *New York Times*.

Peddada, Chetan. 2017, September 7. A Sneak Peek at America's War Plans for North Korea: The Pentagon has been running war games for years, and the results aren't pretty.

Pelz, Stephen. 1983. U.S. Decisions on Korean Policy, 1943-1950: Some Hypotheses. In Cumings, Bruce (ed.), *Child of Conflict: The Korean-American Relationship, 1943-1953*. Seattle and London: University of Washington Press.

Perkovich, G. 2003. Bush's Nuclear Revolution: A Regime Change in Nonproliferation. *Foreign Affairs*, 82(2): 2–8.

Pew Research Center (Global Attitudes & Trends). 2006, September 21. Publics of Asian Powers Hold Negative Views of One Another: China's Neighbors Worry About Its Growing Military Strength. https://www.pewresearch.org/global/2006/09/21/publics-of-asian-powers-hold-negative-views-of-one-another/

Post, Robert C. 2003. *Technology, Transport, and Travel in American History*. Washington, D.C.: American Historical Association.

Rennie, D. 2003. Rumsfeld Calls for Regime Change in North Korea. *The Telegraph*, April 22. http://www.telegraph.co.uk/news/worldnews/asia/northkorea/1428126/Rumsfeld-calls-for-regime-change-in-North-Korea.html.

Renping, Shan. 2019, May 20. Unleashing Economic Potential Key to Winning Protracted Trade War. *Global Times*. http://www.globaltimes.cn/content/1150713.shtml

Richter, William L. 1995. *The ABC-CLIO Companion to Transportation in America*. Santa Barbara, CA: ABC-Clio.

Rizzo, Salvador. 2019, February 25. President Trump's Imaginary Numbers on Military Aid to South Korea. *Washington Post*. https://www.washingtonpost.com/politics/2019/02/25/president-trumps-imaginary-numbers-military-aid-south-korea/

Robin, Sebastien. 2017, April 1. That Time America Went to War in Korea (79 Years before the Korean War): A battle over trade. What could possibly go wrong? *National Interest*,

Roosevelt, Theodore. 1917. *Autobiography*. New York: Harper & Row.

Ross, S. T. 1988. *American War Plans 1945-1950*. New York and London: Garland Publishing, Inc.

Rusk, Dean. 1990. *As I Saw It*. W.W. Norton & Company.

Sato, R. 1994. *The Chrysanthemum and the Eagle: The Future of U.S.-Japan Relations*. New York and London: New York University Press.

Savage-Landor, Arnold Henry. 1895. *Corea or Cho-sen – The Land of the Morning Calm*. Filiquarian Publishing, L.L.C./Qontro.

Selby-Green, Michael. 2018, July 5. The 10 Countries most at Risk from a Trade War between the US and China. *Business Insider*. https://www.businessinsider.com/china-us-trade-war-countries-affected-2018-7

Sheng, Yang. 2019, May 19. Trade war reminds Chinese of Korean War. *Global Times*. http://www.globaltimes.cn/content/1150664.shtml

Shibusawa, N. 2006. *America's Geisha Ally: Reimagining the Japanese Enemy*. Cambridge, Massachusetts and London, England: Harvard University Press.

Shufeldt, Robert Wilson. 1880. The Letter from Shufeldt to R.W. Thompson of 29 May 1880, Robert Wilson Shufeldt Papers, NHF, Box 4 (Mss52688), Manuscript Division, Library of Congress, Washington, D.C.

Sigal, L. 2003. Easing the military confrontation in Korea, PacNet Newsletter, 13, November, Washington D.C.: Center for Strategic and International Studies.

Sigal, Leon. 1998. *Disarming Strangers: Nuclear Diplomacy with North Korea*. Princeton, NJ: Princeton University Press.

Sigal, Leon. 2003, January 15. How to deflate the North Korean crisis: Normalize relations, USA Today.

Sigal, Leon. 2009, June 16. The Only Way Out: Negotiation with North Korea. Minjoktongshin.com (interviewed by Paul Liem on June 8, 2009). http://www.minjoktongshin.com/english/news.php?code=4282 (accessed on December 12, 2009).

Snyder, Scott A. 2018. Chronology of Events Surrounding the Cancellation and Reconfirmation of Trump-Kim Summit, Council on Foreign Relations.

Speelman, Tabitha. 2015, December 15. Looking for Smarter, Sexier Chinese State Media? There's an App for that. *Foreign Policy*. https://foreignpolicy.com/2015/12/15/smarter-sexier-chinese-state-media-pengpai-paper/

Speer, William. 1872. Corea: What shall We do with Her?. Retrieved March 18, 2003, from: http://www.kimsoft.com/2000/speer.htm

Sterner, S. Douglas. 2002. *Shinmiyangyo, The Other Korean War*. By HomeOfHeroes.

Stokes, Bruce. 2016, September 13. Hostile Neighbors: China vs. Japan, View Each Other as Arrogant, Violent; Disagree on WWII Legacy. https://www.pewresearch.org/global/2016/09/13/hostile-neighbors-china-vs-japan/

Storey, Ian. 2020, February 3. Britain, Brexit, and the South China Sea Disputes. *The National Bureau of Asian Research*. https://www.nbr.org/publication/britain-brexit-and-the-south-china-sea-disputes/

Stueck, William. 2002. Revisionism and the Korean War. *Journal of Conflict Studies*, XXII(1): 17–27.

Swartout, Jr. Robert Ray. 1974. The background and Development of the 1871 Korean-American Incident: A Case Study in Cultural Conflict. A thesis submitted in partial fulfillment of the requirements for the degree of MASTER OF ARTS in HISTORY Portland State University.

Swisher, Earl. 1947. Commodore Perry's Imperialism in Relation to America's Present-Day Position in the Pacific. *Pacific Historical Review*, 16(1): 30–40.

The National Interest. 2018, July 19. Why Russia's Iskander Missile is a Killer. https://nationalinterest.org/blog/buzz/why-russias-iskander-missile-killer-26216

The White House. 2017 (December). The National Security Strategy of the United States of America, https://www.whitehouse.gov/wp-content/uploads/2017/12/NSS-Final-12-18-2017-0905-2.pdf

Tikhonov, Vladimir. 2012. The Race and Racism Discourses in Modern Korea, 1890s-1910s. *Korean Studies*, 36: 31–57.

USAID, 2018. U.S. Overseas Loans and Grant, July 1, 1945-September 30, 2018. https://pdf.usaid.gov/pdf_docs/PBAAJ820.pdf

Voorhees, James. 2002. Dialogue Sustained: The Multilevel Peace Process and the Dartmouth Conference, Washington D. C: United States Institute of Peace Press and Washington D.C., Dayton Ohio, and New York, NY: Charles F. Kettering Foundation.

Wakin, Daniel. 2007, December 10. Philharmonic Agrees to Play in North Korea, New York Times. http://www.nytimes.com/2007/12/10/arts/music/10phil.html?pagewanted=print (accessed on December 26, 2007).

Waltz, K. 2000. Structural Realism after the Cold War. *International Security*, 25(1): 5–41.

Ward, Alex. 2019, May 6. North Korea tested a missile over the weekend. The Trump admin flubbed the response. https://www.vox.com/world/2019/5/6/18531121/north-korea-missile-test-trump-pompeo

Watts IV, Robert C. 2020. "Rockets' Red Glare" Why Does China Oppose THAAD in South Korea and What Does It Mean for U.S. Policy? *Naval War College Review*, 71(2): 79–108.

Weathersby, Kathryn. 1993. Soviet Aims in Korea and the Origins of the Korean War, 1945-1950: New Evidence from Russian Archive, Working Paper No. 8., Cold War International History Project, Woodrow Wilson International Center for Scholars, Washington, D.C.

Webb, James E. 1949, May 16. The Acting Secretary of State to the Director of the Bureau of the Budget, Foreign Relations of the United States, 1949, The Far East and Australia, Volume vii, Part 2. https://history.state.gov/historicaldocuments/frus1949v07p2/d248

Wedemeyer, Albert C. 1947. Report to the President, submitted September 1947. Franklin Classics.

Wei, Song. 2019, May 12. China-US rivalry not a clash of civilization. *Global Times*.

William, S. Wells. 1867. "S. Wells Williams to W.H. Seward, No. 44, Peking October 24, 1866," Foreign Relations, Part I, (1867):414-16

Wilmot, Chester. 1955. Stalin's Greatest Victory, in in Fenno, Jr., Richard. F. ed. 1955. *The Yalta Conference*, Boston: D.C. Heath and Company.

Wilz, John Edward. 1985. Did the United States Betray Korea in 1905. *Pacific Historical Review*, 54(3): 243–270.

Wit, J. and Town, J. 2011. Strategic Patience Is Strategic Blunder: Don't Believe the Hype: Obama's North Korea Plan is a Mess. *Foreign Policy*, http://www.foreignpolicy. com/articles /2011/06/16/strategic_patience_is_strategic_blunder.

Wit, Joel S., et al. 2005. *Going Critical: The First North Korean Nuclear Crisis*. Brookings Institution Press.

Wu, A. 2005. What China Whispers to North Korea. *The Washington Quarterly*, 28(2): 35–48.

Yang, Key P. and Henderson, Gregory. 1958. An Outline History of Korean Confucianism: Part I: The Early Period and Yi Factionalism. *The Journal of Asian Studies*, 18(1): 81–101.

Yi, Tae-Jin. 2016. Treaties Leading to Japan's Annexation of Korea: What are the Problems? *Korea Journal*, 56(4): 5–32.

Yonhap News Agency. 2019, November 11. Number of Chinese Tourists Dips 41 pct over 3 Years on THAAD Row. https://en.yna.co.kr/view/AEN20191111 007000320

Index

Page references for figures and tables are italicized

Abe, Shinzo, 163, 194n5
Acheson, Dean: Asian policies, 138; diplomacy of, 126, 216; Press Club speech, 159n18; Truman Doctrine and, 130
Acheson Line, 24, 25, 139, 213, 235, 243
Adams, John Quincy, 158n4
Agreed Framework (1994), 169, 183, 186
Alaska, 20, 21, 96
Aleutian Islands, 96
Allen, Horace Newton, 6, 101, 109n27
Allison, Graham, 223
American defensive perimeter, 24, 28, 29, 129, 138–39, 168, 171, 179
American exceptionalism, 65n10, 116
Andrews, Evan, 241
Anglo-Japanese Treaty of Alliance, 47
Ankel, Sophia, 222
Arduous March, 181–82
Armstrong, Charles, 175
Arriola, Benjamin Vincent, 54
Atahuallpa, Emperor of Incas, 73
Axis of Evil, 13, 165, 173, 179, 186, 193, 194n6, 217
Axis Powers, 50

Barrett, Mark, 234
Barry, P. Mark, 135, 245
Battle on Shangganling Mountain (film), 151
Bell, Henry H., 72, 79, 80
Bellonet, Henri de, 76
Benedict XIV, Pope, 76
Berlinger, Joshua, 174
Biden, Joseph, 1, 163
Bingham, Mr., 35, 37
bipolar international system, 219
Blake, Homer C., 117
Bohlen, Charles E., 126
Bolton, John, 163, 182–83, 194nn5–6
Bonesteel, Charles, 51, 127, 178, 179
Bonifas, Arthur, 234
Booker, William, 144
Borchardt, Kenneth, 144
Bradley, Omar, 53, 229n10
Brazinsky, Gregg, 133
Brown, John McLeavy, 213
Brown, Joseph, 144
Burchett, Wilfred G., 174, 175
Burgess, John, 102
Burnside, C., 237
Burton, David H., 215
Bush, George H. W., 182

267

Bush, George W., 217; North Korean policy, 13, 165, 169, 171, 173, 174, 182, 183, 186
Buss, Claude A., 138
Butler, Ralph E., 144
Byeonginyangyo (French campaign against Korea), 72, 76–77, 107n10, 108n15, 119–20
Byrnes, James, 127

Cairo Declaration (1943), 47, 48, 52, 86, 125, 195n9
Camp Humphrey, 111, 157n2
Carter, Jimmy, 192
Center of Global Nonkilling, 248, 249
Central Intelligence Agency (CIA), 136, 159n17
Cha, Victor, 173
Chang, Gordon H., 115, 123, 124
Chay, John, 75, 82, 98
Chemulpo, Treaty of, 100
Cheney, Dick, 173
Cheonan sinking incident, 190
Chiang, Kai-shek, 195n9
China: cultural influence of, 214, 220; East Asian dominance, 19, 22–23, 189–90; economic rise of, 1, 150, 218–19, 239; Gorbachev's perestroika and, 182; gross domestic product (GDP), 220, *221*; Hong Kong and, 155; Korean policy, 1, 2, 44, 80, 142, 149–50, 189, 247; Korean War and, 154; land size, *221*; languages, *221*; media coverage of Korean War, 151–52; Navy, 156; North Korea's relations with, 54, 172–73, 189; "One Belt, One Road" initiative, 5, 66, 106n2, 139, 149–50, 156, 213, 243; population of, 220, *221*; rivals of, 223–24; Taiwan question, 155–56; territorial claims, 150, 156; trade, 223; U.S.-South Korea relations and, 2, 8, 149; vassals of, 87; views on Japanese contrition, *226*; Xi Jinping's policy, 155

Chinese Civil War, 135, 138
Chosin Reservoir, Battle of, 151, 152
Churchill, Winston, 195n9; "Iron Curtain" speech, 130
Chyo, Min Hui, 101
clash of civilizations, 219–20
Clemens, Walter C., Jr., 60
Clinton, Bill, 165, 182, 183
Clinton, Hillary, 165
Cloman, Jack, 144
Cold War, 11–12, 24, 137, 142, 218
Communist Party of China (CPC), 155
Confucianism, 76, 84–87
Corea. *See* Korea
Cumings, Bruce, 50, 85, 169, 173, 186
Curtius Rufus, Quintus, 241

Daewongun, Regent of King Gojong: anti-Catholic policy, 72, 86, 107n9, 108n15; anti-Western sentiment, 85–86; Heungseon title of, 86, 108n15; isolationist policy, 75–76, 85, 88, 217; official regency, 86–87; reform policy, 108n19
Darwin, Charles, 103
D'Elia, Thomas A., 147
Democratic People's Republic of Korea (DPRK). *See* North Korea
democratization: economic growth and, 237–38
Deng, Xiaoping, 182
Dennett, Tyler, 75, 82, 89, 114, 115, 124
Denyer, Simon, 163
Diamond, Jared: on different courses of history, 9, 10, 13, 15–16, 60, 73; on division of Korea, 61, 74, 106, 112; *Guns, Germs, and Steel*, 210; on relationships between cultures, 55, 113, 123, 171; on U.S.-Korea relations, 68, 243, 246
Dinsmore, Hugh A., 97
division of Korea: Cold War ideology and, 242–43; demarcation line, 127, 128, 133, 158n10, 178–79, 248;

economic impacts, 251n6; United States and, 44, 51, 97, 126–28, 245
Dobbs, Charles M., 244
Dollar, D., 237
Doyle, Michael W., 180, 181
Dragovalovsky, Aleksandr, 162
Drake, Frederick G.: *The Empire of the Seas*, 56
Drew, Edward B., 120
Dulles, Allen, 124–25, 236
Duncan, David Douglas, 207
Dyer, Thomas, 102, 103

East Asia: cultural foundation of, 220, 224; economic interdependence, 222–23; gross domestic product (GDP), 220, *221*; international rivalry, 80, 95, 223–24; land size, *221*; languages, 220, *221*; mutual perception of, 224, *225*; population of, 220, *221*; power politics, 149, 164–65, 189–90, 195n8; tourism, 222, 223; U.S. diplomacy in, 87–88, 232
Eberstadt, Nicholas, 174, 187
EC-121 shootdown incident, 189
Eichengreen, Barry, 62
Eisenhower, Dwight D., 137, 236
Estella, Victor A., 144
Eulsa Treaty. *See* Japan-Korea Treaty (1905)

Febiger, John C., 79, 80
Feng, John, 156
Field, David P., 228, 229n7
First Korean War. *See Shinmiyangyo* (American expedition to Korea)
Fish, Hamilton, 114
Five-Year Economic Development Plans, 197–98
Fong, Leslie, 151
foreign aid: economic development and, 238
France: Catholic missionaries, 107n9; exit form Indochina, 188; war against Korea, 72, 76–77, 108n15

Fry, Michael, 178
Fukuyama, Francis, 62, 235

Gaddis, John, 126
Gadhafi, Moammar, 196n15
Gang, An, 153
Ganghwa Treaty (1876), 93
Gangwha Island, 117, 118
Gasiorowski, M., 13, 184
Gerst, Victor, 144
ginseng root, 71, 81, 84
Gojong, King of Korea: Alice Roosevelt's visit to Korea and, 211; anti-Western views, 85; appeals to the U.S. government, 68, 89, 93, 101; escape to Russia, 109n23; foreign policy of, 212; Great Korean Empire of, 86–87, 109n23; isolationist policy, 86–88, 120, 217; reforms of, 93; USS *General Sherman* incident and, 79
Gorbachev, Mikhail, 182
Graham, Allison, 106n2
Grant, Ulysses S., 70, 73, 106n3
Great Britain: East Asian affairs, 47; Korean policy, 46
Great Circle Route, 20, 43, 124, 125, 231
Greeley, Horace, 121
Gresham, Walter Q., 68
Grew, Joseph, 48
Gries, Peter Hays, 153, 154
Griffis, William Elliot, 57, 81, 85, 117–19; *Corea the Hermit Nation*, 56
Griswold, Whitney, 96, 104
G7 summit (2021), 1
G20 summits, 198, 204
Guterres, António, 250

Hadden, Stanley, 144
Hamel, Hendrik, 83, 108n17
Han, Jongwoo, 169
Han, Woo-keun, 109n21
Harriman, W. Averell, 53
Harris, Thomas C., 144

Harrison, Selig, 169
Harte, Bret, 122
Hay, John, 97, 101
Henderson, Gregory, 175, 179, 239, 244
Herbert, John A., 144
Hickey, Michael, 138
Highly Enriched Uranium (HEU), 173
Hodge, John Reed, 51, 52
Hoff, Rachel, 112
Holy Roman Empire, 54
Hong, Pong-ju, 107n9
Hong Kong, 155
Hopkins, Harry Lloyd, 48–49
Hoth, Edward, 144
Huebner, Andrew J.: "Kilroy is Back: Images of American Soldiers in Korea, 1950–53," 206
Huntington, Samuel, 230n17; *The Clash of Civilizations*, 219
Hurley, Patrick J., 50

ICBM technology, 162, 165, 193n2, 194n3
Inter-American Treaty of Mutual Assistance (Rio Treaty), 231
Inter-Korean Summit, 250
Iraq: regime change, 184; U.S. war in, 187
Iskander missiles, 162, 194n3
Iwakura Mission, 88, 108n20

Japan: cultural and religious roots, 8–9, 214, 230n17; division of Korea and, 178–79; expansionism, 65n11; gross domestic product (GDP), 220, *221*; international perception of, 214, *225*, 246; Iwakura Mission, 88, 108n20; Korean War and, 125; land size, *221*; languages, *221*; Meiji Restoration, 30, 88, 104; modernization of, 30–31; opening of, 88; population of, 220, *221*; rebuilding of, 125; regional hegemony of, 8, 10, 46, 142; relations with China, 46, 82, 224, *226*; relations with Russia, 98, 104; U.S. relations with, 35–36, 44, 82, 125, 214, 235, 244; views of Chinese, *227*; in World War II, 23, 49, 52, 96–97, 126, 195n9, 218
Japan-Korea treaties, 75, 93, 94, 98, 107n7
Johnson, Lyndon, 70, 75
Joseon Korea: Alice Roosevelt's visit to, 210–12, 229n8; anti-Western sentiment, 85–86; Catholic purges in, 72, 76, 86; China's suzerainty over, 1, 19, 22–23, 55, 57, 73, 142; Christianity in, 76, 84, 107n9; Confucian values in, 76, 84–86; decline of, 86; first encounter with the West, 55, 119–20, 217; foreign relations, 82–85; French war against, 72, 76–77, 108n15, 119–20; isolationist policy, 6, 21, 57, 73, 75–76, 115, 217; Japan's relations with, 35, 47, 93–95; medical knowledge, 81; opening of, 3, 5, 8, 20, 26, 39, 57–58, 64n2, 71, 73, 75, 80–82, 88, 109n21, 114, 164; plunder of royal tombs, 76–79; population of, 39–40; Sinocentrism of, 84–87; trade, 80–82; U.S. relations with, 5, 20–21, 24, 28, 42, 58, 80–82, 119, 122–23, 212

Kanagawa, Treaty of, 21, 80
Kang, D., 189
Kang, Woong Joe, 72, 106n4
Kant, Immanuel, 53, 219
Katsura, Tarō, 46, 94, 99, 166
Keat, Wes, 211
Keenan, George: long telegram, 29, 129, 136
Kelly, Robert E., 173, 175
Kentaro, Kaneko, 100
Kilroy, James J., 228n1
Kilroy resurrection. *See* Korean War veterans
Kim, Chaek, 159n15, 193n1
Kim, Dae-jung, 3, 4, 204
Kim, Il-sung: alliance with China, 63; attack on South Korea, 129;

confederation scheme, 61; diplomacy of, 136–37, 175; Korean War, 28, 29, 105, 138; rise to power, 193n1

Kim, Jong-il, 4, 251n3

Kim, Jong-un: Inter-Korean Summit, 250; missile tests, 162; political ambitions of, 164; Trump and, 106, 162–66, 171, 191–92

Kim, Ki-Hoon, 147

Kim, Youngsam, 204

King, Ernest J., 50

Kissinger, Henry A., 174, 188–89

Knack, Stephen, 238

Korea: after World War II, 44, 58–59, 125–26, 236; American betrayal of, 58, 94–101, 166, 168; as buffer state, 230n18; history of, 8–9, 17n1, 107n6; independence movement, 229n7; Japanese rule, 2, 23–24, 51–52, 74–75, 89, 93–95, 124, 166; Three Kingdoms Period, 53–54; Western perception of, 121–22, 207–8, 217. *See also* Joseon Korea; North Korea; South Korea

Korean Peninsula: China's suzerainty over, 1; Cold War on, 142; international powers and, 5, 45, 59, 65n13, 80, 96, 165, 168, 186, 194n7; Japanese strategies in, 93–95; polarization of, 59; rise of China and, 219; Soviet-American occupation of, 121, 126, 127, 132; strategic significance of, 136, 232; U.S. military presence on, 25, 234; voluntary isolation of, 34

Korean Question: American role in, 3, 17, 28–29, 36, 43, 68–69, 105, 179–80, 235, 239–40; conceptualization of, 22, 23, 25–28; internationalization of, 46, 47, 240–41; intrinsic nature of, 195n7; origin of, 1–2, 15, 28, 30, 34; problem of trust in, 27; U.S.-China relations and, 25–27

Korean War (1950–1953): airstrikes, 175; American military casualties, 11, 16, 116–17, 125, 139, 145, 174, 233; armistice, 11, 24, 60, 176, 249, 250; ceasefire, 164; China and, 11, 54, 138, 142, 151–53; civilian deaths, 135; in comparative perspective, 218; consequences of, 53, 144–45, 147, 234–35; critics of, 53; films about, 151, 152; historiography of, 126, 154; Incheon Landing, 218; international relations and, 125; legacy of, 16–17, 105–6, 117, 153, 164, 216–18, 228, 240; media coverage of, 151, 152; outbreak of, 3, 105, 139, 188–89; outcomes of, 24, 105–6; petition to end, 248–51; public memory of, 143, 153, 154; roots of, 24, 26, 52, 124–25, 166, 181, 209, 250; stalemate in, 60, 63; U.N. troops in, 59, 125; use of napalm, 175; U.S. role in, 4, 143; weather, 207

Korean War Legacy Foundation, 207

Korean War veterans: dispatched by state, 200, *201*, 202; experience of, 207, 218; interviews with, 143, 197, 247–48; number of, 200; organizations of, 144, 159n19; public recognition of, 143; reunions of, 144; "Revisit Program," 199, 208

Kraus, Charles, 5

Kreppmeier, Lea, 222

Krishnan, R. R., 50, 52, 65n12, 67

Kroebel, Fraulein Emma, 229n9

Kuril Islands, 20, 96

LaFeber, Walter, 10, 56, 68, 105, 109n26, 110n28, 125, 216

Lamagna, Gabe, 144

Leahy, Admiral, 49

Lee, Myung-bak, 204

LeMay, Curtis Emerson, 174, 176

Lend-Lease Act (1942), 159n20

liberal democracy, 62

Lincoln, Abraham, 75

Lincoln, George, 127

Low, Frederick, 119–24
Low-Rodgers Expedition (1871), 73, 106n3
Lü, Xiang, 153
Lucey, Daniel, Jr., 144
Lugo, Ralph, 144

MacArthur, Douglas, 49, 59, 113–14, 128–29, 137–38, 174, 176
Manchuria: Japan's interests in, 104, 109n26; Russian dominance in, 95
Manifest Destiny, 10–11, 55, 115–16, 123, 158n5
Mao, Zedong, 105, 136
Marshall, George, 49–50, 178
Marshall, Tim, 247
Marshall Plan, 129
Mason, William F., 144
Matray, James I., 137
Mazarr, Michael J., 169, 173
McCallion, Joseph P., 144
McCavitt, William, 144
McCloy, John, 51
McCormack, Gavan, 176, 239
McCune, George M., 5, 244, 245
McCune, Shannon, 89, 251
McMaster, H. R., 177
McWatter, Robert A., 144
Melcher, Ralph W., 144
Minbi, Queen, 211
Molotov, Vyacheslav, 136
Montgomery, A., 186, 187
Moon, Jae-in, 1, 180, 234, 249, 250n5
Murray, Ian, 69, 77, 115
Muslim-majority countries, 220
Mutual Defense Treaty (1953), 8, 12–13, 75, 203–4
Myeongseong (Min), Empress of Joseon, 86, 109n23

Nam, Chong-sam, 107n9
Nathan, Robert R., 9, 145, 146
Neff, Robert, 211
Nelson, Donald E., 144

Nelson, M. Frederick, 89
Neu, Charles E., 104
Newman, Francis G., 211
Nimitz, Chester, 49
Nobuyuki, Abe, 52
Noland, Marcus, 169
Non-Proliferation Treaty (NPT), 181, 251
Norris, William T., 144
North Korea: academic exchange with, 161, 195n10; American hostility to, 239; army, 131; China and, 1, 27, 63, 172–73, 189, 209, 227; Cold War and, 145; communist victory in, 133; economic development, 5, 26, 60–62; food deficit, 61; foreign policy, 3–4; future of, 228; gross domestic product (GDP), *62*, *221*; homicide rate, 61; ICBM technology, 157, 161–63, 165, 177, 180, 192–93, 194n5; ideology of *juche*, 175; infant mortality, 60–61; as international threat, 169, 177, 190; isolationism of, 55; land size, *221*; languages, *221*; major events surrounding, *167*; market activities, 182; nuclear capabilities of, 27, 42, 59, 63, 164–66, 168–69, 177, 181, 185–86, 191, 193, 226, 239–40, 246–47; political regime, 179; population of, 61, *62*, 220, *221*; sanctions against, 162–63, 166; *vs.* South Korea, 60–63; Soviet support of, 9, 12, 131, 168; starvation deaths in, 181–82; trade, *62*, *172*, 172–73; U.S. policy toward, 27, 168, 175, 194n6, 209; withdrawal from Non-Proliferation Treaty, 63
Novikov, Nikolai, 158n12
Nuclear Security Summit (NSS), 204
nuclear weapons programs, 137, 177

Obama, Barack, 74, 150, 165, 171, 182–83, 191
O'Hara, Robert, 144

Olazagasti, Milton H., 144
Oliver, Robert T., 8–9, 86, 97, 98, 138, 230n18, 245, 251n6, 252n7
Operation Paul Bunyan, 234
Opium War, 21, 155, 158n4
Ottoman Empire, 54
Owen, J., 13, 184

Pacific Union: idea of, 219
Pacific War, 44, 52; casualties, 47, 58, 59; cost of, 58; end of, 126; U.S. forces, 135
Paige, Glenn D., 248; *The Korean Decision, June 24–30, 1950*, 247
Pak, Kyusu, 78, 79
Park, Chung-hee, 61
Park, Geun-hye, 204
Park, Jung Eun, 157n2
Parker, Ashley, 163
Parnow, Herbert, 144
Patterson, Arthur T., 144
Patterson, Robert, 130
Pax Americana, 235, 238
Pearl Harbor attack, 23, 229n10, 244
Perc, Joseph J., 144
Philippines: U.S. interests in, 89, 104
Pizarro, Francisco, 73
political regime: definition of, 184
Pompeo, Mike, 163
Poplar Tree Ax incident, 189
Portsmouth, Treaty of, 97–98
Potsdam Conference, 49, 86
Powell, Colin, 190
Pratt, Zadoc, 71, 81, 82
Preston, W. B., 69, 70
proliferation determinist (PD) argument, 186–87
proxy wars, 137
Pruyn, Robert H., 31
Putin, Vladimir, 1, 65n10
Pyeongtaek base, 111

QUAD countries, 156

Reagan, Ronald, 67, 68, 73, 165

regime change, 6, 13–14, 16, 164–65, 173–74, 183–89
regime denial, 6, 13–16, 164, 165, 171, 179, 183–84, 186
regime promotion, 13, 183, 185, 188–89
regime recognition, 6, 14–15, 165, 182, 188, 192
Renping, Shan, 151
Republic of Korea (ROC). *See* South Korea
Rhee, Syngman: advisors of, 245; diplomacy of, 97, 236, 252n7; presidency of, 204; relations with U.S., 5, 67–68, 94, 97, 99
Rice, Spring, 216
Ridgeway, Matthew B., 138
Riggs, Dale W., 144
Ritenour, Charles, 144
Ritttenhouse, C. J., 144
Robeson, George M., 115
Robinson, Joan, 62
Rockhill, William, 101
Rodgers, John, 20, 40, 70, 119
Roh, Tae-woo, 204
Roosevelt, Alice, 210–12, 229n8
Roosevelt, Anna Eleanor, 109n25
Roosevelt, Elliott B., 109n25
Roosevelt, Franklin D.: approach to the Soviet Union, 23, 48–49; Cairo Declaration and, 195n9; diplomacy of, 48, 50; Japanese policy, 217, 235; Korean policy, 29, 44, 47–48, 50, 95, 96, 126, 165; presidency of, 96; statement on Russia, 49
Roosevelt, Theodore: Caribbean policy, 97; containment of Russia, 26, 215, 229n10; expansionism of, 217; Japan-first policy, 28–29, 58, 94, 103–5, 210, 213, 215, 233, 235, 240; Korean affairs of, 5, 13, 15–16, 23, 45, 98, 100–101, 103–5, 166, 245; Nobel Peace Prize, 97; presidency of, 95–96; racism of, 102–3, 110n28, 166; Rhee and, 97, 99; Russo-Japanese War and, 97–98, 215–16;

Taft-Katsura Agreement and, 98–99, 136, 166, 168
Root-Takahira agreement, 104
Rostow, Walter, 133
Roze, Pierre Gustav, 76–77, 79, 82, 108n15
Rumsfeld, Donald, 187–88
Rusk, Dean, 51, 127, 128, 178–79; *As I Saw It*, 178
Russian Empire: decline, 8; Korean policy of, 46, 80; relations with Japan, 98. *See also* Soviet Union
Russo-Japanese War: Britain and, 216; causes of, 93, 99, 126, 132; Japan's victory in, 46, 93; Korea and, 97, 98, 104; peace treaty negotiations, 100, 210, 216; U.S. interests and, 104–6

sadae: ideology of, 175, 195n13
Sandusky, Michael, 135
San Francisco Conference, 126
Sargent, Aaron A., 121
Savage-Landor, Arnold Henry, 17n1, 107n6
Scarselletta, Mario, 144
Second Korean War. *See* Korean War (1950–1953)
Selby-Green, Michael, 209
Seoul Olympics, 248
Seward, George, 20, 31, 70, 78, 80, 114
Seward, William: acquisition of Alaska, 20, 21, 64n7; on commercial interest, 21, 123; correspondence of, 15, 17n2, 30, 64n4, 64n6; diplomacy of, 31, 33–34, 68, 70, 75; ideas of American expansionism, 19–20, 30; Korean Question and, 31–33, 87–88, 114, 165, 214; USS *General Sherman* incident and, 70–71, 80; view of Japan, 31
Seward-Shufeldt (SS) Line: challenges to, 96–97; establishment of, 1, 16, 20–21, 34, 42–43; Korea's place in, 22–23, 25, 29, 233; map of, 22, 64n3; mutual defense treaties within, 231–32; transition to Theodore-Franklin Line, 1, 17, 23–24, 29, 43, 233
Sharif, Nawaz, 177
Sheng, Yang, 152, 153
Shimonoseki, Treaty of, 98
Shinmiyangyo (American expedition to Korea); American forces, 8, 117; casualties, 70; course of war, 117–19; criticism of, 41, 120–21; French fleet, 117; invasion of Ganghwa Island, 113, 118; *vs.* Korean War, 113; media coverage of, 119, 121; outbreak of, 69, 80; outcome of, 6, 56, 70, 113; planning of, 115, 158n8; roots of, 69–70, 73, 123, 208–9
Shufeldt, Robert W.: correspondence of, 15, 30, 34–41; diplomacy of, 17n2, 22–23, 26, 45; ideas of American expansionism, 56, 64n7; Korean Question and, 34, 36, 38–45, 165; on Pacific trade, 38, 39; trade policy, 21; USS *General Sherman* incident and, 41, 72, 73, 79–80
Sigal, Leon, 169
Sino-Japanese War (1894–1895), 22, 29, 46, 98, 109n23
Six-Party Talks, 161, 165, 171, 181, 186, 195n10, 247, 251
Skinner, Kiron, 150
Smith, Allen M., 144
Soules, Charles, 144
South China Sea: Sino-American rivalry in, 44, 150, 156, 208, 216, 219
South Korea: attitude to Japan, 233; auto manufacturing industry, 202; China's relations with, 1, 2, 4, 63, 189, 209, 224, 247; Communist-led revolts, 136; cultural and religious roots, 214; defense treaties, 210; democratization of, 205, 237, 238; demographic performance, 61; economic development of, 4–5, 8, 12, 61, 134, 147, 197–98, *199*, 207, 208, 217, 236, 237; export, *198*,

Index

199–200, *200, 202*; financial aid to, 146, 157n3, 236–38; foreign policy of, 2, 4–5; geopolitical situation of, 205–6; government of, 147; gross domestic product (GDP), 62, *199*, 220, *221*; homicide rate, 61; import, 199, 202; industrialization of, 145, 197; infrastructure, 208; investments, 148, 202–3; land size, *221*; languages, 220, *221*; military aid to, 148; missile defence system, 162, 230n11; *vs.* North Korea, 60–63; political development of, 55, 206; population of, *62*, 220, *221*; post-war reconstruction of, 145, 146, 148, 236–37; presidents of, 204; Russia and, 173; security threat, 5, 132, 156–57, 162, 236; state-society relations, 238; strategic importance of, 131, 233; technology and innovations, 222; tourism, 203, 209–10, 222, 230n11; trade, 19, 62, 146–48, 199, *200*, 202, *202*; U.S. military presence in, 111–12, 157nn1–2, 204, 214; U.S. relations with, 8, 11–12, 27–28, 133–35, 145–46, 180, 192, 217
Soviet Union: collapse of, 26, 63, 168, 176, 190; foreign policy of, 49; nuclear weapons, 137, 138; Pacific War and, 49–50; policy on Korean Peninsula, 9, 12, 29, 97, 105, 235; U.S. policy toward, 185, 189; in World War II, 48, 137
Spanish-American War, 20
Special Measures Agreements (SMAs), 157n3
Stalin, Joseph, 29, 105, 129, 130, 158n12, 195n9
State-War-Navy Coordinating Committee (SWNCC), 51, 127
Status of Forces Agreement (SOFA), 157n3
Steele, Howard M., Jr., 144

Sternburg, Hermann Speck von, 100
Sterner, S. Douglas, 115
Straight, Willard, 212, 229n8
Stucker, LeRoy M., 144
Summers, Harry, 138
Sumner, Charles, 118
Swartout, Robert Ray, Jr., 107n9, 114, 115

Taft, Robert A., 137
Taft, William, 98, 99, 166, 168, 210
Taft-Katsura Agreement, 44, 46, 89, 99, 104, 136, 166, 178, 218
Taiwan: China's policy toward, 156; gross domestic product (GDP) of, *221*; land size of, *221*; languages of, *221*; population of, 220, *221*
Taiwan Strait Crises, 54
Tasca, Henry, 236
Taylor, Maxwell, 236, 237
Terminal High Altitude Area Defense (THAAD) missile system, 162, 210, 230n11
Theodore-Franklin Line, 1, 17, 23–24, 29, 43, 233; establishment of, 1–2; map of, 22, 64n3
Thompson, R. H., 15, 17n2, 30, 34–41
Thrust vector control (TVC), 193n2
Thucydides Trap, 27, 106n2, 213, 218, 223, 243
Tikhonov, Vladimir, 102, 103
Tilton, McLane, 116, 123, 146
Track II diplomacy, 161, 162, 182, 195n10
Treaty of Peace, Amity, Commerce, and Navigation: importance of, 8, 74, 82, 214; legality of, 93, 94; nullification of, 75; provisions of, 11–13, 15, 68, 89, 93, 142, 143, 241; signing of, 130–31
Trevelyan, George O., 215
Truman, Harry S.: Acheson declaration and, 235; decision-making process, 248; foreign affairs of, 23, 29, 130,

216; Korean policy of, 26, 53, 127–28, 131, 133, 136, 185, 188–89; military budget of, 138
Trump, Donald: approach to North Korea, 13, 74, 162–63, 165–66, 183, 194nn4–5; Kim Jong-un and, 74, 105, 106, 162, 164–66, 171, 191–92; Korean public opinion of, 111; South Korean policy, 2, 112, 157n3

United Nations: Korean Peace Settlement and, 250–51; Korean Reconstruction Agency of, 9, 145; North Korea missile tests and, 162, 163; peacekeeping operations, 204
United States: allies, 156; Asian American population, 203; containment policy, 183, 185, 189; defensive perimeter, 24; diplomacy, 8; East Asian policy, 9–11, 89, 96–97, 115, 116, 129–30, 213–14; expansionism of, 6, 8, 19–20, 102; export, 199, *203*, 204, *205*; foreign students in, 203; gross domestic product (GDP), *221*; history of, 82–83, *90–92*; Japan and, 10, 43, 80, 94–95; land size of, *221*; languages of, 220, *221*, 222; military deployments overseas, 157n1; mutual defense treaties, 231–32; nuclear weapons, 137; population of, *221*; racism, 214–15; regime change policy, 165, 183–85; regime promotion policy, 183, 185, 188; Russia and, 1, 95; struggle with communism, 133; trade, 42, 80–82; wars, 52; World War II casualties, 137
United States v. Jenkins, 77
U.S.-China relations: antagonism, 1, 26, 105–6, 106n2, 190; clash of civilizations, 150; Korean Question and, 25–27, 149; trade disputes, 150–53; treaties, 33, 80
U.S. Forces Korea (USFK), 192, 234

U.S.-Korea relations: conceptualization of, *170*; milestones of, 14–16, 69, 74–75, *90–92*, 164–65; timeline of, *7, 140–42*
U.S.-Mexican War, 19
U.S.-North Korea relations: deadlock in, 155, 178, 243; denuclearization and, 162–63, 192, 196n15; evolution of, 2–4, 13–14, 62; hostilities in, 11–12, 162–65, 168–69, 175–78, 183, 189, 226; normalization efforts, 171, 191–93, 240; nuclear weapons in, 16, 161–65; regime change policy, 187–88; regime denial approach, 164, 165, 171, 177, 179, 183–86; Trump's approach to, 13, 74, 162–63, 165–66, 183, 194nn4–5
USS *Colorado*, 117, 158nn7–8
USS *General Sherman* Incident (1866); casualties, 72, 139; as casus belli, 40, 41, 214; consequences of, 79; diplomatic impact of, 8, 71–74, 113, 209, 216–17; roots of, 69, 71, 72, 75–76; Seward's reaction to, 30, 31, 33; ship crew, 106n4; U.S. government investigation of, 6, 70–72, 79–80, 85
U.S.-South Korea relations: Chinese influence of, 2, 8; Cold War and, 11–12; criticism of, 244–45; evolution of, 233–36, 243; military alliance, 2, 75, 204, 227, 232–33, 244; regime promotion approach, 185, 189; trade, 8, *202*
USS *Pueblo*, 189, 217
USS *Shenandoah*, 40
USS *Ticonderoga*, 35, 38–40, 64n8
USS *Wachusetts*, 40, 79

Verbeck, Guido, 88
Vietnam War, 53, 135
Vollings, Herman, 144

Wallace, Harry, 144

Wallerstein, Immanuel, 102
Waltz, K., 13, 189, 190
Wangxia, Treaty of, 33, 54, 80, 157
Ward, Alex, 163
War on Terror, 187
Watson, Herbert, 144
Webb, James, 16, 134–35, 206
Wedemeyer, Albert C., 16, 130–33
Wei, Song, 150
Western international system, 123, 158n4
Westphalia, Treaty of, 93
Wilkinson, Maranda, 64n3
Williams, S. Wells, 71, 72, 78, 85
Wilson, Woodrow, 65n10, 166, 236, 252n7
Wilz, John Edward, 5, 6, 89, 93–95, 99–101, 109n24

Winterstein, Richard, 144
Wood, Leonard, 104
World War II, 23, 44, 48–50, 58–59, 96–97, 125–26, 137, 195n9, 218, 236
Worsham, Wes, 144

Xi, Jinping, 65n16, 155

Yakovlev, Alexander, 182
Yalta Conference, 48, 86, 195n9
Yamamoto, Isoroku, 229n10
Yi, Tae-Jin, 93, 94
Yi, Yong, 229n8

Zhou dynasty, 54
Ziemba, Richard, 144

About the Author

Jongwoo Han (Non-Resident Fellow at the Sejong Institute, R.O.K.) taught in the political science department of the Maxwell School of Citizenship and Public Affairs of Syracuse University after he got his doctoral degree in 1997. He founded the Korean War Veterans Digital Memorial in 2012 and currently serves as president of the World History Digital Education Foundation and the Korean War Legacy Foundation. By 2019, his foundation has completed a Korean War veterans' digital archive of interviews of 22 participant countries, which is the first of its kind. Both foundations have also published several curriculum books with the United States' largest social studies organization, the National Council for Social Studies, on the legacy of the Korean War and modern Korea.

In addition to articles in renowned scholarly journals such as *International Studies Quarterly*, *Australian Journal of International Affairs*, and *Journal of Information Technology & Politics*, he has published with the Lexington Books several books on Korea: *Networked Information Technologies, Elections and Politics*; *Understanding North Korea: Indigenous Perspectives*; *Power, Place and State-Society Relations in Korea: Neo-Confucian and Geomantic Reconstruction of the Developmental State and Democratization*. He is currently a series editor for Lexington Studies on Korea's Place in International Affairs.

As a lay Christian, he also compiled four gospels into one and published *The Gospel: Mark, Matthew, Luke and John in One*. As a president of two foundations on Korea, he also published six curriculum books (including the United States, Great Britain, Canada [coming soon]) on the Korean War, its legacy, and contemporary Korean issues, which are all available digitally in both www.koreanwarlegacy.org and www.worldhistoryde.org.

About the Author

In 2000, Dr. Han ran "Ambassador Pyo Wook Han Lecture Series on Korea-US Affairs," which was established by the Maxwell School of Citizenship and Public Affairs of Syracuse University to commemorate Amb. Han, a Syracuse University graduate of philosophy department in 1942, founder of Korean embassy in Washington DC in 1948. Amb. Han met President Truman for American aid when the Korean War broke out and finished. Jongwoo Han's involvement in Syracuse University's academic exchange program with North Korea's Kim Chaek University of Technology since 2002 led to North Korea's first digital library in 2005, which has still been known as the United States' most successful Track II program with North Korea.

Dr. Han earned a PhD and a master's degree from the department of political science in Syracuse University in 1997 and a graduate of political science of Yonsei University. He finished his military service as professor in the Department of International Relations in the Korean Air Force Academy. He enjoys outdoor activities including his first completion of New York City Marathon in 1999.

www.ingramcontent.com/pod-product-compliance
Lightning Source LLC
Chambersburg PA
CBHW052057300426
44117CB00013B/2175